Fundamentals of
Three-Dimensional
Computer Graphics

Fundamentals of Three-Dimensional Computer Graphics

Alan Watt

University of Sheffield

 **ADDISON-WESLEY PUBLISHING COMPANY**

Wokingham, England · Reading, Massachusetts · Menlo Park, California
New York · Don Mills, Ontario · Amsterdam · Bonn
Sydney · Singapore · Tokyo · Madrid · San Juan

© 1989 Addison-Wesley Publishers Ltd.
© 1989 Addison-Wesley Publishing Company, Inc.

The programs in this book have been included for their instructional value. They
have been tested with care but are not guaranteed for any particular purpose. The
publisher does not offer any warranties or representations, nor does it accept any
liabilities with respect to the programs.

Many of the designations used by manufacturers and sellers to distinguish their
products are claimed as trademarks. Addison-Wesley has made every attempt to
supply trademark information about manufacturers and their products mentioned
in this book. A list of the trademark designations and their owners appears on
p. xvi.

Cover designed by Crayon Design of Henley-on-Thames
using illustrations provided by Digital Pictures Ltd, London and
printed by The Riverside Printing Co. (Reading) Ltd.
Text designed by Lesley Stewart.
Typeset by Columns of Reading.
Printed and bound in Great Britain by The Bath Press, Avon.

First printed 1989.   Reprinted 1990 (twice).

British Library Cataloguing in Publication Data
Watt, Alan H.
  Fundamentals of three-dimensional computer
  graphics.
  1. Computer systems.   Graphic displays.
  Three-dimensional images
  I. Title
  006.6

  ISBN 0–201–15442–0

Library of Congress Cataloging in Publication Data
Watt, Alan H.
  Fundamentals of three-dimensional computer graphics/Alan Watt.
    p.   cm.
  Bibliography: p.
  Includes index.
  ISBN 0–201–15442–0
  1. Computer graphics.   2. Three-dimensional display systems.
  I. Title.
  T385.W38   1989
  006.6–dc20   89–34110
                                                               CIP

To my father
Harry Watt

Preface

This text is a comprehensive introduction to the techniques needed to produce shaded images of three-dimensional solids on a computer graphics monitor. The aim of the book is to give a theoretical understanding of these techniques together with the programming expertise required to implement them.

Three-dimensional computer graphics now embraces a large number of application areas, from the fantasy world of film and television to more practical areas such as CAD of mechanical engineering parts. In this sense three-dimensional graphics is possibly the most important aspect of computer graphics. While certain aspects are locked into particular areas – parametric surface techniques are used almost exclusively in engineering CAD – users as diverse as architects, molecular scientists and television animators use three-dimensional modelling and rendering techniques.

Many of the methods used in three-dimensional graphics are less than 10 years old and, while many excellent textbooks exist, these have mainly been general texts that have dealt with most of the mainstream topic areas in computer graphics. A good deal of the information needed in three-dimensional graphics is to be found only in research papers. This is particularly true of the techniques that have emerged in the last five years; for example, ray tracing and new reflection models. Implementing computer graphics methods from research papers is sometimes a difficult and tedious business. Details that are important to the implementer are quite rightly omitted from such publications, and would-be image synthesizers sometimes find themselves spending an inordinate time rediscovering the important practical tricks that are necessary to produce a rendered image.

Because computer graphics has spawned a large number of different methods, as the applications have grown and diversified, it is now almost impossible to write a comprehensive but standard-length text on the subject. These observations point to the need for more specialist texts that concentrate on important and unifying topics in the subject. This is such a text. Its aim is to deal with one of the mainstream areas of computer graphics and also to provide a level of detail important to implementers. In this respect, nearly all of the technique illustrations have been produced by the author using programs described in the text. Pascal procedures, implementing the crucial parts of methods at their final level of detail, are included. The inclusion of procedures also goes some way to solving the problem of algorithm and method description.

Pascal is chosen for two reasons:

(1) Although it is not the lingua franca that its adherents often claim, it is at least as good as a pseudo-code, and, with the exception of data structures, its translation into other high level languages is straightforward. (A language that has recently become fashionable in computer graphics is C. Although appreciating the practical advantages of C, it is not clear to your author that C offers any significant advantages, as a vehicle for describing algorithms, over Pascal.)

(2) It enables effective data structures to be implemented. The shading and representation of three-dimensional solids are inseparable topics and a text that deals with rendering should also deal, at some length, with three-dimensional data structures.

Currently the most popular hardware arrangement used in high quality rendering applications is a host processor that performs high level programming, driving a graphics terminal that is little more than a screen memory. The host is either in the same box, in which case the term graphics workstation is used, or it is in a separate enclosure and the graphics facility is called a terminal. (By 'high quality' we mean 24-bit screen memories; the most popular arrangement for 8-bit screen memories is the ubiquitous PC, enhanced with some extra hardware.)

For rendering shaded three-dimensional objects the programmer requires just one utility:

Write_Pixel (x, y, R, G, B)

which transfers a three component colour into location (x, y) in the screen memory. Some algorithms also require the 'opposite' utility:

Read_Pixel (x, y, R, G, B)

which reads the current value of a location in the screen memory into a program. This is an advantageous situation for authors of computer graphics textbooks because it means that programming illustrations can be almost completely device independent. Indeed, the programs given in this book will run on any host that accepts standard Pascal and will drive, with trivial alterations, any general-purpose graphics terminal. (Incidentally, since only one or two graphics utilities are used in the entire text the question of graphics standards does not arise. Furthermore, GKS-3D, the recently adopted graphics standard, does not have a convenient equivalent to *Write_Pixel*.)

The processing division between the host and graphics terminal processors is changing rapidly. Terminal utility packages are beginning to offer, for example, interpolative polygon shading and Z-buffer hidden surface removal. The trend is towards integrated workstations and away from the host terminal metaphor. This move is reflected in proposed extensions to the graphics standard PHIGS. PHIGS+ is intended to reflect this trend and includes lighting and shading as well as new three-dimensional primitives.

Efficiency in computer graphics is an important topic. Studios producing three-dimensional animated sequences always have a fixed generation time limit per frame that is imposed by the length of the sequence, the hardware available and the rendering technique used (not to mention the budget). In this text the program procedures are written to illustrate techniques and although efficiency considerations are touched on from time to time, it is difficult to combine such factors with sound theoretical explanations. Efficiency in graphics programming is extremely context dependent and involves such factors as rendering at the lowest appropriate spatial resolution, varying the rendering resolution as a function of the size of the object, using the least expensive reflection model that is appropriate, writing critical code in assembly language and increasing the workload of the graphics terminal processor by loading heavily used routines into it. Although it has been tried, in the text, to avoid gross abuse of processing time, efficiency is generally sacrificed for programming transparency. Efficiency in Phong shading is treated as a topic in its own right.

A significant proportion of the text is devoted to reflection or shading models. The current thrust of research in this area is towards greater and greater realism. Reflection models are continually being refined. The oft-stated goal of such efforts is to produce images that are indistinguishable from images obtained from, say, a television camera. The price that is always paid for more accurate reflection models is, of course, significant increases in computation time. This may not be such a vital consideration in the future, with the continuing decrease in the cost of processing units, but the relentless pursuit of reality in computer graphics does seem to be, in one sense, aimless.

The explosive demand for processor power in computer graphics is also driven by the related factor of increased resolution. Not only do algorithms increase their complexity, but at the same time the spatial resolution of graphics terminals increases, resulting in resource requirements that tend to obey a growth law with an index somewhere between 2 and 3.

One of the major application areas of computer graphics is in the entertainment and advertising industry. Here accurate reality is not necessarily a desirable goal. The appeal of computer graphics in a television commercial or title sequence is the super-reality or computer signature of the images. Images are striking partly because they are recognizably computer generated. To 'reduce' this effect by increasing their authenticity is to reduce their appeal and utility. After all, it is much easier to digitize real scenes using a television camera. In this respect a recent trend is to mix video and computer graphics images.

The treatment in this text of reflection models is restricted to the commonly used methods, although the more advanced and recent methods are not totally ignored. Reflection models are introduced in a sequence that reflects both their historical emergence and their complexity. This is certainly not the best approach from the viewpoint of mathematical propriety and a mathematical unification and discussion of reflection models is given in Appendix E. This can be safely ignored by the reader interested only in implementing a particular method, rather than understanding the mathematical relationship of the model to physical reality.

One of the main aims of the book is to provide implementation details and this means selecting a particular method to implement each part of the rendering process, rather than cataloguing processes and briefly describing each. Hidden surface removal, for example, is a good illustration of a stage in rendering where a choice of algorithms is possible. Where there is such a choice the selection of technique has been motivated by its popularity, acceptance and ease of implementation. In most cases these aims do not conflict with programming efficiency.

Nearly all the screen images in the text have been produced using the basic software described in the text. Some of the images are based on simple and effective ideas or illustrations produced by other computer graphics workers. In such cases accreditation is given to the producer of the original image.

The chapter structure enables the book to be read in any order. Most chapters are self contained. Anti-aliasing is dealt with both in a separate chapter, where the underlying theory is discussed, and in Chapters 7, 10 and 13.

Finally, although the book aims at being a 'how to do it' manual rather than a 'how it has been done' book, there are certain topics which, because of their nature, resist this approach. In particular, the chapter on three-dimensional animation is a description of the major approaches to this topic.

Programs, teaching and learning

The code in this book is in one of three forms; Pascal pseudo-code for the algorithms where this seems appropriate, Pascal procedures for all other algorithms and a complete rendering system in Appendix B and Appendix C. This consists of a wireframe program complete with a viewpoint interface and a comprehensive data structure. Appendix C contains the additional procedures required for a Z-buffer based rendering system with Gouraud shading. The data for the Utah teapot is reproduced in Appendix D – even novice graphics programmers tire of cubes and spheres.

Appendices A, B and C are intended to be an integral part of the book that can be used for more detailed further study. In particular, Appendix A is an example of the use of three-dimensional linear transformations. Appendix B is a study of data structures, wireframe drawing and general viewing systems. Appendix C extends the second appendix with rendering techniques described in Chapter 5.

The software is designed to be a learning aid to the techniques in the text and, with the single exception of ray tracing, all techniques can be grafted onto the supplied rendering system.

If the text is used for teaching or self-study, the student can be supplied with the rendering software to gain basic viewpoint experience, and the techniques covered in each chapter used as exercises. All the procedures have been integrated into the basic rendering system and in most cases no modifications are required to the data structure. Except where otherwise stated all the colour pictures were produced by this software.

Projects, notes and suggestions

The projects are meant to be an integral part of the text and can be usefully read, even if you do not implement them. Many important points are examined that expand on topics in the chapters. Implementation points that are too detailed to be covered in the chapters are dealt with in the context of a project. Some useful background information is also given – Gauss–Seidel in the context of radiosity and Fourier theory for anti-aliasing.

Each project is classified with a heading. Projects marked (*) are fairly lengthy, contain some scope for original work and could be used as a major course assignment.

Have fun.

Acknowledgements

It would have been difficult to have produced this book without the prodigious contributions made by my research students; Keith Harrison, Dave Mitchell and Steve Maddock. They wrote the code, produced the line plotter illustrations and generated all the original colour plates. I am indebted to them for many useful suggestions and criticisms and for the donation of their time. Dave made extensive contributions to Chapter 5 and he and Keith developed the H-test. Steve assisted with Chapter 6. My colleague, Jim McGregor, wrote a recursive ray tracer as an example of recursion for undergraduates and contributed to Chapter 8. Sometime undergraduates – Andy Price and Nigel Rasberry developed the ASL animation project. Bill Sproson (formerly of the BBC, and author of the text *Colour Science in Television and Display Systems*) checked Chapter 14.

But I should mention my collaborators at Addison-Wesley. Sarah Mallen has been a source of encouragement in a world of slipped deadlines; the production staff and Lynne Balfe coped with the usual tiresome preproduction problems and endless author alterations with great efficiency and cheerfulness; and finally, Kathryn Kergozou – the world would be a duller place without her sox.

Alan Watt

University of Sheffield
August 1989

Contents

Preface   vii

Chapter One   Basic three-dimensional theory   1
1.1   Manipulating three-dimensional structures   1
1.2   The basics: linear transformations   2
1.3   Structure-deforming transformations   10
1.4   Projecting three-dimensional objects onto a view plane   13
1.5   Viewing systems   16
1.6   Three-dimensional viewing pipeline   26
1.7   An aside on graphics languages   29
1.8   Polygon mesh models and wireframe representation   31
       Projects, notes and suggestions   38

Chapter Two   A basic reflection model   45
2.1   Simple reflection – the Phong model   46
2.2   Diffuse reflection   48
2.3   Ambient light   49
2.4   Distance   50
2.5   Specular reflection   50
2.6   Geometric considerations   53
2.7   Colour   55
2.8   Summary of the Phong model   55
2.9   The 20 spheres – an example   56
2.10   Using look-up tables with reflection models   59
2.11   Empirical transparency   62
       Projects, notes and suggestions   63

Contents

Chapter Three   A more advanced reflection model   65

3.1   The Cook and Torrance model   65
3.2   Illumination source models   78
      Projects, notes and suggestions   81

Chapter Four   Incremental shading techniques   83

4.1   Gouraud shading   84
4.2   Phong interpolation   87
4.3   Comparison of Gouraud and Phong shading   89
4.4   Speeding up Phong shading   90
      Projects, notes and suggestions   93

Chapter Five   The rendering process   97

5.1   Rasterization   98
5.2   Order of rendering   102
5.3   Hidden surface removal   104
5.4   Compositing three-dimensional images   111
      Projects, notes and suggestions   112

Chapter Six   Parametric representation of three-dimensional objects   115

6.1   Parametric representation of three-dimensional curves   116
6.2   Parametric representation of three-dimensional surfaces   127
6.3   Scan converting parametric surfaces   139
      Projects, notes and suggestions   147

Chapter Seven   Ray tracing   151

7.1   Basic algorithm   152
7.2   A historical digression – the optics of the rainbow   154
7.3   Recursive implementation of ray tracing   156
7.4   A remark on efficiency   161
7.5   Ray tracing geometry – intersections   162
7.6   Ray tracing geometry – reflection and refraction   165
7.7   Reflection–illumination model   167
7.8   Shadows and ray tracing   173
7.9   Distributed ray tracing   174
7.10 Ray tracing and anti-aliasing operations   176
      Projects, notes and suggestions   178

Chapter Eight   Advanced ray tracing   181

8.1   Adaptive depth control   181
8.2   Bounding volume extensions   184
8.3   First-hit speed up   187
8.4   Spatial coherence   187
8.5   Data structures for ray tracing: octrees   190
8.6   Data structures for ray tracing: BSP trees   195
      Projects, notes and suggestions   198

Chapter Nine   Diffuse illumination and the development of the radiosity method   201
9.1   Radiosity theory   202
9.2   Form factor determination   205
9.3   Further development of the radiosity method   209
      Projects, notes and suggestions   216

Chapter Ten   Further realism: shadows, texture and environment mapping   219
10.1   Shadows   219
10.2   Texture   227
10.3   Environment mapping   247
       Projects, notes and suggestions   251

Chapter Eleven   Functionally based modelling   255
11.1   Particle systems   256
11.2   Fractal systems   257
11.3   Functions suitable for three-dimensional texture   261
       Projects, notes and suggestions   264

Chapter Twelve   Anti-aliasing techniques   267
12.1   Aliasing artefacts and Fourier theory   269
12.2   Supersampling or postfiltering   273
12.3   Prefiltering or area sampling techniques   275
12.4   A mathematical comparison   277
12.5   Stochastic sampling   278
       Projects, notes and suggestions   281

Chapter Thirteen   Three-dimensional animation   285
13.1   Approaches: three-dimensional key frame systems   288
13.2   Approaches: parametric systems   291
13.3   Approaches: programmed animation and scripting systems   292
13.4   Approaches: simulated or model-driven systems   295
13.5   Temporal anti-aliasing   300
       Projects, notes and suggestions   301

Chapter Fourteen   Colour science and computer graphics   309
14.1   Applications of colour in computer graphics   311
14.2   Monitor models   313
14.3   Television transmission spaces   315
14.4   Colour models   318
14.5   Basic colorimetry concepts   331
14.6   The CIE standard   339
14.7   Realistic rendering and reflection models   353
       Projects, notes and suggestions   354

Appendix A Viewing transformation for a simple four-parameter viewing system   357

Appendix B A wireframe system   363
B.1   Introduction   363
B.2   Data structure   364
B.3   Program   371

Appendix C An implementation of a renderer   389

Appendix D The Utah teapot   395

Appendix E Some theoretical concepts   399
E.1   Introduction   399
E.2   Useful definitions   400
E.3   Hall's model   400
E.4   The rendering equation   403

Appendix F Highlight detection – the H test   405
F.1   Introduction   405
F.2   The tests   407
F.3   Example timings   410

References   413

Index   421

Trademark notice
Luxo^{TM} is a trademark of Jac Jacobson Industries.
Kodak^{TM} is a trademark of Eastman Kodak Company.

CHAPTER ONE

Basic Three-Dimensional Theory

Linear transformations are important tools in generating three-dimensional scenes. They are used to move objects around in an environment, and also to construct a two-dimensional view of the environment for a display surface. This chapter deals with basic three-dimensional transformations, introduces some useful shape-changing transformations, looks at viewing techniques and considers techniques for representing and displaying a wireframe of an object.

1.1 Manipulating three-dimensional structures

In computer graphics the most popular method for representing an object is the polygon mesh model. This form of representation is either exact or an approximation depending on the nature of the object. A cube, for example, can be represented exactly by six squares. A cylinder, in contrast, can only be approximated by polygons; say six rectangles for the curved surface and two hexagons for the end faces. The number of polygons used in the approximation determines how accurately the object is represented and this has repercussions in modelling cost, storage and rendering cost and quality. The popularity of the polygon mesh modelling technique in computer graphics is undoubtedly due to its inherent simplicity and the development of inexpensive shading algorithms that work with such models.

A polygon mesh model consists of a structure of vertices, each vertex being a three-dimensional point in so-called world coordinate space or definition space. Later we shall be concerned with how vertices are connected to form polygons and how polygons are structured into complete objects, but to start with we shall consider objects just as a set of three-dimensional vertices and look at how these are transformed in three-dimensional space using linear transformations.

1.2 The basics: linear transformations

Objects are defined in a world coordinate system which is conventionally a right-handed system. Right-handed and left-handed three-dimensional coordinate systems are shown in Figure 1.1. As we shall see later, objects in the right-handed world coordinate system are transformed into a left-handed view plane and view surface coordinate system.

It is sometimes convenient to define objects in their own local coordinate system. There are three reasons for this. When a three-dimensional object is modelled it is useful to build up the vertices with respect to some reference point in the object. In fact a complex object may have a number of local coordinate systems, one for each subpart. It may be that the same object is to appear many times in a scene and a definition with a local origin is the only sensible way to set this up. Instancing an object by applying a mix of translations, rotation and scaling transformations can then be seen as transforming the local coordinate system of each object to the world coordinate system. Finally, when an object is to be rotated, it is easier if the rotation is defined with respect to a local reference such as an axis of symmetry. (This philosophy is adopted, for example, in the graphics standard PHIGS where the programmer defines structures in the modelling coordinate system. Modelling transformations define the mapping from this coordinate space to world coordinate space.)

A set of vertices or three-dimensional points belonging to an object can be transformed into another set of points by a linear transformation.

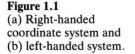

Figure 1.1
(a) Right-handed coordinate system and (b) left-handed system.

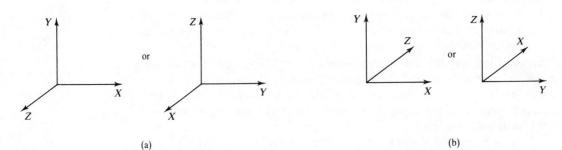

(a)

(b)

Both sets of points remain in the same coordinate system. Matrix notation is used in computer graphics to describe the transformations and the *de facto* convention in computer graphics is to have the point or vector as a row matrix, followed by the transformation matrix **M**. (This convention is the reverse of that adopted in many other fields.)

Using matrix notation, a point **V** is transformed under translation, scaling and rotation as:

$$\mathbf{V}' = \mathbf{V} + \mathbf{D}$$
$$\mathbf{V}' = \mathbf{V} \, \mathbf{S}$$
$$\mathbf{V}' = \mathbf{V} \, \mathbf{R}$$

where **D** is a translation vector, and **S** and **R** are scaling and rotation matrices.

These three operations are the most commonly used linear transformations in computer graphics and, to enable them to be treated in the same way and combined, we use homogeneous coordinates. In a homogeneous system a vertex **V** (x, y, z) is represented as **V** (X, Y, Z, w) for any scale factor $w \neq 0$. The three-dimensional cartesian coordinate representation is:

$$x = X/w$$
$$y = Y/w$$
$$z = Z/w$$

In computer graphics w is always taken to be 1 and the vector representation of a point is $[x\,y\,z\,1]$. Translation can now be treated as matrix multiplication, like the other two transformations, and becomes

$$\mathbf{V}' = \mathbf{VT}$$

$$[x'\,y'\,z'\,1] = [x\,y\,z\,1] \begin{bmatrix} 1 & 0 & 0 & 0 \\ 0 & 1 & 0 & 0 \\ 0 & 0 & 1 & 0 \\ T_x & T_y & T_z & 1 \end{bmatrix}$$

$$= [x\,y\,z\,1] \, \mathbf{T}$$

This specification implies that the object is translated in three dimensions by applying a displacement T_x, T_y and T_z to each vertex that defines the object. The matrix notation is a convenient and elegant way of writing the transformation. As a set of three equations the transformation is:

$$x' = x + T_x$$
$$y' = y + T_y$$
$$z' = z + T_z$$

The set of transformations is completed by scaling and rotation. First scaling:

$$\mathbf{V}' = \mathbf{VS}$$

$$\mathbf{S} = \begin{bmatrix} S_x & 0 & 0 & 0 \\ 0 & S_y & 0 & 0 \\ 0 & 0 & S_z & 0 \\ 0 & 0 & 0 & 1 \end{bmatrix}$$

Here S_x, S_y and S_z are scaling factors. For uniform scaling $S_x = S_y = S_z$; otherwise, scaling occurs along those axes for which the scaling factor is non-unity. Again the process can be expressed less succinctly by a set of three equations:

$$x' = xS_x$$
$$y' = yS_y$$
$$z' = zS_z$$

applied to every vertex in the object.

To rotate an object in three-dimensional space we need to specify an axis of rotation. This can have any spatial orientation in three-dimensional space, but it is easiest to consider rotations that are about one of the coordinate axes. The transformation matrices for counter-clockwise rotation about the X, Y and Z axes respectively are (looking towards the origin in all cases in a right-handed system):

$$\mathbf{R}_x = \begin{bmatrix} 1 & 0 & 0 & 0 \\ 0 & \cos\theta & \sin\theta & 0 \\ 0 & -\sin\theta & \cos\theta & 0 \\ 0 & 0 & 0 & 1 \end{bmatrix}$$

$$\mathbf{R}_y = \begin{bmatrix} \cos\theta & 0 & -\sin\theta & 0 \\ 0 & 1 & 0 & 0 \\ \sin\theta & 0 & \cos\theta & 0 \\ 0 & 0 & 0 & 1 \end{bmatrix}$$

$$\mathbf{R}_z = \begin{bmatrix} \cos\theta & \sin\theta & 0 & 0 \\ -\sin\theta & \cos\theta & 0 & 0 \\ 0 & 0 & 1 & 0 \\ 0 & 0 & 0 & 1 \end{bmatrix}$$

The Z axis matrix specification is equivalent to the following set of three equations:

$$x' = x\cos\theta - y\sin\theta$$
$$y' = x\sin\theta + y\cos\theta$$
$$z' = z$$

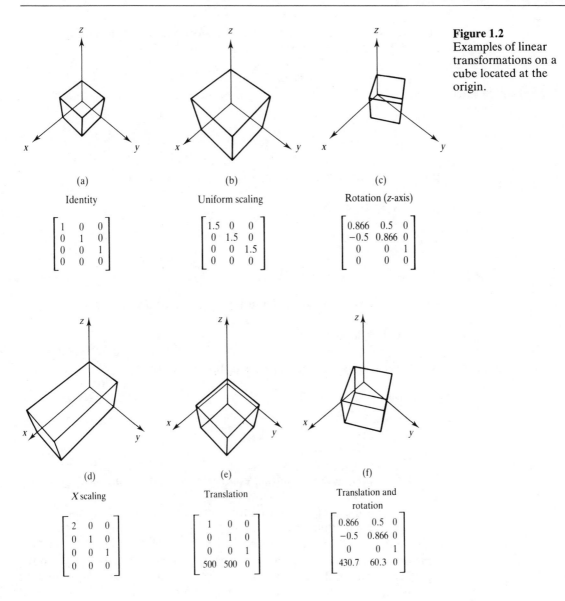

Figure 1.2
Examples of linear transformations on a cube located at the origin.

(a)

Identity

$$\begin{bmatrix} 1 & 0 & 0 \\ 0 & 1 & 0 \\ 0 & 0 & 1 \\ 0 & 0 & 0 \end{bmatrix}$$

(b)

Uniform scaling

$$\begin{bmatrix} 1.5 & 0 & 0 \\ 0 & 1.5 & 0 \\ 0 & 0 & 1.5 \\ 0 & 0 & 0 \end{bmatrix}$$

(c)

Rotation (z-axis)

$$\begin{bmatrix} 0.866 & 0.5 & 0 \\ -0.5 & 0.866 & 0 \\ 0 & 0 & 1 \\ 0 & 0 & 0 \end{bmatrix}$$

(d)

X scaling

$$\begin{bmatrix} 2 & 0 & 0 \\ 0 & 1 & 0 \\ 0 & 0 & 1 \\ 0 & 0 & 0 \end{bmatrix}$$

(e)

Translation

$$\begin{bmatrix} 1 & 0 & 0 \\ 0 & 1 & 0 \\ 0 & 0 & 1 \\ 500 & 500 & 0 \end{bmatrix}$$

(f)

Translation and rotation

$$\begin{bmatrix} 0.866 & 0.5 & 0 \\ -0.5 & 0.866 & 0 \\ 0 & 0 & 1 \\ 430.7 & 60.3 & 0 \end{bmatrix}$$

Figure 1.2 shows examples of these transformations operating on a cube with one of its vertices originally at the origin.

The inverse of these transformations is often required. $\mathbf{T}^{-1}$ is obtained by negating T_x, T_y and T_z. Replacing S_x, S_y and S_z by their reciprocals gives $\mathbf{S}^{-1}$ and negating the angle of rotation gives $\mathbf{R}^{-1}$.

Any set of rotations, scalings and translations can be multiplied or concatenated together to give a **net** transformation matrix, that describes a combined transformation. For example if:

$$[x'\, y'\, z'\, 1] = [x\, y\, z\, 1]\ \mathbf{M}_1$$

and

$$[x''\, y''\, z''\, 1] = [x'\, y'\, z'\, 1]\ \mathbf{M}_2$$

then the transformation matrices can be concatenated:

$$\mathbf{M}_3 = \mathbf{M}_1\mathbf{M}_2$$

and

$$[x''\, y''\, z''\, 1] = [x\, y\, z\, 1]\ \mathbf{M}_3$$

Although translations are commutative, rotations are not and

$$\mathbf{R}_1\mathbf{R}_2 \neq \mathbf{R}_2\mathbf{R}_1$$

A general transformation matrix will be of the form:

$$\begin{bmatrix} a_{11} & a_{12} & a_{13} & 0 \\ a_{21} & a_{22} & a_{23} & 0 \\ a_{31} & a_{32} & a_{33} & 0 \\ t_x & t_y & t_z & 1 \end{bmatrix}$$

The 3×3 upper left submatrix $\mathbf{A}$ is the net rotation and scaling while (t_x, t_y, t_z) gives the net translation.

A typical use of transformation matrices in computer graphics is to build up a scene that consists of instances of predefined objects. An example of two scenes, two views of each, built up from instances of the same objects is given in Figure 1.3 (viewing system information is given in the illustrations and described later in the chapter). The absolute or precise effect of the transformations is unimportant; the two scenes should be compared so that a general feel for the effect of the transformations is obtained.

Three objects are subject to transformations, from positions centred on the origin, as follows:

(1) First cube:
     scale   (0.4, 0.4, 0.4) (S_x, S_y, S_z)
     rotation   (0, 0, 0) (counter clockwise in degrees about
                                 X, Y and Z axes)

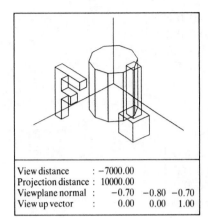 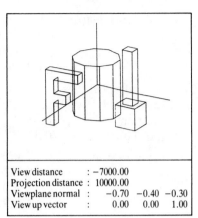

View distance	: −7000.00		
Projection distance	: 10000.00		
Viewplane normal	: −0.70	−0.80	−0.70
View up vector	: 0.00	0.00	1.00

View distance	: −7000.00		
Projection distance	: 10000.00		
Viewplane normal	: −0.70	−0.40	−0.30
View up vector	: 0.00	0.00	1.00

(a)

Figure 1.3
Building up a scene using three-dimensional transformations to instance objects: (a) two views of scene 1 and (b) two views of scene 2 (see text for details).

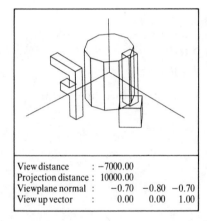

View distance	: −7000.00		
Projection distance	: 10000.00		
Viewplane normal	: −0.70	−0.80	−0.70
View up vector	: 0.00	0.00	1.00

View distance	: −7000.00		
Projection distance	: 10000.00		
Viewplane normal	: −0.70	−0.40	−0.30
View up vector	: 0.00	0.00	1.00

(b)

translation $(0.5, 1.7, -0.6)$ (T_x, T_y, T_z)

composite matrix
$$\begin{bmatrix} 0.4 & 0.0 & 0.0 & 0.0 \\ 0.0 & 0.4 & 0.0 & 0.0 \\ 0.0 & 0.0 & 0.4 & 0.0 \\ 0.5 & 1.7 & -0.6 & 1.0 \end{bmatrix}$$

(2)   F:

scale $(1, 1, 1)$

rotation $(0, 0, 0)$

translation $(1.7, -0.4, 0)$

composite matrix $\begin{bmatrix} 1.0 & 0.0 & 0.0 & 0.0 \\ 0.0 & 1.0 & 0.0 & 0.0 \\ 0.0 & 0.0 & 1.0 & 0.0 \\ 1.7 & -0.4 & 0.0 & 1.0 \end{bmatrix}$

(3)   Second cube:
        scale   (0.2, 0.2, 1)
        rotation   (0, 0, 0)
        translation   (0.5, 1.7, 0.8)

composite matrix $\begin{bmatrix} 0.2 & 0.0 & 0.0 & 0.0 \\ 0.0 & 0.2 & 0.0 & 0.0 \\ 0.0 & 0.0 & 1.0 & 0.0 \\ 0.5 & 1.7 & 0.8 & 1.0 \end{bmatrix}$

(4)   Cylinder:
        scale   (0.9, 0.9, 1)
        rotation   (0, 0, 0)
        translation   (0, 0, 0)

composite matrix $\begin{bmatrix} 0.9 & 0.0 & 0.0 & 0.0 \\ 0.0 & 0.9 & 0.0 & 0.0 \\ 0.0 & 0.0 & 1.0 & 0.0 \\ 0.0 & 0.0 & 0.0 & 1.0 \end{bmatrix}$

For comparison the second scene data (this time without the composite matrix) is given:

(1)   First cube:
        scale   (0.4, 0.4, 0.4)
        rotation   (0, 0, 45)
        translation (0.5, 1.7, −0.6)

(2)   F:
        scale   (1, 1, 1)
        rotation   (0, 0, 180)
        translation (1.7, −0.4, 0)

(3)   Second cube:
        scale   (0.2, 0.2, 1)
        rotation   (0, 0, 0)
        translation (0.5, 1.7, 0.8)

(4)   Cylinder:
        scale   (0.9, 0.9, 1)
        rotation   (0, 0, 0)
        translation (0, 0, 0)

The ability to concatenate transformations to form a net transformation matrix is useful because it gives a single matrix specification for any linear transformation. For example, consider rotating a body about a

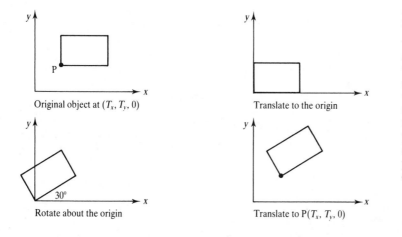

Original object at $(T_x, T_y, 0)$

Translate to the origin

Rotate about the origin

Translate to $P(T_x, T_y, 0)$

Figure 1.4
The stages in building up the rotation of an object about one of its own vertices. The rotation is about an axis parallel to the Z axis at point $(T_x, T_y, 0)$. A two-dimensional projection (with the Z axis coming out of the paper) is shown for clarity.

line parallel to the Z axis which passes through the point $(T_x, T_y, 0)$ and also passes through one of the vertices of the object. Here we are implying that the object is not at the origin and we wish to apply rotation about a reference point in the object. We cannot simply apply a rotation matrix because this is defined with respect to the origin and an object not positioned at the origin would rotate and translate – not usually the desired effect. Instead we have to derive a net transformation matrix as follows:

(1)   translate the object to the origin,
(2)   apply the desired rotation, and
(3)   translate the object back to its original position.

The net transformation matrix is:

$$
\mathbf{T_1 R T_2} =
\begin{bmatrix}
1 & 0 & 0 & 0 \\
0 & 1 & 0 & 0 \\
0 & 0 & 1 & 0 \\
-T_x & -T_y & 0 & 1
\end{bmatrix}
\begin{bmatrix}
\cos\theta & \sin\theta & 0 & 0 \\
-\sin\theta & \cos\theta & 0 & 0 \\
0 & 0 & 1 & 0 \\
0 & 0 & 0 & 1
\end{bmatrix}
\begin{bmatrix}
1 & 0 & 0 & 0 \\
0 & 1 & 0 & 0 \\
0 & 0 & 1 & 0 \\
T_x & T_y & 0 & 1
\end{bmatrix}
$$

$$
=
\begin{bmatrix}
\cos\theta & \sin\theta & 0 & 0 \\
-\sin\theta & \cos\theta & 0 & 0 \\
0 & 0 & 1 & 0 \\
-T_x\cos\theta + T_y\sin\theta + T_x & -T_x\sin\theta - T_y\cos\theta + T_y & 0 & 1
\end{bmatrix}
$$

This process is shown in Figure 1.4 where θ is 30°.

9

Figure 1.5
Two links with local
origins at joints.

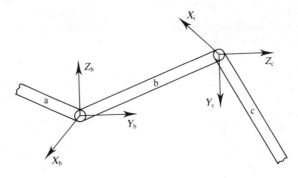

The ability to concatenate transformations is also useful in describing objects that have a natural hierarchy. For example, a stylization of a human figure used in animation would have a set of local coordinate systems based on limb joints. The object would be described by a hierarchy based on these joints. The rationale is that it is sensible to specify, say, movement of a hand with respect to the wrist joint and the movement of the lower arm with respect to the elbow joint. Local coordinate systems are related to each other and eventually to a single world coordinate system via a series of transformation matrices.

Consider two links b and c, with local coordinate systems at each joint, in a series of links constituting, say, a chain system with one end fixed (at the world coordinate origin) and the other end free (Figure 1.5). $\mathbf{T}_{cb}$ is the matrix that specifies the current location of c with respect to the origin of c – a coordinate system attached to b. If $\mathbf{T}_{ba}$ is the matrix that specifies the location of b with respect to its local coordinate system – a coordinate system attached to a – then

$$\mathbf{T}_{ca} = \mathbf{T}_{cb}\mathbf{T}_{ba}$$

is the transformation matrix specifying the position of c with respect to a. Moving b will alter $\mathbf{T}_{ba}$ and $\mathbf{T}_{ca}$ will change. Similarly, all the descendants of c will also change. Thus, to move any link in the system, a movement is specified with respect to the local coordinate system and all the descendants of this link will move appropriately.

1.3   Structure-deforming transformations

The above linear transformations either move an object (rotation and translation) or scale the object. Uniform scaling preserves shape. Using different values of S_x, S_y and S_z the object is stretched or squeezed along particular coordinate axes. In this section a set of transformations that deform the objects in other ways are introduced. These are fully described by Barr (1984) where they are termed global deformations. The particular deformations detailed in this paper are tapering, twisting and bending.

Barr uses a formula definition for the transformations:

$$X = F_x(x)$$
$$Y = F_y(y)$$
$$Z = F_z(z)$$

where (x, y, z) is a vertex in an undeformed solid and (X, Y, Z) is the deformed vertex. Using this notation the scaling transformation above is:

$$X = S_x(x)$$
$$Y = S_y(y)$$
$$Z = S_z(z)$$

Tapering is easily developed from scaling. We choose a tapering axis and differentially scale the other two components, setting up a tapering function along this axis. Thus to taper an object along its Z axis:

$$X = rx$$
$$Y = ry$$
$$Z = z$$

where $r = f(z)$ is a linear or non-linear tapering profile or function.

Global axial twisting can be developed as a differential rotation just as tapering is a differential scaling. To twist an object about its Z axis we apply:

$$X = x \cos \theta - y \sin \theta$$
$$Y = x \sin \theta + y \cos \theta$$
$$Z = z$$

where $\theta = f(z)$ and $f'(z)$ specifies the rate of twist per unit length along the Z axis.

A global linear bend along an axis is a composite transformation comprising a bent region and a region outside the bent region where the deformation is a rotation and a translation.

Barr defines a bend region along the Y axis as:

$$y_{min} \leqslant y \leqslant y_{max}$$

The radius of curvature of the bend is $1/k$ and the centre of the bend is at $y = y_0$. The bending angle is:

$$\theta = k(y' - y_0)$$

where:

$$y' = \begin{cases} y_{min} & \text{if } y \leqslant y_{min} \\ y & \text{if } y_{min} < y < y_{max} \\ y_{max} & \text{if } y \geqslant y_{max} \end{cases}$$

Figure 1.6
Structure-deforming
transformations.

The deforming transformation is given by:

$$X = x$$

$$Y = \begin{cases} -\sin\theta \ (z - 1/k) + y_0 & y_{min} \leqslant y \leqslant y_{max} \\ -\sin\theta \ (z - 1/k) + y_0 + \cos\theta \ (y - y_{min}) & y < y_{min} \\ -\sin\theta \ (z - 1/k) + y_0 + \cos\theta \ (y - y_{max}) & y > y_{max} \end{cases}$$

$$Z = \begin{cases} \cos\theta \ (z - 1/k) + 1/k & y_{min} \leqslant y \leqslant y_{max} \\ \cos\theta \ (z - 1/k) + 1/k + \sin\theta \ (y - y_{min}) & y < y_{min} \\ \cos\theta \ (z - 1/k) + 1/k + \sin\theta \ (y - y_{max}) & y > y_{max} \end{cases}$$

Figure 1.6 shows an example of each of these transformations. The deformation on the cube is an intuitive reflection of the effects and the same transformations are applied to the Utah teapot. Plate 1 shows a rendered version of a polygon mesh object (a corrugated cylinder) that has been twisted and tapered.

Non-constrained, non-linear deformations cannot be applied to polygon meshes in general. One problem is the connectivity constraints between vertices. For example, we cannot twist a cube, represented as six surfaces without limit, and retain a structure suitable for rendering. Another problem is that deformations where vertices move apart have the effect of reducing the polygonal resolution of the original model, giving rise to a degradation in silhouette edge aliasing (dealt with in detail later). Thus the polygonal resolution of the object model constrains the nature of the deformation and this can only be overcome by subdivision of the original mesh as a function of the 'severity' of the deformation.

1.4 Projecting three-dimensional objects onto a view plane

Although various three-dimensional display devices exist, most computer graphics view surfaces are two dimensional. Thus a three-dimensional pipeline – the jargon term used to describe the various processes in converting from three-dimensional world coordinate space to a two-dimensional representation – must contain at least a projective transformation and a viewing transformation.

For reasons that will become clear, it is easiest to consider the transformation of the set of vertices representing an object onto a two-dimensional view surface in two parts. We can consider a transformation from a world coordinate system to a viewing coordinate system (x_v, y_v, z_v). Here vertices are expressed in a left-handed coordinate system with the origin sometimes known as the view point or view reference point. Separating the transformations in this way means that we can isolate the

Figure 1.7
Two points projected
onto a plane using
parallel and perspective
projections.

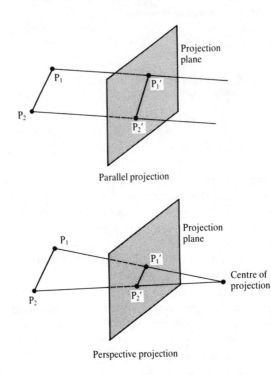

Parallel projection

Perspective projection

geometry of the projections from the fact that, in general, the projection plane can have any orientation in world coordinate space.

Because the viewing surface in computer graphics is deemed to be flat, we consider the class of projections known as planar geometric projections. Two basic projections, perspective and parallel, are now described. These projections and the difference in their nature are illustrated in Figure 1.7.

A perspective projection is the more popular or common choice in computer graphics because it incorporates foreshortening. In a perspective projection relative dimensions are not preserved, and a distant line is displayed smaller than a nearer line of the same length (Figure 1.8). This effect enables human beings to perceive depth in a two-dimensional photograph or a stylization of three-dimensional reality. A perspective projection is characterized by a point known as the centre of projection and the projection of three-dimensional points onto the view plane is the intersection of the lines from each point to the centre of projection. These lines are called projectors.

Figure 1.9 shows how a perspective projection is derived. Point $\mathbf{P}(x_v, y_v, z_v)$ is a three-dimensional point in the viewing coordinate system. This point is to be projected onto a view plane normal to the z_v axis and

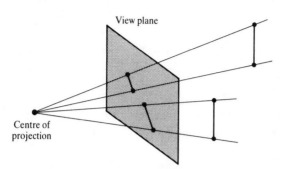

Figure 1.8
In a perspective projection a distant line is displayed smaller than a nearer line of the same length.

positioned at a distance d from the origin of this system. Point $\mathbf{P}'$ is the projection of this point in the view plane and has two-dimensional coordinates (x_s, y_s) in a view plane coordinate system with the origin at the intersection of the z_v axis and the view plane. The view plane is effectively the view surface or screen.

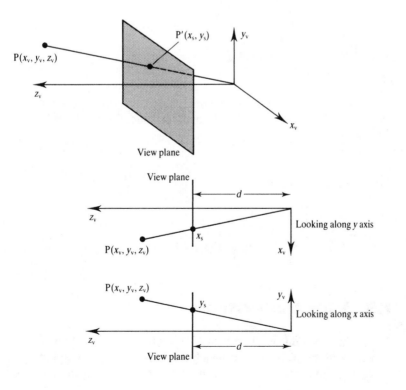

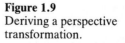

Figure 1.9
Deriving a perspective transformation.

15

Similar triangles give:

$$\frac{x_s}{d} = \frac{x_v}{z_v} \qquad \frac{y_s}{d} = \frac{y_v}{z_v}$$

$$x_s = \frac{x_v}{z_v/d} \qquad y_s = \frac{y_v}{z_v/d}$$

To express this transformation as a 4×4 matrix we have:

$$[x_s \ y_s \ d \ 1] = \left[\frac{x_v}{z_v/d} \quad \frac{y_v}{z_v/d} \quad d \quad 1 \right]$$

Expressing the left-hand side using homogeneous coordinates $[X Y Z W]$ we can write

$$[X/w \ Y/w \ Z/w \ 1] = [x_s \ y_s \ d \ 1]$$
$$[X \ Y \ Z \ W] = [x_v \ y_v \ z_v \ z_v/d]$$
$$= \mathbf{PT}_{pers}$$

where

$$\mathbf{T}_{pers} = \begin{bmatrix} 1 & 0 & 0 & 0 \\ 0 & 1 & 0 & 0 \\ 0 & 0 & 1 & 1/d \\ 0 & 0 & 0 & 0 \end{bmatrix}$$

in a parallel projection; if the view plane is normal to the direction of projection then the projection is orthographic and we have:

$$x_s = x_v \qquad y_s = y_v$$

Expressed as a matrix:

$$\mathbf{T}_{ort} = \begin{bmatrix} 1 & 0 & 0 & 0 \\ 0 & 1 & 0 & 0 \\ 0 & 0 & 0 & 0 \\ 0 & 0 & 0 & 1 \end{bmatrix}$$

1.5 Viewing systems

A viewing system is a set of parameters that enables a series of transformations to be set up which have the effect of mapping points in world coordinate space onto the view surface. Such a system allows a user to specify a projective transform, previously described, and it enables the view plane to be positioned anywhere in world coordinate space.

A full viewing system will also determine a view volume, that subset of world coordinate space which is to be included in the transformation process. This definition enables a user to select particular regions of interest within the world coordinate space.

Three systems are described; an extremely simple but limited four-parameter system, a practical system and a completely general system based on, but not identical to, the GKS and PHIGS model. Working through the evolution of a more and more complex viewing system will also help in understanding the extra factors involved in general viewing systems.

1.5.1 A note on practical approaches to viewing systems

At the time of writing, GKS-3D and PHIGS have just been formally ratified as standards and a graphics programmer will have to either implement a viewing system and work with two-dimensional line-drawing utilities, or use a standard or general viewing system and work with three-dimensional line-drawing utilities. There seems to be no alternative at the moment but to describe both approaches. Thus simple viewing systems are described and implementation details are given and the general systems are treated from an interpretive point of view only, in the hope that, if you are interested in a full system, you will already have access to one. Details of the implementation of a full system – three-dimensional clipping and so on – are given in Chapter 8 of Foley and Van Dam (1982).

1.5.2 A simple four-parameter viewing system

In this system a user specifies a view point or eye point (three parameters or a vector) and a view plane distance (one parameter). A viewing direction or view plane normal is established by the line from the view point to the world coordinate origin. This constraint is fine for single-object scenes, where the object is disposed about the world coordinate origin, but is an unworkable constraint in the case of multi-object scenes.

A view coordinate system (x_v, y_v, z_v) is established at the view point, with the direction of y_v being parallel to y_s in the view plane. A perspective projection is used with the centre of projection at the view point and the fourth parameter is the distance d from the view point to the view plane. This set-up is shown in Figure 1.10. An easy and intuitive user interface is possible if a spherical coordinate system is used to specify the view point position. (See Appendix A.) Consider the line from the

Figure 1.10
A simple four-parameter viewing system. A view coordinate system is established at the view point with y_v parallel to y_s and z_v pointing to the world coordinate origin.

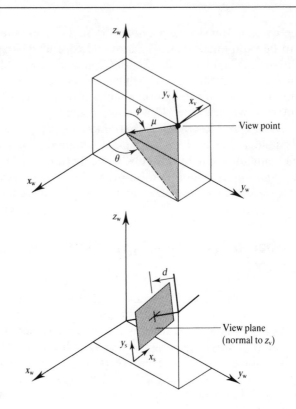

view point to the world coordinate origin. μ is the distance from the world coordinate origin to the view point along this line, θ is the angle that the plane containing the line makes with the x axis and ϕ is the angle the line makes with the z axis. Smart readers will have noticed that this system contains a singularity when the view point lies on the z axis.

The following transformation transforms the world coordinate points to view coordinate points:

$$[x_v\, y_v\, z_v\, 1] = [x_w\, y_w\, z_w\, 1] \begin{bmatrix} -\sin\theta & -\cos\theta\,\cos\phi & -\cos\theta\,\sin\phi & 0 \\ \cos\theta & -\sin\theta\,\cos\phi & -\sin\theta\,\sin\phi & 0 \\ 0 & \sin\phi & -\cos\phi & 0 \\ 0 & 0 & \mu & 1 \end{bmatrix}$$

$$= [x_w\, y_w\, z_w\, 1]\; \mathbf{T}_{\text{view}}$$

A complete derivation of this viewing transformation is given as an example in Appendix A. Viewing transformations in subsequent sections can be derived in a similar way. It is not unreasonable to assume that most three-dimensional computer graphics practitioners will be using a graphics language that already contains a viewing system and the emphasis in this chapter is on the description and the interpretation of the viewing parameters, rather than the derivation of transforms.

1.5.3 A practical viewing system

The problem with three-dimensional viewing systems is that as the system becomes more and more general, to include, for example, oblique projections, the number of parameters required to specify a view grows, and makes a user interface consequently more difficult. A compromise system, which does not allow full generality, but which overcomes the limitation of the first system and allows a reasonably easy interface, is now described.

The second system is best introduced by considering a synthetic camera (Figure 1.11). In this viewing system we can point the camera in

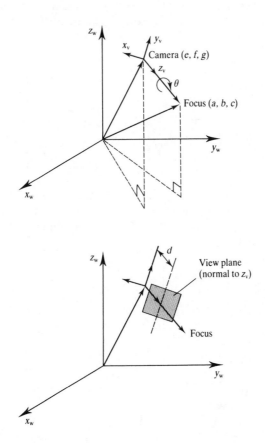

Figure 1.11
A practical viewing system using two vectors (camera and focus point), a twist angle θ and a view plane distance d.

any direction; the view plane normal or viewing direction is no longer constrained to point at the origin of the world coordinate system. Also, the camera can be rotated about the view plane normal.

We establish a camera position, which is the view reference point or origin of the view coordinate system and the centre of projection. A view plane normal to the z_v axis is specified at a distance d from this origin (as Section 1.4). The direction in which the camera is pointing is determined by a point of interest or focus point. These two points $\mathbf{C}$ and $\mathbf{F}$ define the z_v axis of the viewing coordinate system, and a twist angle establishes the rotation of the camera about this axis and the direction of the y_s axis in the view plane. The system requires a user to specify two vectors or three-dimensional points $\mathbf{C}$ and $\mathbf{F}$, a twist angle and a view plane distance d (a total of eight parameters: two three-dimensional points, an angle and a distance).

The notion of a camera is especially useful in three-dimensional animation where the path of one camera (or a number of cameras) may be choreographed as part of a sequence.

The viewing transformation can be derived from the following steps. First, if the camera is positioned at the world coordinate origin, pointing in a direction defined by the point of interest (a, b, c), then it can be shown that:

$$
\mathbf{V} = \begin{bmatrix} \dfrac{b}{(1-c^2)^{1/2}} & \dfrac{-ac}{(1-c^2)^{1/2}} & a & 0 \\[2ex] \dfrac{-a}{(1-c^2)^{1/2}} & \dfrac{-bc}{(1-c^2)^{1/2}} & b & 0 \\[2ex] 0 & (1-c^2)^{1/2} & c & 0 \\[1ex] 0 & 0 & 0 & 1 \end{bmatrix}
$$

If we then generalize the camera position, placing it at point (e, f, g), and include rotation through an angle θ counterclockwise about $\mathbf{C}$ (looking away from the origin), then the three components of the view transformation matrix are:

$$
\mathbf{V}_1 = \begin{bmatrix} \cos\theta & -\sin\theta & 0 & 0 \\ \sin\theta & \cos\theta & 0 & 0 \\ 0 & 0 & 1 & 0 \\ 0 & 0 & 0 & 1 \end{bmatrix}
$$

$$\mathbf{V}_2 = \mathbf{V} \quad \text{(above)}$$

$$
\mathbf{V}_3 = \begin{bmatrix} 1 & 0 & 0 & 0 \\ 0 & 1 & 0 & 0 \\ 0 & 0 & 1 & 0 \\ -e & -f & -g & 1 \end{bmatrix}
$$

and

$$\mathbf{T}_{\text{view}} = \mathbf{V}_1 \mathbf{V}_2 \mathbf{V}_3$$

This viewing transformation will cope with most situations in computer graphics and it avoids the difficult user interface associated with general viewing systems described next.

1.5.4 General viewing systems

Completely general viewing systems are adopted by the GKS-3D and PHIGS models. In the previous two systems we have located a centre of projection on the view plane normal (or on a line parallel to the view plane normal). The centre of projection was then termed a view point and the line from the centre of projection to the view plane origin established the view plane normal and viewing direction. In a general system oblique projections are allowed. Here the line from the centre of projection to the view plane origin is not in general parallel to the view plane normal.

1.5.5 The view plane in more detail

The position and orientation of a view plane are defined by the view reference point (VRP) and the view plane normal (VPN) (see Figure 1.12). The viewing direction is thus set by the VPN. Compared with the previous system, which used the camera and a focus point to establish the VPN and a distance d, we now use two vectors – the VRP and the VPN (plus a distance, the view distance which displaces the VRP from the view plane). Unlike the previous two systems where the VRP was also used as

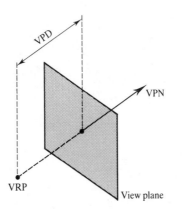

Figure 1.12
Parameters required to establish the viewplane in a general viewing system. The viewplane can be positioned anywhere and have any orientation.

21

Figure 1.13
A *u–v* coordinate system is established in the viewplane forming a three-dimensional left-handed (right-handed for GKS-3D and PHIGS) system with the VPN.

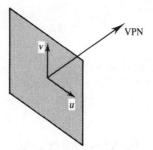

a centre of projection (COP), the COP has to be separately specified. The VRP is now just a reference point for a coordinate system and can be placed anywhere that is convenient. It can, for example, form the view plane origin, or it can be placed at the world coordinate origin, or at the centre of the object of interest. Placing it other than at the view plane origin has the advantage that the view plane distance (VPD) has some meaning as a view distance. If the VRP is located in the view plane the VPD becomes zero and is redundant as a parameter. Also, to move further or nearer to an object, only the VPD needs changing.

A view plane can be positioned anywhere in world coordinate space. It can be behind, in front of or cut through objects. Having established the position and orientation of a view plane we now proceed to set up a *u–v* coordinate system in the view plane with the VRP (or its projection on the view plane) as origin (Figure 1.13). The two-dimensional *u–v* coordinate system and the VPN form a three-

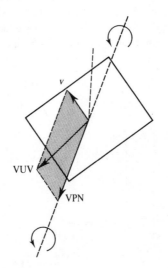

Figure 1.14
The VUV establishes the direction of the *v* axis allowing the viewplane to 'twist' about the VPN.

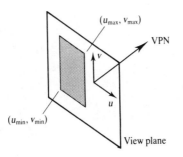

Figure 1.15
Establishing a
two-dimensional window
in the viewplane.

dimensional left-handed coordinate system in which a viewing window
will be defined. The orientation of the *u–v* axes is determined by the view
up vector (VUV) which defines a 'twist' about the VPN (Figure 1.14).
The general effect of this vector is to determine whether the scene is
viewed upright, upside down or whatever. The direction of the *v* axis is
determined by the projection of the VUV parallel to the VPN onto the
view plane.

With a two-dimensional coordinate system established in the view
plane a two-dimensional window can be set (Figure 1.15). This takes care
of the mapping from the unconstrained or application-oriented vertex
values in world coordinate space to appropriate values in the view plane
extent. All other things being equal, this window setting determines the
size of the object(s) on the view surface.

General viewing systems also allow a three-dimensional subset of
world coordinate space to be selected to undergo the viewing system transformations. This space is known as the view volume. Without clipping
planes, the view volume for a perspective projection is a rectangular pyramid with the apex at the centre of projection (Figure 1.16).

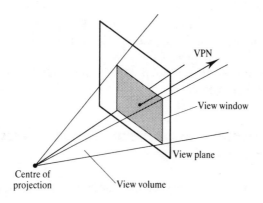

Figure 1.16
View volume formed by
the view window and the
centre of projection.

Figure 1.17
Using clip planes to establish a finite view volume. Distances are measured along the VPN and clip planes are normal to this vector.

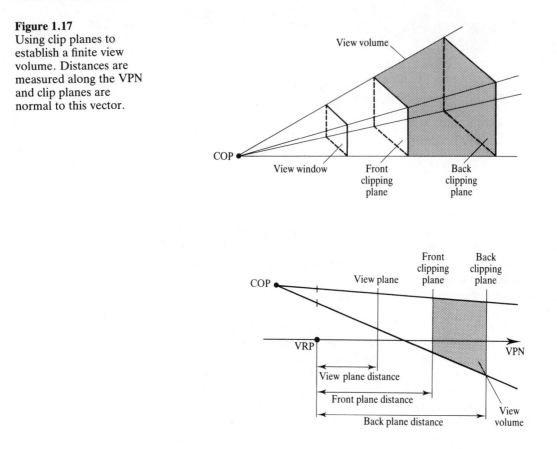

Every vertex contained in this semi-infinite region is projected onto the view plane. A finite view volume is defined by using a front and back clipping plane. This restricts the view volume to a doubly truncated pyramid formed by the four lines through the centre of projection and the view window corners, and the clip planes. These are shown in Figure 1.17 together with the setting distances. The orientation of these planes is always parallel to the view plane.

An example of a shaded object 'interacting' with various view volumes is given in Plate 2.

1.5.6 Summary of general viewing system parameters

Table 1.1 shows a summary of the parameters used in general viewing systems.

Table 1.1 General viewing system parameters.

Parameter	Specification	Conventional default	Function effect
View reference point (VRP)	Three-dimensional point in world coordinate space	0, 0, 0	Reference point used to establish view plane and clip plane positions
View plane distance (VPD)	Scalar	0	Distance from the VRP to the view plane along the VPN
View plane normal (VPN)	Three-dimensional vector	0, 0, −1 0, 0, +1	Establishes the orientation of the view plane
View up vector (VUV)	Three-dimensional vector	0, 1, +1	Establishes the direction of the v axis in the view plane
Front plane distance	Scalar	0	Distance from the VRP to the front clip plane
Back plane distance	Scalar	1	Distance from the VRP to the back clip plane
Projection type			Defines the projection to be parallel or perspective
Projection point (COP)	Three-dimensional point relative to VRP	0, 0, 0	Defines a centre for a perspective projection
Projection direction	Three-dimensional vector		Direction for a parallel projection
View plane window	Two two-dimensional points	0, 1, 0, 0.75	Defines the mapping from world coordinate space to view plane space

1.5.7 General viewing systems: examples

We now consider a few examples of the use of the parameters in Table 1.1 (Figure 1.18). These were produced on the SunCore system, which is almost compatible with PHIGS and GKS-3D. (The example system uses a left-hand UVN coordinate system in the view plane, GKS-3D and PHIGS use a right-hand coordinate system.) The examples are intended merely to give a feel for a comprehensive viewing system and are reproduced without comment concerning their ease of use and understanding. All projections are perspective. (This is the only machine–system-dependent example in the text.)

The VRP is set equal to (0, 0, 0), the world coordinate origin and centre of the object of interest. The caption associated with each example contains information extracted from the viewing system parameters and is compressed to ease interpretation. The view distance (VPD) is negative because it is measured with respect to the direction of the VPN. The COP information given (projection distance) is the distance from the VRP to the COP.

(1)   This is the reference figure. The F is defined in a cube $(-1, -1, -1)$ to $(1, 1, 1)$ in world coordinate space.

(2)   The viewing distance is increased, decreasing the size of the object.

(3)   The view up vector is given a non-zero Y component. This vector can be perceived as the orientation of the screen with respect to the projection. Using the camera analogy, this is equivalent to rotating the camera about the direction it is pointing in.

(4)   The view plane normal is changed by rotating it about the Z axis (increasing its Y component).

(5)   The projection distance approaches the region of the object and the perspective effect is greatly exaggerated because the two distances are comparable with the extent of the object.

1.6   Three-dimensional viewing pipeline

The complete series of transformations involved in going from three-dimensional world coordinates to a display on a view surface is usually referred to as the three-dimensional viewing pipeline. This is a set of standard transformations, some of the components of which are set by the user, with others that are invisible to the user. Although it is not strictly necessary for a high level graphics programmer to be familiar with these transformations, it is always judicious to be aware of them and an

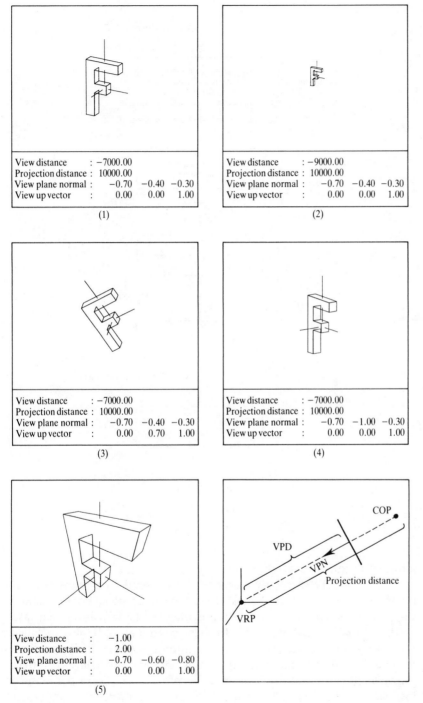

View distance	: −7000.00		
Projection distance :	10000.00		
View plane normal :	−0.70	−0.40	−0.30
View up vector	: 0.00	0.00	1.00

(1)

View distance	: −9000.00		
Projection distance :	10000.00		
View plane normal :	−0.70	−0.40	−0.30
View up vector	: 0.00	0.00	1.00

(2)

View distance	: −7000.00		
Projection distance :	10000.00		
View plane normal :	−0.70	−0.40	−0.30
View up vector	: 0.00	0.70	1.00

(3)

View distance	: −7000.00		
Projection distance :	10000.00		
View plane normal :	−0.70	−1.00	−0.30
View up vector	: 0.00	0.00	1.00

(4)

View distance	: −1.00		
Projection distance :	2.00		
View plane normal :	−0.70	−0.60	−0.80
View up vector	: 0.00	0.00	1.00

(5)

Figure 1.18
Examples of the use of a general viewing system.

Figure 1.19
Three-dimensional
viewing pipeline.

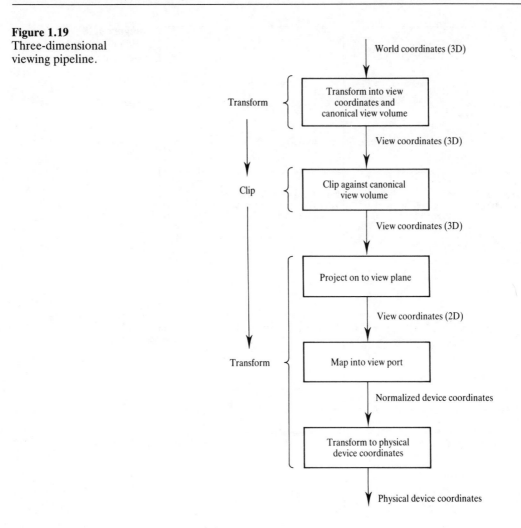

informal treatment now follows.

Figure 1.19 shows the pipeline. It is essentially a transform–clip–transform sequence, with the last three transforms being combined into a single operation. The first operation is the viewing transformation taking vertices in world coordinates into view coordinates. It also includes a transformation of the view volume into a so-called canonical view volume. This transformation simplifies the clipping procedure. Its effect is shown in Figure 1.20 for a perspective projection. Two operations are involved; first a shear to bring the centre of projection onto a line perpendicular to the centre of the view window. A scaling transform,

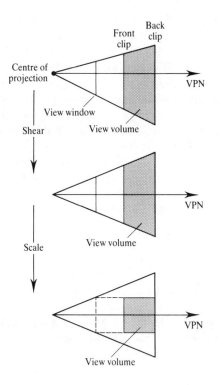

Figure 1.20
Producing a canonical
view volume for a
perspective projection.

inversely proportional to the distance from the view window, then converts the view volume into a rectangular parallelepiped. Clipping is now simple because each surface is perpendicular to one of the coordinate axes. Standard two-dimensional clipping algorithms are easily extended into this three-dimensional context.

The final two steps in the three-dimensional pipeline are the standard final processes in a two-dimensional pipeline. These involve transforming the view window contents into the view port (the part of the display surface selected) and finally transforming these coordinates into physical device coordinates.

1.7 An aside on graphics languages

High level programming of raster graphics terminals is facilitated either by using a set of manufacturer's utilities embedded in a high level language such as C or Pascal, or by using a standard such as GKS or PHIGS, bound to a high level language. The use of manufacturer's utilities is still the most popular approach because raster graphics terminals are evolving rapidly and the standards do not reflect the new hardware facilities that are available. As discussed in the Preface, rendering software requires very few graphics utilities. The current three-dimensional facilities in PHIGS and GKS-3D do not include any lighting or shading options and so the choice of programming approach is largely academic except for the case of line drawing in three dimensions. The new proposed standard, or extension, PHIGS+ includes lighting, shading and depth cueing, as well as curve and surface primitives (PHIGS, 1988).

The GKS–PHIGS philosophy on line drawing departs from the 'traditional' approach used in computer graphics. Any two-dimensional figure made up of a set of line segments can be constructed from the pair of utilities:

> *move_to* (x, y)
> *line_to* (x, y)

where the parameters refer, say, to absolute screen coordinates. These utilities function by referring to a current position register. *Line_to* (x, y) draws a straight line from the current position to the point (x, y) and updates the current position to (x, y). *Move_to* (x, y) updates the current position register. In systems that provide three-dimensional wireframe facilities, this approach is extended to:

> *move_to3D* (x, y, z)
> *line_to3D* (x, y, z)

which 'plot' lines in world coordinate space that are projected onto the screen using the viewing parameters set up by the user.

The GKS–PHIGS approach is a single utility:

> *polyline* (*list*)

This single statement constructs a complete line segment figure given a set of two-dimensional vertices or line segment end-points in *list*.

It is this philosophy that has been extended into GKS-3D and PHIGS as:

> *polyline3* (*list*)

This draws a figure made up of three-dimensional line segments from a list of three-dimensional world coordinates. These appear as a wireframe model on the screen after passing through the three-dimensional pipeline, the viewing parameters of which are defined by the user. This single statement together with model definitions and viewing parameter initialization are all that is required to define a wireframe in such a system.

1.8 Polygon mesh models and wireframe representation

1.8.1 Wireframes and polygon meshes

A popular representation of three-dimensional objects is the wireframe model. Here the object is displayed as a set of straight lines that join vertices together. Compared with shading an object, drawing a wireframe model is very fast. It will use, say, a few hundred calls to the basic line-drawing utility, and the complete model will be drawn in the order of seconds rather than the minutes generally required for a shaded representation. This speed is the main reason for its ubiquity. Hidden lines can be removed or left in as required and the interpretation of wireframes can be enhanced by the judicious use of colour and depth cueing.

Wireframes are used as a preview facility when the final image is to consist of a scene made up of shaded objects and they are used extensively in CAD applications both as a preview and as a final representation.

Three-dimensional computer animation makes extensive use of wireframe previews. The choreography of objects and the virtual camera needs to be worked out and evaluated using wireframe sequences before a set of frames is rendered. Current workstations can cope easily with wireframes of complex scenes in real time, and the images impart sufficient information for the animator to evaluate the sequence. In fact wireframe animation sequences are a pure analogy of the pencil or line test employed by traditional animators. Here the animator draws a sequence of outline drawings with no colour fill to test the dynamics of the movement.

A wireframe model is the simplest visualization of an object represented as a polygon mesh model. Although a polygon mesh model is a simple concept, its exact form and the data structure in which it is embedded depend on the use to which it is to be put. To produce a wireframe model a simple data structure suffices for the polygon mesh. However, to produce a shaded model a more complex data structure, dealt with in Appendix B, is necessary.

One of the simplest ways to represent a polygon mesh structure is to define each surface by pointers into a list of polygons and each polygon by pointers into a list of vertices. This means that each vertex – a list of three floating point numbers – is only stored once (Figure 1.21).

An object is made up of a set of polygons and it is convenient to define a two-level hierarchy in which an object is made up of surfaces that consist of polygons. A data structure used in a program that draws a wireframe model is given in Appendix B. A conceptual reflection of the structure is shown in Figure 1.22. This shows an object – a cylinder –

31

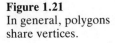

Figure 1.21
In general, polygons
share vertices.

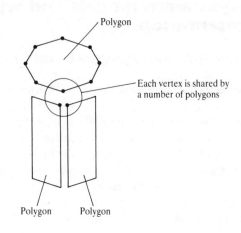

made up of three surfaces. The end surfaces are single polygons and the
curved surface is made up of a set of polygons (rectangles in this case).
The number of polygons used to represent a curved surface determines
the visual accuracy of the final display. This consideration is critically
important when a shaded model is to be produced; it is less important for
wireframe models.

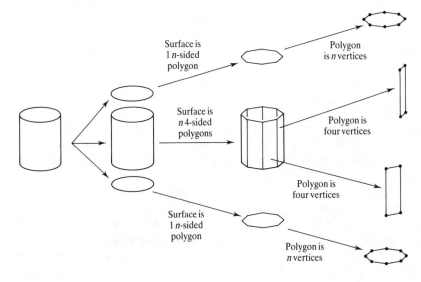

Figure 1.22
Hierarchical structure for
polygon mesh models.

Incidentally, a major problem with polygon mesh models, when the data is not derived analytically but produced manually or from a three-dimensional digitizer, is deciding on the 'polygonal resolution' for surface areas that are not of constant curvature. More polygons per unit area need to be used in regions where the curvature varies rapidly.

The final procedures in the program that draws a wireframe model are reproduced in Program 1.1. The hierarchy in the code reflects the hierarchy in the data structure. The procedure *DrawObject* extracts the required surfaces from the data structure and calls *DrawSurface*. This procedure fetches the polygons for a surface and calls *DrawPolygon*. *DrawPolygon* moves to the first vertex, fetches vertices in sequence and draws to them. The draw and move procedures apply the view point transformation. These procedures are extracted from a complete wireframe system. The reproduced code is given simply to underline the hierarchy in Figure 1.22. It is part of a complete system detailed in Appendix B and contains machine–system dependent utilities. These are three-dimensional versions of the *move_to* and *line_to* utilities mentioned previously and they work in conjunction with a set of predefined viewing parameters. Thus, at the moment, two approaches to wireframe drawing are possible:

(1)   Use your own world-to-screen coordinate viewing system and use (two-dimensional) *line_to* and *move_to* utilities.

(2)   If you have a viewing system already (this will usually be the full general system already described) use this together with associated three-dimensional versions of *line_to* and *move_to*.

A disadvantage of the object surface polygons pointing directly into a vertex list is that edges are not shared, and in general each edge will be plotted twice, the complete wireframe taking twice as long to draw. This is clearly a disadvantage in such applications as animation and the significance of this disadvantage increases with the complexity of the model. An advantage of storing each vertex once is that memory space is saved. Also, it is easy to change the coordinate values of a vertex (because there is guaranteed to be only one occurrence of a vertex in the list). This is important in interactive CAD where the user of an interactive data entry program may want to edit the model by changing a vertex.

An alternative common representation that avoids edge duplication is the representation of a polygon as a list of pointers into an edge list (rather than as a list of pointers into a vertex list). Each edge only occurs once and is stored as a list of two vertices together with two polygons that share the edge. A wireframe of this representation is constructed by drawing all the edges.

Program 1.1 Procedures for drawing wireframe models.†

```
procedure DrawSurface(Surface: SurfacePtr);
var
  Polygon: PolygonPtr;

  procedure DrawPolygon(Polygon: PolygonPtr);
  var
    VList: VertexList;
    StartPos: Vector;

    procedure DrawVNormal(Vertex: VertexPtr);
    var
      tvec: Vector;
    begin
      with Vertex^ do
      begin
        tvec.x := WorldPosition.x + 0.1*Normal.x;
        tvec.y := WorldPosition.y + 0.1*Normal.y;
        tvec.z := WorldPosition.z + 0.1*Normal.z;
        MoveTo3D(WorldPosition);
        DrawTo3D(tvec);
      end;
    end   {DrawVNormal};

  begin   {DrawPolygon}
    with Polygon^ do
      if not Culled then
      begin
        VList := Vertices;
        StartPos := VList^.Vertex^.WorldPosition;
        MoveTo3D(StartPos);
        VList := VList^.Rest;
        while VList < > nil do
        begin
          DrawTo3D(VList^.Vertex^.WorldPosition);
          VList := VList^.Rest;
        end;
        DrawTo3D(StartPos);
        if DrawVertexNormals then
        begin
          VList := Vertices;
          while VList < > nil do
          begin
            DrawVNormal(VList^.Vertex);
            VList := VList^.Rest;
          end;
        end;
      end;
  end   {DrawPolygon};
```

```
begin   {DrawSurface}
  with Surface^ do
  begin
    Polygon := PolygonHead;
    while Polygon < > nil do
    begin
      DrawPolygon(Polygon);
      Polygon := Polygon^.Next;
    end;
  end;
end   {DrawSurface};
```

```
procedure DrawObject(Object: ObjectPtr);
var
  Surface: SurfacePtr;

    procedure MoveTo3D(p: vector);
    var
      f: integer;
    begin
      with p do
        f := moveabs3(x, y, z);
    end   {MoveTo3D};

    procedure DrawTo3D(p: vector);
    var
      f: integer;
    begin
      with p do
        f := lineabs3(x, y, z);
    end   {DrawTo3D};

    procedure DrawSurface(Surface: SurfacePtr);
    { . . . body of procedure . . . }

begin   {DrawObject}
  with Object^ do
  begin
    Surface := SurfaceHead;
    while Surface < > nil do
    begin
      DrawSurface(Surface);
      Surface := Surface^.Next;
    end;
  end;
end   {DrawObject};
```

† See Appendix B for variable definitions.

1.8.2 Back face elimination (culling) and polygon normals

A particular advantage of structuring a polygon mesh model as described in Section 1.8.1 is that it allows back-facing surfaces to be culled. A back-facing surface is one that cannot possibly be seen from the view point. This operation will remove a significant proportion of the hidden lines from the wireframe display. If the object is convex then all the hidden lines are removed. Culling is a low cost-operation and is always applied as a preprocessing operation prior to general hidden surface removal and scan conversion in shaded models.

In a complex multi-object scene culling will typically remove about 50% of the surfaces, leaving the general problems that would result from, for example, overlapping objects, to more expensive hidden surface removal algorithms. In the context of a wireframe model, Figure 1.23 shows the lines that are removed by culling (dashed lines in the diagram) and the lines that would be removed by a general hidden surface removal algorithm (dotted lines in the diagram).

Given a view point (in a general viewing system using a perspective projection this will be the centre of projection) we determine whether or not a polygon is visible from the view point. Polygon visibility is determined by calculating the angle between the polygon surface normal and the 'line-of-sight' vector, which is simply the line from the base of the surface normal to the viewpoint. The surface is visible if, and only if, the angle between these two vectors is less than 90°. That is:

$$\text{visibility} := N \cdot V > 0$$

where V is the line-of-sight vector. Figure 1.24 shows a cube, two polygons or surfaces of which are visible and one which is invisible.

Figure 1.23
Culling wireframe images:
---, lines that are removed by culling;
....., lines that can only be removed by a general hidden surface removal algorithm.

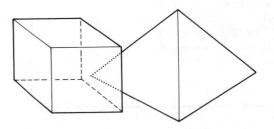

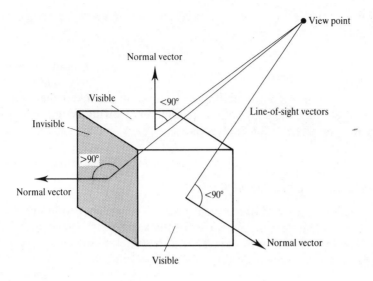

Figure 1.24
Back face elimination:
two visible polygons and
one invisible polygon.

A polygon surface normal can be calculated from three non-collinear vertices. These define two vectors contained in the plane of the polygon, the cross-product of which gives the surface normal (Figure 1.25). Provided that the three points occur in a counterclockwise direction around the polygon, when looking from the outside, the normal will point outwards as required for this test. Note that removing a surface from a wireframe display removes hidden lines.

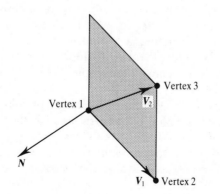

Figure 1.25
Normal vector N is
calculated from the cross-product of the vectors V_1
and V_2.

Projects, notes and suggestions

1.1 Wireframe drawing

Write a program to draw a wireframe of a simple asymmetric object, using two-dimensional line drawing utilities, the simple (four-parameter) viewing system and a hierarchical data structure of surfaces and polygons.

1.2 Scene generation and linear transformations

Build a scene from a limited number of objects using simple linear transformations. Adapt your data structure to handle multiple copies of the same object by storing a transform matrix for each instance of each object. Thus a scene consisting of say n objects will only access m unique object descriptions (where $m < n$).

1.3 Interacting with a wireframe object (*)

Write a simple modelling program that enables a user to select a vertex of a wireframe model displayed on the screen and to pull the vertex around in three-dimensional space to alter the shape of the object.

The project highlights a number of problems with this type of interaction. First you will possibly only have access to a two-dimensional locator device, and this has to be used both as a three-dimensional pick to select a vertex and as a three-dimensional locator to move the vertex around.

Vertex selection can be reduced to a two-dimensional problem if the vertices do not overlap in screen space. Maintaining a list of (x_s, y_s) positions of each vertex in the object, for a particular view, together with a spatial tolerance will enable a vertex to be selected in two-dimensional screen space.

To move the vertex around, the two-dimensional locator needs to be used in three-dimensional space. An obvious approach is to use, say, a mouse in two operational modes; one the normal coupled x, y mode, which will allow movement in an x_w, y_w plane, the other mode simulating a potentiometer and allowing movement up and down the z_w axis. (Extending the use of a mouse to accommodate three-dimensional graphics is a relatively unexplored topic. Three-dimensional locator devices exist but they are uncommon.)

Moving the vertex around means re-drawing, say in a different colour, those edges that join at the vertex. If your workstation is powerful enough then you can implement this animated feedback loop by re-drawing the entire object. Otherwise two-dimensional line-drawing utilities need to be animated in an 'erase–draw' sequence, under control of an exclusive-or Raster_op so that moving lines do not erase stationary lines.

The vertex dragging needs to be operated in two modes, move and fix. See Foley and Van Dam (1982) for full details on two-dimensional interactive techniques.

1.4 Viewing system interface

Design a view port that maintains a current line-drawing representation of the viewing system parameters; this should be a two-dimensional projection of the viewing system from an appropriate view point (see, for example, Figure A.2). We now have two view points: a primary view point used in the main view port for looking at the object and a view point used for the interaction view port that looks at the primary view point embedded in its spherical coordinate system. This enables a user to move the view point in an intuitive manner from its current position to a new position.

Note that the choice of the view point for the viewing system representation is not arbitrary. If the projection of the viewing system is going to be useful, then a view point should be chosen that is itself a function of the main viewing parameters.

1.5 Volume sweeping

Volume sweeping is a common technique in CAD for generating ducted solids. For example, a toroid can be generated by sweeping a circle around the circumference of another circle.

Generate a wireframe model of, say, a toroid in this manner. A polygon mesh representation can be obtained, for the purposes of a wireframe, by sweeping a cross-sectional polygon with, say, n vertices around a circle and generating n polygons (on the fly) as the cross-section is moved from one incremental position to the other.

A parametric representation for the purpose of vertex generation is:

$$x = (R + r \cos \phi) \cos \theta$$
$$y = (R + r \cos \phi) \sin \theta$$
$$z = r \sin \phi$$

This scheme is shown in Figure 1.26 and will result in the standard program structure, for this method of a nested loop.

Note that, in general, there are potential problems with this technique that you may have to consider. For example, with the toroid, the size of the polygons on the inside is less than those on the outside and this discrepancy is a function of both the generating radius and the radius of the cross-section. Such discrepancies can cause visible shading defects.

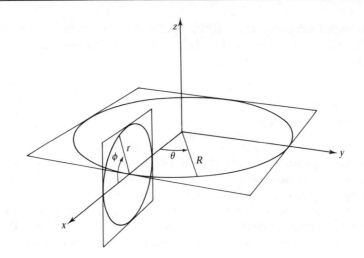

Figure 1.26   Parametric scheme for generating a wireframe toroid.

Investigate variations on the toroid; for example, modulate the generating radius with a sine wave (whose amplitude is small with respect to the radius).

1.6   Volume sweeping and modelling

Using suitable two-dimensional interactive techniques (see, for example, rubber-banding in Foley and Van Dam (1982)) design a system that enables any two-dimensional piecewise linear shape to be developed.

Input this shape as a cross-section to a module that derives a three-dimensional polygon mesh model by rotating the cross-section around a selected circumference.

1.7   Ducting (extruding and rotating)

Use circular cross-sections to generate a polygon mesh model of a fibre optics cable as shown in Figure 1.27. This particular model is not well visualised by a wireframe. Short of rendering how can the wireframe display be improved?

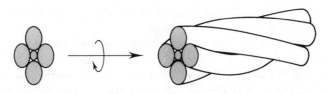

Figure 1.27   General ducting, creating a fibre optics cable by translating or extruding the cross-section and rotating.

1.8 Quadric surfaces

Using a similar technique to Project 1.5 build up a library of polygon mesh objects from quadric surfaces such as those shown in Figure 1.28 whose definitions are:

- Ellipsoid

$$x^2/a^2 + y^2/b^2 + z^2/c^2 - 1 = 0$$

where a, b and c are the semi-axes of the ellipse. $(0, 0, 0)$ is the centre of the ellipsoid and the solid can be generated by revolving:

$$x^2/a^2 + z^2/c^2 - 1 = 0, \; y = 0$$

contained in the x–z plane about the z axis.

- Hyperboloid:

$$x^2/a^2 + y^2/b^2 - z^2/c^2 - 1 = 0$$

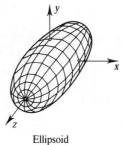

Ellipsoid

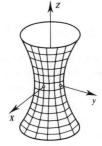

Hyperboloid

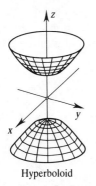

Hyperboloid

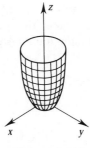

Elliptic paraboloid

Figure 1.28 Quadric surfaces.

and

$$x^2/a^2 + y^2/b^2 - z^2/c^2 + 1 = 0$$

$(0, 0, 0)$ is the centre of the object and the hyperboloid is obtained by revolving:

$$x^2/a^2 - z^2/c^2 \pm 1 = 0, \ y = 0$$

about the z axis.

- Elliptic paraboloid:

$$x^2/a^2 + y^2/b^2 = z$$

rotate:

$$x^2/a^2 - z = 0, \ y = 0$$

about the z axis.

1.9 Animated sequences

If you have a powerful enough workstation or a simple model, generate an animated sequence by choreographing a virtual camera (the view point). You might try a flight around an object combined with a zoom in and a zoom out. Investigate possibilities for virtual camera animation in both a simple and a general viewing system.

In a simple viewing system what happens when the view point moves inside the object?

1.10 Animated sequences and Barr's transformations

Generate an animated sequence showing a wireframe model of, say, a rectangular solid deforming. Do this by controlling a single parameter in one of Barr's transformations. Investigate the possibility of controlling two parameters, say bending and twisting, simultaneously.

1.11 Drawing surfaces

A common technique to display functions of the form:

$$z = f(x, y)$$

is to plot, say, the value of the function for constant y in x–z planes positioned at increasing values of y.

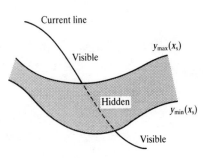

Figure 1.29   Maintaining two buffers that enable hidden portions to be removed from the line currently being plotted.

Maintaining two screen space buffers y_{max} (x_s) and y_{min} (x_s) enables hidden lines to be removed (Figure 1.29), the function only being drawn if the current value to be plotted (x_s, y_s) is such that:

$$y_s > y_{max} (x_s)$$

or

$$y_s < y_{min} (x_s)$$

Using this technique, write a program to plot

$$z = 3 \sin(x^2 + y^2)^{1/2}$$

CHAPTER TWO

A Basic Reflection Model

In this chapter we introduce the geometry of a simple and commonly used reflection model. A reflection model describes the interaction of light with a surface, in terms of the properties of the surface and the nature of the incident light. A reflection model is the basic factor in the look of a three-dimensional shaded object. It enables a two-dimensional screen projection of an object to look real – in the sense that a two-dimensional image such as a photograph is an acceptable representation of three-dimensional reality to human visual perception.

Conversely, an illumination model defines the nature of the light emanating from a source – the geometry of its intensity distribution etc. Outside research laboratories, most computer graphics shaders use simple reflection models and extremely simplified illumination models – usually a point source. This works because it works – it produces acceptable results using currently available hardware power and display devices.

The purpose of reflection models in computer graphics is to render three-dimensional objects in two-dimensional screen space such that reality is mimicked to an acceptable level. The phrase 'acceptable level' depends on the context of the application. The higher the degree of reality required, the more complex the reflection model and the greater the processing demands. For example, simple models are used in computer-generated imagery for flight simulators. Even with large multiple processors the prodigious demands of such systems constrain the accuracy of the reflection models and the geometric representation of the solids. Also, an accurate shading model in a flight simulator may not be as important as texturing a surface. Textures are important depth cues in flight simulators and texture mapping may place as heavy demands on the processor as reflection. In contrast, a television commercial comprising a short animated sequence may demand, for aesthetic reasons, a much richer reflection model and tens of minutes may be spent in generating each frame in the sequence on a single processor. Somewhere between these two extremes is the shading of solid models in CAD packages. Here a machine part may be designed interactively using a solid modelling capability. In the design loop a user of such a system may operate with wireframe models. To visualize the finished object most three-dimensional CAD systems have a shading option. This will use a basic reflection model to shade the surfaces of the object. Such a process running on a CAD workstation may run in real time or take tens of seconds to a few minutes to complete, depending on the capability of the workstation. Current workstations with hardware shaders are capable of shading hundreds of thousands of polygons per second.

A reflection model, not as basic as those used in flight simulation, nor as rich as the current research models in image synthesis, has been in use in computer graphics since the mid 1970s. It is with this model that we begin.

2.1 Simple reflection – the Phong model

Simple reflection models attempt to synthesize the way in which light interacts with a surface. The 'standard' model in computer graphics that compromises between acceptable results and processing cost is the Phong model (Phong, 1975a). This models reflected light in terms of a diffuse and specular component together with an ambient term. (The inadequacies of modelling reflection using these three terms are discussed later.) The intensity at a point on a surface is taken to be the linear combination of these three components.

Simple reflection models in computer graphics are subject to two distinct approximations. First there are geometric approximations to cut down on processing time, then there are physical approximations that constrain the complexity of the model. Geometric approximations are dealt with in context; here we briefly digress to discuss the nature of the physical model constraints.

First we consider an obvious equation:

light incident at a surface = light reflected
+ light scattered
+ light absorbed
+ light transmitted

This is shown diagrammatically in Figure 2.1. Computer graphics attends in most detail to reflected light and also models transmitted light. Note

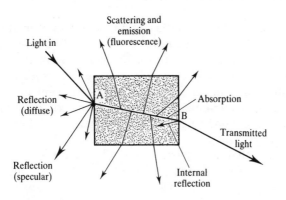

Figure 2.1
Light interactions with a solid.

from the diagram that a reflected component can also result from the transmitted component. The intensity and wavelength of light reflected from a surface depend on incident wavelength, the angle of incidence, the nature (roughness) of the surface material and its electrical properties (permittivity, permeability and conductivity). The exact interaction is extremely complex. For example, the same surface may be smooth for some wavelengths and rough for others; or for the same wavelength, it may be rough or smooth for different angles of incidence. Also we have the well-known empirical fact that any surface, regardless of its roughness, will reflect specularly at grazing incidence. Generally, we can define a bidirectional reflection function that is a function of the incident and the reflected angle: $R_{bd}(\phi_{in}, \theta_{in}, \phi_{out}, \theta_{out})$ where (ϕ, θ) is a direction in spherical coordinates. In the Phong reflection model we split R_{bd} into two components, dropping the directional dependence of the diffuse component.

Diffuse and specular light are both reflected components from the same surface. In the case of specular light we are viewing along or near to the mirror direction:

$$(\phi_{out}, \theta_{out}) = (\phi_{mirror}, \theta_{mirror})$$

and a smoothish surface tends to reflect a high intensity of incident light along this direction. Diffuse light is scattered in all directions and is also responsible for the colour of the object. This component of reflected light is due to incident light that has been both reflected and selectively absorbed according to material-dependent properties.

2.2 Diffuse reflection

Most objects that we see around us do not emit light of their own. Rather they absorb daylight, or light emitted from an artificial source, and reflect part of it. This reflection is due to molecular interaction between the incident light and the surface material. A green object, for example, absorbs white light and reflects the green component in the light. The detailed nature of such interactions need not concern us, but we note that a surface reflects coloured light when illuminated by white light and the coloured reflected light is due to diffuse reflection.

A surface that is a perfect diffuser scatters light equally in all directions. This means that the amount of reflected light seen by the viewer does not depend on the viewer's position. Such surfaces are dull or matt and the intensity of diffuse reflected light is given by Lambert's law:

$$I_d = I_i k_d \cos \theta \qquad 0 \leqslant \theta \leqslant \pi/2 \tag{2.1}$$

I_i is the intensity of the light source. θ is the angle between the surface normal and a line from the surface point to the light source (considered as a point source). The constant k_d is an approximation to the diffuse reflectivity which depends on the nature of the material and the wavelength of the incident light.

In Figure 2.2, surface 1 is parallel to the light beam and θ is 90°. Surface 2 is normal to the light source and θ is 0°. For surface 3, θ is less

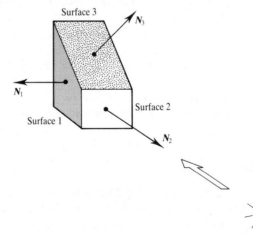

Figure 2.2
Three diffuse reflecting surfaces.

than 90°. Thus surface 1 would not be illuminated and surface 2 would be brighter than surface 3. k_d is a constant between 0 and 1 that depends on the material.

Equation 2.1 can be written as the dot product of two unit vectors:

$$I_d = I_i k_d \ (L \cdot N)$$

where N is the surface normal and L the direction vector from the light source to the point on the surface. If there is more than one light source then

$$I_d = k_d \sum_n I_{i,n} \ (L_n \cdot N)$$

where L_n is the direction vector from the nth light source to the point on the surface.

2.3 Ambient light

In Figure 2.2 surface 1 is parallel to the light source (and therefore invisible to it) but visible to the viewer. Such a surface is made visible by ambient light, otherwise it would be rendered black. Scenes illuminated by a point light source are unnatural and hard, like illuminating a scene at night with a thin flashlight beam. Also, it is clearly unsatisfactory that surfaces that are visible from the view point, but invisible from the light source, are rendered black. This is a state of affairs not normally encountered naturally.

Ambient light is the result of multiple reflections from walls and objects, and is incident on a surface from all directions. It is modelled as a constant term for a particular object using a constant ambient reflection coefficient. Combination of the diffuse and ambient terms gives:

$$I = I_a k_a + I_i k_d \ (L \cdot N) \tag{2.2}$$

The approximation here is again the constancy of the term. Ambient light originates from the interaction of diffuse reflection from all the surfaces in the scene. Considering ambient light intensity as a global term, constant over all the three-dimensional space of the scene, is a first approximation to modelling diffuse light globally. In effect, this simplification means that we are considering the objects as if they are floating in free space, with no interactions between objects themselves, or between objects and backgrounds.

2.4 Distance

At this stage in the development of the model we consider the role of distance. We can add a term that reduces light intensity as a function of the distance of the surface from the light source. This ensures that surfaces of the same colour, but at different distances from the light source, are not assigned the same intensity. For reasons that are explained later, light sources are considered to be at infinity and a measure equal to the distance from the view point to the surface can be used instead. Equation 2.2 becomes:

$$I = I_a k_a + I_i k_d \ (\textbf{L·N})/(r + k) \tag{2.3}$$

where r is the distance to the view point and k is a constant. In applications where efficiency is critical this denominator need not be used. It has little effect on the final look of the image. In contexts where depth cueing is important, for example flight simulation, a more complex model is used to simulate atmospheric haze and fading.

2.5 Specular reflection

Most surfaces in real life are not perfectly matt and do not behave as perfect diffusers of light. Surfaces usually have some degree of glossiness. A perfect glossy surface is a mirror. Glossy surfaces are different from matt surfaces in a number of important respects. Firstly, light reflected from a glossy surface leaves the surface at angle θ, where θ is the angle that the incident beam makes with the surface (Figure 2.3). This means that the degree of specular reflection seen by a viewer depends on the viewing direction. Consider the case of a perfect glossy surface illuminated by a single point source. All the light from the source is reflected along one particular direction, the mirror direction, and will only be seen when the surface is viewed from this direction. The surface will only appear bright for a single viewing direction and dark for all

Figure 2.3
For a perfect mirror surface the angle of reflection is equal to the angle of incidence.

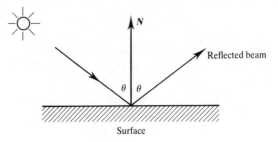

50

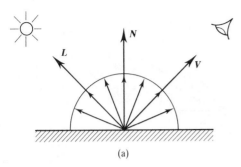

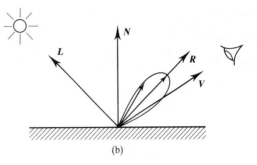

(a)

(b)

Figure 2.4
(a) Diffuse reflection – light is scattered in all directions from a point on the surface.
(b) Specular reflection – light is concentrated around the mirror direction **R**.

others. In practice, specular reflection is not perfect and reflected light can be seen for viewing directions close to the direction of the reflected beam (Figure 2.4). The area over which specular reflection is seen is commonly referred to as a highlight and this phrase describes a second important aspect of this type of reflection: the colour of the specularly reflected light is different from that of the diffuse reflected light. In simple models of specular reflection the specular component is assumed to be the colour of the light source. If, say, a green surface is illuminated with white light then the diffuse reflection component is green but the highlight is white.

For a single ray or a single point on the surface we can model specularly reflected light by considering two more vectors. In Figure 2.5 **L** and **N** are as before, **R** is the direction along which specular light is reflected and **V** is the viewing direction. ϕ is the angle between the viewing vector and the reflection vector (both unit vectors). For a perfect mirror this angle must be zero for any specular light to be seen. In practice, as we have already mentioned, specular reflection is seen over a range of ϕ that depends on the glossiness of the surface. Bui-Tuong Phong (1975a) modelled this behaviour empirically by a term $\cos^n \phi$. For a perfect reflector n is infinite. A very glossy surface produces a small highlight area and n is large (Figure 2.6). As a surface becomes more and

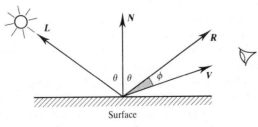

Surface

Figure 2.5
ϕ and **V** used in the calculation of the specular term.

Figure 2.6
(a) Large n simulates a glossy surface, (b) small n simulates a less glossy surface.

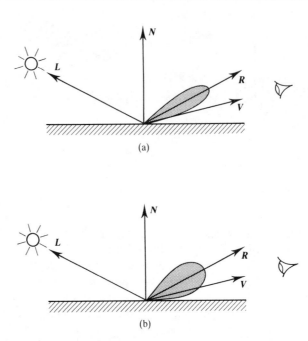

(a)

(b)

more matt the highlight areas become more spread out and their intensity diminishes in relation to the diffuse reflection component. Equation 2.3 becomes:

$$I = I_a k_a + I_i [k_d \ (\boldsymbol{L \cdot N}) + k_s \ \cos^n \phi] / (r + k)$$
$$= I_a k_a + I_i [k_d \ (\boldsymbol{L \cdot N}) + k_s \ (\boldsymbol{R \cdot V})^n] / (r + k) \qquad (2.4)$$

k_s is the specular reflection coefficient, usually taken to be a material-dependent constant. (Bui-Tuong Phong (1975a) uses $W(i)$ as the specular reflectivity, where W is actually a function of i, the incidence angle, but he gives no details on the nature of this dependence, and Equation 2.4, with constant k_s, is usually quoted as the Phong model.) Figure 2.7 shows the variation in light intensity at a point P on a surface calculated using Equation 2.4. The intensity variation is shown as a profile – a function of the orientation of V. The intensity at P is given by the length of V from P to its intersection with the profile. The semicircular part of the profile is the contribution from the ambient and diffuse terms. The specular part of the profile is shown for different values of n. Note that large values of n are required for a tight highlight to be obtained.

Like the diffuse term this simple model of specular reflection is a local model. Only the interaction at a surface point from the light sources is considered. Light reflected onto the surface that originates from

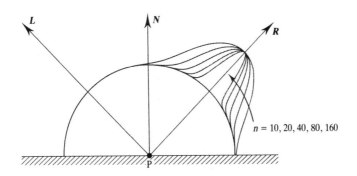

Figure 2.7
The light intensity at point P as a function of the orientation of the viewing vector **V**.

specular reflections in other objects is not considered. This is a much more severe constraint than the locality of the diffuse term. It excludes reflections of other objects in the surface of the object being rendered. This is solved by using a simple but extremely expensive global model for specular reflection called ray tracing. This is discussed in detail in Chapter 7.

2.6   Geometric considerations

The expense of Equation 2.4 can be considerably reduced by making some geometric assumptions and approximations. Firstly, if the light source and the viewpoint are considered to be at infinity then **L** and **V** are constant over the domain of the scene. The vector **R** is expensive to calculate and, although Bui-Tuong Phong gives an efficient method for calculating **R**, it is better to use a vector **H**. This appears to have been first introduced by Blinn (1977). The specular term then becomes a function of $N \cdot H$ rather than $R \cdot V$. **H** is the unit normal to a hypothetical surface that is oriented in a direction halfway between the light direction vector **L** and the viewing vector **V** (Figure 2.8):

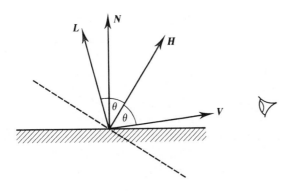

Figure 2.8
H is the normal to a surface orientation that would reflect all the light along **V**.

53

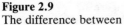

Figure 2.9
The difference between using (a) $R \cdot V$ and (b) $N \cdot H$ for a fixed value of n. Note the difference in the intensity in direction V.

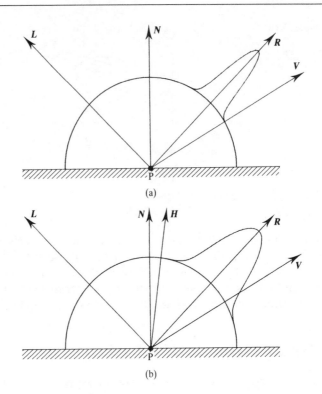

$$H = (L + V)/2$$

This is the required orientation for a surface to reflect light along the direction V. It is easily seen that the angle between R and V is twice the angle between N and H but this can be compensated for, if necessary, by adjusting n. Figure 2.9 shows the difference in the highlight for a single value of n. The use of $N \cdot H$ 'spreads' the highlight over a greater area. Equation 2.4 now becomes:

$$I = I_a k_a + I_i [k_d(L \cdot N) + k_s(N \cdot H)^n]/(r + k) \tag{2.5}$$

This now means that the intensity I is solely a function of the surface normal N. If L and V are constant vectors then so is H. There are two implications of placing the light source at infinity. First, there is no variation of shading over a planar surface (ignoring the effect of the distance denominator $(r + k)$), because L is now a constant and N does not change over the surface. Second, the shape of the specular highlight changes. In general the variation in $N \cdot H$ over a surface is less if H is a constant than if H is calculated from a varying L.

2.7 Colour

For coloured objects the easiest approach is to model the specular highlights as white (for a white light source) and to control the colour of the objects by appropriate setting of the diffuse reflection coefficients. We use three intensity equations to drive the monitor:

$$I_r = I_a k_{ar} + I_i[k_{dr}(L \cdot N) + k_s(N \cdot H)^n]$$
$$I_g = I_a k_{ag} + I_i[k_{dg}(L \cdot N) + k_s(N \cdot H)^n]$$
$$I_b = I_a k_{ab} + I_i[k_{db}(L \cdot N) + k_s(N \cdot H)^n]$$

Note that the specular term is common to all three equations. Summarizing these three equations as a single expression gives:

$$I(r, g, b) = I_a k_a(r, g, b) + I_i[k_d(r, g, b)(L \cdot N) + k_s(N \cdot H)^n] \qquad (2.6)$$

It should be mentioned at this stage that this three-sample approach to colour is a crude approximation and accurate treatment of colour requires far more than three samples. This point is dealt with at some length in Chapter 14.

2.8 Summary of the Phong model

The following points summarize the model. Most of the inadequacies or assumptions of the model will be dealt with in the course of the text.

- Light sources are assumed to be point sources. Any intensity distribution of the light source is ignored.
- All geometry except the surface normal is ignored (that is, light source(s) and viewer are located at infinity).
- The diffuse and specular terms are modelled as local components.
- An empirical model is used to simulate the decrease of the specular term around the reflection vector modelling the glossiness of the surface.
- The colour of the specular reflection is assumed to be that of the light source (that is, highlights are rendered white regardless of the material).
- The global term (ambient) is modelled as a constant.

Finally, note that because of its simplicity and the geometric constraints this much-loved reflection model, although it imparts a degree of realism sufficient for many applications, does carry a recognizable computer signature. The overall effect of the lack of interaction between objects in a scene is that they appear plastic like and floating. Shadows and approximate approaches to global illumination are dealt with in the course of the text and these two additions to the model mediate the floating effect. Also, note that the lack of shadows means not only that objects do not cast a shadow on other objects, but self-shadowing within an object is omitted. Concavities in an object that are hidden from the light source are erroneously shaded simply on the basis of their surface normal.

2.9 The 20 spheres – an example

This case study is a simple application of the Phong model and shows the effect of varying the proportion of specular to diffuse reflection and n, the specular modelling index, for a simple surface. Plate 3 shows the results of the program. It is based on an illustration by Roy Hall (Program of Computer Graphics, Cornell University, 1981). Twenty spheres are rendered using different values of k_d, k_s and n for a single-intensity equation for I_g. The tightness of the specular highlight, achieved by increasing n, varies vertically. Horizontal variation is the ratio of k_s to k_d. At the right-hand side k_d is unity and k_s is zero. k_d is then reduced to zero and k_s is increased to unity. Also in the plate is a set of intensity profiles for four of the spheres showing, for each sphere, in a plane through the highlight maximum, the contributions from the ambient term (fine dotted line), the diffuse term (dotted line) and the specular term (full line). For a particular point on the surface of the sphere (or that part of the surface cut by the plane through the highlight centre), the intensity is given by the sum of each profile (that is, the sum of the values from the centre to each profile).

The geometric model for this example is straightforward. We assume that the view point is located along the positive z axis at infinity and that the (x, y) values of the surface can be used directly as screen coordinates. The three-dimensional coordinates of points on the surface of the (visible) hemisphere are calculated and are used to produce the light intensity. This intensity, calculated for a point (x, y, z) on the surface of the hemisphere, is then displayed as pixel (x_s, y_s), where:

$$x_s = x$$
$$y_s = y$$

Incidentally, making up a special geometric, or programming model, for a particular set of objects to be rendered is a valid and much-used approach. Such are the processing overheads of three-dimensional modelling that a designer or programmer may use context-dependent techniques rather than a general-purpose system. This is particularly so in the case of an animated sequence, where a large number of frames have to be generated using variations of the same model.

The rendering program (Program 2.1) given uses two procedures: *ShadeSphere* initially calculates a point on the surface of the sphere. The surface normal at a point on the surface is simply (x, y, z). This is passed into *CalculateLNandNnH*. In this procedure the light direction vector L, the distance of the light source from the object d, and the vector H are declared as constants. The first calculation in this procedure is the dot product $L \cdot N$. If this is less than zero then the point under consideration is not visible from the light source, as discussed in Chapter 1. Alternatively, we can say that the angle between the surface normal N and the light direction vector L is greater than 90°. (It is instructive to examine the effect of omitting this **if** statement.) Note that if $L \cdot N$ is negative then that point on the surface is not visible to the light source and $L \cdot N$ is set to zero.

Finally, note that it is usually necessary to twiddle the intensity to produce a nice result. The brightest highlight in the illustration is maximum intensity white. Theoretically this is wrong. We are viewing along the positive z axis and the highlight intensity should only be the maximum value if we were viewing along the light reflection vector, that is if $V = R$. If, for example, we were producing an animated sequence and

Program 2.1   *Procedures for shading spheres.*

```
procedure ShadeSphere (Kd, Ks: real;
    SpecIndex, Xcentre, Ycentre, radius: integer);
const
    Ilight = 140;
    K = 70.0;
    IaKa = 0.2;
    Hx = 0.325058; Hy = 0.325058; Hz = 0.888074;
    dx = 110.0; dy = 110.0; dz = 110.0;
    Lx = 0.57735; Ly = 0.57735; Lz = 0.57735;
var
    Ig, Irb, x, y, z: integer;
    rsquare, xsquare, ysquare, zsquare, denom, xn, yn, zn, LdotN, NnH,
        dist, distfactor, ambientterm, diffuseterm, specularterm: real;

    procedure CalculateLNandNnH (x, y, z, SpecIndex: integer;
        xn, yn, zn: real; var LdotN, dist, NnH: real);
    var
        NH: real;
```

```
    begin
      LdotN := xn*Lx + yn*Ly + zn*Lz;
      if LdotN <= 0.0 then LdotN := 0.0
      else
      begin
        dist := sqrt (sqr (dx − x) + sqr (dy − y) + sqr (dz − z));
        NH := Hx*xn + Hy*yn + Hz*zn;
        NnH := exp (SpecIndex*ln (NH));
      end;
    end;   {CalculateLNandNnH}

begin   {ShadeSphere}
  rsquare := sqr (radius);
  for y := −radius to radius do
  begin
    ysquare := sqr (y);
    for x := −radius to radius do
    begin
      xsquare := sqr (x);
      if (xsquare + ysquare) <= rsquare then
      begin
        z := round (sqrt (rsquare − xsquare − ysquare));
        zsquare := sqr (z);
        denom := sqrt (xsquare + ysquare + zsquare);
        xn := x/denom; yn := y/denom; zn := z/denom;
        CalculateLNandNnH (x, y, z, SpecIndex, xn, yn, zn, LdotN, dist,
          NnH);
        ambientterm := IaKa;
        if LdotN <= 0.0 then
        begin
          Ig := round (255*ambientterm);
          Irb := 0;
        end
        else
        begin
          distfactor := Ilight/(dist + K);
          diffuseterm := distfactor*Kd*LdotN;
          specularterm := distfactor*Ks*NnH;
          Ig := round (255*(ambientterm + diffuseterm + specularterm));
          Irb := round (255*specularterm);
        end;
        WritePixel (Xcentre + x, Ycentre + y, Irb, Ig, Irb);
      end;
    end;
  end;
end; {ShadeSphere}
```

intended to move the view point around the sphere, then the highlight seen from the z axis would be dimmer than that seen when viewing along the light reflection vector. Another point in this connection is saturation of the highlight. If k_s is adjusted so that the calculated highlight intensity never exceeds the light source intensity or the maximum (RGB) value then for a sphere only one pixel will be rendered at maximum white. It may be desirable to allow the highlight intensity to saturate and render an area of pixels at maximum white. The visual effect of this factor worsens with increasing n.

One of the points of this case study is to demonstrate that a straightforward implementation of simple reflection models will not always produce acceptable results. As we have seen a considerable degree of *ad hoc* adjustment is necessary.

2.10 Using look-up tables with reflection models

A video look-up table (LUT) or colour table is a hardware table interposed between the screen memory and the image display system. Its original *raison d'être* was to 'extend' the colour range of a graphics terminal. For example, with an 8-bit screen memory a pixel on the screen can have one out of 256 colours. This range can be extended to any 256 colours out of a 'palette' of 2^{24} (16 million) by using an 8×24-bit LUT (Figure 2.10). In this system the pixel intensity, instead of appearing directly on the screen, is used to address a row in the LUT, the contents of which are displayed as an intensity on the screen. The fact that the entire contents of an LUT can be changed in real time leads to a number of uses in different areas of computer graphics.

An implication of the simplifications that reduce the reflected intensity to a function of N, that is $I = f(N)$, is that it is possible to

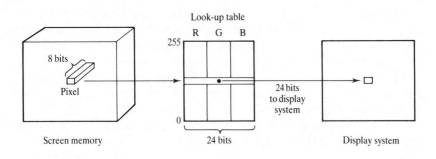

Figure 2.10
An 8-bit screen memory accessing an 8-bit × 24-bit look-up table.

59

precalculate a set of I values, to store these in a table and to use the surface normal to index the table. A (perhaps fairly rare) animation situation in which this method can provide a real-time or near-real-time sequence is where a three-dimensional scene is to remain static while the illumination sources move or change in some way; for example, in intensity or colour characteristics. If the scene remains static, then the surface normals do not change with time. Here the scene is stored in the screen memory as a set of surface normals. Changing the way in which the scene is illuminated is then easily accomplished, in real time, by changing the contents of the table storing the set of I values.

Bass (1981) used this method with a 12-bit LUT. This means that a total of 4096 different normal vectors can be used. In this is embedded the disadvantage of the method. 'Vector quantization noise' results, which manifests itself in coherent interference in the final image. The solution is, of course, to increase the entry dimension of the LUT at extra hardware cost.

The same basic idea can be used with a software table to reduce the calculation of I to an evaluation of the normalized surface normal. This has the disadvantage that a separate table must be stored for each object in the scene that has a different set of reflection coefficients. This will have the effect of considerably expanding the object database in most contexts. The method is useful in scenes consisting of many identical objects (for example, in rendering molecular models) where there will be a large number of occurrences of each possible surface normal.

A novel use of LUTs is described in Warn (1983). The idea here is to allow a degree of interactive control over the final appearance of the image; that is, the colour and the proportion of specular to diffuse reflection. Warn uses Phong's model but assumes that the intensity at a point on a surface consists of a diffuse and specular contribution, and that a particular intensity corresponds to exactly one combination of diffuse and specular components. (This is a simplification that appears to work in practice.) The calculated intensity is stored in a 10-bit frame buffer that is then used to access an LUT. The LUT is loaded with a set of diffuse colours of increasing intensity that blend into a set of specular colours (Figure 2.11). The diagonal line in Figure 2.11 represents the transition from diffuse colour to specular colour. Both the specular and diffuse colours can be changed interactively via a suitable user interface. (It will be shown later that it is not always a good approximation to have white specular highlights.) The 'blend' intensity, the threshold at which specular highlights start to occur, can also be changed interactively, altering the area of visible specular highlights and therefore the look of the image, without having to recalculate from the shading equation.

One disadvantage of this approach is that a separate partition is required in the LUT for each surface type. For a 10-bit table this places

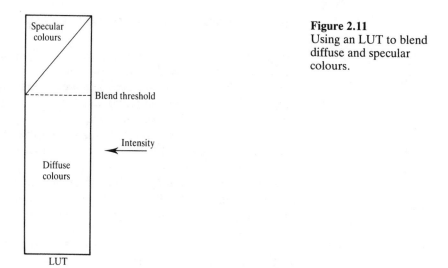

Figure 2.11
Using an LUT to blend
diffuse and specular
colours.

obvious restrictions on the number of surface types and the colour range within a surface type.

Plate 4 shows a demonstration of this process used in conjunction with a simple interactive technique for changing LUT contents. All three illustrations were obtained from one rendering process by changing LUT entries. Dividing the LUT into three columns, the red, green and blue components of the colour of an entry (the detailed use of the RGB colour model in computer graphics is dealt with extensively in Chapter 14), we rubber band the RGB profiles to set the entire contents of the LUT. Changing entries below the blend threshold alters the colour of the object, changing entries above this threshold alters the colours of the highlights and changing the value of the blend threshold alters the degree of specular reflection.

Each illustration shows an object together with its accompanying LUT profiles. The first illustration shows how both the colour of the object and the colour of the highlight are easily changed to simulate a metallic object – where the highlight colour is not necessarily white. In the second illustration the blend intensity is changed and the degree of specular to diffuse reflection altered. Special effects are easily obtained as shown in the final illustration.

This is a useful technique when a scene is being composed. Re-rendering by changing coefficients in the Phong equation can take minutes and if colour aesthetics are important then real-time interaction is vital.

2.11 Empirical transparency

Simple transparency effects in computer graphics are almost as common as simple reflection models. If refraction is ignored then transparency can be grossly (but effectively) approximated using a linear parameter t to mix the object colour with the intensity of a single background. For partially transparent objects that are hollow, t can be 'modulated' by the z component of the normalized surface normal of the projected object (Kay and Greenberg, 1979). We are then saying that t is a transparency factor that attenuates anything behind the object (further z) according to an amount that can be approximated by multiplying by N_z. For the paths shown in Figure 2.12, P_1 is longer than P_2 and point s on the surface of the object should exhibit a lower intensity of background colour than point r. t is given by:

$$t = t_{min} + (t_{max} - t_{min})N_z \tag{2.7}$$

The object colour I_0 is computed in the normal way using a reflection model. In the simplest case the background colour I_b can be a constant. The final intensity I is given by the mix:

$$I = tI_b + (1 - t)I_0 \tag{2.8}$$

If refractive effects are to be taken into account and the scene is simple –

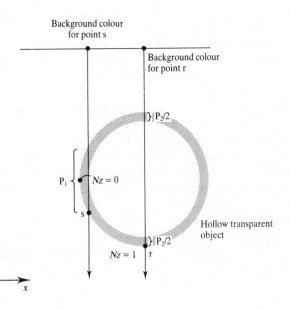

Figure 2.12
Mixing background colour and object colour as a function of N_z, the z component of the surface normal.

say a single planar background – then a simple special case ray tracing scheme (where rays terminate on the background) is easily implemented (see Chapter 7).

Finally, the main problem with transparency is that it cannot be easily integrated with the preferred rendering method – a Z-buffer based approach. Another empirical transparency model (Hall, 1983) is discussed in Section 7.8.

Projects, notes and suggestions

2.1 Shading spheres

Implement the program that shades spheres, for more than one light source. Alter Equation 2.6 so that different coloured light sources are possible (I now has red, green and blue components) and experiment with coloured light sources.

What are the problems involved in extending this scheme for shading spheres to any quadric surface and why is the general philosophy of combining a screen space procedure and a world space implicit definition unsatisfactory?

2.2 Light source interaction

Develop an interaction view port for the previous project, showing a view of a single sphere together with the light sources, that enables a user to change the position of each light source.

2.3 Reflection model representation

Write a program that generates a wireframe model of a three-dimensional version of Figure 2.7. This will show the variation in intensity over the hemispherical space surrounding a single point whose reflected intensity is calculated from Equation 2.5.

Ensure that the polygonal resolution is increased sufficiently in the region of the specular bump.

2.4 Transparency

Implement the empirical transparency scheme given by Equations 2.7 and 2.8 by shading a hollow transparent sphere in front of a suitable background.

2.5 Postprocessing shaded images

Write a program that postprocesses a shaded image using LUTs. Design an interface that allows a user to rubber-band LUT profiles as suggested by Plate 4.

CHAPTER THREE

A More Advanced Reflection Model

The first significant development in reflection models after the Phong model involved a physically based rather than an empirical specular term. This was first proposed by Blinn (1977) and was based on a surface model introduced by Torrance and Sparrow (1967). Cook and Torrance (1982a, 1982b) then enhanced this model to account for energy equilibrium and the change of colour within a specular highlight. In particular they directed their attention to the accurate rendering of different metallic and non-metallic surfaces. This development is a good example of the continuing quandary that faces image renderers – is the pursuit of more and more accurate physical models (which inevitably incur higher processing costs) worth the extra computing expense? A computer graphics image is, after all, an artifice created in the main for effect. Undoubtedly images that are accurately realistic have a place in computer graphics, but this does not imply that greater and greater realism is necessarily justified. Indeed, at the time of publication, it is almost certainly the case that most images are rendered with the Phong model.

3.1 The Cook and Torrance model

The Cook and Torrance model is distinguished from the Phong model by the following factors:

- It is based on a consideration of incident energy rather than intensity.

Figure 3.1
The value of the specular
intensity for high and low
angles of incidence.

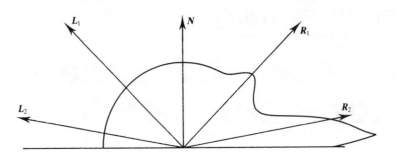

- The specular term is based on a physical microfacet model.
- Colour change within the highlight is based on Fresnel's law and measured characteristics of the material.

The model contains Blinn's treatment (Blinn, 1977) which includes the second factor but excludes the third. The model consists of three terms: the specular and diffuse reflection due to direct illumination and the global ambient component. In this respect, and the fact that it models light due to direct illumination only, it is similar to Phong's approach. One of the original aims of the model was to render polished metallic surfaces correctly. The Phong model gives the impression of coloured plastic surfaces. Also, it is inaccurate in the specular term for illumination at low angles of incidence. Physically, the amplitude of the specular 'bump' is a function of the angle the light source makes with the surface. Figure 3.1 shows the value of the reflected intensity for a light source at a high and low angle of incidence (L_1 and L_2) obtained using the improved model described in this chapter (using the Phong model, equal specular bumps would be produced at R_1 and R_2). That this behaviour occurs in reality is easily confirmed by viewing low incidence light reflected from a sheet of paper. In addition, for low angles of incidence, the maximum value of the specular bump is not coincident with the reflection vector R. The Cook and Torrance model corrects this defect, and this results in a change in the shape of the specular highlights for illumination at low incidence angles. Modelling the specular highlight correctly is particularly important in animated sequences that involve specular reflection.

The surface model on which this improved specular term is based is given in Torrance and Sparrow (1967). Blinn (1977) used this new specular term to account for the dependence of the magnitude of the specular highlight on the angle of incidence, and retained the approximation that the colour of the highlight is that of the light source. Cook and Torrance include the wavelength dependence of the specular reflection coefficient in the model.

In general the colour of a specular highlight depends on physical characteristics of the material except when the illumination is at a low angle of incidence. In the Phong model the highlight colour is the colour of the light source, usually white, and the change from a white highlight to a region exhibiting diffuse reflection means a change of colour that depends on the relative magnitudes of the diffuse and specular terms. As the specular term reduces to zero the colour surrounding the highlight would approach the colour given by the diffuse coefficients. Consider the spheres shown in Plate 3. As the intensity of the specular term reduces, the diffuse term predominates and the colour changes from white to green. This colour change is an effect that will only occur in practice for green-coloured plastic. Other materials will behave differently. In the Cook and Torrance model it is possible to represent, for example, highly polished metallic surfaces with a diffuse contribution of zero. A change in both the colour and the intensity of the highlight term is controlled by the value of the specular reflection coefficient.

The Cook and Torrance model is developed from a reflectance definition that relates the brightness of an object to the intensity and size of each light source that illuminates it. The basis of the model is the bidirectional reflectance R_{bd} which relates incident energy E_i to reflected intensity I_r:

$$R_{bd} = I_r / E_i$$

E_i is defined as energy incident on a surface element per unit time per unit area and is:

$$E_i = I_i(N \cdot L)\ dw_i$$

where dw_i is the solid angle of the incident light beam. This is equal to the projected area of the light source divided by the square of the distance to the light source and approximates a constant for a distant source. Thus:

$$I_r = R_{bd}E_i$$
$$= R_{bd}I_i(N \cdot L)\ dw_i$$

(Note that I_r depends on incident energy because the incoming beam is spread over a wide range of angles.) It is important to note that this is the reflected intensity for one particular direction and that R_{bd} varies over the hemispherical surface that specifies all reflecting directions. The bidirectional component is split into a diffuse and a specular contribution and we have:

$$R_{bd} = sR_s + dR_d \qquad \text{(where } s + d = 1)$$

This accounts for that component of illumination seen in a particular direction – the viewing direction, for example – originating from a direct source or a number of direct sources. To this must be added, as with the previous model, a term due to ambient illumination.

In the Phong model ambient illumination was modelled as a constant. In fact ambient illumination can be viewed as the inverse of the diffuse illumination process. A perfect diffuser reflects light equally in all directions. Light reflected along the viewing direction is considered to be the same as that reflected in any other direction in the hemispherical reflection space. Conversely, ambient light is incident on a surface element from every direction in the hemispherical reflection space. The amount of light reflected along the viewing direction from any particular incoming ambient direction is small, and is the incoming ambient intensity times R_a, the ambient reflectance for this direction. If we assume that R_a is a constant over the hemispherical space, then the total ambient illumination reflected along a particular direction is R_a times the integral of I_a, the incoming ambient intensity. If we assume that I_a is a constant over the space then the ambient term is again a constant and equal to $I_a R_a$. Since the ambient term can be considered to be the reflected intensity (diffuse and specular) from an infinity of low intensity direct light sources, R_a must be a linear combination of R_s and R_d. Such an approach reduces the model to a modified version of the Phong model – applicable to isolated objects floating in free space. In practice I_a depends on the proximity of objects to each other. An approximation to accurate computation of the global ambient term is to include a blocking fraction f. This is the fraction of the hemisphere that is not blocked by nearby objects. We then have:

global ambient term $= I_a R_a f$

and the complete model for the intensity at a point is:

$$I = I_a R_a f + \sum_n I_{i,n} \ (N \cdot L_n) \ \mathrm{d}w_{i,n} \ (d R_d + s R_s)$$

This model is distinguished from the previous by the fact that it contains a reflectance definition that relates the brightness of an object to the intensity and size of the light source that illuminates it. The other major distinction of the Cook and Torrance model is incorporated in the specular term. In the Phong model the angular spread of the specular contribution about the reflection vector R was modelled empirically using an exponentiated cosine term. Here the model is physical, based on a microfacet description of the surface introduced by Torrance and Sparrow (1967). This is based on the notion of a reflecting surface that consists of a large number of microfacets, each with perfectly reflecting or mirror faces (Figure 3.2). The geometric extent of a surface element – the unit of

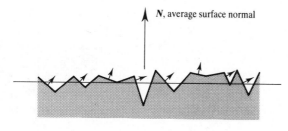

Figure 3.2
Microfacet model of a
reflecting surface: a set of
symmetric V-shaped
grooves whose
orientation can be
modelled by a
distribution about a
particular direction.

surface area from which a reflected intensity is calculated – means that it is made up of a collection of such microfacets. These can be described by a distribution function of the slope or orientation of the reflecting planes of the microfacets. The specular term in terms of this geometric surface model is:

$$R_s = \frac{FDG}{\pi \, (N{\cdot}V) \, (N{\cdot}L)} \qquad\qquad (3.1)$$

The influence of the terms F, D and G and $N{\cdot}V$ is now explained. The specular intensity along the V direction originates from those microfacets with planes oriented in the H direction. This is determined by a microfacet orientation distribution function. The function used by Torrance and Sparrow was a simple Gaussian:

$$D = k \, exp \, [-(\alpha/m)^2]$$

where k is a constant, α is the angle of the microfacet with respect to the normal of the (mean) surface, that is the angle between N and H, and m is the root mean square slope of the microfacets. For low values of m the surface is shiny or glossy. (If m is 0 the surface is a perfect mirror and H must be equal to N for there to be any contribution of the specular reflection along V.) A high value for m implies that the surface is dull. D quantifies the dependence of R_s on the angle between N and H. The Cook and Torrance model uses a distribution proposed by Beckmann and Spizzichino (1963):

$$D = \frac{1}{m^2 \, cos^4\alpha} \, exp \left[-\left(\frac{tan^2\alpha}{m^2} \right) \right]$$

This is computationally more expensive but is a function of m and α only and does not include an arbitrary constant. Lobes are shown in Figure 3.3 for Gaussian and Beckmann distributions for different values of m. The value of D is given as a distance from the surface element (to the outside

Figure 3.3
(a) Microfacet orientation distributions; (b) Gaussian distributions with m varying from 0.2 to 0.8.

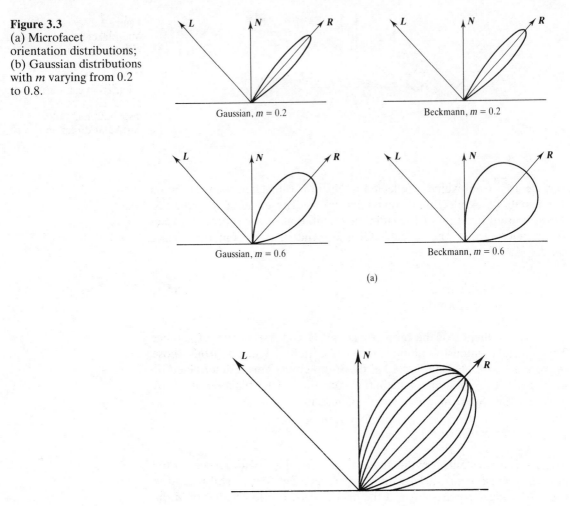

Gaussian, $m = 0.2$

Beckmann, $m = 0.2$

Gaussian, $m = 0.6$

Beckmann, $m = 0.6$

(a)

(b)

of the lobe) and is a maximum along the reflection vector R.

The inverse dependence of R_s on $N \cdot V$ can now be seen. As the angle between N and V is increased more of the surface is seen along the viewing direction. A greater proportion of the microfacets oriented in the H direction will be seen. If the surface is viewed normally then only a very small area will be seen. If, however, the surface is viewed at a low angle then a large number of microfacets will be seen along the surface. This effect is counteracted by the next factor.

The next term to be considered is G. This is an attenuation factor due to the effect of shadowing by the microfacets. Figure 3.4 shows the

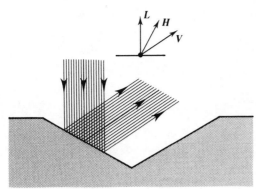

Figure 3.4
The interaction of light
with a microfacet
reflecting surface.

Case 1. No interference : angle between *L* and *V* is small – all light
falling on the microfacet escapes.

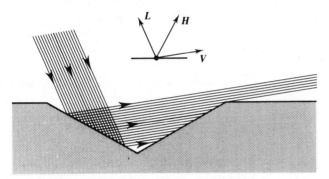

Case 2. Some reflected light is trapped – 'masking'.

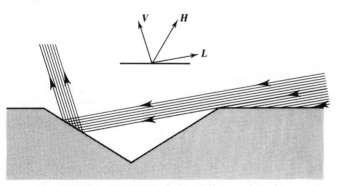

Case 3. Some incident light is 'shadowed' (inverse of case 2).

three possible cases which depend on the relative positions of *L* and *V*
with respect to the microfacets. The term 'shadowing' is used to describe
interference in the incident light and 'masking' to describe interference in
the reflected light. The degree of masking and shadowing is dependent on

Figure 3.5
Amount of light which
escapes depends on
$(1 - l_1/l_2)$.

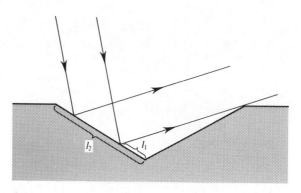

the ratio l_1/l_2 (Figure 3.5) which describes the proportion of the facets contributing to reflected light that is given by:

$$G = 1 - l_1/l_2$$

In the case where l_1 reduces to zero then all the reflected light escapes and

$$G = 1$$

A detailed derivation of the dependence of l_1/l_2 on L, V and H is given in Blinn (1977). For masking:

$$G_m = \frac{2\ (N \cdot H)\ (N \cdot V)}{V \cdot H}$$

For shadowing the situation is geometrically identical with the roles of the vectors L and V interchanged. For shadowing we have:

$$G_s = \frac{2\ (N \cdot H)\ (N \cdot L)}{V \cdot H}$$

The value of G that must be used is the minimum of G_s and G_m:

$$G = \mathrm{min\_of}(1, G_s, G_m)$$

F, the Fresnel term in R_s, accounts for the colour change of the specular highlight as a function of the angle of incidence of the light source ϕ. This equation expresses the reflectance of a perfectly smooth mirror surface in terms of the refractive index of the material, η, and the angle of incidence of the light source ϕ:

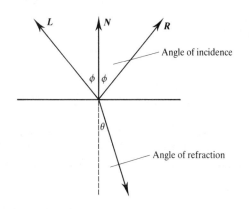

Figure 3.6
The angles used in the
Fresnel equation.

$$F = \frac{1}{2} \frac{\sin^2 (\phi - \theta)}{\sin^2 (\phi + \theta)} + \frac{\tan^2 (\phi - \theta)}{\tan^2 (\phi + \theta)} \qquad \text{(3.2)}$$

where ϕ is the angle of incidence, that is $\cos^{-1} (\boldsymbol{L \cdot H}) = \cos^{-1} (\boldsymbol{V \cdot H})$, and θ is the angle of refraction, with $\sin \theta = (\sin \phi)/\eta$, where η is the refractive index of the material. Here we are considering light moving through air (refractive index ≈ 1) striking a material of refractive index η.

These angles are shown in Figure 3.6. F is minimum, that is most light is absorbed, when $\phi = 0$ (normal incidence). No light is absorbed by the surface and F is equal to unity for $\phi = \pi/2$. The wavelength-dependent property of F comes from the fact that η is a function of wavelength. This dependence is not normally known and Cook and Torrance suggest a practical compromise which is to fit the Fresnel equation to the measured normal reflectance for a polished surface.

The Fresnel equation is rewritten as:

$$F = \frac{1}{2} \frac{(g - c)^2}{(g + c)^2} \left\{ 1 + \frac{(c (g + c) - 1)^2}{(c (g - c) + 1)^2} \right\}$$

where

$$c = \cos \phi = \boldsymbol{V \cdot H}$$

and

$$g^2 = \eta^2 + c^2 - 1$$

for $\phi = 0$, that is normal incidence,

$$F = \frac{(\eta - 1)^2}{(\eta + 1)^2}$$

giving

$$\eta = \frac{1 + F_0^{1/2}}{1 - F_0^{1/2}}$$

This then gives values for η as a function of wavelength from the measured values of F_0 and this can be substituted into Equation 3.2 to give F for any angle of incidence ϕ. A method to approximate the colour changes in the highlight as a function of ϕ is to proceed as follows:

(1) $F_{0,\,red}$, $F_{0,\,green}$ and $F_{0,\,blue}$ are obtained from measured values (Purdue University, 1970), giving η_{red}, η_{green} and η_{blue}.

(2) These values of η are then substituted into Equation 3.2 to obtain $F_{red}(\phi)$, $F_{green}(\phi)$ and $F_{blue}(\phi)$. These slices through $F(\phi, \lambda)$ are shown in Figure 3.7.

(3) These values of F are used in the three (red, green, blue) intensity equations.

In general, both R_d and F (and thus R_s) vary with the geometry of reflection. Cook and Torrance assume that R_d is the bidirectional reflectance for normal illumination and restrict dependence on illuminating angle to F. The dependence of F on incidence angle ϕ and wavelength λ is shown in Figure 3.7 for a polished copper surface. From this it can be seen that significant colour changes only occur when ϕ approaches $\pi/2$. Also note that it is inaccurate to attempt to model 'realistic' colour by working with three sets of coefficients at the red, green and blue wavelengths. Accurate rendering of the colour and colour changes that simulate real metals requires consideration of the complete spectral variation of F and the spectral distribution of the light source. These considerations are described in detail in Chapter 14.

Plate 5 shows sets of three spheres obtained using this technique. The illustrations are exaggerated to show how the model controls the rendering of shiny metallic objects. In this respect the diffuse contributions have been deliberately set equal to zero. In practice a non-zero diffuse contribution would produce a more 'recognizable' effect. The message is that shiny metallic objects behave almost as mirror spheres, the only difference being the colour of the specular highlight. In the illustration each sphere is illuminated by a perfect white illuminant at normal incidence and at an angle of 77°. The top sphere was produced by a form of Phong shading exhibiting no change in intensity between the centre and edge highlight. The colour was controlled (given that k_d is zero) by setting the light source colours to the object colour. The centre

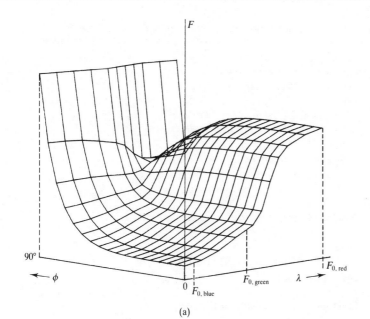

(a)

Figure 3.7
(a) Reflectance *F* as a
function of wavelength
(λ) and angle of
incidence (polished
copper). (b) The
dependence of *F* on φ for
red, green and blue
wavelengths.

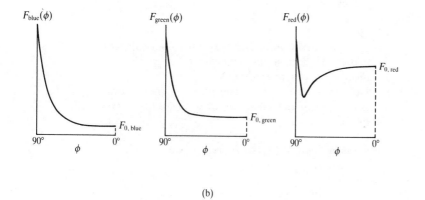

(b)

sphere is rendered using the Cook and Torrance model but the *F* term dependence on angle of incidence in R_s is omitted. This sphere exhibits an edge highlight of higher intensity than the centre highlight and is of markedly different shape from the Phong edge highlight. Finally the bottom sphere includes the *F* term which produces a distinct colour change – the edge highlight tending to white.

Program 3.1 is fairly straightforward code that rendered the bottom sphere in each case. It contains data for polished copper (illuminated at normal incidence) defined at red, green and blue wavelengths.

Program 3.1 Code for rendering the bottom spheres in Plate 4.

```
program Fresnel (input, output);

  var
    dw, m, kd,ks, F0r, F0g, F0b: real;
    Rar, Rag, Rab, Rdr, Rdg, Rdb: real;
    V, L, H: vector;
    mur, mug, mub: real;
    Il, Ia: real;
    col: C;

function GetMu (F0: real): real;

begin
  GetMu := (1 + sqrt (F0))/(1 − sqrt (F0));
end   {GetMu};

function GetF (phi, mu: real): real;

  var
    theta: real;

begin
  {Fresnel curves are nearly horizontal for small phi}
  if phi < 0.005 then phi := 0.005;
  theta := arcsin (sin (phi)/mu);
  GetF := (sqr (sin (phi − theta))/sqr (sin (phi + theta))
          + sqr (tan (phi − theta))/sqr (tan (phi + theta)))/2;
end   {GetF};

procedure EvalCol (N, L, H: vector; var col: C);

  var
    alpha, phi: real;
    D, Gs, Gm, G, F: real;
    Rs, Rsr, Rsg, Rsb: real;
    Ir, Ig, Ib: real;

begin
  alpha := arccos (dot (N, H));
  D := 1/sqr (m)/sqr (sqr (cos (alpha)))*exp (− sqr (tan (alpha))/sqr (m));
  if alpha > pi/2 then D := 0;

  Gs := 2*dot (N, H)*dot (N, V)/dot (V, H);
  Gm := 2*dot (N, H)*dot (N, L)/dot (V, H);
  if Gs < Gm then G := Gs else G := Gm;
  if G > 1 then G := 1;
  if G < 0 then G := 0;
```

```
Rs := D*G/pi/dot (N, V)/dot (N, L);
phi := arccos (dot (N, L));

F := GetF (phi, mur);
Rsr := F*Rs;
F := GetF (phi, mug);
Rsg := F*Rs;
F := GetF (phi, mub);
Rsb := F*Rs;

Ir := Ia*Rar + Il*dot (N, L)*dw*(kd*Rdr + ks*Rsr);
Ig := Ia*Rag + Il*dot (N, L)*dw*(kd*Rdg + ks*Rsg);
Ib := Ia*Rab + Il*dot (N, L)*dw*(kd*Rdb + ks*Rsb);

if Ir < 0 then Ir := 0;
if Ig < 0 then Ig := 0;
if Ib < 0 then Ib := 0;

if Ir > 255 then Ir := 255;
if Ig > 255 then Ig := 255;
if Ib > 255 then Ib := 255;

with col do
    begin
        r := round (Ir);
        g := round (Ig);
        b := round (Ib);
    end;
end   {EvalCol};


procedure ShadeObject;

begin
    {
        This is specific to a particular object, see for example ShadeSphere in
        previous Chapter. The procedure has to repeatedly call EvalCol
        supplying a surface normal. The value returned is the colour of the
        pixel.
    }
end   {ShadeObject};


begin
    Il := 650000;
    dw := 0.0001;

    ks := 1.0;
    F0r := 0.755;   {Fresnel coefficients for copper}
    F0g := 0.490;
    F0b := 0.095;
    m := 0.3;
```

```
kd := 0.0;
Rdr := F0r;
Rdg := F0g;
Rdb := F0b;

Ia := 0.00001*Il;
Rar := pi*Rdr;
Rag := pi*Rdg;
Rab := pi*Rdb;

mur := GetMu (F0r);
mug := GetMu (F0g);
mub := GetMu (F0b);

with V do
   begin
     x := 0; y := 0; z := 1;
   end;
with L dp
   begin
     x := -5; y := 0; z := 10;
   end;
Normalize (L);
AddVector (V, L, H); Normalize (H);

ShadeObject;

end.
```

3.2 Illumination source models

Modelling the attributes of illumination sources is another neglected topic in computer graphics. This is because most scenes modelled consist of either a single object or a few objects, and apparently different lighting conditions can be achieved by adjusting coefficients in the Phong reflection model. Also, the Phong reflection model functions ideally with simple point light sources. Consider the 20 spheres example in Chapter 2. Visually these effects could result from changing the characteristics of the source, rather than altering the nature of the material, and it is likely that most people would identify changes in this example as being due to changes in lighting conditions rather than a change in surface glossiness.

In scenes of complex environments (interiors of rooms and so on) realism can only be attained by taking into account the attributes of light sources. Rooms are lit either by artificial light or by daylight streaming in through a window. In either case we can identify the following attributes of a light source:

(1)   its geometry – whether, for example, it is a fluorescent or incandescent source or a window,

(2)   its luminous intensity distribution, which will be a function of the geometry, and

(3)   its spectral distribution; fluorescent lights have a distinctly different spectral distribution from both incandescent lights and daylight.

The main problem with modelling light sources accurately is the computational expense. A different L vector must be calculated for each point on the surface and an emitted intensity I calculated from $I(L)$ the luminous intensity distribution of the source. Certain empirical approaches have evolved that deal with the first two factors, the simplest of which is Warn's method (Warn, 1983).

The third factor is dealt with in depth in Chapter 14. For the moment we can note that a coloured light source can be approximately modelled by making I_i a function of wavelength.

3.2.1   Warn's method for modelling illumination sources

This is a simple method for modelling a spotlight as an empirical intensity distribution – the cosine model (Phong) of reflected light. Light is assumed to emanate from a source whose predominant direction is specified by a vector L_N. Given that L is the vector from the source to the object point, the intensity reflected from a point due to a source is:

$$I = \text{source intensity} \times [k_d\ (N{\cdot}L) + k_s\ (N{\cdot}H)^n]$$

The source intensity in this case (Figure 3.8):

$$\text{source intensity} = [I_i\ (L_N{\cdot}L)^s]$$

This illumination model provides control over the concentration and the direction of the light source. Warn points out that point light sources are difficult to position to produce highlights in a desired area of the object. In this model the light source is fixed in position, but its direction is changed by changing L_N. The concentration of the light source and hence the area (and generally the shape) of the highlight it produces is controlled by adjusting the index s. Low exponents simulate floodlights whereas high s values will tend to simulate spotlights. The model is

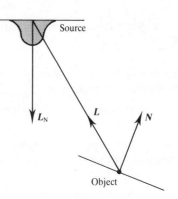

Figure 3.8
Warn's method of representing a light source as a specularly reflecting surface.

exactly equivalent to representing the light source as a surface receiving light from a point light source and specularly reflecting it according to Phong's model.

Warn extends this model to generate special effects by limiting the spatial extent of the light to provide sharp cut-offs. This is equivalent to studio lights that have flaps or barn doors. Such devices can be used in practice to emphasize a crease in an object, by lining up a flap with the crease so that the object is illuminated above the crease but not below. Rather than have the complex geometry that would result from implementing these as actual flaps, Warn models their effect as parallel extents in the X, Y and Z axes in world coordinate space, defining a rectangularly shaped illumination volume.

Another benefit that easily accrues from this model is that variable cone-shaped sources can be simulated. This can be implemented by comparing the angle that L makes with L_N against a cone threshold, simulating a point source with a conical intensity distribution.

3.2.2 Using goniometric diagrams

Verbeck and Greenberg (1984) introduced a comprehensive light source model. Although this is now somewhat overshadowed by Greenberg's radiosity method (Chapter 9), it is a model that uses the Phong diffuse component, modulated by an intensity value that is computed from a goniometric diagram of the source. Verbeck and Greenberg point out that the extensions to the standard intensity computations are quite simple, yet dramatic improvements in image quality can be achieved.

The luminous intensity distribution is a three-dimensional field and a goniometric diagram is a slice through this field. Generalizing the Phong

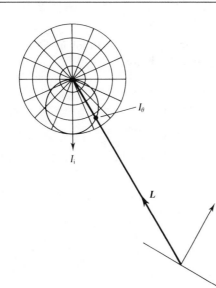

Figure 3.9
Using a goniometric
diagram to modulate the
calculated intensity.

diffuse term to include a reflection coefficient that is a function of wavelength, we have:

$$I = k_d (\lambda) \sum_n (N \cdot L_n) I_{i,n}$$

the intensity due to n point light sources. To include the luminous intensity distribution, $I_{i,n}$ is replaced with $I_{i\theta,n}$ and we have:

$$I = k_d (\lambda) \sum_n (N \cdot L_n) I_{i\theta,n} S_n$$

where $I_{i\theta,n}$ is the relative intensity of the nth light source which is now a function of θ specified by the goniometric diagram (Figure 3.9). Also included is S_n an occlusion factor that takes values of 0 or 1.

This is an equation that extends the Phong reflection model to cope with point sources with particular intensity distributions expressed as goniometric diagrams. It can be used to simulate a light source of any geometry by treating the light source as a sum of m point sources.

Projects, notes and suggestions

3.1 Reflection model solid

Repeat Project 2.3 but this time use Equation 3.1 to determine the reflected intensity.

3.2 Cook and Torrance model

Investigate the visual effect of the Cook and Torrance model using a sphere and light sources at different angles as suggested by Plate 5.

CHAPTER FOUR

Incremental Shading Techniques

Most images currently generated in computer graphics apply the Phong reflection model, described in Chapter 2, to polygon mesh models. Polygon mesh models are distinguished by the fact that the geometric information is only available at the vertices of a polygon. Incremental or interpolative shading techniques apply simple reflection models to polygons, calculating intensities at the vertices, and then interpolating values for interior points. Interior points are evaluated in scan line order and the schemes are easily integrated into a Z-buffer or a scan line hidden-surface removal algorithm. Incidentally, on terminology, the term 'shading' is loosely used to signify the application of a 'point' reflection model over the entire surface of an object. The term 'rendering' appears to be used to mean the complete process of going from an object database to the final shaded object on a screen. This chapter deals only with the problem of applying simple reflection models to polygon mesh objects. The next chapter looks at how these methods are integrated with scan conversion and hidden surface removal to form a complete rendering system.

Two incremental shading techniques are common; Gouraud interpolation (Gouraud, 1971) and Phong interpolation (Phong, 1975a). Phong interpolation gives more accurate highlights and is generally the preferred model. The Gouraud method tends to be confined to applications where the diffuse component is sufficient, or to preview images prior to final rendering.

Phong shading is more expensive than Gouraud shading and obeys the first law of computer graphics, which appears to be that the required processing time grows exponentially with perceived image quality. However, Gouraud shading has become almost standard in recent graphics hardware and Phong shading is also available. This trend is reflected in the proposed standard PHIGS+ which contains Gouraud and Phong shading utilities (PHIGS, 1988).

This chapter deals with both these methods and a final section describes how to combine these methods and to speed up the shading process without losing quality. Doing shading calculations efficiently is a neglected topic in computer graphics. Phong calculations can greatly exceed more than 50% of the total rendering time and addressing the problem of shading using an efficient method should be considered to be just as important as the quality of the reflection model. It is mandatory in areas such as three-dimensional animation where large numbers of frames have to be generated.

Another problem that must be addressed by interpolative shading techniques is final polygon visibility. Polygon boundaries should be invisible in the final shaded version and some impression of the original surface that the polygon mesh approximates restored. We can thus identify two functions of a shading scheme for polygon meshes:

(1)   to use some interpolative method for interior points, and

(2)   to diminish the visibility of the polygon mesh approximation.

The first shading schemes to be used in computer graphics were developed by Bouknight (1970) and Wylie et al. (1967). Wylie et al.'s method calculated an intensity at the vertices of triangular facets on the basis of distance from the viewpoint and then used linear interpolation to assign an intensity to interior points. In Bouknight's work the emphasis was on hidden surface removal and the polygons were 'constant' shaded. That is, a single intensity was calculated for each polygon and used over its entire area. This method, although it certainly imparts an impression of three dimensionality (see Plate 6), leaves the polygon mesh structure glaringly obvious.

4.1 Gouraud shading

The generally acknowledged first scheme that overcame the disadvantages of constant shading of polygons uses bilinear intensity interpolation. This is known as Gouraud shading (Gouraud, 1971). It is a simple and economic scheme that does not entirely eliminate the visibility of polygons. It suffers from Mach banding – where piecewise linear intensity

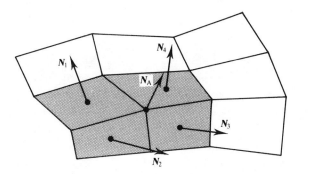

Figure 4.1
The vertex normal N_A
is the average of the
normals N_1, N_2, N_3 and
N_4, the normals of the
polygons that meet at
the vertex.

changes across a polygon boundary trigger the human visual system into perceiving the boundary as a bright band. The standard explanation for this is that the human visual system is sensitive to the second derivative of intensity because of our need to detect and enhance edges.

The Gouraud scheme is normally restricted to the diffuse component of the reflection model developed in Chapter 2. This is because the shape of the specular highlights, using this scheme, depends strongly on the underlying polygon mesh. An obvious highlight example that Gouraud shading misses altogether is the case of a highlight in the middle of a polygon. If there is no highlight component at any vertex then there is no way that the highlight will be recovered by the interpolation. The diffuse component from Equation 2.3 is:

$$I_i \, k_d \, (L \cdot N)/(r + k)$$

If we assume the light source is at infinity then $L \cdot N$ is constant over the surface of the polygon. The only variable is r, the distance of the view point. If we ignore the fact that the variation of r over the polygon is non-linear (or even ignore r altogether), then we can calculate intensities at the vertices and use bilinear interpolation to calculate all other intensities.

The technique first calculates the intensity at each vertex of the polygon by applying Equation 2.3. The normal N used in this equation is the so-called vertex normal and this is calculated as the average of the normals of the polygons that share the vertex (Figure 4.1). This is an important feature of the method and the vertex normal is an approximation to the true normal of the surface (which the polygon mesh represents) at that point. Plate 6 shows a wireframe object with the vertex normals superimposed.

A pass through the data structure storing the object will calculate an intensity I_v for each vertex. The interpolation process that calculates the intensity over a polygonal surface can then be integrated with a scan

Figure 4.2
The notation used for the intensity interpolation equations.

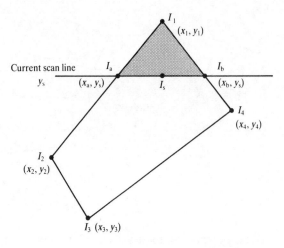

conversion algorithm that evaluates the screen position of the edges of a polygon from the vertices in the data structure. The intensities at the edge of each scan line are calculated from the vertex intensities and the intensities along a scan line from these (Figure 4.2). The interpolation equations are as follows:

$$I_a = \frac{1}{y_1 - y_2} [I_1(y_s - y_2) + I_2(y_1 - y_s)]$$

$$I_b = \frac{1}{y_1 - y_4} [I_1(y_s - y_4) + I_4(y_1 - y_s)]$$

$$I_s = \frac{1}{x_b - x_a} [I_a(x_b - x_s) + I_b(x_s - x_a)]$$

For computational efficiency these equations are implemented as incremental calculations. This is particularly important in the case of the third equation, which is evaluated for every pixel. If we define Δx to be the incremental distance along a scan line then ΔI, the change in intensity, from one pixel to the next is

$$\Delta I_s = \frac{\Delta x}{x_b - x_a} (I_b - I_a)$$

$$I_{s,n} = I_{s,n-1} + \Delta I_s$$

Apart from Mach banding, two well-known errors that can be introduced in Gouraud shading are:

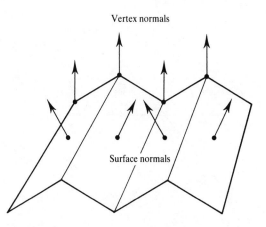

Vertex normals

Surface normals

Figure 4.3
A regularly corrugated
surface producing
identical vertex normals
from non-identical
surface normals.

- Anomalies can appear in animated sequences because the intensity interpolation is carried out in screen coordinates from vertex normals calculated in world coordinates. This is not invariant with respect to transformations such as rotation and in animated sequences frame-to-frame disturbances can be caused by this.

- The process of averaging surface normals to provide vertex normals for the intensity calculation can cause errors which result in, for example, corrugations being smoothed out. Figure 4.3 shows three normals all pointing in the same direction. This would result in a visually flat surface. Although this can be a problem, it should not occur providing a sufficiently high polygonal solution has been used in the model.

4.2 Phong interpolation

A method due to Bui-Tuong Phong (1975a) overcomes some of the disadvantages of Gouraud shading and specular reflection can be successfully incorporated in the scheme. In particular we can now have a specular highlight in the middle of a polygon despite the fact that each of the vertex normal angles would not produce a highlight. The features of the method are:

- Bilinear interpolation is still used so that points interior to polygons can be calculated incrementally.

- The attributes interpolated are the vertex normals, rather than vertex intensities. These are calculated, as before, by averaging the normal vectors of the surfaces that share the vertex.

- A separate intensity is evaluated for each pixel from the interpolated normals.

Figure 4.4
In the Phong method
vector interpolation
replaces intensity
interpolation.

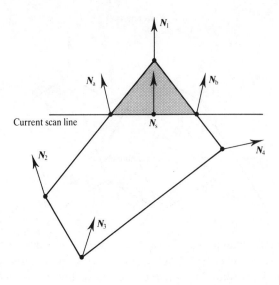

Figure 4.4
In the Phong method
vector interpolation
replaces intensity
interpolation.

- Again we need to assume that both the light source and the viewpoint are at infinity so that the intensity at a point is a function only of the interpolated normal.

The first stage in the process is the same as for the Gouraud method – for any polygon we evaluate the vertex normals. For each scan line in the polygon we evaluate by linear interpolation the normal vectors at the end of each line (Figure 4.4). These two vectors N_a and N_b are then used to interpolate N_s. We thus derive a normal vector for each point or pixel on the polygon that is an approximation to the real normal on the curved surface approximated by the polygon. This feature accounts for the quality of Phong shading. N_s, the interpolated normal vector, is then used in the intensity calculation. This idea is represented in Figure 4.5 which shows that vector interpolation tends to restore the curvature of the original surface that has been approximated by a polygon mesh.

Referring to the notation used in Figures 4.2 and 4.4 we have:

$$N_a = \frac{1}{y_1 - y_2} [N_1(y_s - y_2) + N_2(y_1 - y_s)]$$

$$N_b = \frac{1}{y_1 - y_4} [N_1(y_s - y_4) + N_4(y_1 - y_s)]$$ (4.1)

$$N_s = \frac{1}{x_b - x_a} [N_s(x_b - x_s) + N_b (x_s - x_a)]$$

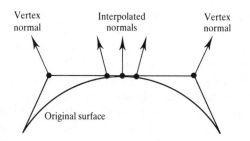

Figure 4.5
Vector interpolation
tends to 'restore'
curvature.

These are vector equations that would each be implemented as a set of three equations, one for each of the components of the vectors in world space. This makes the interpolation phase three times as expensive as Gouraud shading. In addition there is an application of the Phong model intensity equation at every pixel. Incremental computations can be employed as with intensity interpolation, and Equation 4.1, for example, would be implemented as:

$$N_{sx,n} = N_{sx,n-1} + \Delta N_{sx}$$
$$N_{sy,n} = N_{sy,n-1} + \Delta N_{sy}$$
$$N_{sz,n} = N_{sz,n-1} + \Delta N_{sz}$$

where N_{sx}, N_{sy} and N_{sz} are the components of a general scanline normal vector N_s and

$$\Delta N_{sx} = \frac{\Delta x}{x_b - x_a} (N_{bx} - N_{ax})$$

$$\Delta N_{sy} = \frac{\Delta x}{x_b - x_a} (N_{by} - N_{ay})$$

$$\Delta N_{sz} = \frac{\Delta x}{x_b - x_a} (N_{bz} - N_{az})$$

Plate 6 is a composite illustration showing the same object after constant shading, Gouraud shading and Phong shading.

4.3 Comparison of Gouraud and Phong shading

Gouraud shading is effective for shading surfaces which reflect light diffusely. Specular reflections can be modelled using Gouraud shading, but the shape of the specular highlight produced is dependent on the relative positions of the underlying polygons. The advantage of Gouraud shading is that it is computationally the less expensive of the two models, only requiring the evaluation of the intensity equation at the polygon vertices, and then bilinear interpolation of these values for each pixel.

Phong shading produces highlights which are much less dependent on the underlying polygons. However, more calculations are required, involving the interpolation of the surface normal and the evaluation of the intensity function for each pixel. These facts suggest a straightforward approach to speeding up Phong shading by combining Gouraud and Phong shading.

4.4 Speeding up Phong shading

In any practical context, such as the production of an animated sequence, the application of a speed-up method to Phong shading is a vital adjunct to a Phong reflection and interpolation scheme. This section describes two useful speed-up techniques. Unfortunately the mathematical detail associated with the second technique is somewhat greater than that of the reflection model and interpolation technique. This is given in Appendix F and can be skipped over if desired and the speed-up function, given below, used as presented.

Speed-up techniques generally fall into one of two categories: geometric and numerical. Geometric approaches are to be found in Bui-Tuong (1975b) and Bergman *et al.* (1986). Phong's method is based on the reflection vector and an extra coordinate transformation to align the light source (assuming there is only one) along the *z* axis. Bergman *et al.* use a simple test which compares the directions of the polygon's vertex normals with the direction of maximum highlight. This will detect only those specular highlights which correspond to the simplest case (case 1) given in Appendix F. Although most highlighted polygons fall into this category the remainder are aesthetically significant. It is particularly important in animated sequences to detect all highlighted polygons, otherwise highlights may 'switch' on and off. The emphasis in Bergman *et al.* (1986) is on the high-speed interactive development of single images, where a simple highlight test will suffice.

A numerical approach to efficient shading has been investigated in Duff (1979) and Bishop (1986). These are mathematical optimizations of the basic Phong method. Bishop, for example, uses a two-dimensional Taylor series to approximate the Phong equation, claiming that no penalty is incurred in doing this since the Phong normal interpolation is itself an approximation. The technique results in a method that evaluates an ambient, diffuse and specular term for each pixel with five additions plus one memory access per pixel.

We now describe two methods that speed up shading by combining Gouraud and Phong shading. The first is an extremely simple technique that results in approximately 35% saving in the shading phase. The second method – the H test – is a far more elaborate geometric approach that detects those polygons in which a highlight will appear. This results in even greater savings that are detailed in Section 4.4.2. Both methods are effectively combinations of Gouraud and Phong shading.

4.4.1   Simple Phong shading speed up

In Phong shading one vertex normal is linearly interpolated towards the other, one pixel step at a time. At each pixel the vertex normal is normalized, and an intensity calculated from the standard Phong intensity equation.

There is virtually no loss of image quality if double-step interpolation is used, with intermediate pixels being calculated from simple averaging. Note that this is equivalent to Gouraud interpolative shading where each polygon projects onto a three-pixel-wide screen area. At this resolution, of course, the disadvantages of using Gouraud shading disappear. You will recall that Gouraud shading cannot be used for highlights, in general, because the large polygon areas over which the interpolation is performed lead to bad highlights.

4.4.2   Highlight detection – the H test

Generally, an object will have relatively few highlighted polygons. Therfore it would be computationally more efficient to Phong shade the highlighted polygons and to Gouraud shade the remainder. In practice, however, the diffuse components produced for a particular pixel by the two interpolation methods differ slightly, and it is necessary to Gouraud shade the entire object. The Phong specular term can then be evaluated on the highlighted polygons, and combined with the Gouraud diffuse value.

To enable the implementation of the combined shading algorithm, a test has to be determined in order to ascertain which of the polygons are partially or fully within an area of specular highlight. This test is known as the highlight test or H test (Harrison *et al.*, 1988).

The algorithm is now given (Program 4.1) in the form of a Pascal function. This tests a single polygon for highlights. Further details on the test are given in Appendix F.

Program 4.1 The H test algorithm.

```
function H_test (T: real; Hv: vector): boolean;

  type vector = record
                      xc, yc, zc: real;
                    end;
  var
      a, b, c, d, e, f, g, h: real;
      all_edges_max: boolean;
      highlight: boolean;
      Av, Bv, Hv: vector;

begin
  all_edges_max := true;
  highlight := false;

  while more_vertices and not highlight do
    begin
      get_next_normal (Av);
      if dot (Av, Hv) > T then      {the current vertex is within the}
        highlight := true           {range of a specular highlight}
    end;
  reset_polygon_data;

  while more_vertices and not highlight do
    begin
      get_next_pair_of_normals (Av, Bv);
      a := dot (Av, Hv); b := dot (Bv, Hv);
      c := dot (Av, Bv);
      d := b*c − a; e := a*c − b;
      f := d*e;

      if f > 0 then    {the specular intensity reaches a maximum along}
                       {the current edge}
        begin
          g := a*d + b*e;
          if d*g > 0 then    {the maximum is greater than zero}
            if g*g >= T*T*(d*d + 2*c*f + e*e) then   {the maximum is
              highlight := true                       greater than the
                                                      threshold}

        end
      else    {the current edge did not have a maximum}
        all_edges_max := false
    end;
  H_test := highlight or all_edges_max;
end {H_test};
```

Projects, notes and suggestions

The projects for this chapter inevitably require a rendering system described in Chapter 5. They are mostly concerned with the quality–speed trade-off in incremental shading techniques. As usual each project is classified with a heading and those marked (*) are longish and can be used as a major course assignment or project.

4.1   Phong shading

Extend the code given in Appendix C to include Phong shading and, for an object, produce a display similar to Plate 6 which shows:

(1)   a wireframe plus vertex normals,

(2)   a flat or constant shaded version,

(3)   a Gouraud-shaded object, and,

(4)   a Phong-shaded object.

Isolate the time your program spends in actual shading and compare timings for (2), (3) and (4).

4.2   Mach band visualization (*)

Investigate the relationship between Mach band visibility and polygonal resolution. This can be done by generating a variable number of polygons, for, say, a toroid by volume sweeping, Gouraud shading the object and postprocessing the image so that the Mach bands can be visualized.

Mach bands can be highlighted by spatially differentiating the image twice and thresholding the high intensity values. To differentiate once, we can use the following approximation. For all pixels:

$$E' := \{[(A + B + C) - (G + H + I)]^2 + [(A + D + G) - (C + F + I)]^2\}^{1/2}$$

where E' is the new value for pixel E and A, B, . . ., I are a 3×3 array of pixels centred on E:

A B C
D E F
G H I

You should find that the 'strength' of the Mach bands increases as the 'polygonal resolution' decreases. Why is this so?

4.3 Simple Phong speed up

Implement the double-step interpolation method for Phong speed up as described in Chapter 4 and investigate the efficacy of the method by doing a comparison of timing and image quality between the speed-up method and the standard method.

For image quality comparisons, generate a normal Phong-shaded image and an image of the same scene using the speed up technique. Subtract the two images and display a difference image.

4.4 Vertex intensity

For a polygon mesh object with a regular quadrilateral structure, a useful texture effect can be achieved by reducing the vertex intensities in diagonally opposite vertices to zero as shown in Figure 4.6. The non-zero vertex intensities can be set to equal values and Gouraud shading used to render the object.

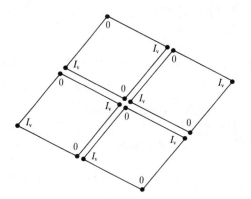

Figure 4.6   Using Gouraud shading and the polygon mesh structure as a texture effect.

4.5 Vertex intensity

In a Gouraud-shaded object, map the variation in intensity into a hue variation using a suitable path in HSV space (see Chapter 14). Note that this should be done by pre-calculating the HSV path, storing the results in an LUT and using a single-equation Gouraud scheme to index into the LUT.

4.6 Phong speed up

Implement the H test (see Appendix F) and compare its performance against numeric methods (Bishop, 1986).

4.7   Reflection model solid

Produce a rendered version of the wireframe reflection model solids (Projects 2.3 and 3.1). Add thin cylinders and cones in a different colour to represent the vectors *L*, *N* and *R* (see, for example, Foley and Van Dam (1982), pages 579 and 580).

4.8   Illumination source model (*)

Implement Warn's method (Warn, 1983) for controlling the nature and direction of a light source. Use the Phong reflection model together with a suitable light source interaction viewport.

Extend the scheme to include light flaps and cones.

CHAPTER FIVE

The Rendering Process

This chapter brings together material in the previous chapters, integrating it into the rendering process. Rendering is a general term that describes the overall process of going from a database representation of a three-dimensional object to a shaded two-dimensional projection on a view surface. It involves a number of separate processes:

(1)   setting up a data structure for polygon models that will contain all the information which is subsequently required in the shading process;

(2)   applying linear transformations to the polygon mesh model, for example transformations to position objects within a scene, and viewing transformations;

(3)   culling back-facing polygons;

(4)   scan converting or rasterizing polygons, that is converting the vertex-based model into a set of pixel coordinates;

(5)   applying a hidden surface removal algorithm;

(6)   shading the individual pixels using an interpolative or incremental shading scheme.

In practice, operations (4), (5) and (6) are carried out simultaneously. However, computer graphics textbooks normally fragment the rendering process. They usually contain a chapter comparing hidden surface removal algorithms without regard to how these algorithms are integrated with the other processes. In this text we have ignored the classification and description of the many hidden surface removal algorithms in favour of an integrated approach to the entire latter half of the rendering process. So rather than dealing with them as unconnected processes, we shall wherever possible, try to show how they work together.

It would appear that most rendering systems have settled for some variation of the Z-buffer approach, and indeed graphics workstations are now available with hardware Z-buffers. Other hidden surface removal algorithms find applications in special contexts such as flight simulators.

A complete rendering system based on the approach recommended in this chapter is given in Appendix C. This consists of a set of rendering procedures to be added to the code given in Appendix B.

5.1   Rasterization

First, it is necessary to discuss rasterization, or scan conversion. This is the process of finding which pixels an individual polygon covers or, at a more basic level, which pixels an edge of a polygon lies on. This second aspect will be dealt with first.

5.1.1   Rasterizing edges

There are two different ways of rasterizing an edge, based on whether line drawing or solid area filling is being used. Line drawing is not covered in this book, since we are interested in solid objects. However, the main feature of line-drawing algorithms (for example, Bresenham's algorithm (Bresenham, 1965)) is that they must generate a linear sequence of pixels with no gaps (Figure 5.1(a)). For solid area filling, a less rigorous approach suffices. We can fill a polygon using horizontal line segments; these can be thought of as the intersection of the polygon with a particular scan line. Thus, for any given scan line, what is required are the left- and right-hand limits of the segment, that is the intersections of the scan line with the left- and right-hand polygon edges. This means that, for each edge, we need to generate a sequence of pixels corresponding to the edge's intersections with the scan lines (Figure 5.1(b)). This sequence may have gaps, when interpreted as a line, as shown by the right-hand edge in the diagram.

The conventional way of calculating these pixel coordinates is by use of what is grandly referred to as a 'digital differential analyser' or (DDA). All this really consists of is finding how much the x coordinate increases per scan line, and then repeatedly adding this increment.

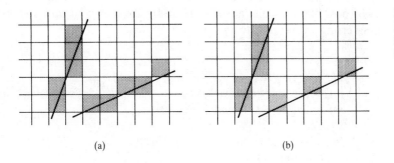

Figure 5.1
Pixel sequences required
for (a) line drawing and
(b) polygon filling.

(a)   (b)

Let (xs, ys), (xe, ye) be the start and end points of the edge (we assume that $ye > ys$). The simplest algorithm for rasterizing, sufficient for polygon edges is:

$x := xs$
$m := (xe - xs)/(ye - ys)$
for $y := ys$ **to** ye **do**
   $output$ $(round$ $(x), y)$
   $x := x + m$

The main drawback of this approach is that m and x need to be represented as floating-point values, with a floating-point addition and real-to-integer conversion each time around the loop. A method due to Swanson and Thayer (1986) provides an integer-only version of this algorithm. It can be derived from the above in two logical stages. First we separate out x and m into integer and fractional parts. Then, each time round the loop, we separately add the two parts, adding a carry to the integer part should the fractional part overflow. Also, we initially set the fractional part of x to -0.5 to make rounding easy, as well as simplifying the overflow condition. In pseudo-code:

$xi := xs$
$xf := -0.5$
$mi := (xe - xs)$ **div** $(ye - ys)$
$mf := (xe - xs)/(ye - ys) - mi$

for $y := ys$ **to** ye **do**
   $output$ (xi, y)
   $xi := xi + mi$
   $xf := xf + mf$
   if $xf > 0.0$ **then** $\{$ $xi := xi + 1$; $xf := xf - 1.0$ $\}$

Because the fractional part is now independent of the integer part, it is possible to scale it throughout by $2*(ye-ys)$, with the effect of converting everything to integer arithmetic:

$$xi := xs$$
$$xf := -(ye-ys)$$
$$mi := (xe-xs) \textbf{ div } (ye-ys)$$
$$mf := 2*[(xe-xs) \textbf{ mod } (ye-ys)]$$

for $y := ys$ **to** ye **do**
  $output\ (xi, y)$
  $xi := xi + mi$
  $xf := xf + mf$
  if $xf > 0$ **then** $\{\ xi := xi + 1;\ xf := xf - 2*(ye-ys)\ \}$

Although this appears now to involve two divisions rather than one, they are both integer rather than floating point. Also, given suitable hardware, they can both be evaluated from the same division, since the second (**mod**) is simply the remainder from the first (**div**). Finally it only remains to point out that the $2*(ye-ys)$ within the loop is constant and would in practice be evaluated just once outside it.

5.1.2 Rasterizing polygons

Now that we know how to find pixels along the polygon edges, it is necessary to turn our attention to filling the polygons themselves. Since we are concerned with shading, 'filling a polygon' means finding the pixel coordinates of interior points and assigning to these a value calculated using one of the incremental shading schemes described in the previous chapter. We need to generate pairs of segment end points and to fill in horizontally between them. This is usually achieved by constructing an 'edge list' for each polygon. In principle this is done using an array of linked lists, with an element for each scan line. Initially all the elements are set to *nil*. Then each edge of the polygon is rasterized in turn, and the x coordinate of each pixel (x, y) thus generated is inserted into the linked list corresponding to that value of y. Each of the linked lists is then sorted in order of increasing x. The result is something like that shown in Figure 5.2. Filling in of the polygon is then achieved by, for each scan line, taking successive pairs of x values and filling in between them (because a polygon has to be closed, there will always be an even number of elements in the linked list). Note that this method is powerful enough to cope with concave polygons with holes.

In practice, the sorting of the linked lists is achieved by inserting values in the appropriate place in the first place, rather than performing a big sort at the end. Also, as well as calculating the x value and storing it

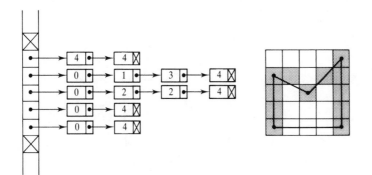

Figure 5.2
An example of a linked
list maintained in polygon
rasterization.

for each pixel on an edge, the appropriate shading values would be calculated and stored at the same time (for example, intensity value for Gouraud shading; x, y and z components of the interpolated normal vector for Phong shading).

If the object contains only convex polygons then the linked x lists will only ever contain two x coordinates; the data structure of the edge list is simplified and there is no sort required. It is not a great restriction in practical computer graphics to constrain an object representation to convex polygons.

One thing that has been slightly glossed over so far is the consideration of exactly where the borders of a polygon lie. This can manifest itself in adjacent polygons either by gaps appearing between them or by their overlapping. For example, in Figure 5.3, the width of the polygon is 3 units, so it should have an area of 9 units, whereas it has been rendered with an area of 16 units. The traditional solution to this problem, and the one usually advocated in textbooks, is to consider the sample point of the pixel to lie in its centre, that is at $(x + 0.5, y + 0.5)$. (A pixel can be considered to be a rectangle of finite area with dimensions 1.0×1.0, and its sample point is the point within the pixel area where the scene is sampled in order to determine the value of the pixel.) So for example the intersection of an edge with a scan line is calculated for $y + 0.5$, rather than for y, as we assumed above. This is messy, and excludes the possibility of using integer-only arithmetic. A simpler solution is to assume that the sample point lies at one of the four corners of the pixel; we have chosen the top right-hand corner of the

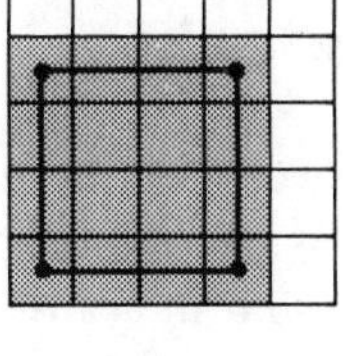

Figure 5.3
Problems with polygon
boundaries – a 9-pixel
polygon fills 16 pixels.

Figure 5.4
Three polygons
intersecting a scan line.

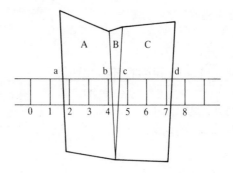

pixel. This has the consequence that the entire image is displaced half a pixel to the left and down, which in practice is insignificant. The upshot of this is that it provides the following simple rasterization rules:

(1)   horizontal edges are simply discarded;

(2)   an edge which goes from scan line y_{bottom} to y_{top} should generate x values for scan lines y_{bottom} through to $y_{top} - 1$ (that is, missing the top scan line);

(3)   similarly, horizontal segments should be filled from x_{left} to $x_{right} - 1$ (with no pixels generated if $x_{left} = x_{right}$).

Incidentally, in rules (2) and (3), whether the first or last element is ignored is arbitrary, and the choice is based around programming convenience. The four possible permutations of these two rules define the sample point as one of the four corners of the pixel. The effect of these rules can be demonstrated in Figure 5.4. Here we have three adjacent polygons A, B and C, with edges a, b, c and d. The rounded x values produced by these edges for the scan shown are 2, 4, 4 and 7 respectively. Rule (3) then gives pixels 2 and 3 for polygon A, none for polygon B, and 4–6 for polygon C. Thus, overall, there are no gaps, and there is no overlapping. Horizontal edges are discarded because the adjacent edges will have already contributed the x values to make up the segment (for example the base of the polygon in Figure 5.2 – note also that, for the sake of simplicity, the scan conversion of this polygon was not performed strictly in accordance with the rasterization rules mentioned above).

5.2 Order of rendering

There are two basic ways of ordering the rendering of a scene. These are: on a polygon-by-polygon basis, where each polygon is rendered in turn, in isolation from all the rest; and in scan-line order, where the segments of all polygons in that scene which cross a given scan line are rendered, before moving on to the next scan line. In standard textbooks, this classification has the habit of becoming hopelessly confused with the classification of hidden surface removal algorithms. In fact the order of rendering a scene places restrictions on which hidden surface algorithms can be used, but it is of itself independent of the method employed for hidden surface removal. To skip ahead briefly, these are the common hidden surface removal algorithms that are compatible with the two methods:

- by polygon: Z-buffer
- by scan line: Z-buffer; scan line Z-buffer; spanning scan line algorithm

By-polygon rendering has a number of advantages. It is simple to implement, and it requires little data active at any one time. Because of this, it places no upper limit on scene complexity, unlike scan line rendering, which needs to hold simultaneously in memory, rasterization, shading, and perhaps texture information for all polygons which cross a particular scan line. The main drawback of simple by-polygon rendering is that it does not make use of possible efficiency measures such as sharing of information between polygons (for example, most edges in a scene are shared between two polygons). The method can only be used with the Z-buffer hidden surface algorithm which, as we shall see, is rather expensive in terms of memory usage. Also, scan line based algorithms possess the property that the completed image is generated in scan line order, which has advantages for hardware implementation and anti-aliasing operations.

An important difference between the two rendering methods is in the construction of the edge list. This has been described in terms of rendering on a polygon-by-polygon basis. If, however, rendering is performed in scan line order, two problems arise. One is that rasterizing all edges of all polygons in advance would consume a vast quantity of memory, setting an even lower bound on the maximum complexity of a scene. Instead, it is usual to maintain a list of 'active edges'. When a new scan line is started, all edges which start on that scan line are added to the list, while those which end on it are removed. For each edge in the active list, current values for x, shading information and so on, are stored, together with the increments for these values. Each time a new edge is added, these values are initialized; then the increments are added for each new scan line.

The other problem is in determining segments, since there are now multiple polygons active on a given scan line. In general, some extra information will need to be stored with each edge in the active edge list, indicating which polygon it belongs to. The exact details of this depend very much on the hidden surface removal algorithm in use. Usually an active polygon list is maintained that indicates the polygons intersected by the current scan line, and those therefore that can generate active edges. This list is updated on every scan line, new polygons being added and inactive ones deleted.

The outline of a polygon-by-polygon renderer is thus:

> **for** {*each polygon*} **do**
>   {*construct an edge list from the polygon edges*}
>   **for** *y* := *ymin* **to** *ymax* **do**
>   **for** {*each pair* (x_I, x_{I+1}) *in EdgeList* [*y*]} **do**
>   {*shade the horizontal segment* (x_I, y) **to** (x_{I+1}, y)}

while that of a scan line renderer is:

> clear active edge list
> **for** {*each scan line*} **do**
>   **for** {*each edge starting on that scan line*} **do**
>   {*add edge to active edge list;*
>   *initialize its shading and rasterization values*
>   *and their increments*}
>   {*remove edges which end on that scan line;*
>   *parse active edge list to obtain and render segments;*
>   *add the increments to all active edges*}

Finally, it is worth pointing out that it is possible to achieve a hybrid of these two methods. Often it is possible to split a scene up into a number of unconnected objects. If the scene is rendered on an object-by-object basis, using scan line ordering within each object, then the advantage of shared information is realized within each object, and there is no upper limit on scene complexity, only on the complexity of each individual object.

5.3 Hidden surface removal

The major hidden surface removal algorithms are described in most computer graphics textbooks and are classified in an early, but still highly relevant, paper by Sutherland *et al.* (1974). In this paper algorithms are characterized as to whether they operate primarily in object space or image (screen) space and the different uses of 'coherence' that the algorithms employ. Coherence is a term used to describe the process where geometrical units, such as areas or scan line segments, instead of single points are operated on by the hidden surface removal algorithm.

There appear to be two popular approaches to hidden surface

removal. These are scan line based systems and Z-buffer based systems. Other approaches to hidden surface removal such as area subdivision (Warnock, 1969), or depth list schemes (Newell *et al.*, 1972) are not particularly popular now or are reserved for special-purpose applications such as flight simulation.

5.3.1 The Z-buffer algorithm

We start by considering the easier of the two approaches – the Z-buffer renderer. The Z-buffer algorithm, developed by Catmull (1975), is as ubiquitous in computer graphics as the Phong reflection model and interpolator, and the combination of these represents the most popular rendering option. Using Sutherland's classification scheme (Sutherland *et al.*, 1974) it is an algorithm that operates in image or screen space.

Pixels in the interior of a polygon are shaded, using an incremental shading scheme, and their depth is evaluated by interpolation from the z values of the polygon vertices after the viewing transformation has been applied. Thus we can imagine a three-dimensional screen space, where the (x, y) values are pixel coordinates and the z value is the interpolated viewing space depth.

The Z-buffer algorithm is equivalent, for each point (x, y), to a search through the associated z values of each interior polygon point to find that point with the minimum z value. This search is conveniently implemented by using a Z-buffer that holds for a current point (x, y) the smallest z value so far encountered. During the processing of a polygon we either write the intensity of a point (x, y) into the frame buffer or not, depending on whether the depth z, of the current point is less than the depth so far encountered as recorded in the Z-buffer.

The overwhelming advantage of the Z-buffer algorithm is its simplicity of implementation. Its main disadvantage is the amount of memory required for the Z-buffer. The size of the Z-buffer depends on the accuracy to which the depth value of each point (x, y) is to be stored, which is a function of scene complexity. 20–32 bits are usually deemed sufficient and the scene has to be scaled to this fixed range of z so that accuracy within the scene is maximized. Note that for frame buffers smaller than 24 bits per pixel, say, the Z-buffer will in fact be larger than the frame buffer. In the past Z-buffers have tended to be part of the main memory of the host processor, but now graphics terminals are available with dedicated Z-buffers and this represents the best solution.

The Z-buffer imposes no constraints on database organization (other than those required by the shading interpolation) and in its simplest form can be driven on a polygon-by-polygon basis, with polygons being presented in any convenient order.

In principle, for each polygon we compute:

(1) the (x, y) value of the interior pixels,

(2) the z depth for each point (x, y), and

(3) the intensity I for each point (x, y).

Thus we have three concurrent bilinear interpolation processes and a triple nested loop. The z values and intensities I are available at each vertex and the interpolation scheme for z and I is distributed between the two inner loops of the algorithm.

An extended version of the by-polygon algorithm with Z-buffer hidden surface removal is as follows:

```
for {all x, y} do
    Z-Buffer [x, y] := maximum_depth

for {each polygon} do
    {construct an edge list from the polygon edges
    (that is, for each edge, calculate the values of x, z and I for each
    scan line by interpolation and store them in the edge list)}
    for y := ymin to ymax do

        for {each segment in EdgeList[y]} do
            {get Xleft, Xright, Zleft, Zright, Ileft, Iright}

            for x := Xleft to Xright do
                {linearly interpolate z and I between
                Zleft, Zright and Ileft, Iright respectively}
                if z < Z_Buffer[x, y] then
                    {Z_Buffer[x, y] := z
                    frame_buffer[x, y] := I}
```

The structure of the algorithm reveals the major inefficiency of the method in that shading calculations are performed on hidden pixels which are then either ignored or subsequently overwritten. The extent of this duplication will be a function of the overall order in which the polygons in the scene are examined. If preprocessing is possible, so that those polygons nearest the view point are processed first, considerable savings can be made.

If Phong interpolation is used then the final reflection model calculations, which are a function of the interpolated normal, should also appear within the innermost loop; that is, interpolate N rather than I, and replace the last line with:

$$frame\_buffer[x, y] := ShadingFunction\ (N)$$

Procedures that implement the above techniques are given in Appendix C. Adding these procedures to the code in Appendix B results in a complete rendering system.

5.3.2 Scan line Z-buffer

There is a variation of the Z-buffer algorithm for use with scan line based renderers, known (not surprisingly) as a scan line Z-buffer. This is simply a Z-buffer which is only one pixel high, and is used to solve the hidden surface problem for a given scan line. It is re-initialized for each new scan line. Its chief advantage lies in the small amount of memory it requires relative to a full-blown Z-buffer; in fact it is very common to see a scan line Z-buffer-based program running on systems which do not have sufficient memory to support a full Z-buffer.

5.3.3 Spanning hidden surface removal

A spanning hidden surface removal algorithm attempts, for each scan line, to find 'spans' across which shading can be performed. The hidden surface removal problem is thus solved by dividing the scan line into lengths over which a single surface is dominant. This means that shading calculations are performed only once per pixel, removing the basic inefficiency inherent in the Z-buffer method. Set against this is the problem that spans do not necessarily correspond to polygon segments, making it harder to perform incremental shading calculations (the start values must be calculated at an arbitrary point along a polygon segment, rather than being set to the values at the left-hand edge). The other major drawback is in the increase in complexity of the algorithm itself, as will be seen.

It is generally claimed that spanning algorithms are more efficient than Z-buffer based algorithms, except for very large numbers of polygons (Foley and Van Dam, 1982; Sutherland *et al.*, 1974). However, since extremely complex scenes are now becoming the norm, it is becoming clear that, overall, the Z buffer is more efficient, unless a very complex shading function is being used.

5.3.4 A spanning scan line algorithm

The basic idea, as has been mentioned, is that, rather than solving the hidden surface problem on a pixel-by-pixel basis using incremental z calculation, the spanning scan line algorithm uses spans along the scan line over which there is no depth conflict. The hidden surface removal process uses coherence in x and deals in units of many pixels. The processing implication is that a sort in x is required for each scan line and the spans have to be evaluated.

The easiest way to see how a scan line algorithm works is to consider the situation in three-dimensional screen space (x_s, y_s, z_s). A

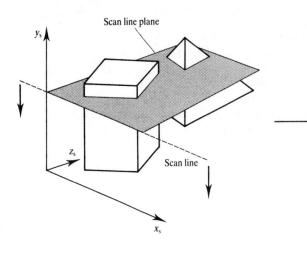
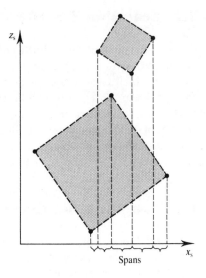

Figure 5.5
A scan line plane is moved down through the scene producing line segments and spans.

scan line algorithm effectively moves a scan line plane, that is a plane parallel to the (x_s, z_s) plane, down the y_s axis. This plane intersects objects in the scene and reduces the hidden surface problem to two-dimensional space (x_s, z_s). Here the intersections of the scan line plane with object polygons become lines (Figure 5.5). Note that the precise orientation of this plane, with respect to the objects in world coordinates, depends on the transformations used. If a perspective transformation is employed then the objects would be distorted in three-dimensional screen space. These line segments are then compared to solve the hidden surface problem by considering 'spans'. A span is that part of a line segment that is contained between the edge intersections of all active polygons. A span can be considered a coherence unit within the extent of which the hidden surface removal problem is 'constant' and can be solved by depth comparisons at either end of the span. Note that a more complicated approach has to be taken if penetrating polygons are allowed.

It can be seen from this geometric overview that the first stage in a spanning scan line algorithm is to sort the polygon edges by y_s vertex values. This results in an active edge list which is updated as the scan line moves down the y_s axis. If penetrating polygons are not allowed, then each edge intersection with the current scan line specifies a point on the scan line where 'something is changing', and so these collectively define all the span boundary points.

By going through the active edge list in order, it is possible to generate a set of line segments, each of which represents the intersection of the scan line plane with a polygon. These are then sorted in order of increasing x_s.

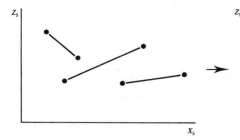

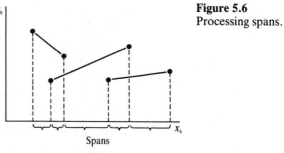

Figure 5.6
Processing spans.

Active line segments produce span boundaries

Which are used to subdivide a line

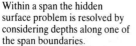

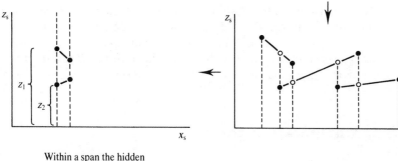

Within a span the hidden
surface problem is resolved by
considering depths along one of
the span boundaries.

The innermost loop then processes each span in the current scan line. Active line segments are clipped against span boundaries and are thus subdivided by these boundaries. The depth of each subdivided segment is then evaluated at one of the span boundaries and hidden surface removal is effected by searching within a span for the closest subdivided segment. This process is shown in Figure 5.6.

In pseudo-code the algorithm is:

for {*each polygon*}
    {*Generate and bucket sort in y_s the polygon edge information.*}

for {*each scanline*}
    for {*each active polygon*}
        {*Determine the segment or intersection of the scan plane and polygon.*
        Sort these active segments in x_s.
        Update the rate of change per scan line of the shading parameters.}

> {*Generate the span boundaries.*}
>   **for** {*each span*}
>   {*Clip active segments to span boundaries.*
>
>   *Evaluate the depth for all clipped segments at one of the span boundaries.*
>
>   *Solve the hidden surface problem for the span by finding the segment with minimum z_s.*
>
>   *Shade the visible clipped line segment.*
>
>   *Update the shading parameters for all other line segments by the rate of change per pixel times the span width.*}

Note that integrating shading information is far more cumbersome than with the Z-buffer. Records of values at the end of clipped line segments have to be kept and updated. This places another scene complexity overhead (together with the overhead of the absolute number of polygons) on the efficiency and memory requirements of the process.

5.3.5 Comparative points

From an ease of implementation point of view the Z-buffer is best. It has significant memory requirements, particularly for high resolution frame buffers. However, it places no upwards limit on the complexity of scenes, an advantage that is now becoming increasingly important. It renders scenes one object at a time and for each object one polygon at a time. This is both a natural and a convenient order as far as database considerations are concerned.

An important restriction it places on the type of object that can be rendered by a Z-buffer is that it cannot deal with transparent objects without costly modification. A partially transparent polygon may:

(1)   be completely covered by an opaque nearer polygon, in which case there is no problem, or

(2)   be the nearest polygon, in which case a list of all polygons behind it must be maintained so that an appropriate combination of the transparent polygon and the next nearest can be computed (the next nearest polygon is not of course known until all polygons are processed).

Compared with scan line algorithms, anti-aliasing solutions, particularly hardware implementations, are more difficult. (This aspect is dealt with in some detail in Chapter 12.)

Cook *et al.* (1987) point out that a Z-buffer has an extremely important 'system' advantage. It provides a 'back door' in that it can combine point samples with point samples from other algorithms that have other capabilities such as radiosity or ray tracing.

If memory requirements are too prodigious then a scan line Z-buffer is the next best solution. Unless a renderer is to work efficiently on simple scenes, it is doubtful whether it is worth contemplating the large increase in complexity that a spanning scan line algorithm demands.

Historically there has been a shift in research away from hidden surface problems to realistic image synthesis. This has been motivated by the easy availability of high spatial and colour resolution terminals. All the 'classic' hidden surface removal algorithms were developed prior to the advent of shading complexities and it looks as if the Z-buffer will be the most popular survivor for conventional rendering.

5.4 Compositing three-dimensional images

An important advantage of Z-buffer based algorithms is that the z value associated with each pixel can be retained and used to enable the compositing of separately generated scene elements.

Three-dimensional images are often built up from separate subimages. A system for compositing separate elements in a scene, pixel by pixel, was proposed by Porter and Duff (Porter and Duff, 1984; Duff, 1985). This simple system is built round an RGBαZ representation for pixels in a subimage. At the time of writing (1988) 24-bit frame stores with associated z memories are becoming increasingly common – hardware confirmation of the popularity of Z-buffer based rendering systems. Also, at least one company (PIXAR) has now incorporated an α memory or channel allowing this fifth parameter to be associated with each pixel. This parameter allows subimages to be built up separately and combined, retaining subpixel information that may have been calculated in the rendering of each subimage.

Composites are built up by using a binary operator that combines two subimages:

$$c = f \ \textbf{op} \ b$$

For example, consider the operator $\mathbf{Z}_{min}$. We may have two subimages, say of single objects, that have been rendered separately, the Z values of each pixel in the final rendering contained in the Z channel. Compositing in this context means effecting hidden surface removal between the objects and is defined as:

$$RGB_c = (\text{if } Z_f < Z_b \text{ then } RGB_f \text{ else } RGB_b)$$
$$Z_c = \min (Z_f, Z_b)$$

for each pixel.

The α parameter ($0 \leqslant \alpha \leqslant 1$) is the fraction of the pixel area that the object covers. It is used as a factor that controls the mixing of the colours in the two images. The use of the α channel effectively extends area anti-aliasing across the compositing of images. Of course this parameter is not normally calculated by a basic Z-buffer renderer and, because of this, the method is only suitable when used in conjunction with the A-buffer hidden surface removal method (Carpenter, 1984), an anti-aliased extension to the Z-buffer described in Chapter 12.

The operator **over** is defined as:

$$RGB_c = RGB_f + (1 - \alpha_f) \, RGB_b$$
$$\alpha_c = \alpha_f + (1 - \alpha_f) \, \alpha_b$$

This means that, as α_f decreases, more of RGB_b is present in the pixel.

The compositing operator **comp** combines both the above operators. This evaluates pixel results when Z-value comparisons at the corners of pixels are different between RGB_f and RGB_b. Z_f is compared with Z_b at each of the four corners. There are 16 possible outcomes to this and, if the Z values are not the same at the four corners, then the pixel is said to be confused. Linear interpolation along the edges takes place and a fraction β is computed (the area of the pixel of which f is in front of b). We then have the **comp** operator:

$$RGB_c = \beta \, (\text{f } \mathbf{over} \text{ b}) + (1 - \beta) \, (\text{b } \mathbf{over} \text{ f})$$

Another example of compositing in three-dimensional image synthesis is given in Nakamae *et al.* (1986). This is a montage method, the point of which is to integrate a three-dimensional computer-generated image, of say a new building, with a real photograph of a scene. The success of the method is due to the fact that illuminance for the generated object is calculated from measurements of the background photograph and because atmospheric effects are integrated into the finished image.

Projects, notes and suggestions

5.1   Z-buffer by-polygon renderer

Implement the rendering system described in Appendix C. If you are short of memory space for the Z-buffer a possibility is to use half the screen memory as a

Z-buffer for the other half. If the screen memory is used for depth, the Z-buffer image can be displayed using a pseudo-colour enhancement technique (Chapter 14). That is, map the depth variations in the Z-buffer into colour changes so that the depth variations are more visible than they would otherwise be if they were left as intensity variations in the screen memory.

5.2   Simple rendering using flat-shaded polygons

Implement a simple rendering scheme that flat-shades polygons with an average intensity, using a fast polygon fill utility. Handle hidden surface removal by building up a polygon list that contains an average intensity and average depth and sorts the list by depth. The polygons are then shaded in order of depth – the furthest polygon being dealt with first.

What constraints does this method of hidden surface removal place on the nature of the scene or the objects?

5.3   Transparency

The rendering method employed in Project 5.2 can easily be adapted to handle partially transparent surfaces. Adapt the program of Project 5.2 to do this.

5.4   Z-buffer resolution

Investigate the relationship between scene complexity and Z-buffer resolution (that is, element resolution, not spatial resolution). You could do this by setting up an object formed from the intersection of two objects (say, for example, a sphere and a cylinder) and observing the effect of truncating the Z-buffer to lower and lower ranges on the curve of intersection between the two objects.

5.5   Scan line Z-buffer (*)

A scan line Z-buffer is a particular form of the general Z-buffer algorithm where the rendering proceeds one scan line at a time. All those polygons that cover the current scan line must be processed and this means maintaining a list of active polygons together with the current state of the intensity and depth interpolation for each polygon. When the intersection of a scan line and an active polygon is initiated, the interpolations are restarted and the Z-buffer comparison is made.

Implement this approach and find out the extent of the extra processing over the conventional Z-buffer method.

CHAPTER SIX

Parametric Representation of Three-dimensional Objects

The parametric representation of solids and curves is now an established tool in computer graphics, particularly in computer-aided design (CAD). Techniques that were originally developed to model car bodies and aircraft shapes are now applied in the many diverse branches of computer graphics. For example, the techniques are used in object modelling and subsequent interactive design and in animation key framing.

One of the most popular parametric formulations is the Bezier patch, developed in the 1960s by Pierre Bezier for use in the design of Renault car bodies. His CAD system, UNISURF, in use by 1972, was no doubt responsible for the many varied models emerging from Renault's factories in the 1970s. In fact Bezier's work may have been preceded by the efforts of P. de Casteljau at Citroen in the early 1960s. However his internal reports lay undiscovered until 1975. We may not be referring to de Casteljau patches today, but his name is nonetheless familiar in an algorithm that is widely used to design and display curves and surfaces.

The usual approach in considering parametric representations is to begin with a description of three-dimensional curves and then to generalize to surfaces. We shall adopt this trend, concentrating on Bezier and B-spline formulations. In Section 6.2 we use the de Casteljau algorithm to display Bezier curves and discuss the different rendering techniques employed for visualizing parametrically defined surfaces.

6.1 Parametric representation of three-dimensional curves

A simple practical example of a three-dimensional space curve is a point moving in space (Figure 6.1). Its position is defined by a vector r, a function of time t. This gives a so-called parametric description of the curve as a set of three equations in t:

$$x = x(t)$$
$$y = y(t)$$
$$z = z(t)$$

Following from this we can describe any space curve parametrically and a cubic curve is given by:

$$
\begin{aligned}
x(u) &= a_x u^3 + b_x u^2 + c_x u + d_x \\
y(u) &= a_y u^3 + b_y u^2 + c_y u + d_y \\
z(u) &= a_z u^3 + b_z u^2 + c_z u + d_z
\end{aligned}
\tag{6.1}
$$

where $0 \leqslant u \leqslant 1$, and each of x, y and z is a cubic polynomial of the parameter u.

Cubics are used in computer graphics as a compromise. Quadratics do not exhibit sufficient shape flexibility and going to higher degree polynomials means greater computation and a more cumbersome description.

There are a number of reasons for using parametric descriptions in computer graphics rather than implicit functions. (An implicit function is $f(x, y, z) = 0$; for example, the implicit function description of a sphere is $x^2 + y^2 + z^2 - r^2 = 0$.) Firstly, points on a curve can be computed sequentially, rather than by solving non-linear equations for each point in

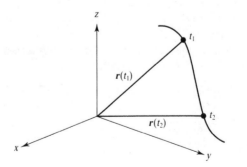

Figure 6.1
A point moving in three-dimensional space.

an implicit definition. Parametric curves (and surfaces) are easily transformed. Applying a linear transform to the parametric representation of the curve transforms the curve itself. Most design applications involve complex curves (and/or surfaces) which cannot be described by simple functions, whereas a parametric representation allows piecewise descriptions and a curve or a surface can be a set of piecewise polynomials. (Polynomials of high degree can describe complex curves but require a large number of coefficients and may introduce unwanted oscillations into the curve.)

6.1.1 Bezier curves

We now look at a particular form of parametric representation: the Bezier cubic curve. The Bezier formulation of a cubic curve involves specifying a set of **control points** from which the cubic polynomial is derived. This form is derived, in most texts, by starting with blending or basis functions (see below). Foley and Van Dam (1982) give a comprehensive derivation showing the relationship between the Bezier formulation and Hermite or Ferguson cubics.

Rewriting Equations 6.1 as a single vector equation gives:

$$P(u) = au^3 + bu^2 + cu + d$$

and this is the normal way to express a parametric cubic polynomial. Using the Bezier basis or Bernstein blending functions (these are discussed more fully below):

$$(1 - u)^3$$
$$3u(1 - u)^2$$
$$3u^2(1 - u)$$
$$u^3$$

the polynomial is expressed in terms of these functions and four control points:

$$P(u) = P_0(1 - u)^3 + P_1 \times 3u(1 - u)^2 + P_2 \times 3u^2(1 - u) + P_3 u^3$$

or in matrix notation:

$$P(u) = \mathbf{UBP} = [u^3 \ u^2 \ u \ 1] \begin{bmatrix} -1 & 3 & -3 & 1 \\ 3 & -6 & 3 & 0 \\ -3 & 3 & 0 & 0 \\ 1 & 0 & 0 & 0 \end{bmatrix} \begin{bmatrix} P_0 \\ P_1 \\ P_2 \\ P_3 \end{bmatrix}$$

Figure 6.2
A bicubic Bezier curve
and its control
polyhedron.

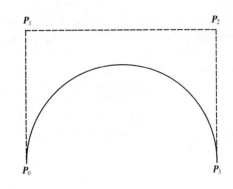

From an intuitive point of view the matrix formulation is not particularly useful and the blending function definition, given below, is preferred; however, a matrix formulation is useful when considering hardware implementation.

P_0, P_1, P_2 and P_3 are four control points that specify the curve, P_0 and P_3 being the end-points. They are called control points because moving them around in space controls or influences the shape of the curve. The polygon formed by joining the control points together is sometimes called the characteristic or control polygon. Figure 6.2 shows a curve and its characteristic polygon.

The Bezier form is an ingenious reformulation of a Hermite cubic polynomial form. It allows the shape of the curve to be determined entirely from the position of the four control points. In particular, the user does not have to specify or control the tangent vectors, or first derivatives, required for the Hermite specification. A geometric interpretation of the way in which the control points work now follows. This can easily be omitted if you are only interested in the practical use of Bezier segments.

By differentiating the basis functions with respect to u it can be shown that:

$$P_u(0) = 3(P_1 - P_0)$$
$$P_u(1) = 3(P_3 - P_2)$$

These are the tangent vectors to the curve at the end-points and it can be seen that P_1 and P_2 lie on these vectors. Altering the four control points will thus allow the position and shape of the curve to be controlled as they effectively alter the end-points and the two tangent vector values.

Figure 6.3 attempts to show the way in which the control points

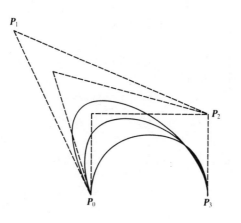

Figure 6.3
Effects of moving control point P_1.

influence the curve shape and Figure 6.4 shows a curve and its tangent vectors. Writing a short interactive program and experimenting with the position of the control points will give an intuitive appreciation of this geometric interpretation. In particular you will see that the middle two control points appear to exercise a 'pull' on the curve. Say, for example, that we required a design method that reproduced the shape of a 'simple' hand-drawn curve. We could proceed as follows:

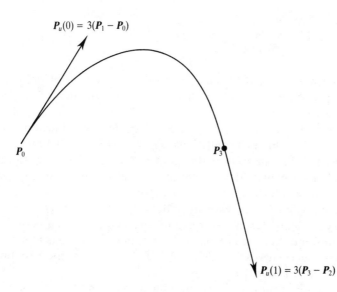

Figure 6.4
The relationship between Bezier control points and tangent vectors.

Figure 6.5
Cubic Bezier basis
functions.

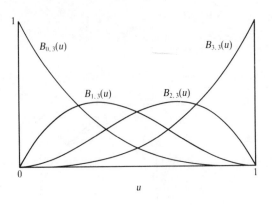

(1)   'Approximate' the shape of the curve by forming a control polygon.

(2)   Use this to draw the associated Bezier curve.

(3)   Adjust the control points.

(4)   Repeat (2) and (3) until satisfied with the shape.

A number of texts prefer a mathematical interpretation in terms of the four basis functions, which in this context are called blending functions because they blend the control points to form the curve. The four basis functions are shown in Figure 6.5 and for this interpretation the curve is usually specified by:

$$P(u) = \sum_{i=0}^{3} P_i \, B_{i,3}(u)$$

where each term in the sum is a product of a control point P_i and a blending function B_i which in this case is a polynomial of degree three. These curves show the 'influence' that each control point has on the final curve form. For a particular value of u we sum the values obtained from each of the four blending functions. P_0 is most influential at $u = 0$ ($B_{1,3}$, $B_{2,3}$ and $B_{3,3}$ are all zero at this point). As u is increased 'towards' P_1, $B_{0,3}$ and $B_{1,3}$ mainly determine the curve shape, with $B_{2,3}$ and $B_{3,3}$ exerting some influence. The control points P_1 and P_2 have most effect when $u = 1/3$ and $2/3$ respectively. Note that moving any control point will influence, to a greater or lesser extent, the shape of all parts of the curve. Another important point is that parametric representations allow multiple-valued curves. For example, if $P_0 = P_3$ then the resulting curve will be a closed loop.

The set of basis or blending functions given for cubic polynomials:

$$B_{0,3}(u) = (1-u)^3$$
$$B_{1,3}(u) = 3u(1-u)^3$$
$$B_{2,3}(u) = 3u^2(1-u)$$
$$B_{3,3}(u) = u^3$$

are a particular case of basis function of any degree n, where:

$$P(u) = \sum_{i=0}^{n} P_i \, B_{i,n}(u)$$

and:

$$B_{i,n}(u) = C(n, i)u^i(1-u)^{n-i}$$

and $C(n, i)$ is the binomial coefficient:

$$C(n, i) = n!/(i!(n-i)!)$$

Note that this increases the number of control points to $n + 1$ in general. There are, however, problems associated with increasing the number of control points by increasing the degree of the blending functions, and these difficulties are one reason for preferring B-splines.

At this point it is useful to consider all the ramifications of representing a curve with control points. The most important property, as far as interaction is concerned, is that moving the control points gives an intuitive change in curve shape. Another way of putting it is to say that the curve mimics the shape of the control polygon. An important property from the point of view of the algorithms that deal with curves (and surfaces) is that a curve is always enclosed in the convex hull formed by the control polygon. With regard to transformations, since the curves are defined as linear combinations of the control points, the curve is transformed by any affine transformation (rotation, scaling, translation and so on) in three-dimensional space by applying the appropriate transformations to the set of control points. Thus to transform a curve we transform the control points then compute the points on the curve. In this context note that it is not easy to transform a curve by computing the points and then transforming (as we might do with an implicit description). For example, it is not clear in scaling how many points are needed to ensure a smoothness when the curve has been magnified. Note here that perspective transformations are non-affine, so we cannot map control points to screen space and compute the curve there.

Although we have discussed the cubic Bezier form, this is only a special case of a set of Bernstein–Bezier polynomial curves. Cubics are used most often because they are reasonably simple, but are still

Figure 6.6
Positional continuity
between Bezier curves.

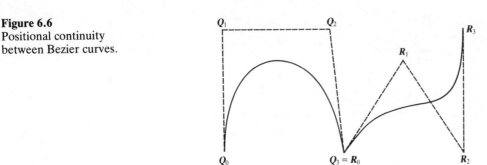

sufficiently flexible for interactive design work. The advantages of higher order curves relate to the degree of continuity that can be achieved between curve segments (see the next section). Apart from the computational expense, the relationship between the characteristic polygons formed by the control points and the curve becomes weaker as higher order curves are used.

6.1.2 Joining Bezier curve segments

Curve segments defined by a set of four control points can be joined to make up 'more complex' curves than those obtainable from a cubic polynomial form. This results in a piecewise polynomial curve. An alternative method of representing more complex curves is to increase the order of the polynomial, but this has computational and mathematical disadvantages and it is generally considered easier to split the curve into cubic segments. Connecting curve segments implies that constraints must apply at the joins. The default constraint is that first-order continuity must be maintained at the join. The difference between zero-order and first-order continuity is shown diagrammatically in Figures 6.6 and 6.7. Zero-order continuity means that the end point of the first segment is coincident with the start point of the second. First-order continuity means that the edges of the characteristic polygon are collinear as shown in the figure. This means that the tangent vectors at the end of one curve and the start of the other match to within a constant. In shaded surfaces, maintaining only zero-order continuity would possibly result in the 'joins' being visible in the final rendered object.

If the control points of the two segments are Q_i and R_i then first-order continuity is maintained if:

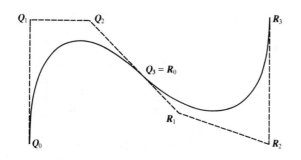

Figure 6.7
Tangential continuity between Bezier curves.

$$(Q_3 - Q_2) = k(R_1 - R_0)$$

Using this condition, a composite Bezier curve is easily built up by adding a single segment at a time. However, the advantage of being able to build up a composite form from segments is somewhat negated by the constraints on local control that now apply because of the joining conditions. This can only be alleviated by increasing the degree of the polynomial or by splitting a segment into two or more smaller segments.

6.1.3 B-spline curves

Two drawbacks associated with Bezier curves that are overcome by using B-spline curves are their non-localness and the relationship between the degree of the curve and the number of control points. The first property – non-localness – implies that, although a control point heavily influences that part of the curve most close to it, it also has some effect on all the curve and this can be seen by examining Figure 6.5. The second disadvantage means that we cannot fit a Bezier cubic curve through, in general, n points without the inconvenience of using multiple curve segments.

Originally, a spline was a draughtsman's aid. It was a thin metal (or wooden) strip that was used to draw curves through certain fixed points by adding weights at points called nodes or 'knots'. The resulting curve is smooth and minimizes the internal strain energy in the splines. The mathematical equivalent is the cubic polynomial spline.

Like a Bezier curve, a B-spline curve does not pass through the control points. A B-spline is really a piecewise cubic polynomial. It is a cubic over a certain interval and, on going from one interval to the next, the coefficients change. From one interval to the next we can compare the B-spline formulation with the Bezier formulation by using the same matrix notation.

The B-spline formulation is:

$$P(u) = \mathbf{UB_sP}$$

$$= [u^3 \ u^2 \ u \ 1] \ \frac{1}{6} \begin{bmatrix} -1 & 3 & -3 & 1 \\ 3 & -6 & 3 & 0 \\ -3 & 0 & 3 & 0 \\ 1 & 4 & 1 & 0 \end{bmatrix} \begin{bmatrix} P_{i-1} \\ P_i \\ P_{i+1} \\ P_{i+2} \end{bmatrix}$$

where $2 \leq i \leq n - 2$, and from this we can see that $\mathbf{P}$ is a set of four points in a sequence of control points. The formulation exhibits both first and second derivative continuity between the piecewise cubic polynomial segments. At this point we mention a confusion that appears in some of the literature on B-splines. The term 'B-spline' is sometimes used confusingly in computer graphics literature to describe both a single cubic polynomial segment and a set or sequence of cubic polynomials. Since the general advantage of a sequence of B-spline cubic polynomials is that the number of controls points can be increased to overcome the disadvantage of the Bezier form, it seems sensible that the term should relate to a set rather than a single curve.

In terms of its blending functions a B-spline curve is specified by:

$$P(u) = \sum_{i=0}^{n} P_i N_{i,k}(u)$$

where again P_i is a set of control points. Here $n + 1$ is the total number of $(k - 1)$-degree B-spline basis functions (n depends on k and the number of knot values $m + 1$ in the knot vector). We are now representing a curve by a number of segments – a piecewise polynomial curve – and the values of the parameter u that correspond to the joints between segments are called knots. The sequence of knots is called a knot vector. The key difference between Bezier blending functions and B-spline blending functions is that the number of control points can be increased without increasing the degree of the curve. We can set up the blending functions of degree $k - 1$ by using a recursive definition over various sub-intervals for the range of the parameter u:

$$N_{i,1}(u) = \begin{cases} 1 & \text{if } t_i \leq u \leq t_{i+1} \\ 0 & \text{otherwise} \end{cases}$$

$$N_{i,k}(u) = \frac{(u - t_i) \ N_{i,k-1}(u)}{t_{i+k-1} - t_i} + \frac{(t_{i+k} - u) \ N_{i+1,k-1}(u)}{t_{i+k} - t_{i+1}}$$

This recursive definition is known as the Cox–deBoor algorithm. A knot vector is non-periodic if the first and last knots are repeated with multiplicity k. In this case the knot vectors have the form:

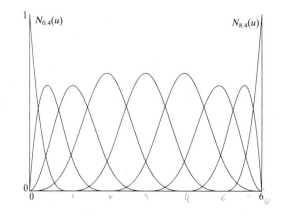

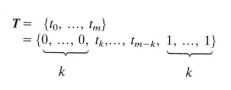

Figure 6.8
Nine cubic B-spline basis functions defined by the knot vector 0, 0, 0, 0, 1, 2, 3, 4, 5, 6, 6, 6, 6.

$$
\begin{aligned}
\boldsymbol{T} = \;& \{t_0, \ldots, t_m\} \\
= \;& \{\underbrace{0, \ldots, 0,}_{k}\; t_k, \ldots, t_{m-k},\; \underbrace{1, \ldots, 1}_{k}\}
\end{aligned}
$$

where $m = n + k$ is the number of knots in the knot vector.

This is a special case of non-uniform B-splines, but this family of B-spline curves is the one that is usually described in computer graphics texts. The reasons for its popularity are that the end-points of the curve become coincident with the first and last control vertices (just as for Bezier curves) and the tangent vector at the beginning of a curve lies along the line segment connecting the first and second control vertices. If uniform B-splines are used, then the curve end-points are not coincident with the end control vertices, and control vertices appear before and after the curve.

When knots are repeated a quotient of 0/0 can occur in the Cox–deBoor definition and this is deemed to be zero. Computationally the numerator is always checked for zero and the result set to zero irrespective of the denominator value. The choice of a particular knot set in commercial CAD systems that use B-splines is usually a predefined part of the system.

For open curves a non-periodic B-spline is used and the knot values from t_n to $t_n + k$ are chosen as follows:

$$
\begin{aligned}
t_i &= 0 && \text{if } i < k \\
t_i &= i - k + 1 && \text{if } k \leqslant i \leqslant n \\
t_i &= n - k + 2 && \text{if } i > n
\end{aligned}
$$

To obtain $n + 1$ basis functions we define $n + 5$ knots over an interval of length $n - 2$. Figure 6.8 shows the nine B-spline basis functions defined

Figure 6.9
Four versions of a cubic
B-spline curve and its
control points.

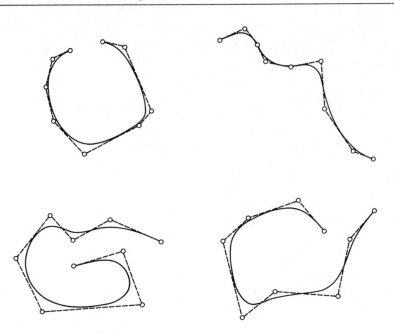

over the interval from 0 to 6. The 13 knots are:

$$0, 0, 0, 0, 1, 2, 3, 4, 5, 6, 6, 6, 6$$

This diagram also gives an interpretation of the knots. As u moves past the knot values one basis function (and the associated control point) 'switches off' and another 'switches on'. For example, at the knot value $u = 1$ in Figure 6.8, $N_{0,4}$ switches off and $N_{4,4}$ switches on. Figure 6.9 shows a cubic B-spline curve and its control polygon.

Reputedly B-splines derived their name from the shape of the basis functions and comparison of Figure 6.8 with Figure 6.5 shows that, for the Bezier blending functions, each basis function is non-zero over the whole interval from 0 to 1 whereas the B-spline basis functions are zero over a large proportion of the interval of definition. In fact when a control point is moved it affects the curve only in k knot spans. The degree of locality is a function of the number of knots and can be increased by knot insertion.

It is often claimed in computer graphics literature that Bezier curves exhibit global control while B-spline curves exhibit local control. Bartels *et al.* (1988) point out that this is misleading because it is not a comparison of like with like but a comparison of a single-segment Bezier curve (which may have the control vertex set extended and the degree of the curve raised) with a piecewise or composite B-spline curve. A single-segment Bezier curve is subject to global control because moving a control point affects the complete curve. In a composite B-spline curve moving a control point only affects a few segments of the curve. The comparison should be between multisegment Bezier curves and B-splines. The difference here is that to maintain continuity between Bezier segments the movement of the control points must satisfy constraints, while the control points of a B-spline composite can be moved in any way.

Finally, a knot vector:

$$T = \{\underbrace{0, \ldots, 0,}_{k} \underbrace{1, \ldots, 1}_{k}\}$$

yields the $(k - 1)$th degree Bezier–Bernstein basis function. From this we can see that a Bezier curve is a B-spline curve defined on a knot vector with no interior knots.

As for a Bezier curve, an affine transformation is applied to the curve by applying it to all the control points.

Since a B-spline curve is already a set of cubic segments with first- and second-order derivative continuity between segments, there is no need to consider joining conditions as we did for Bezier curves.

6.2 Parametric representation of three-dimensional surfaces

6.2.1 Biparametric cubic surfaces

The treatment of parametric cubic curve segments given in the foregoing section is easily generalized to bi-parametric cubic surface patches. A point on the surface patch is given by a bi-parametric function and a set of blending or basis functions are used for each parameter. A cubic Bezier patch is defined as:

$$P(u, v) = \sum_{i=0}^{3} \sum_{j=0}^{3} P_{ij} \, B_{i,3} \, (u) \, B_{j,3} \, (v)$$

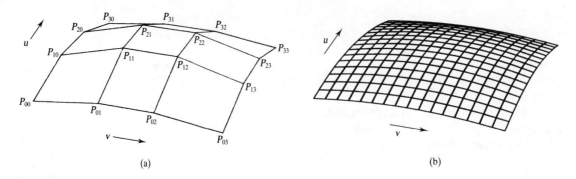

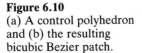

(a)

(b)

Figure 6.10
(a) A control polyhedron
and (b) the resulting
bicubic Bezier patch.

Mathematically the three-dimensional surfaces are said to be generated from the cartesian product of two curves. A Bezier patch and its control points are shown in Figure 6.10 where the patches are displayed using isoparametric lines. The 16 control points form a characteristic polyhedron and this bears a relationship to the shape of the surface, in the same way that the characteristic polygon relates to a curve segment. From Figure 6.10(a) it can be seen intuitively that 12 of the control points are associated with the boundary edges of the patch (four of them specifying the end-points) and the four interior points specify the internal shape. Only the corner vertices lie in the surface. The properties of the Bezier curve formulation are extended into the surface domain. Figure 6.11 shows a patch being deformed by the 'pulling out' of a single control point. The intuitive feel for the surface through its control points and the ability to ensure first-order continuity are maintained. The surface patch is transformed by applying transformations to each of the control points.

The way in which the control points work can be seen by analogy with the cubic curve. The geometric interpretation is naturally more difficult than that for the curve and, of course, the purpose of the Bezier formulation is to protect the designer against having to manipulate tangent vectors etc., but it is included for completeness.

The matrix specification is:

$$\boldsymbol{P}(u, v) = [u^3 \ u^2 \ u \ 1] \ [\mathbf{BPB^T}] \begin{bmatrix} v^3 \\ v^2 \\ v \\ 1 \end{bmatrix}$$

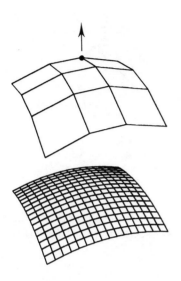
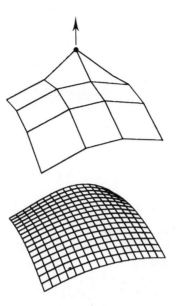
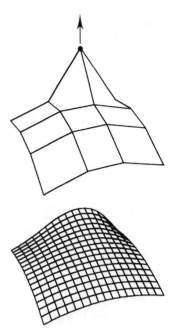

Figure 6.11
The effect of 'lifting' one of the control points of a Bezier patch.

where

$$\mathbf{B} = \begin{bmatrix} -1 & 3 & -3 & 1 \\ 3 & -6 & 3 & 0 \\ -3 & 3 & 0 & 0 \\ 1 & 0 & 0 & 0 \end{bmatrix}$$

$$\mathbf{P} = \begin{bmatrix} P_{00} & P_{01} & P_{02} & P_{03} \\ P_{10} & P_{11} & P_{12} & P_{13} \\ P_{20} & P_{21} & P_{22} & P_{23} \\ P_{30} & P_{31} & P_{32} & P_{33} \end{bmatrix}$$

Note that the matrix, $\mathbf{BPB}^T$, can be subdivided into four regions:

end-points	based on tangent vectors at each end-point along the v parametric direction
based on tangent vectors at each end-point along the u parametric direction	based on the cross-derivatives at each end-point

Figure 6.12
Tangent vector at P_{00}.

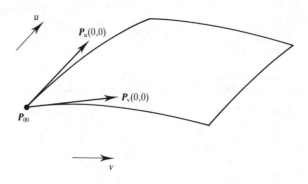

For example, consider the corner $u = v = 0$. The relationship between the control points and the vectors or derivatives associated with the vertex P_{00} is as follows:

$$P_u\,(0,0) = 3(P_{10} - P_{00})$$
$$P_v\,(0,0) = 3(P_{01} - P_{00})$$
$$P_{uv}(0,0) = 9(P_{00} - P_{01} - P_{10} + P_{11})$$

Figure 6.12 shows these vectors at a patch corner. The cross-derivatives at each end-point, sometimes called twist vectors, specify the rate of change of the tangent vectors with respect to u and v. They are vectors normal to the plane containing the tangent vectors.

For shading calculations we need to calculate certain surface normals. One of the easiest ways to shade a patch is to subdivide it until the products of the subdivision are approximately planar (this technique is discussed fully later in the chapter). The patches can then be treated as planar polygons and Gouraud or Phong shading applied. Polygon normals are calculated from the cross-product of the two tangent vectors at the vertex. For example:

$$a = P_{01} - P_{00}$$
$$b = P_{10} - P_{00}$$
$$N = a \times b$$

A normal can be computed at any point on the surface from the cross-product of the two partial derivatives $P_u(u, v)$ and $P_v(u, v)$ but shading a patch by exhaustive calculation of internal points from the parametric description is computationally expensive and is subject to other problems (described below). The advantages of using a parametric patch description of a surface are not contained in the fact that a precise world coordinate is available for every point in the surface – the cost of this information is generally too high – but in advantages that patch representation has to offer in object modelling.

6.2.2 Joining Bezier surface patches

Maintaining first order continuity across two patches is a simple extension of the curve-joining constraints and is best considered geometrically. Figure 6.13 shows two patches, Q and R, sharing a common edge. For positional or zero-order continuity:

$$Q(1, v) = R(0, v) \qquad \text{for } 0 \leqslant v \leqslant 1$$

This condition implies that the two patches require a common boundary edge characteristic polygon and:

$$Q_{33} = R_{03}$$
$$Q_{32} = R_{02}$$
$$Q_{31} = R_{01}$$
$$Q_{30} = R_{00}$$

or

$$Q_{3i} = R_{0i} \qquad i = 0, \ldots, 3$$

To satisfy first-order continuity the tangent vectors at $u = 1$ for the first patch must match these at $u = 0$ for the second patch for all v. This implies that each of the four pairs of polyhedron edges that straddle the boundary must be collinear (Figure 6.14). That is:

$$Q_{3i} - Q_{2i} = k(R_{1i} - R_{0i}) \qquad i = 0, \ldots, 3$$

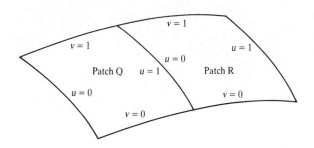

Figure 6.13
Joining two patches.

131

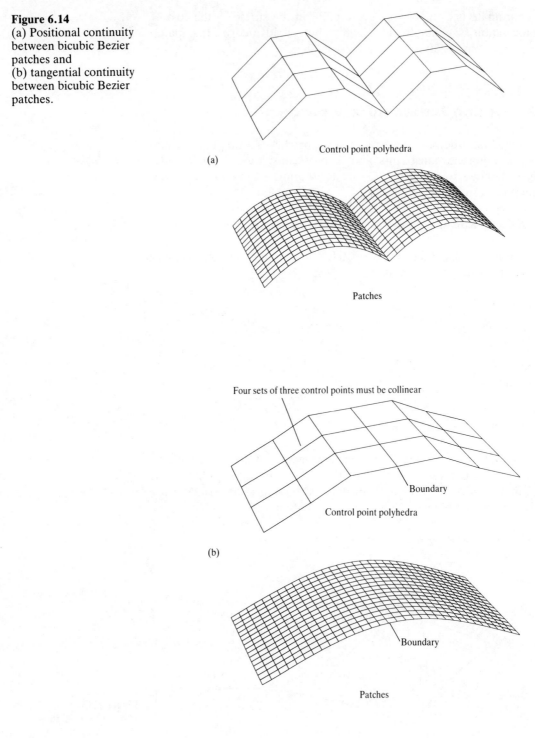

Figure 6.14
(a) Positional continuity between bicubic Bezier patches and
(b) tangential continuity between bicubic Bezier patches.

Control point polyhedra

(a)

Patches

Four sets of three control points must be collinear

Boundary

Control point polyhedra

(b)

Boundary

Patches

Faux and Pratt (1979) point out that, in CAD contexts, this constraint is severe if a composite surface is constructed from a set of Bezier patches. For example, a composite surface might be designed by constructing a single patch and working outwards from it. Joining two patches along a common boundary implies that 8 of the control points for the second patch are already fixed and joining a patch to two existing patches implies that 12 of the control points are fixed.

A slightly less restrictive joining condition was developed by Bezier (1972). In this, patch corners have positional but not gradient continuity. However, tangent vectors of edges meeting at a corner must be co-planar. Even with this marginally greater flexibility, there are still problems with the design of composite surfaces and one solution is to use patches of higher degree than cubic.

It should be mentioned that, although the foregoing treatment has dealt with rectangular patches, such patches cannot represent all shapes. Consider, for example, a spherically shaped object. Rectangular patches must degenerate to triangles at the poles. Triangular patches do not suffer from such degeneracies and are a more appropriate choice for complex shapes.

Farin (1988) points out that perhaps the main reason for the predominance of rectangular patches in most CAD systems is that the first applications of patches in car design were to the design of the outer body panels. Those parts have a rectangular geometry and it was natural to break them down into smaller rectangles and to use rectangularly shaped patches.

6.2.3 B-spline surface patches

B-spline surfaces patches are related to B-spline curves in the same way that Bezier patches are related to Bezier curves. The definition in terms of blending functions is:

$$P(u, v) = \sum_{i=0}^{n} \sum_{j=0}^{m} P_{i,j} N_{i,k}(u) N_{j,l}(v)$$

The easiest 'type' of B-spline surface patch to imagine is where the univariate basis functions contributing to the tensor product basis functions are based on knot vectors with multiple end-points. This means that the corner points of the $(n + 1) \times (m + 1)$ control vertices are coincident with the corner points of the patch. Otherwise the net of control points exists over a larger region than the extent of the patch.

The advantages of B-splines over Bezier curves are possibly more important in the surface domain. The non-localness of the control point influence in Bezier curves is a disadvantage in deforming or modelling contexts and the joining condition for multipatch segments imposes tedious constraints and makes user interfaces difficult. Another of the major disadvantages of the 16-vertex Bezier patch is that it can only represent a surface element with a simple topography. In contrast, with a B-spline surface there is no limit on the number of vertices defining the characteristic polyhedron and it is possible to represent far more complex surfaces using a single B-spline patch compared with a single Bezier patch. However, again problems of a user interface for object deformation or modelling arise as the number of control points increases.

A more general problem arises when modelling with B-spline surface patches. Because a patch does not interpolate or pass through its control points there is a difficulty in obtaining an initial surface approximation, from say a network of modelling points, for subsequent deformation. This has to be done by an initial interpolation process which yields a set of control vertices.

Since a cubic B-spline surface patch is already a network of patches all of which are cubic in each of the two parametric directions and which everywhere exhibit first- and second-order continuity, there is no need to consider joining conditions as we did for the Bezier patches.

6.2.4 Extending the control: NURBS and ß-splines

Two important surface representation schemes exist that extend the control of shape beyond movement of control vertices. These are NURBS (non-uniform rational B-splines) and β-splines. In the case of NURBS a control vertex is extended to a four-dimensional coordinate, the extra 'parameter' being a weight that allows a subtle form of control which is different in effect to moving a control vertex. In the simplest form of β-spline control, two 'global' parameters are introduced that affect the whole curve. These are 'bias' and 'tension' controls.

NURBS

A non-uniform B-spline curve is a curve defined on a knot vector where the interior knot spans are not equal. For example, we may have interior knots with multiplicity greater than 1 (that is, knot spans of length zero). Some common curves and surfaces, such as circles and cylinders, require non-uniform knot spacing and the use of this option generally allows better shape control and the ability to model a larger class of shapes.

A rational B-spline curve is defined by a set of four-dimensional control points:

$$P_i^w = (w_i x_i, w_i y_i, w_i z_i, w_i)$$

The perspective map of such a curve in three-dimensional space is called a rational B-spline curve.

$$P(u) = H\left[\sum_{i=0}^{n} P_i^w N_{i,k}(u) \right]$$

$$= \sum_{i=0}^{n} P_i w_i N_{i,k}(u) \Big/ \sum_{i=0}^{n} w_i N_{i,k}(u)$$

$$= \sum_{i=0}^{n} P_i R_{i,k}(u)$$

where

$$R_{i,k}(u) = N_{i,k}(u) \; w_i \Big/ \sum_{j=0}^{n} N_{j,k}(u) \; w_j$$

Rational B-splines have the same analytical and geometric properties as non-rational B-splines and if:

$$w_i = 1 \qquad \text{for all } i$$

then

$$R_{i,k}(u) = N_{i,k}(u)$$

The w_i associated with each control point are called weights and can be viewed as extra shape parameters. It can be shown that w_i affects the curve only locally. If, for example, w_j is fixed for all $j \neq i$, a change in w_i only affects the curve over k knot spans (just as moving a control point only affects the curve over k spans). w_i can be interpreted geometrically as a coupling factor. The curve is pulled towards a control point P_i if w_i increases. If w_i is decreased the curve moves away from the control point.

A specialization of rational B-splines is the generalized conic segment important in CAD. Faux and Pratt (1979) show that a rational quadratic form can produce a one-parameter (w) family of conic segments.

ß-splines

β-splines are a formulation (Barsky and Beatty, 1983) of B-spline curve segments. Barsky introduced two new degrees of freedom – bias and tension – which can be applied either uniformly to the whole curve (uniformly shaped B-splines) or non-uniformly by varying their values along the curve (continuously shaped B-splines). Note that, if the former technique is employed, then one of the useful properties of a B-spline – localness of control – is abandoned. For appropriate values of bias and tension, the β-spline formulation reduces to a uniform cubic B-spline.

A β-spline curve is defined by a sequence of $m - 2$ curve segments, the ith of which is:

$$P_i(u) = \sum_{r=-2}^{1} P_{i+r} \, b_r(\beta_1, \beta_2, u)$$

where P_i is a set of control points $[P_0, P_1, ..., P_m]$

$$0 \leqslant u < 1$$
$$i = 2, ..., m - 1$$

b_r (β_1, β_2, u) is a cubic polynomial called the rth β-spline basis function. By relaxing the first and second derivative continuity requirement (C^2) for B-spline curves to unit tangent and curvature vector continuity (G^2), Barsky gives the following formulae for the values of the four basis functions for each curve segment:

$$b_{-2} \, (\beta_1, \beta_2, u) = \frac{2\beta_1^3}{\delta}(1 - u)^3$$

$$b_{-1}(\beta_1, \beta_2, u) = \frac{1}{\delta}[2\beta_1^3 \, u(u^2 - 3u + 3)$$
$$+ 2\beta_1^2(u^3 - 3u^2 + 2)$$
$$+ 2\beta_1(u^3 - 3u + 2)$$
$$+ \beta_2(2u^3 - 3u^2 + 1)]$$

$$b_0(\beta_1, \beta_2, u) = \frac{1}{\delta}[2\beta_1^2 \, u^2(-u + 3) + 2\beta_1 \, u(-u^2 + 3)$$
$$+ \beta_2 u^2 \, (-2u + 3) + 2(-u^3 + 1)]$$

$$b_1(\beta_1, \beta_2, u) = \frac{2u^3}{\delta}$$

where

$$\delta = 2\beta_1^3 + 4\beta_1^2 + 4\beta_1 + \beta_2 + 2$$

When $\beta_1 = 1$ the curve is said to be unbiased. Increasing β_1 causes the curve to skew to one side, approaching the control polygon in an unsymmetric way. Replacing β_1 by a reciprocal value causes the curve to be skewed in the opposite manner. The β_2 parameter affects the curve symmetrically and is called tension. As β_2 is increased the curve approaches the control polygon. When $\beta_1 = 1$ and $\beta_2 = 0$ the β-spline reduces to the uniform cubic B-spline. Barsky categorized such a B-spline curve, in terms of his definition, as an unbiased, untensed β-spline.

A singular disadvantage of a β-spline is that it does not pass through any control points (including the end-points).

Both these curve methods can be extended to tensor product surfaces in the same way that the Bezier and B-spline curve definitions were used as a surface basis.

6.2.5 Objects and bicubic parametric patches

The use of bicubic parametric patches in computer graphics tends to be restricted to CAD and research areas. In the mainstream of three-dimensional image synthesis, the polygon mesh representation still predominates. There are a number of reasons for this. For most applications object modelling or building a data structure representation of a three-dimensional object is more difficult when bicubic patches are used. For example, quite complex real objects are easily polygonized by using a three-dimensional digitizer and operating software. Without the aid of large CAD packages it is difficult to build up a representation of an object in terms of surface patches.

Set against these disadvantages, there are a number of advantages that give surface patches their use in CAD. Firstly, the representation is 'fluid' and, by using software to adjust the position of the control points, the shape of an object can be adjusted. However, this is not as easy as it sounds because depending on the basis used it may be necessary to maintain the continuity conditions between patches. Although considerable effort is devoted to the mathematics of bicubic parametric patches in texts, there is little emphasis on using control point polyhedra in a practical context. For example, if we consider an object made up of Bezier patches, then one way of moving control points and maintaining adjoining patch continuity constraints is to move groups of nine control points as a single unit, as shown in Figure 6.15. This automatically

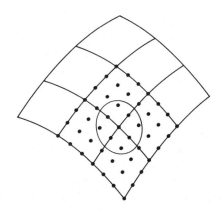

Figure 6.15
Four adjoining Bezier patches and their control points. Continuity constraints imply that the central control point cannot be moved without considering its eight neighbours. All nine points can be moved together and continuity maintained.

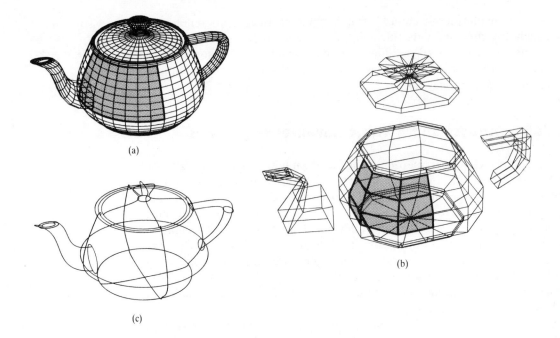

(a)

(b)

(c)

Figure 6.16
The Utah teapot.
(a) Lines of constant
u and v. The teapot is
made up of 32 Bezier
patches. A single patch is
shown shaded. (b) A
wireframe of the control
points. The shaded
region shows the control
polyhedron for the
shaded patch. (c) A
wireframe of the patch
edges.

ensures patch continuity but it is not too convenient from the point of
view of free deformation. 'Steps' easily appear in the surface between
areas controlled by these nine-point groups.

B-spline editors also have problems in user interface design. The
general principles of B-spline editors are discussed by Forsey and Bartels
(1988). An editing method is presented that encompasses what are likely
to be common requirements in most contexts – the need to mix broad-
scale surface manipulations with manipulations of a finer nature. Forsey
meets these requirements by using a hierarchical scheme allowing a
designer to manipulate a surface at any level of detail. The method is
completely general and is suitable for any parametric surface defined in
terms of control vertices.

Another advantage of bicubic patch representation is that, because
it is an exact analytical form, mass properties such as volume, surface
area and moments of inertia can be extracted from the description. This
property is fully exploited in CAD systems.

Finally, it should be mentioned that object representations at high
three-dimensional resolution can demand large memory volumes. This
means both high memory cost and database transfer time penalties. When
rendering complex multi-object scenes, database accesses can become
significant. A bicubic parametric patch object database, an exact
representation, is in contrast extremely economical.

The Utah teapot will suffice as an example here. A wireframe of
lines of constant u and v is shown in Figure 6.16. The object is made up

of 32 Bezier patches given in Appendix D. A single patch is shown as a shaded region. (Also shown in this figure is a composite control point polyhedron and a wireframe of the patch boundaries.) This representation consists of:

> 32 patches × 16 control points/patch
> = 288 vertices (approximately; most patches share 12 control points)
> = 288 × 3 real numbers (say)

In contrast, a 'reasonable' polygon mesh representation would be:

> approximately 2048 × four-sided polygons
> = 2048 × 3 real numbers (1 vertex for each polygon)

Thus the polygon mesh model, an inaccurate representation, uses more than seven times as much memory.

A related advantage here concerns rendering distant objects that project onto a small screen area. Using a fixed resolution polygon mesh model means paying the same database transfer penalty irrespective of the number of pixels occupying the final projection. A subdivision scheme of parametric patches would be more economical in this respect (although invoking higher scan conversion time penalties).

6.3 Scan converting parametric surfaces

Algorithms that scan convert surfaces represented by bicubic parametric patches divide naturally into two categories:

- those that render directly from the parametric description, and
- those that approximate the surface by a polygon mesh and use a planar polygon scan converter to render this approximation.

Currently the second approach appears to be the most popular. It is certainly the easier to implement and is computationally less expensive. Examples of the first are to be found in Blinn (1978a), Whitted (1978), Schweitzer and Cobb (1982), and Griffiths (1984). Lane *et al.* (1980) give a comparative description of these methods and describe an implementation of the second approach.

Scan conversion of parametrically defined surfaces is difficult because attributes of a polygon mesh, used in 'standard' polygon scan conversion, are not available from parametrically defined patches. Those attributes of a polygon that make for simple scan conversion are defined in Lane *et al.* (1980) as:

(1) the maximum and minimum Y screen coordinates are easily obtained

(2)   incremental equations can be used to track each of the polygon edges as functions of Y, and

(3)   incremental equations can be used to calculate the screen depth Z as a function of X.

A parametrically defined surface has none of these properties. The maximum and minimum Y coordinates will not in general be on the boundary or edges of the surface and a patch will often exhibit a silhouette edge. Silhouette edges are difficult because they are not necessarily the actual patch edges but could be, say, part of a central bump obscuring an actual edge. With parametrically defined surfaces both the boundary edge and the silhouette edge need to be tracked. A further complication is that a silhouette edge and a boundary edge may intersect. Finally, in general, neither the boundary nor silhouette edges will be monotonic in X or Y.

A parametrically defined surface, or surface patch, can be specified by three bivariate functions:

$$x = X(u, v)$$
$$y = Y(u, v)$$
$$z = Z(u, v)$$

where both u and v vary between 0 and 1. The boundaries of a surface patch are defined by the values $u = 0$, $u = 1$, $v = 0$ and $v = 1$. This results in a four-sided patch.

One way of looking at scan conversion in the context of bicubic parametric patches is that it is an algorithm which operates on curves formed by the intersection of the X–Z scan plane with the surface. In general the curve is between two boundary points or between a boundary point and a silhouette edge. With planar polygons this curve is a straight line and it is only necessary to store the end-points. In the case of parametric surfaces all points on the intersection curve need to be determined.

Blinn's algorithm (Blinn, 1978a) for parametric scan conversion is a straightforward algebraic approach and involves solving equations (using iterative techniques) for the intersection of the boundary curves and the silhouette edge with each scan line. The intersection of a scan line Y_s with the boundary of a patch is given by:

$$Y_s = Y(0, v)$$
$$Y_s = Y(1, v)$$
$$Y_s = Y(u, 0)$$
$$Y_s = Y(u, 1)$$

The silhouette edge intersections are given by:

$$Y_s = Y(u, v)$$
$$0 = N_z(u, v)$$

where N_z is the z component of the surface normal to the patch. A silhouette edge is defined by those points on the surface that exhibit a surface normal with zero z component. Local maxima and minima are determined from:

$$Y_u(u, v) = 0$$
$$Y_v(u, v) = 0$$

The points on the curve between these points are given by:

$$Y(u, v) - Y_s = 0$$
$$X(u, v) - X_s = 0$$

Solving these equations yields a set of points (u, v) in parameter space that can be substituted into the X and Z functions to yield the X and Z values of the edge on the current scan plane. This procedure is followed for each patch or surface, yielding successive pairs of boundaries representing areas to be shaded. As the scan plane moves down the screen, the boundary and silhouette edges must be tracked and their connectivity maintained. This is not an easy process and Blinn gives an instructive example using saddle points. Detection of a local maximum implies that a new intersection curve is added to an intersection curve list. Curves are deleted at Y minima. The effect of this process is to partition the surface patch into regions that are monotonically decreasing in Y and single valued in Z. It is pointed out in Lane *et al.* (1980) that there are numerous problems with this approach but that for most shapes the algorithm is robust. Thus, as with planar polygon scan conversion, the outer Y scan loop tracks boundary and silhouette edges and the inner X scan loop 'fills in' points on the intersection curve in the Y scan plane. Blinn further modifies this process by trading off accuracy against speed, approximating the intersection curve by straight line segments. Finally, if this approach is adopted then the surface normals have to be calculated, both for silhouette edge detection and for use in the reflection model applied to shade the patch.

Whitted's, Schweitzer's and Griffith's methods are all variations of this basic approach.

6.3.1 Approximation to a surface patch using a polygon mesh

A planar polygon mesh is easily generated from a surface patch. The patch can be divided using isoparametric curves. (Splitting up a patch into isoparametric curves is a common method of display in CAD systems, permitting a wireframe visualization of the surface sufficient for the requirements of such systems.) This yields a net or mesh of points at the intersection of these curves with each other and the boundary edges. This net of points can be used to define the vertices for a mesh of planar polygons which can then be scan converted using a planar polygon scan converter. There are two basic flaws in this rudimentary approach. Visible boundary edges and silhouette edges may exhibit discontinuities. In general a finer polygon resolution will be necessary to diminish the visibility of piecewise linear discontinuities on edges than is necessary to maintain smooth shading within the patch. Also, internal silhouette edges in the patch will generally be of higher degree than cubic.

Connected with this is the question: how fine should the isoparametric division be? Too fine a subdivision is computationally expensive, and too coarse implies visible discontinuities. A possible approach is to relate the number of divisions to the area projected by the patch on the screen.

A subtler approach is varying 'resolution'. Areas of the patch that are 'flattish' are subject to few subdivisions. Areas where the local curvature is high are subject to more subdivisions. Effectively the patch is subdivided to a degree that depends on local curvature. This is the approach adopted by Lane *et al.*, (1980).

Patches are subdivided until the products of the subdivision satisfy a flatness criterion. Such patches are now considered to be approximately planar polygons and are scan converted by a normal polygon renderer using the corner points of the patches as vertices for rectangles in the polygon mesh. The set of patches representing the surface can be preprocessed, yielding a set of polygons which are then scan converted as normal. This is the approach adopted in Clark (1979). Lane integrates this patch-splitting approach with a scan conversion algorithm.

There are two significant advantages to patch splitting:

- it is fast, and,
- the speed can be varied by altering the depth of the subdivision. This is important for interactive systems.

A disadvantage of non-uniform subdivision is that holes can appear between patches owing to the approximation of a patch boundary by a

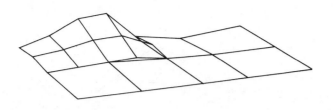

Figure 6.17
Tears produced by non-uniform subdivision of patches.

straight line. An example of this degenerative process is shown in Figure 6.17.

Subdivision algorithms are best considered for a curve. These are then easily extended or generalized to deal with a patch. The crux of the method is that, rather than evaluate points along a curve, the curve is approximated by a piecewise linear version obtained by subdividing the control points recursively. This gives a finer and finer approximation to the curve. The level of subdivision–recursion terminates when a linearity criterion is satisfied. Lane and Riesenfeld (1980) show that the piecewise linear approximation to the curve will eventually 'collapse' onto the curve provided that enough subdivisions are undertaken.

A subdivision formula for the Bezier basis (or, in general, the Bernstein basis) is given in Lane *et al.* (1980) and derived in Lane and Riesenfeld (1980). This is based on the de Casteljau algorithm mentioned at the beginning of the chapter. A Bezier curve is subdivided into two curves by subdividing the control points, forming two new sets of control points Q_i and R_i. The point Q_3 or R_0 is the end-point of the first curve and the start of the second. The formula is:

$$Q_0 = P_0 \qquad\qquad R_0 = Q_3$$
$$Q_1 = (P_0 + P_1)/2 \qquad\qquad R_1 = (P_1 + P_2)/4 + R_2/2$$
$$Q_2 = Q_1/2 + (P_1 + P_2)/4 \qquad\qquad R_2 = (P_2 + P_3)/2$$
$$Q_3 = (Q_2 + R_1)/2 \qquad\qquad R_3 = P_3$$

Figure 6.18 shows how, after a single subdivision, the piecewise linear curve joining the two new sets of control points is a better approximation to the curve than the original. The approximation after three levels of subdivision is shown in Figure 6.19.

This efficient formula (that uses only additions and divide by twos) makes the subdivision rapid. The depth of the subdivision is easily controlled using a linearity criterion. The Bezier basis functions sum identically to 1:

$$\sum_{i=0}^{3} B_{i,n}(u) = 1$$

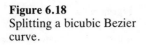

Figure 6.18
Splitting a bicubic Bezier
curve.

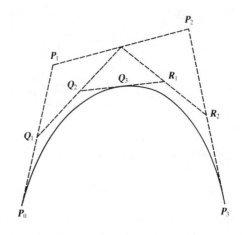

This means that the curve lies in the convex hull formed by the control points P_i. The piecewise linear subdivision product will coincide with the curve when it approaches the line joining the two end-points. The degree to which this is achieved, that is the linearity of the line joining the four control points, can be tested by measuring the distance from the middle two control points to the end-point joining line (Figure 6.20).

The philosophy of this test is easily extended to surface patches. A plane is fitted through three non-collinear control points. The distance of each of the other 13 control points from this plane is then calculated. If one of these distances lies outside a prespecified tolerance, then the patch is further subdivided.

A practical problem that occurs when considering non-uniform subdivision (subdivision until a flatness criterion is satisfied) compared with uniform subdivision to some predetermined level is the cost of the flatness test. It is debatable whether it is a simpler and better, but less

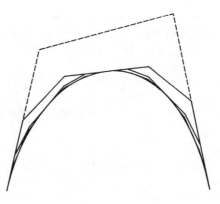

Figure 6.19
Drawing the control
points at each level of
subdivision.

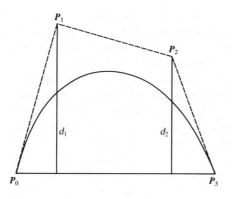

Figure 6.20
A cubic Bezier curve with control points P_0, P_1, P_2, P_3.

elegant approach, simply to adopt uniform subdivision and to ignore the fact that some areas are going to be unnecessarily subdivided (because they are already almost flat). Plate 7 shows a uniform subdivision approach for the Utah teapot at subdivisions of depth one, two and three. This shows predictably that the difference in quality between the rendered images is mainly visible along silhouette edges. If uniform subdivision is adopted then rendering bicubic patches can reduce to a preprocessing phase of a normal Z-buffer renderer. This method requires a large database memory for the subdivision products. If sufficient memory is not available, and the extra complexity of a scan line algorithm is to be introduced, then it is not a big step to use non-uniform subdivision.

The overall structure of a scan line algorithm such as the Lane–Carpenter algorithm is as follows:

(1)   Sort the patches by maximum possible Y value. This value, as already stated, may be a corner point, a point on a boundary edge, or a point on a silhouette edge. The only quick way to an estimate of this value is to take the maximum Y value of the convex hull of the control points.

(2)   For each scan line, lists of inactive and active patches are updated. For each active patch, subdivision is performed until either a flatness criterion is satisfied, or any one subdivision product no longer straddles a scan line. 'Flat' polygons are added to an active polygon list and scan converted in the normal way. Subdivision products that no longer overlap the scan line can be added to the inactive patch list. Thus we have an active and inactive list of parametric patches together with an active list of flat polygons.

One of the practical points that has to be dealt with is the problem of tears. Tears are a natural consequence of recursive or non-uniform subdivision. If one part of a surface patch is subdivided along a boundary shared by another patch that requires no further subdivision, then a gap between the two parts will naturally result. This tear is then an unrepresented area and will appear as a gap or hole in the final rendering phase (Figure 6.17). The Lane–Carpenter algorithm does not deal with this problem. It can be minimized by making the flatness criterion more rigorous but herein lines the usual computational paradox. The philosophy of the subdivision approach is that areas of a surface are subdivided to a degree that corresponds to local curvature. Large flat areas are minimally subdivided. Areas exhibiting fast curvature changes will be subdivided down to sufficiently small polygons. Tightening the flatness criterion means that many more polygons are generated and the final rendering phase takes much longer.

Clark's method deals with this problem in a more elegant way by adopting a subdivision method that is initially constrained to the boundary curves. There are three steps involved:

(1)   The convex curve hull criterion is applied to the boundary edges $u = 1$ and $u = 0$ and the patch is subdivided along the v direction until this is satisfied.

(2)   The same method is then applied to the $v = 1$ and $v = 0$ boundaries.

(3)   Finally, the normal convex hull test is applied to the subdivision products and the process is continued, if necessary, either along the u or v direction.

Once a boundary satisfies the convex hull criterion it is assumed to be a straight line. Any further subdivision along this boundary will thus incur no separation.

A possible advantage of subdividing in the direction of the u or v boundaries is that with some objects this will result in fewer patches. Consider, for example, subdividing a 'ducted' solid – a cylinder is a trivial example of such an object. Subdividing the cylinder along a direction parallel to its long axis will lead this algorithm to converge more quickly and with fewer patches, than if the subdivision proceeds in both parametric directions. A disadvantage with this approach is that it is difficult to integrate with a scan line algorithm. A scan line algorithm 'drives' or controls the order of subdivision depending on how the patches lie with respect to the scan lines.

Another aspect that requires consideration is the calculation of surface normals. These are, of course, required for shading. They are easily obtainable from the original parametric description of any point (u, v) on the surface by computing the cross-product of the u and v

derivatives. However, if a subdivision method is being used to scan convert, then the final polygon rendering is going to utilize a Phong interpolation method and the vertex normals are easily calculated by taking the cross-products of the tangent vectors at the corner points. This will, in general, depending on the level of the subdivision, give non-parallel vertex normals for the 'flat' polygons, but all polygons contributing to a vertex will have the same normal. Two consequences can result from the fact that 'flat' polygons are being sent to a shader with non-parallel vertex normals. Firstly, erroneous shading effects can occur at low levels of subdivision. Secondly, the question of which vertex normal to use for culling arises. Problems arise because not all the polygons surrounding a vertex may be available, since subdivision is taking place on the fly, and an average vertex normal cannot be calculated as in polygon meshes. Cases can result where one normal subtends an angle greater than 90° with the view vector and another from the same polygon subtends an angle less than 90°. The only safe course of action is to cull a polygon by testing, each of its vertex normals. If any vertex normal is 'visible' the polygon is not culled.

An earlier approach by Catmull (1974) subdivided patches until they approximated the size of a single pixel, writing the results into a Z-buffer. This straightforward but computationally expensive approach sidesteps yet another problem – relating the extent of the subdivision to the projected screen size of the patch. Clearly there is no point in subdividing to a greater and greater depth if, when projected into screen space, the patch only covers a few pixels. Clark relates the subdivision test to the depth coordinates of the control points of the patches.

Finally, these subdivision methods differ in the basis used. The Lane–Carpenter algorithm uses a cubic Bernstein or Bezier basis. Clark uses a Taylor series expansion and central differences to derive more efficient subdivision formulae and to utilize a flatness test that is available directly from the subdivision components.

Projects, notes and suggestions

6.1 A patch editor (*)

Write an interactive editor that facilitates the deformation of a Bezier curve or a Bezier surface patch. The editor should allow the user to grab and manipulate control points. Project 1.3 discusses the general problems of using a two-dimensional locator device in three-dimensional space.

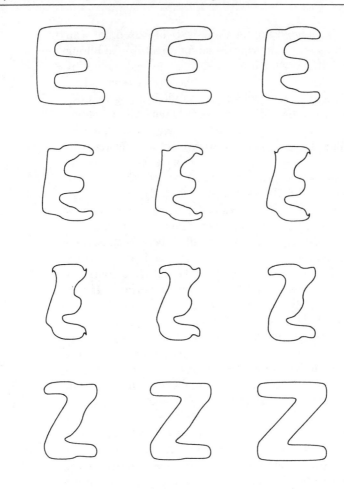

Figure 6.21   A multi-segment Bezier curve representing letter E changing into a curve representing the letter Z.

6.2   Control point animation (*)

By using a suitable interpolation procedure with the control points that specify a shape made up, say, of piecewise Bezier segments, write a program to 'in-between' the transformation of one arbitrary shape into another. For example, Figure 6.21 shows a multisegment Bezier curve forming the letter 'E' changing into a curve forming the letter 'Z'. Repeat this procedure using B-splines. Extend the procedure to deal with surfaces.

6.3 Rendering bicubic patches

Using the rendering software of Chapter 5, write a uniform subdivision algorithm that converts bicubic parametric patches into polygons. Compare the cost of the uniform subdivision with non-uniform subdivision.

6.4 Modelling and representational methods – a comparison (*)

Consider an example of a non-trivial solid, such as, say, that formed from the union of three mutually perpendicular cylinders. Use a solid such as this in a study that compares the following representational methods.

(1) A polygon mesh model:
The polygon mesh model adopted in this text is just one of a number of possible schemes generally known as boundary representations. Such schemes differ in the way in which edges and vertices are represented and connected, and in the entities, other than polygons, that appear in the representation.

(2) Quadric surfaces:
Use a set of implicit equations for a library of quadric functions (Project 1.8).

(3) A bicubic parametric patch model:
Use a net of an appropriate number of bicubic parametric patches to represent the surface.

(4) A CSG tree:
CSG denotes constructive solid geometry and is a form used mainly in CAD applications. It is beyond the scope of this text but any graphics practitioner should be aware of it.
   A CSG tree represents an object by decomposing it into a number of primitive three-dimensional objects. These primitives – solids such as cubes, cylinders and spheres, are combined using three-dimensional boolean set operations such as union, intersection and set differences, together with linear transformations. An object is represented by a tree whose leaves are the primitive object specifications and whose nodes are the combination operations. For example, the tree for the aforementioned solid would contain a single union node and three leaves each specifying the parameters of (transformed) cylinders.

(5) Octrees:
Discussed in Chapter 8, octrees are used extensively, for example, in medical imaging, where consecutive cross-sectional images are merged to form a three-dimensional data field represented by an octree.

Points that you may consider in the comparison are:

- The generality of the representation. What are the limitations on the type of three-dimensional shape that can be represented?
- The relative difficulty in building or specifying the structure initially.
- The ability to derive a representation from automatically collected data such as an object scanned by a laser ranger.
- The data storage requirements.
- The ability of the method to accommodate an interactive editing scheme.
- The ease of rendering the object. For example, how would you go about extracting a surface from an octree representation? Clearly a Z-buffer renderer can cope with a union operator in a CSG representation, but how well can a Z-buffer renderer generally cope with a CSG tree?
- The generality of the method with respect to applications. For example, can CSG methods be applied in 'creative' three-dimensional graphics where the polygon mesh model tends to predominate?

This project should involve a wide search through the literature and references have been deliberately omitted.

CHAPTER SEVEN

Ray Tracing

It is oft stated that ray tracing has produced the most realistic images to date in computer graphics. It is more the case that ray tracing has produced extremely impressive images of scenes that are carefully chosen to demonstrate the attributes of the ray tracing model; for example, the ability of the technique to deal with multiple reflections. Thus most examples contain mixtures of highly reflective and highly transparent procedurally defined objects. These scenes, examples of which abound in the literature on ray tracing, are also characterized by the frequent occurrence of spheres – for reasons that will later become clear. Both the choice of objects that tend to appear in ray traced scenes, and the fact that ray tracing is only a partial solution to the global illumination–reflection problem, result in images that are indisputably impressive but which exhibit a ray-traced 'signature'. The nature of and reasons for this signature will become apparent as this chapter proceeds, and the difficulties and limitations of ray tracing are revealed.

Ray tracing is currently the most complete simulation of an illumination–reflection model in computer graphics. The surface reflection models introduced earlier can be seen as simplifications of ray tracing. In both simple surface reflection models and ray tracing, light is simulated as rays travelling in a straight line through homogeneous media. The difference between a simple reflection model and a ray-traced model is the 'depth' to which interaction between light rays and objects in the scene is examined.

The basic philosophy of ray tracing is that an observer sees a point on a surface as a result of the interaction of the surface at that point with rays emanating from elsewhere in the scene. In simple surface reflection models, only the interaction of surface points with direct illumination from light sources is considered. In general, however, a light ray may reach the surface indirectly via reflection in other surfaces, transmission through partially transparent objects or a combination of these. This is often referred to as global illumination – light that originates from the environment rather than from local interaction of the surface with direct illumination from the light source or sources.

The method possesses a number of disadvantages, the most important being extremely high processing overheads. Ray-traced images typically take many minutes, hours or even days to compute. Its significant advantage is that it is a partial solution to the global illumination problem, elegantly combining in a single model:

- *hidden surface removal;*
- *shading due to direct illumination;*
- *shading due to global illumination;*
- *shadow computation.*

The present chapter is concerned with the theoretical and practical details necessary to implement a very simple ray tracing program. The next chapter is devoted to looking at various established extensions to ray tracing. Because ray tracing is best implemented using recursion, there are certain subtle details that have to be taken care of concerning the structure of the program. These are dealt with by developing a recursive procedure in Pascal and generally apply to any language that supports recursion.

7.1 Basic algorithm

Ray tracing is an algorithm that works entirely in object space. At a given point in the image plane, the surfaces visible, and hence colour and intensity, at that point are obtained by tracing a ray backwards from the eye through the point into the scene. If this ray intersects an object, then local colour calculations will determine the colour that is the result of direct illumination at that point. This is light from a light source directly reflected at the surface. If the object is partially reflective, partially transparent or both, the colour of the point in the image plane should include a contribution from reflected and transmitted rays. These must be traced backwards to discover their contribution. Determining a colour for each of these rays may itself require the tracing of further rays at other

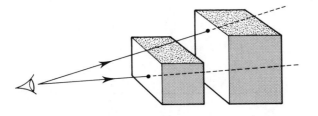

Figure 7.1
Terminating a ray trace
at the first intersection
gives hidden surface
removal.

intersections with objects. To determine completely the colour of the original point in the viewing plane, this set of rays must be traced backwards through the scene. The trace of a particular ray in the set terminates if it intersects the background, or if so many surface intersections separate it from the observer that its colour contribution to the image is likely to be negligible.

A ray is started from the observer through each point that is to be defined in the viewing plane, or image plane. In a simple program a ray is traced through the centre of each pixel in the image plane. This means that the scene is sampled in object space by infinitesimally thin rays. The process uses zero spatial coherence and the sampling produces aliasing. However, the fact that each ray calculation is independent of all others makes implementation in parallel processing hardware trivial. The process is easily distributable; for example, a recent implementation of a standard ray tracing program on transputers is given in Atkin (1986).

Ray tracing was originally used in computer graphics by Appel (1968). Here it was used only as a solution to the hidden surface problem in a general rendering system for three-dimensional objects. The ray tracing in this case stops at the first intersection of the ray and a surface (Figure 7.1). Such intersections are then categorized as visible points in the screen image. A simple implementation of this algorithm would search for an intersection between the ray and all surfaces in the scene, the intersection nearest to the viewer being the one required. These initial rays are sometimes called viewer rays, hidden surface rays or first-level rays.

Note at this point that in a scene containing highly reflective objects the 'conventional' hidden surface solution is no longer apt. Surfaces of an object, which would be back surfaces if the object was isolated, may be reflected in the front surfaces of an adjacent object (Figure 7.2). Culling or depth sorting techniques cannot be used for such scenes.

The first use of a ray tracing model to trace beyond the initial ray–surface intersection and to incorporate reflection, refraction and shadows was developed in 1979 (Kay, 1979; Whitted, 1980) and most simple ray tracing procedures use the model detailed in these reports.

Figure 7.2
In a ray-traced scene 'back' surfaces of an object may be visible. Here a back surface of the cube is reflected in the sphere.

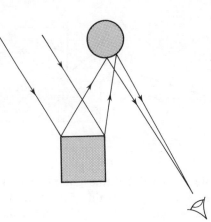

7.2 A historical digression – the optics of the rainbow

Many people associate the term 'ray tracing' with a novel technique but in fact it has always been part of geometric optics. For example, an early use of ray tracing in geometric optics is René Descartes's treatise, published in 1637, explaining the shape of the rainbow. From experimental observations involving a spherical glass flask filled with water, Descartes used ray tracing as a theoretical framework to explain the phenomenon. Descartes used the already-known laws of reflection and refraction to trace rays through a spherical drop of water.

Rays entering a spherical water drop are refracted at the first air–water interface, internally reflected at the water–air interface and finally refracted as they emerge from the drop. As shown in Figure 7.3, horizontal rays entering the drop above the horizontal diameter emerge at an increasing angle with respect to the incident ray. Up to a certain maximum the angle of the exit ray is a function of the height of the incident ray above the horizontal diameter. This trend continues up to a certain ray, when the behaviour reverses and the angle between the incident and exit ray decreases. This ray is known as the Descartes ray, and at this point the angle between the incident and exit rays is 42°. Incident rays close to the Descartes ray emerge close to it and Figure 7.3 shows a concentration of rays around the exiting Descartes ray. It is this concentration of rays that makes the rainbow visible.

Figure 7.4 demonstrates the formation of the rainbow. An observer looking away from the sun sees a rainbow formed by '42°' rays from the sun. The paths of such rays form a 42° 'hemicone' centred at the observer's eye. (An interesting consequence of this model is that each observer has his own personal rainbow.)

154

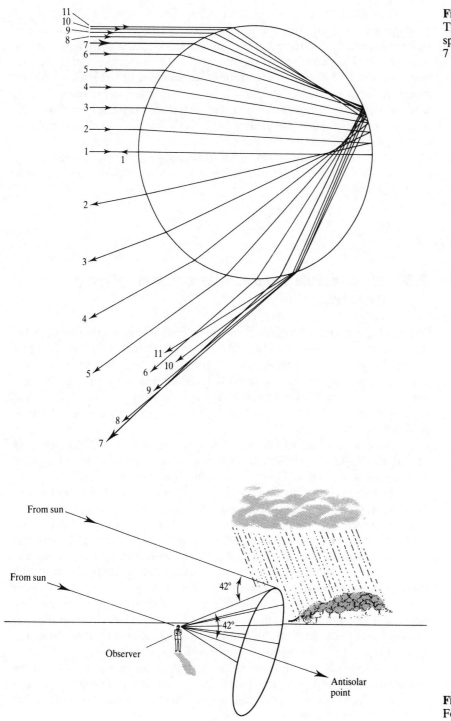

Figure 7.3
Tracing rays through a spherical water drop (ray 7 is the Descartes ray).

Figure 7.4
Formation of a rainbow.

155

This early, elegant use of ray tracing did not, however, explain that magical attribute of the rainbow – colour. Thirty years would elapse before Newton discovered that white light contained light at all wavelengths. Together with the fact that the refractive index of any material varies for light of different wavelength, Descartes's original model is easily extended. About 42° is the maximum angle for red light, while violet rays emerge after being reflected and refracted through 40°. The model can then be seen as a set of concentric hemicones, one for each wavelength, centred on the observer's eye.

This simple model is also used to account for the fainter secondary rainbow. This occurs at 51° and is due to two internal reflections inside the water drops.

7.3 Recursive implementation of ray tracing

The implementation of a general ray tracing algorithm is quite difficult for two reasons. The geometrical calculations are elaborate and the execution time is long. Execution time can be reduced for test runs by generating images at a lower spatial resolution than finally required, but this process may mask errors whose effect is slight and only visible in the final resolution image. A simple ray tracer for scenes of restricted geometry is straightforward.

In this section, we discuss the implementation of a simple ray tracing model in Pascal. Ray tracing is best implemented in a language that supports recursion. To see this, first consider Figure 7.5.

In Figure 7.5, a ray (ray 1) is being traced backwards from the eye through a pixel on the screen into an environment containing semi-transparent spheres (that is, objects that reflect and refract transmitted light). The colour to be seen along this ray will be the result of an analysis of its intersection with the first object surface encountered during the backwards trace of the ray. The colour seen coming along the ray from the surface (and hence the colour required at the pixel) is made up of three contributions: local colour due to illumination of the surface by direct and ambient light; a colour contribution from the reflection of a ray coming from the reflection direction; and a colour contribution from the transmission of a ray coming from the refraction direction.

The colour contribution from the reflection ray (ray 2) can be discovered by tracing this ray backwards to its first intersection (if any) with an object. The colour at this intersection will itself be made up of

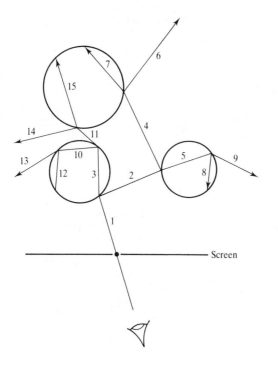

Figure 7.5
A simple example demonstrating the recursive nature of ray tracing.

three contributions: local, reflected and transmitted. The reflected and transmitted contributions at this intersection are obtained by backward tracing rays 4 and 5, and so on. The transmitted contribution to ray 1 needs to be calculated in the same way by tracing ray 3 back to its next intersection, and so on.

Figure 7.6 shows the analysis that takes place at each intersection of a ray with a surface. The tree of Figure 7.7 shows the complete pattern of intersection analyses that need to be done to discover the colour perceived along ray 1. In Figure 7.7, we have assumed a trace depth of 4. This implies the assumption that, beyond four intersections, any colour contribution to the first level ray will be negligible. Whether or not this is a reasonable assumption is discussed in Chapter 8.

Program 7.1 presents an outline of the main tasks to be handled by a simple recursive ray tracing procedure. In order to discover the colour of the pixel corresponding to ray 1 in Figure 7.5, a call of this procedure would be made with parameters representing the start point and direction of this ray, together with a depth value to indicate the depth to which the trace should be carried out:

Figure 7.6
Details of three
contributions to the
intensity of a point on a
surface.

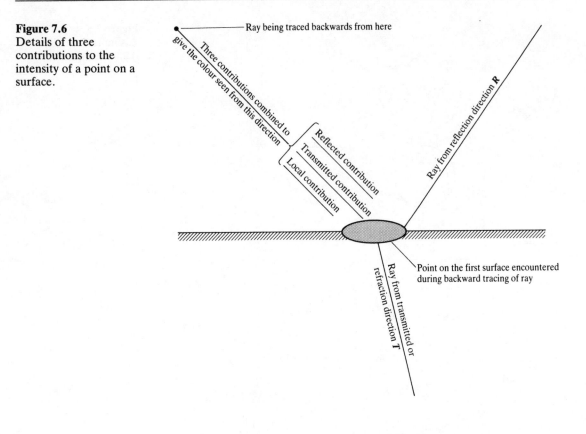

$$TraceRay(viewing\text{-}position,\ pixel\text{-}position$$
$$-viewing\text{-}position,\ 4,\ pixel\text{-}colour)$$

The eventual result of the trace will be returned as a triplet of RGB
values in the parameter *pixel-colour*.

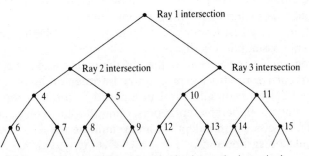

Figure 7.7
Ray tracing as a tree.

Program 7.1 An outline of a simple recursive ray tracing procedure.

```
procedure TraceRay(start, direction: vectors;
                       depth: integer; var colour: colours);

var intersection-point, reflected-direction,
       transmitted-direction: vectors;
    local-colour, reflected-colour,
       transmitted-colour: colours;

begin
  if depth > maxdepth then colour := black
  else
  begin
    { Intersect ray with all objects and find intersection
    point (if any) that is closest to start of ray }
    if {no intersection} then colour := background-colour
    else
    begin
      local-colour := {contribution of local colour model
                          at intersection-point}
      {Calculate direction of reflected ray}
      TraceRay(intersection-point, reflected-direction,
         depth + 1, reflected-colour);
      {Calculate direction of transmitted ray}
      TraceRay(intersection-point, transmitted-direction,
         depth + 1, transmitted-colour);
      Combine(colour,
         local-colour, local-weight-for-surface,
         reflected-colour, reflected-weight-for-surface,
         transmitted-colour, transmitted-weight-for-surface)
    end
  end
end   { TraceRay };
```

Figure 7.8 shows the tree of procedure calls that results from the above top level call. The activation of the procedures in this tree takes place depth first and left to right. Thus, for example, the procedure calls for ray 2 and all its subsidiary rays are obeyed before the call for ray 3 is entered.

The procedure outline presented as Program 7.1 describes the situation at a general intersection point and this model is used at every intersection point involved in the trace started by ray 1 in Figure 7.5.

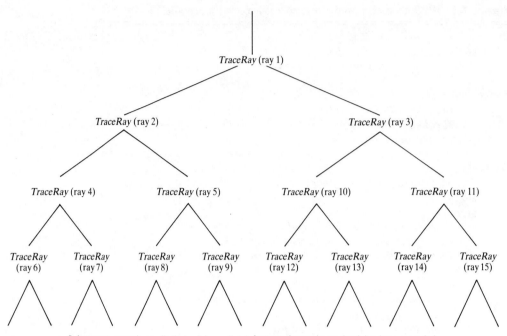

Subsequent procedure calls that exit immediately because the maximum depth has been exceeded

Figure 7.8
Tree of procedure calls
executed by Program 7.1

Each procedure activation has its own private copy of the workspace required for its parameters and local variables and this, together with the recursive control mechanism of a language such as Pascal, relieves the user of many of the book-keeping tasks that would otherwise be associated with an implementation of ray tracing.

Plate 8 shows a ray-traced image of a rather contrived scene containing a mix of reflective and refractive spheres against a striped background. The background colour in all other directions is blue. Each sphere displays a different mix of local colour, reflection and refraction. The sphere at the bottom left is red. The spheres in the bottom row become increasingly reflective from left to right. The sphere at the bottom right is wholly reflective. Moving upwards, the spheres become more transparent. The sphere at the top left is partially (50%) transparent and completely non-reflective. The sphere at the top right is completely transparent and looks rather strange. Completely transparent objects are only encountered in ray-traced images. The other spheres illustrate intermediate cases.

The trace depth used to produce Plate 8 (*top*) was 6. The full effect of this can best be seen in the reflective sphere at the bottom right. This sphere contains an image of the rest of the scene (constructed with a trace depth of 5).

Note that with respect to the horizontal variation 'increasing reflectivity' actually refers to the relative proportions of local and global contributions. This, for example, changes the glossy red sphere into a perfect mirror sphere. On the left the local weight is unity and the global weight is zero. On the right these proportions are reversed. In practice, going along the bottom row, we should still always see the light source and it should end up as a point in the perfectly reflecting sphere. Problems such as this arise in this simple approach to ray tracing and are entirely due to the hybrid nature of the model and the incorrect mixing of a spreading term (local illumination) with a non-spreading term (global illumination). This particular deficiency can be overcome by enhancing the algorithm so that the traced rays are checked for intersection with the light source.

Plate 8 (*centre*) shows a ray-traced image of three balls on a table, two reflective and one not. This image was also generated by tracing to maximum depth 6.

7.4 A remark on efficiency

The structure of the procedure of Program 7.1 has certain drawbacks in terms of efficiency. In many recursive procedures the simplest structure is obtained by making the test for the terminating condition at the start of the procedure and exiting immediately if this condition is satisfied. At the terminal branches of the tree of procedure calls, this involves unnecessary calls that terminate immediately. If the overheads in making the redundant calls are not too high, then this is often an acceptable price to pay for program simplicity and transparency. In this case, making these extra calls involves doing the reflection and refraction geometry calculations for the calls. These calculations involve substantial real arithmetic.

The unnecessary procedure calls, and hence these calculations, can be eliminated by using the alternative structure of Program 7.2. An activation of this procedure does the local colour calculations first and then checks the current depth value to see whether it is appropriate to make the calculations and procedure calls for the reflected and transmitted rays. This is the version of the ray tracing procedure that would be used in practice.

Program 7.2 Improved efficiency in a naive ray tracing procedure.

```
procedure TraceRay (start, direction: vectors;
                         depth: integer; var colour: colours);

var intersection-point, reflected-direction,
         transmitted-direction: vectors;
     local-colour, reflected-colour,
         transmitted-colour: colours;

begin
  {Intersect ray with all objects and find intersection
     point (if any) that is closest to start of ray}
  if {no intersection} then colour := background-colour
  else
  begin
    local-colour := {contribution of local colour model
                          at intersection-point}
    if depth = maxdepth then
    begin
      reflected-colour := black; transmitted-colour := black
    end
    else
    begin
      {Calculate direction of reflected ray}
      TraceRay(intersection-point, reflected-direction,
          depth + 1, reflected-colour);
      {Calculate direction of transmitted ray}
      TraceRay(intersection-point, transmitted-direction,
          depth + 1, transmitted-colour);
    end;
    Combine(colour,
        local-colour, local-weight-for-surface,
        reflected-colour, reflected-weight-for-surface,
        transmitted-colour, transmitted-weight-for-surface)
  end
end { TraceRay };
```

7.5 Ray tracing geometry – intersections

Originally a ray traced backwards from the eye is tested against all objects in the scene for an intersection. The coordinates of the intersection points are retained and the one nearest the viewpoint will be on the surface that is nearest to the viewer. This is the first intersection of the initial ray with the scene. This ray spawns (possibly) two more rays

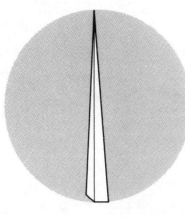

Figure 7.9
A sphere is an inefficient
bounding volume for a
long thin object.

and each of these needs to be tested against all objects in the scene for intersection. Each node in the ray history tree is obtained in this way and it is easily seen that the program will spend a large proportion of its time testing for intersections between a ray and an object. Whitted (1980) estimated that, for scenes of moderate complexity, up to 95% of the processing time is spent in intersection calculations.

Whitted originally used a scheme of bounding volumes to speed up intersection calculations. First suggested by Clark (1976), each object in the scene has a bounding volume associated with it. An object of arbitrary complexity can be enclosed by a simple bounding volume whose intersections with a straight line are easily calculated. If a ray does not intersect the bounding volume, it cannot intersect the object. For an object represented by a large number of polygons this saves testing every polygon in the object against the ray.

Spheres have mostly been used as bounding volumes, although their suitability is critically dependent on the nature of the object. For example, long thin objects (Figure 7.9) will result in a situation where most rays that intersect the bounding sphere do *not* intersect the object. Because spherical objects and their bounding volumes coincide, early ray traced images tend to contain only spheres. Bounding volumes are discussed further in Chapter 8.

As an example of an intersection calculation we now deal with the simple case of the sphere. The intersection between a ray and a sphere is easily calculated. If the end-points of the ray are (x_1, y_1, z_1) and (x_2, y_2, z_2) then the first step is to parametrize the line:

$$x = x_1 + (x_2 - x_1)t = x_1 + it$$
$$y = y_1 + (y_2 - y_1)t = y_1 + jt \qquad \textbf{(7.1)}$$
$$z = z_1 + (z_2 - z_1)t = z_1 + kt$$

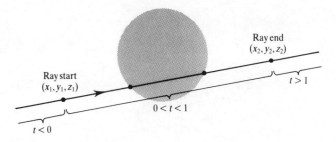

Figure 7.10
Values of parameter t
along a ray.

A sphere at centre (l, m, n) of radius r is given by:

$$(x - l)^2 + (y - m)^2 + (z - n)^2 = r^2 \tag{7.2}$$

Substituting for x, y and z gives a quadratic equation in t of the form:

$$at^2 + bt + c = 0 \tag{7.3}$$

where:

$$a = i^2 + j^2 + k^2$$
$$b = 2i(x_1 - l) + 2j(y_1 - m) + 2k(z_1 - n)$$
$$c = l^2 + m^2 + n^2 + x_1^2 + y_1^2 + z_1^2 + 2(-lx_1 - my_1 - nz_1) - r^2$$

If the determinant of this quadratic is less than 0 then the line does not intersect the sphere. If the determinant equals 0 then the line grazes or is tangential to the sphere. The real roots of the quadratic give the front and back intersections. Substituting the values for t into the original parametric equations yields these points. Figure 7.10 shows that the value of t also gives the position of the points of intersection relative to (x_1, y_1, z_1) and (x_2, y_2, z_2). Only positive values of t are relevant and the smallest value of t corresponds to the intersection nearest to the start of the ray.

If a ray intersects a bounding sphere (or in general any bounding volume) then it must be checked for intersection with the object. The method used here will depend on the way the object is represented in the data structure. If a boundary representation is used and the object is represented by a set of polygons then the straightforward approach for each polygon is:

(1)   obtain an equation for the plane containing the polygon, and
(2)   check for an intersection between this plane and the ray;
(3)   check that this intersection is contained by the polygon.

For example, if the plane containing the polygon is:

$$ax + by + cz + d = 0$$

and the line is defined parametrically as before, then the intersection is given by:

$$t = -(ax_1 + by_1 + cz_1 + d)/(ai + bj + ck)$$

(If the denominator is equal to zero the line and plane are parallel.) The straightforward method that tests a point for containment by a polygon is simple but expensive. The sum of the angles between lines drawn from the point to each vertex is 360° if the point is inside the polygon, but not if the point lies outside.

If the objects are procedurally defined, then the method used depends on the type of the definition. Kajiya (1983) gives efficient methods for three procedurally defined types: fractal surfaces, prisms and surfaces of revolution. A prism is a surface defined by translating a plane curve orthogonally and Kajiya points out that many objects used in computer graphics can be defined as (collections of) prisms. For example, block letters, machine parts formed by extrusion and simple models of urban architecture.

Details on intersecting a ray with bicubic patches are to be found in Joy and Bhetanabhotla (1986), Barr (1986), Steinberg (1984), Hanrahan (1983), Kajiya (1982), Potmesil and Chakraverty (1981) and Whitted (1980). Whitted (1980) uses an expensive approach which extends the bounding sphere approach to bicubic patches. Each patch on a surface is enclosed in a bounding sphere. If the sphere is intersected by a ray the patch is subdivided using a standard patch subdivision algorithm, and each patch subdivision product is enclosed in a bounding sphere. This process is continued until either a bounding sphere, of preset minimum radius, is reached or the ray does not intersect the sphere. This recursive process of subdivision, enclosure in a bounding sphere and checking for intersection between the ray and the sphere will eventually produce a point of intersection whose accuracy is determined to within the radius of the minimum bounding sphere. In contrast, Kajiya (1982) uses a direct numerical approach to ray–patch intersection.

7.6 Ray tracing geometry – reflection and refraction

The formulae presented in this section are standard formulae in a form that is suitable for incorporation into a simple ray tracer.

Each time a ray intersects a surface it produces, in general, a

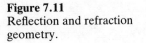
Figure 7.11
Reflection and refraction
geometry.

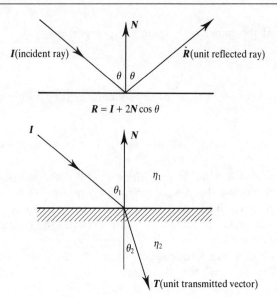

reflected and refracted ray. The reflection direction, a unit vector, is
given by:

$$R = I + 2N \cos \theta$$

where I and N are unit vectors representing the incident ray direction and
the surface normal respectively. I, R and N are co-planar. These vectors
are shown in Figure 7.11.

A ray striking a partially or wholly transparent object is refracted
owing to the change in the velocity of light in different media. The angles
of incidence and refraction are related by Snell's law:

$$\frac{\sin \theta_1}{\sin \theta_2} = \frac{\eta_2}{\eta_1}$$

where the incident and transmitted rays are co-planar with N. The
transmitted ray is represented by T and this is given by

$$T = \frac{1}{\eta} I - (\cos \theta_2 - \frac{1}{\eta} \cos \theta_1) N$$

$$\eta = \frac{\eta_2}{\eta_1}$$

$$\cos \theta_2 = [1 - \frac{1}{\eta^2}(1 - \cos^2 \theta_1)]^{1/2}$$

as shown in Figure 7.11. These formulae are given in Heckbert and

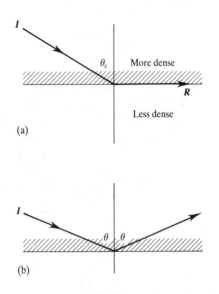

Hanrahan (1984). They are equivalent to those used in Whitted (1980) but the formulae for the refracted ray are simpler.

If a ray is travelling from a more to a less dense medium then it is possible for the refracted ray to be parallel to the surface (Figure 7.12). θ_c is known as the critical angle. If θ is increased then total internal reflection occurs.

7.7 Reflection—illumination model

At this stage it is useful to reiterate the difference between direct and global illumination and to look at how these considerations can be built in to a model that calculates intensity at a surface element. Direct illumination is light incident on a scene from a light source or a number of light sources. A surface element receives light directly from a source. However, if illumination from direct sources 'enters' a scene, and is incident on a surface element after interaction with another object or objects, then that illumination is categorized as global. Global illumination arises from the interaction of direct light with reflective and transparent objects.

In the Phong model for direct illumination, three terms are used:

$$I_{\text{phong}} = \frac{\text{diffuse}}{\text{term}} + \frac{\text{specular}}{\text{term}} + \frac{\text{ambient}}{\text{term}}$$

Each term in this equation is, of course, a vector of three **RGB** values.

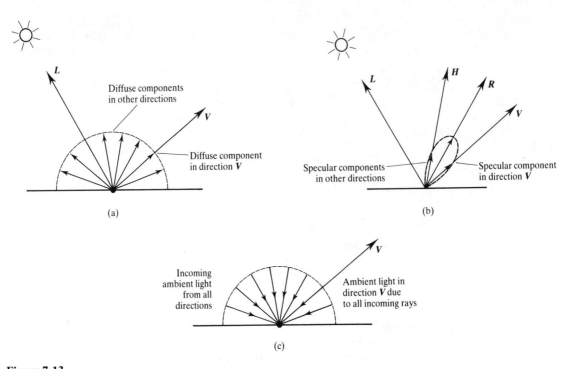

Figure 7.13
Diagrammatic
representations of local
reflection components.

The diffuse term and the specular term result from direct illumination and the ambient term results from diffuse light originating from the rest of the scene. In the Phong model the ambient term is modelled as a constant.

Figure 7.13 shows schematically how these reflection contributions are considered in computer graphics. A surface element exhibiting diffuse reflection radiates light equally in all directions, and specular reflection is concentrated around the reflection vector. The ambient term can be considered to originate from an infinity of incoming rays (or, equivalently, elemental light sources). Each one of these rays is reflected from the surface, and the overall sum of the reflections gives the ambient term. It is important to realize that, although these effects are simulated in the local contribution, they are not in the global contribution. No diffuse interaction between objects is considered and the specular interaction involves simply tracing infinitesimally thin rays that are not spread (as are the rays from light sources in the local contribution).

The local component is calculated as before, using the Phong reflection model, which is extended by another term that accounts for transparent objects; see Hall (1983). This is light that is seen through a transparent object due to a light source located at the other side of it.

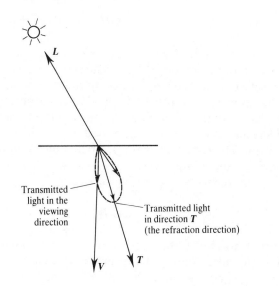

Figure 7.14
Extending the Phong
model to account for the
spread of transmitted
light in a transparent
object.

This term generalizes the direct illumination component of the model. The scattering of light transmitted through a medium blurs the image of a point light source, just as a surface that is not perfectly smooth reflects a highlight that is a spread or blur of a point source. The scattering can be modelled in the same empirical manner:

$$I_{\text{direct transmitted}} = k_t \, (\boldsymbol{N \cdot H'})^n$$

Recall that $\boldsymbol{H}$, the bisector of the angle between the light source vector and the viewer, is the angle at which the surface microfacets have to be oriented to reflect light maximally to the viewer. Similarly, $\boldsymbol{H'}$ is the orientation that surface microfacets must possess to maximally refract light to the viewer, that is, the orientation that the microfacets would need to possess for $\boldsymbol{T}$ and $\boldsymbol{V}$ to coincide (Figure 7.14). $\boldsymbol{H'}$ is thus a function of $\boldsymbol{L}$, $\boldsymbol{V}$, and the relative index of refraction:

$$\boldsymbol{H'} = \frac{-\boldsymbol{L} - (\eta_2/\eta_1)\boldsymbol{V}}{(\eta_2/\eta_1 - 1)} = \frac{-\boldsymbol{L} - \eta\boldsymbol{V}}{\eta - 1}$$

(Note: to avoid complicating the expression $\boldsymbol{H'}$ has been left un-normalized.) In ray tracing models it is useful to forget that the ambient term (which is anyway modelled as a constant) is technically a global term, and to categorize all these terms as local. Local terms are those that are calculated at each surface intersection owing to direct illumination and ambient light. Our comprehensive local model is now:

$$I_{\text{local}} = I_a k_a + I_i \left[k_d (N \cdot L) + k_s (N \cdot H)^{n_s} + k_t (N \cdot H')^{n_t} \right] \qquad \textbf{(7.4)}$$

Note that for a given light source only one of the last two terms can be active. Extending the necessary program check described in Chapter 2 enables a selection of the appropriate term depending on the sign of $(N \cdot L)$. In ray tracing, to this model are added two more terms, described as global. These are the contributions from a reflected ray incident on the surface element and from a transmitted ray incident on the surface element (if the object is transparent), originating from elsewhere in the scene. Both of these are traced rays whose colour contributions are returned by the recursive ray tracing procedure:

$$I = I_{\text{local}} + k_r I_{\text{reflected}} + k_t I_{\text{transmitted}}$$

It is important to realize that this expresses the summation of the three values at a particular point in the recursive process. $I_{\text{transmitted}}$ invokes an equivalent expression at the next surface intersected by the transmitted ray, and $I_{\text{reflected}}$ invokes an equivalent expression at the next surface intersected by the reflected ray. Thus in any multi-object scene we can consider that reflection from a visible surface element will originate from three sources:

(1) ambient light – a surface element will always receive ambient light;

(2) direct light source(s) – a surface element will receive illumination from such a source if it is visible to the source: in our treatment (1) and (2) are considered as local terms;

(3) traced rays of light concentrated along particular directions due to interaction between objects.

Ray tracing is essentially a hybrid model – some rays are traced, others are not. In the direct specular term, spread is calculated empirically, rather than by ray tracing. In contrast, in the ray-traced global terms, the transmitted and reflected rays are not spread. Thus rays from direct illumination are spread (empirically) but rays from the eye (traced rays) are not. This is an inherent contradiction in the model and again underlines the fact that models in computer graphics are a combination of theoretical and empirical 'fixes' that are tuned until an acceptable image generation tool is achieved. Reflections in an object, from other items in the scene, appear as if that object was a perfect mirror. Similarly, rays traced through objects appear as if the object was a perfect transmitter. This effect is somewhat diminished, because the image of one object in the other is usually less in size and intensity than the original, but it does contribute to the ray-traced signature of sharp reflections, refractions and shadows.

The final expression for a simple ray tracing model is:

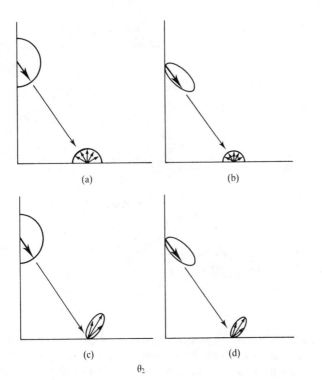

Figure 7.15
The four 'mechanisms' of
light transport: (a) diffuse
to diffuse; (b) specular to
diffuse; (c) diffuse to
specular; (d) specular to
specular. (After Wallace
et al. (1987)).

$$I = I_{\text{local}} + I_{\text{global}}$$
$$= I_a k_a + I_i \left[k_d (N \cdot L) + k_s (N \cdot H)^{n_s} + k_t (N \cdot H')^{n_t} \right] + k_t I_t + k_r I_r \qquad (7.5)$$

k_a and k_d are functions of wavelength, as before, and the local contribution would be evaluated for RGB components. Note that I_t and I_r are in fact RGB vectors since they are returning intensities that may have a local component. Also note that this equation does not explicitly reflect the recursive nature of the process used to obtain the I_t and I_r value, but gives a value for I at one stage in the recursive process. Finally, note that Equation 7.5 also reflects the different theoretical domains of the two contributions. In practice k_s should equal k_r, but in this simple model it is convenient use k_s to control the intensity of any highlight due to direct illumination and k_r to control the mirror reflectivity of objects in any multiple reflecting path.

A useful abstraction that puts the above model in perspective is Figure 7.15 which is based on an illustration by Wallace *et al.* (1987). In the model just described only 'mechanism' (d) is implemented, but without the spread. Mechanism (b) is partially contained in the model in that diffuse spread from direct illumination is modelled in the local part of the equation.

Figure 7.16
Ray tracing a simple two-dimensional scene.

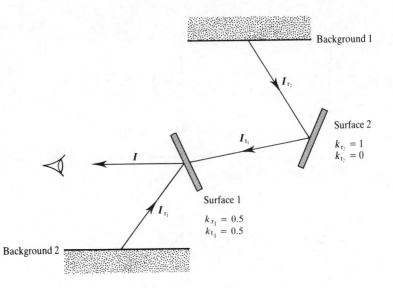

Finally, consider a simple example. Figure 7.16 shows a two-dimensional slice of a simple scene consisting of two opaque background surfaces, a semitransparent surface and a totally reflecting surface. The calculation will proceed recursively to a depth of three.

$$I = I_{\text{local surface1}} + k_{r1}I_{r1} + k_{t1}I_{t1}$$

I_{r1} and I_{t1} are then calculated using the same expression, giving:

$$I_{r1} = I_{\text{local background2}} + 0 + 0$$
$$I_{t1} = I_{\text{local surface2}} + k_{r2}I_{r2} + 0$$

The recursion now terminates with the evaluation of I_{r2}:

$$I_{r2} = I_{\text{local background1}} + 0 + 0$$

The contribution made to an image by the different levels of the trace can be seen in Plate 8 (*bottom*). This contains four images of the portion of the scene marked in Plate 8 (*centre*). These four images were produced with maximum trace depths of 1, 2, 3 and 4. A black region in one of these images represents an object at which the trace was terminated 'prematurely' at a reflective surface. Tracing to depth 1 results in both reflective spheres appearing dark. All the detail that should be seen in the spheres has to be obtained by tracing rays that have been reflected (rays at depth 2 or beyond). Similarly, with maximum trace depth set to 2, reflections of mirror spheres appear black, and so on. A satisfactory level of detail in the reflected images is obtained for this scene with a maximum trace depth of 4.

With the adaptive depth modification discussed in the next chapter, the depth of trace would vary for different parts of the scene. In some places, a depth of 1 would be adequate, in others a depth of 4 or more might be necessary.

7.8 Shadows and ray tracing

Shadows are easily incorporated into the reflection–illumination model described in the previous section. At each ray intersection I_{local} is computed. As described in the previous section this assumes that L, the light source vector (or vectors if there is more than one light source), is not interrupted by any objects in its path. If L is so interrupted then the current surface point lies in shadow. Whether other objects lie in the path of L is determined by creating an additional ray (called a shadow feeler) from the point to the light source (or to each light source in turn). If a wholly opaque object lies in the path of the shadow feeler then I_{local} is reduced to the ambient value. An attenuation in I_{local} is calculated if the intersecting object is partially transparent. Note that it is no longer appropriate to consider L as a constant vector (light source at infinity) and the so-called shadow feelers are rays whose direction is that of L.

Strictly speaking, a shadow feeler intersecting partially transparent objects should be refracted. It is not possible to do this, however, in the simple scheme described. The shadow feeler is initially calculated as the straight line between the surface intersection and the light source. This is an easy calculation and it would be difficult to trace a ray from this point to the light source and to include refractive effects.

Finally, note that, as the number of light sources increases from unity, the computational overheads for shadow testing rapidly predominate. This is because the 'main' rays are only traced to an average depth of between 1 and 2 (see Section 8.1). However, each ray–surface intersection spawns n shadow feelers (where n is the number of light sources) and the object intersection costs for a shadow feeler are exactly the same as for a main ray.

A recent development (Haines and Greenberg, 1986) uses a 'light buffer' as a shadow testing accelerator. Shadow testing times were reduced, using this procedure, by a factor of between 4 and 30.

The method precalculates, for each light source, a light buffer which is a set of cells or records, geometrically disposed as two-dimensional arrays on the six faces of a cube surrounding a point light source (Figure 7.17). To set up this data structure all polygons in the

Figure 7.17
Shadow testing
accelerator of Haines and
Greenberg (1986).

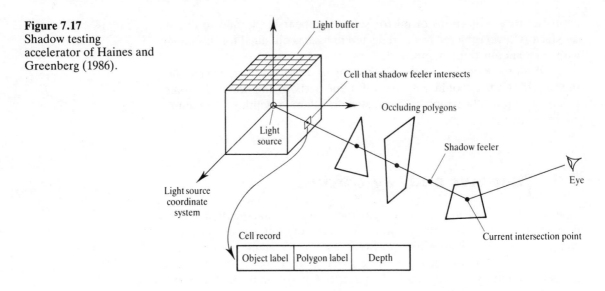

scene are cast or projected onto each face of the cube, using as a projection centre the position of the light source. Each cell in the light buffer then contains a list of polygons that can be seen from the light source. The depth of each polygon is calculated in a local coordinate system based on the light source, and the records are sorted in ascending order of depth. This means that, for a particular ray from the eye, there is immediately available a list of those object faces that may occlude the intersection point under consideration.

Shadow testing reduces to finding the cell through which the shadow feeler ray passes, accessing the list of sorted polygons, and testing the polygons in the list until occlusion is found, or the depth of the potentially occluding polygon is greater than that of the intersection point (which means that there is no occlusion because the polygons are sorted in depth order).

The method deals with point light sources and the resulting images do not contain soft shadows or penumbrae. Storage requirements are prodigious and depend on the number of light sources and the resolution of the light buffers.

7.9 Distributed ray tracing

Earlier it was pointed out that there are inherent contradictions in the reflection–illumination model that is used in standard ray tracing algorithms. In particular, the traced rays are not spread but continue from intersection to intersection as infinitely thin beams. This results in standard aliasing artefacts together with sharp shadows, sharp reflection and sharp refraction resulting in a super-real signature for conventional ray traced images.

Some of these problems can be overcome by increasing both the number of initial rays and spawning extra rays at intersections but this approach very soon becomes completely impractical because of the overheads. Distributed ray tracing, developed by Cook *et al.* (1984), is an elegant method that circumvents the straightforward solution of adding a large number of extra rays. Both the anti-aliasing problem and the modelling of what Cook calls fuzzy phenomena are solved by distributed ray tracing. Algorithmically the anti-aliasing function is inherent to the process and is described in this section. However, the underlying theory of stochastic anti-aliasing – the method used – is presented in Chapter 12.

The motivation for distributed ray tracing can easily be seen by examining a conventional ray-traced image (see, for example, Plate 8). The ray-traced surreal signature originates from the assumption of perfect reflection and transmission for the global component. Reflecting surfaces produce, in general, blurred reflections as a result of surface imperfections; similarly, transmitting surfaces blur transmitted rays owing to scattering in the material. As we discussed above, the hybrid nature of a naive ray tracer allows reflections from a direct light source to cause a blurred reflection (or specular highlight) but global reflection–transmission is deemed to be perfect. In Cook *et al.* (1984) these problems are overcome by causing the rays to follow paths other than that predicted by the exact reflection and transmission direction. This produces blurred reflection and transmission. The same model incorporates new effects – blurred shadows, depth of field, motion blur and anti-aliasing (Cook, 1986). The method uses 16 rays per pixel and its main attributes are:

- The process of distributing rays means that stochastic anti-aliasing becomes an integral part of the method.
- Distributing reflected rays produces blurry reflections.
- Distributing transmitted rays produces translucency.
- Distributing shadow rays results in penumbrae.
- Distributing ray origins over the camera lens area produces depth of field.
- Distributing rays in time produces motion blur (temporal anti-aliasing).

Consider, for example, reflection and transmission. A spatially randomized set of initial rays is generated in the image plane by jittering (see Chapter 12). At a surface intersection a reflected and a transmitted ray

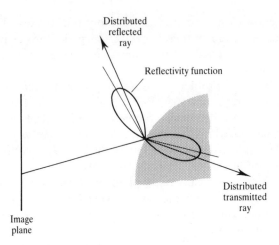

Figure 7.18
Distributed ray tracing.

are spawned, but the outgoing direction is distributed and jittered by indexing into a look-up table. The rays are distributed by using importance sampling. This means that the outgoing direction is chosen on the basis of the specular reflection function. The probability of a certain sample's being chosen is based on the magnitude of the specular reflection function at that point. For an incoming angle (between the incident ray and the surface normal) the look-up table will store a range of reflection angles plus a jitter magnitude for determining an exact reflection angle. Jittering is still necessary to avoid the aliasing that would occur as a result of using a selected reflection angle that is chosen from a small number of table entries. The general process is shown in Figure 7.18.

A similar form of distributed ray tracing is used by Wallace *et al.* (1987) to integrate ray tracing with the radiosity method and overcome one of the disadvantages of radiosity – that it does not handle specular interaction.

7.10 Ray tracing and anti-aliasing operations

Ray tracing is a sampling method and suffers from the classic aliasing artefacts. However, the cost of ray tracing makes unintelligent over-sampling an impractical solution.

A certain improvement is possible if rays are originated at pixel corners and averaged. Theoretically nothing is gained from this approach; the same number of rays are originated, and we trade aliasing artefacts against blurring. Generating more rays by uniform subdivision of pixels is extremely expensive because the normal execution time is just multiplied by the subdivision factor. A better approach is to use the corner samples to control the subdivision. If a corner intensity differs from the other corner intensities by more than a certain amount, then this quarter of the pixel is subdivided and seven more rays are originated. Stochastic sampling, described in Chapter 12, is possibly the best anti-aliasing method to use in ray tracing.

A more general approach to non-uniform over-sampling is given by Mitchell (1987). The method has two important attributes:

- It is a context-dependent approach devoting most effort to areas of the image that require it.
- The anti-aliasing module is algorithmically separate from the ray tracing module and it can therefore be used in conjunction with a standard ray tracer or indeed any ray tracer.

The anti-aliasing operations take place in three stages:

(1) A ray tracing solution is constructed at a low sampling density, say, for example, one ray per pixel.

(2) This solution is used to determine those areas that should be supersampled.

(3) An image is constructed from those non-uniform samples by using an appropriate reconstruction filter.

Mitchell suggests a two-level sampling approach, where the super-sampling is carried out at either four or nine samples per pixel (making this approach cheaper than distributed ray tracing). Whether to supersample or not is a decision that must be taken by examining small areas of the low resolution samples (3×3 areas are used in Mitchell (1987)). Mitchell points out that this approach is not infallible (nor theoretically correct). It will detect edges, where a 3×3 area straddles an edge, but it is likely to miss small isolated features. A contrast measure is used to make the decision. This is:

$$C = (I_{max} - I_{min})/(I_{max} + I_{min})$$

This yields three values of C in a conventional RGB ray tracer and different thresholds are used for R, G and B different wavelengths of 0.4, 0.3 and 0.6 respectively. This enables a gross simulation of the fact that the eye's sensitivity to noise or aliasing artefacts is a function of colour. The method thus produces non-uniform samples in both the image and the RGB domain.

In the final reconstruction phase the choice of a reconstruction filter (see Chapter 12) is made difficult by the sudden changes in sampling density. Mitchell uses a multistage filter with characteristics for each stage that copes with the nature of the samples.

Projects, notes and suggestions

7.1   First-hit ray tracing

Implement a 'first-hit' ray tracer in which a ray is traced only as far as its first intersection with an object. The structure of the main procedure should be based on Program 7.1, but without the calculations for reflected and transmitted ray directions and without the recursive calls to trace these rays. This means that all the objects in the scene will appear to be completely opaque. Such a program will simply act as an expensive solution to the hidden surface removal problem. The advantage of doing this is that it will enable you to familiarize yourself with the basic structure of a ray tracing program without the added complication of handling recursion and calculations for reflection and transmission. Problems to be dealt with include:

- Intersection calculations: limit the objects in the scene to spheres and base the intersection calculations on Equations 7.1, 7.2 and 7.3.
- Colour calculations: use a simple local colour model based on Equation 7.4 without the last two terms for the specular components (one light source, no shadows).
- Data structures: the representation of each object will have to contain information about its position, its geometry and its surface properties. The objects will have to be linked together in some way to form a data structure representation of the scene.

7.2   Shadow calculations

Incorporate shadow feelers in the above simple model. This involves tracing an additional ray from each intersection with an object towards the light source. If that ray intersects an object on the way, then only the ambient term in Equation 7.4 should be used for colouring the point of intersection.

7.3   Intersection geometry

Implement data structures and intersection tests for other types of object. For example, a polygon mesh can be tested for intersection using the approach described earlier in this chapter.

There are various special cases for which intersection calculations can be speeded up. For example, intersection of a ray with a rectangular surface can be done more efficiently by expressing the coordinates of the point of intersection in a coordinate system whose z axis is perpendicular to the surface and whose x–y axes are parallel to the edges of the rectangle. The test for containment then becomes a simple x–y comparison. The coefficients for the coordinate transformation can be stored as part of the data structure for the surface. For a rectangular box, all six surfaces can be treated this way using a common set of axes.

A surface that is a circle can be treated in a similar way, using a coordinate system whose z axis is perpendicular to the surface and passes through the centre of the circle. This simplifies the test for containment of the point of intersection in the circle. For a cylinder, we can use a coordinate system whose z axis is the axis of the cylinder.

Simple shapes, such as spheres, cylinders and rectangular boxes, are often used as 'bounding volumes'. These are used to speed up intersection calculations for more complex surfaces and are discussed in the next chapter.

7.4 Specular highlights

Extend the local colour model to include specular highlights (the last two terms in Equation 7.4). The data structure for each object will have to be extended to include reflection and transmission coefficients for the object.

7.5 Recursive ray tracing

Extend the local colour model to include the two global terms of Equation 7.5. Evaluating these terms will involve recursive calls of the ray tracing procedure. The program you have developed so far will be slow. During the development phase, you should test it on a small subset of the screen and with a fairly shallow depth of trace (2 or 3). The number of objects in the scene will also have to be small. Methods of speeding up a naive ray tracer are discussed in the next chapter.

7.6 Anti-aliasing

Implement the context-dependent anti-aliasing scheme due to Mitchell (1984) described in this chapter. The only problem with this method is in the choice of a reconstruction filter that copes with unevenly spaced sample points. Mitchell suggests the use of a multi-stage filter with a progressively lower cut-off frequency. In practical terms this means filtering the image with a box filter a quarter of a pixel wide. The output from this is then processed with a filter half a pixel wide, followed by a filter one pixel wide. This scheme copes with the fact that different areas of the image will exhibit a different two-dimensional frequency spectrum depending on the spatial sampling density.

CHAPTER EIGHT

Advanced Ray Tracing

A conventional naive ray tracer is hopelessly impractical. Image generation time can be hours or even days. Much research has been devoted to ways of improving this situation. Several techniques that have gained wide acceptance are now described. The first, simplest and most inexpensive is a context-dependent constraint on the recursive depth, or the depth to which the ray is traced. This is an easy extension and should always be incorporated. The other approaches are more difficult to implement.

8.1 Adaptive depth control

In a naive ray tracer it is necessary to set up a maximum depth to which rays are traced. The recursive process is terminated when this depth is reached. For a particular scene this maximum depth is preset to a certain value which will depend on the nature of the scene. A scene containing highly reflective surfaces and transparent objects will require a greater maximum depth than a scene that consists entirely of poorly reflecting surfaces and opaque objects. If the depth is set equal to unity then the ray tracer functions exactly as a conventional renderer, which removes hidden surfaces and applies a local reflection model.

It is pointed out in Hall and Greenberg (1983) that the percentage of the scene that consists of highly transparent and reflective surfaces is, in general, small and it is thus inefficient to trace every ray to a maximum depth. Hall suggests using an adaptive depth control that depends on the

Figure 8.1
Reflected rays appear to
the left at each node. Ray
4 contribution at the top
level is attenuated by
$k_{t_1} \times k_{r_2} \times k_{r_3}$.

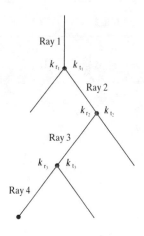

properties of the materials with which the rays are interacting. The context of the ray being traced now determines the termination depth, which can be any value between unity and the maximum preset depth.

Rays are attenuated in various ways as they pass through a scene. When a ray is reflected at a surface, it is attenuated by the global specular reflection coefficient for the surface. When it is refracted at a surface, it is attenuated by the global transmission coefficient for the surface. For the moment, we consider only this attenuation at surface intersections. A ray that is being examined as a result of backward tracing through several intersections will make a contribution to the top level ray that is attenuated by several of these coefficients. Figure 8.1 illustrates this. Any contribution from ray 4 to the colour at the top level is attenuated by the product of the global coefficients: $k_{t1}k_{r2}k_{r3}$. If this value is below some threshold, there will be no point in tracing back further than ray 4.

In general, of course, there will be three colour contributions (RGB) for each ray and three components to each of the attenuation coefficients. For tutorial purposes, we assume a single coefficient at each intersection.

Program 8.1 shows a new structure for the recursive ray tracing procedure that will implement this adaptive depth control. Each activation of this procedure is given a cumulative weight parameter that indicates the final weight that will be given at the top level to the colour returned for the ray represented by that procedure activation. The correct weight for a new procedure activation is easily calculated by taking the cumulative weight for the ray currently being traced and multiplying it by the reflection or transmission coefficient for the surface intersection at which the new ray is being created.

In Program 8.1, the tests on the cumulative weight and recursive depth parameters take place at the start of the procedure. The remarks on efficiency made about Program 7.1 still apply. Unnecessary procedure

Program 8.1 Adaptive depth control in a recursive ray tracing procedure.

```
procedure TraceRay (start, direction: vectors;
                        depth: integer; var colour: colours;
                        cumulative-weight: real);

var intersection-point, reflected-direction,
        transmitted-direction: vectors;
    local-colour, reflected-colour,
        transmitted-colour: colours;

begin
    if cumulative-weight < weight-threshold then colour := black
    else if depth > maxdepth then colour := black
    else
    begin
        {Intersect ray with all objects and find intersection
            point (if any) that is closest to start of ray}
        if {no intersection} then colour := background-colour
        else
        begin
            local-colour := {contribution of local colour model
                                at intersection-point}
            {Calculate direction of reflected ray}
            TraceRay(intersection-point, reflected-direction,
                depth + 1, reflected-colour, cumulative-weight*reflected-weight-for-
                    surface);
            {Calculate direction of transmitted ray}
            TraceRay(intersection-point, transmitted-direction,
                depth + 1, transmitted-colour, cumulative-weight*transmitted-
                    weight-for-surface);
            Combine(colour,
                local-colour, local-weight-for-surface,
                reflected-colour, reflected-weight-for-surface,
                transmitted-colour, transmitted-weight-for-surface)
        end
    end
end   { TraceRay };
```

calls could again have been eliminated by a slightly messy restructuring of Program 8.1.

Another way in which a ray can be attenuated is by passing for some distance through an opaque material. This can be dealt with by associating a transmittance coefficient with the material composing an object. Colour values would then be attenuated by an amount determined by this coefficient and the distance a ray travels through the material. A simple addition to the intersection calculation in the ray tracing procedure would allow this feature to be incorporated.

The use of adaptive depth control will prevent, for example, a ray that initially hits an almost opaque object spawning a transmitted ray that is then traced through the object and into the scene. The intensity returned from the scene may then be so attenuated by the initial object that this computation is obviated. Thus, depending on the value to which the threshold is preset, the ray could, in this case, be terminated at the first hit.

For a highly reflective scene with a maximum tree depth of 15, Hall and Greenberg (1983) report that this method results in an average depth of 1.71, giving a large potential saving in image generation time. The actual saving achieved will depend on the nature and distribution of the objects in the scene.

8.2 Bounding volume extensions

As discussed in the previous chapter, the increase in efficiency gained by using bounding volumes depends critically on the choice of the bounding volume and how well the bounding volume encloses the complex object. Spheres are a popular choice because of the simplicity of the associated intersection test, but we have seen that spheres are unsuitable bounding volumes of long thin objects.

Weghorst *et al.* (1984) point out that the simplicity of the intersection test should not be the sole criterion in the selection of a bounding volume. They define a 'void' area, of a bounding volume, to be the difference in area between the orthogonal projections of the object and bounding volume onto a plane perpendicular to the ray and passing through the origin of the ray (see Figure 8.2). They show that the void

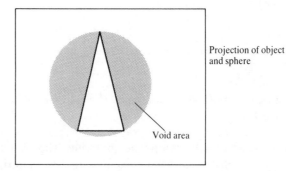

Figure 8.2
The void area of a bounding sphere.

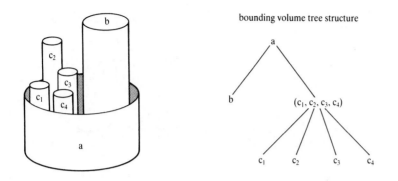

bounding volume tree structure

Figure 8.3
A simple scene and the associated bounding cylinder tree structure.

area is a function of object, bounding volume and ray direction and define a cost function for an intersection test:

$$T = bB + iI$$

where:

- T is the total cost function;
- b is the number of times that the bounding volume is tested for intersection;
- B is the cost of testing the bounding volume for intersection;
- i is the number of times that the item is tested for intersection (where $i \leqslant b$);
- I is the cost of testing the item for intersection.

It is pointed out by the authors that the two products are generally interdependent. For example, reducing B by reducing the complexity of the bounding volume will almost certainly increase i. A quantitive approach to selecting the optimum of a sphere, a rectangular parallelepiped and a cylinder as bounding volumes is given.

A common extension to bounding volumes, first suggested by Rubin and Whitted (1980) and discussed in Weghorst *et al.* (1984), is to attempt to impose a hierarchical structure of such volumes on the scene. If it is possible, objects in close spatial proximity are allowed to form clusters, and the clusters are themselves enclosed in bounding volumes. For example Figure 8.3 shows a container (a) with one large object (b) and four small objects (c_1, c_2, c_3 and c_4) inside it. The tree represents the hierarchical relationship between seven boundary extents: a cylinder enclosing all the objects, a cylinder enclosing (b), a cylinder enclosing (c_1, c_2, c_3, c_4) and the bounding cylinders for each of these objects. A ray traced against bounding volumes means that such a tree is traversed from

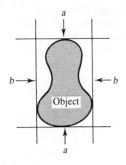

Bounding volume defined
by plane-set (a, b)

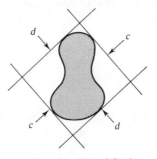

Bounding volume defined
by plane-set (c, d)

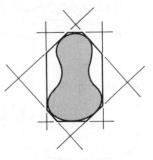

'Tight' bounding volume
defined by plane-set (a, b, c, d)

Figure 8.4
Defining a bounding
volume from the
maximum and minimum
extents of a projection of
the object.

the topmost level. A ray that happened to intersect c_1 in the above example would, of course, be tested against the bounding volumes for c_1, c_2, c_3 and c_4, but only because it intersects the bounding volume representing that cluster. This example also demonstrates that the nature of the scene should enable reasonable clusters of adjacent objects to be selected if substantial savings over a non-hierarchical bounding scheme are to be achieved. Now the intersection test is implemented as a recursive process, descending through a hierarchy, only from those nodes where intersections occur. Thus a scene is grouped, where possible, into object clusters and each of those clusters may contain other groups of objects that are spatially clustered. Ideally, high-level clusters are enclosed in bounding volumes that contain lower level clusters and bounding volumes. Clusters can only be created if objects are sufficiently close to each other. Creating clusters of widely separated objects obviates the process. The potential clustering and the depth of the hierarchy will depend on the nature of the scene; the deeper the hierarchy the more the potential savings.

The disadvantage of this approach is that it depends critically on the nature of the scene. Also, considerable user investment is required to set up a suitable hierarchy.

Kay and Kajiya (1986) introduce a new type of bounding volume which can be made to fit tightly the convex hulls of objects. The authors also claim that the ray intersection test requires little computation. Their method thus overcomes the void area problem while retaining the advantages of a hierarchical bounding volume scheme. Objects are enclosed by bounding volumes made from polyhedra consisting of pairs of parallel planes. Computation and storage are constrained by restricting the orientation of the plane sets to preset directions. The position of pairs of planes is determined from the maximum and minimum extents of the object in a projection plane normal to the plane pair under consideration (Figure 8.4).

8.3 First-hit speed up

Earlier it was pointed out that, even for highly reflective scenes, the average depth to which rays were traced was between 1 and 2. This fact led Weghorst *et al.* (1984) to suggest a hybrid ray tracer, where the intersection of the initial ray is evaluated during a preprocessing phase, using a hidden surface algorithm. The implication here is that the hidden surface algorithm will be more efficient than the general ray tracer for the first hit. Weghorst suggests executing a modified Z-buffer algorithm, using the same viewing parameters. Simple modifications to the Z-buffer algorithm will make it produce, for each pixel in the image plane, a pointer to the object visible at that pixel. Ray tracing, incorporating adaptive depth control, then proceeds from that point. Thus the expensive intersection tests associated with the first hit are eliminated.

Results in Weghorst *et al.* (1984) show that incorporation of all these methods (adaptive depth control, hierarchical bounding volumes and first-hit speed up) results in improvements that appear to be inversely dependent on scene complexity. For a scene of reasonable complexity the computation time is approximately half that of a naive ray tracer using spherical bounding volumes.

8.4 Spatial coherence

Currently, spatial coherence is the only approach that looks like making ray tracing a practical proposition for routine image synthesis. For this reason the use of spatial coherence is discussed in some detail.

Recent developments in ray tracing attempt to address the problem of unrealistic computation time by exploiting the spatial coherence of objects. Until recently object coherence in ray tracing has generally been ignored. The reason is obvious. By its nature a ray tracing algorithm spawns rays of arbitrary direction anywhere in the scene. It is difficult to use such 'random' rays to access the object data structure and to extract efficiently those objects in the path of a ray. Unlike an image space scan conversion algorithm where, for example, active polygons can be listed, there is no *a priori* information on the sequence of rays that will be spawned by an initial or view ray. Naive ray tracing algorithms execute an exhaustive search of all objects, perhaps modified by a scheme such as bounding volumes, to constrain the search.

The idea behind spatial coherence schemes is simple. The space occupied by the scene is subdivided into regions. Now, rather than check a ray against all objects or sets of bounded objects, we attempt to answer the question: is the region, through which the ray is currently travelling, occupied by any objects? Either there is nothing in this region, or the region contains a small subset of the objects. This group of objects is then tested for intersection with the ray. The size of the subset and the accuracy to which the spatial occupancy of the objects is determined varies, depending on the nature and number of the objects and the method used for subdividing the space.

This approach, variously termed spatial coherence, spatial subdivision or space tracing has been independently developed by several workers, notably Glassner (1984), Kaplan (1985) and Fujimoto *et al.* (1986). All of these approaches involve preprocessing the space to set up an auxiliary data structure that contains information about the object occupancy of the space. Rays are then traced using this auxiliary data structure to enter the object data structure. Note that this philosophy (of preprocessing the object environment to reduce the computational work required to compute a view) was first employed by Schumacker (1969) in a hidden surface removal algorithm developed for flight simulators. In this algorithm, objects in the scene are clustered into groups by subdividing the space with planes. The spatial subdivision is represented by a binary tree. Any view point is located in a region represented by a leaf in the tree. An on-line tree traversal for a particular view point quickly yields a depth priority order for the group clusters. The important point about this algorithm is that the spatial subdivision is computed off line and an auxiliary structure, the binary tree representing the subdivision, is used to determine an initial priority ordering for the object clusters. The motivation for this work was to speed up the on-line hidden surface removal processing and to enable image generation to work in real time.

Dissatisfaction with the bounding volume or extent approach to reducing the number of ray object intersection tests appears in part to have motivated the development of spatial coherence methods (Kaplan, 1985). One of the major objections to bounding volumes has already been pointed out. Their 'efficiency' is dependent on how well the object fills the space of the bounding volume. A more fundamental objection is that such a scheme may increase the efficiency of the ray object intersection search, but it does nothing to reduce the dependence on the number of objects in the scene. Each ray must still be tested against the bounding extent of every object and the search time becomes a function of scene complexity. Also, although major savings can be achieved by using a hierarchical structure of bounding volumes, considerable investment is required to set up an appropriate hierarchy and, depending on the nature and disposition of objects in the scene, a hierarchical description may be difficult or impossible. The major innovation of methods described in this section is to make the rendering time constant (for a particular image space resolution) and to eliminate its dependence on scene complexity.

The various schemes that use the spatial coherence approach differ mainly in the type of auxiliary data structure used. Kaplan (1985) lists six properties that a practical ray tracing algorithm should exhibit if the technique is to be used in routine rendering applications. Kaplan's requirements are:

- Computation time should be relatively independent of scene complexity (number of objects in the environment, or complexity of individual objects), so that scenes having realistic levels of complexity can be rendered.

- Per-ray time should be relatively constant, and not dependent on the origin or direction of the ray. This property guarantees that overall computation time for a shaded image will be dependent only on overall image resolution (number of first-level rays traced) and shading effects (number of second-level and higher level rays traced). This guarantees predictable performance for a given image resolution and level of realism.

- Computation time should be 'rational' (say, within an hour) on currently available minicomputer processors, and should be 'interactive' (within a few minutes) on future affordable processor systems.

- The algorithm should not require the user to supply hierarchical object descriptions or object clustering information. The user should be able to combine data generated at different times, and by different means, into a single scene.

- The algorithm should deal with a wide variety of primitive geometric types, and should be easily extensible to new types.

- The algorithm's use of coherence should not reduce its applicability to parallel processing or other advanced architectures. Instead, it should be amenable to implementation on such architectures.

Kaplan summarizes these requirements by saying, '. . . in order to be really usable, it must be possible to trace a large number of rays in a complex environments in a rational, predictable time, for a reasonable cost.'

Two related approaches to an auxiliary data structure have emerged. These involve an octree representation (Fujimoto *et al.*, 1986; Glassner, 1984) and a data structure called a BSP (binary space partitioning). The BSP tree was originally proposed by Fuchs (1980) and is used in Kaplan (1985).

8.5 Data structures for ray tracing: octrees

8.5.1 Octrees

An octree is an established hierarchical data structure that specifies the occupancy of cubic regions of object space. The cubic regions are often called 'voxels'. The octree has been used extensively in image processing and computer graphics (see, for example, Doctor and Torborg (1981), Jackins and Tanimoto (1980), Meager (1982) and Yamaguchi *et al.* (1984)).

An octree is a data structure that describes how the objects in a scene are distributed throughout the three-dimensional space occupied by the scene. The ideas involved in an octree representation can be more easily demonstrated by using a 'quadtree' to represent the occupancy of a two-dimensional region. Figure 8.5 shows a two-dimensional region

Figure 8.5
Quadtree representation of a two-dimensional scene at the pixel level. A similar method is used to represent a three-dimensional scene by an octree.

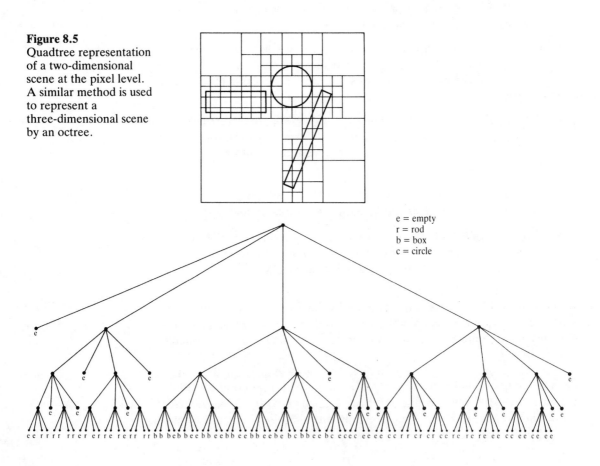

e = empty
r = rod
b = box
c = circle

Figure 8.6
Ordering scheme for
child nodes in quadtree
illustrations.

containing some simple objects together with a quadtree representation of the region and the objects. The tree is created by starting with a square region representing the whole of the occupied space. This region is represented by the node at the top of the tree. (In the three-dimensional case, the region would be a cube.) Because the region is occupied by objects, it is subdivided into four subregions, represented by the four child nodes in the tree. Figure 8.6 indicates the ordering scheme used for the child nodes. (In the three-dimensional case, a region would be subdivided into eight subregions, and the node representing the region would have eight children – hence the term octree.) Any subregion that is occupied by objects is further subdivided until the size of the subregion corresponds to the maximum resolution required of the representation scheme.

Thus there are two types of terminal node in the tree. Some terminal nodes correspond to subregions that are unoccupied by objects, while others correspond to cells of minimum size that are occupied by part of an object. Note that, in the two-dimensional case, we have represented objects by their boundaries and the interior of an object counts as unoccupied space. In the three-dimensional case, objects are represented by their surfaces and we would only subdivide regions that contain parts of the surface.

There are actually two ways in which the octree decomposition of a scene can be used to represent the scene. Firstly, an octree as described above can be used in itself as a complete representation of the objects in the scene. The set of cells occupied by an object constitutes the representation of the object. However, for a complex scene, high resolution work would require the decomposition of occupied space into an extremely large number of cells and this technique requires enormous amounts of data storage. A common alternative is to use a standard data structure representation of the objects and to use the octree as a representation of the distribution of the objects in the scene. In this case, a terminal node of a tree representing an occupied region would be represented by a pointer to the data structure for any object intersecting that region. Figure 8.7 illustrates this possibility in the two-dimensional case. Here the region subdivision has stopped as soon as a region is encountered that intersects only one object. A region represented by a

Figure 8.7
Quadtree representation of a two-dimensional scene down to the level of cells containing at most a single object. Terminal nodes for cells containing objects are represented by a pointer to a data structure representation of the object.

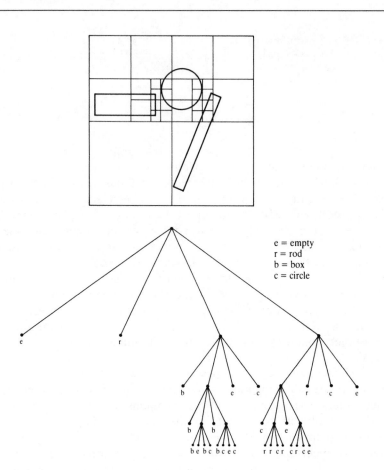

e = empty
r = rod
b = box
c = circle

terminal node is not necessarily completely occupied by the object associated with that region. The shape of the object within the region would be described by its data structure representation. In the case of a surface model representation of a scene, the 'objects' would be polygons or patches. In general, an occupied region represented by a terminal node could intersect with several polygons and would be represented by a list of pointers into the object data structures.

8.5.2 Use of an octree in ray tracing

An octree is a representation of the objects in a scene that allows us to exploit spatial coherence – objects that are close to each other in space are represented by nodes that are close to each other in the octree.

When tracing a ray, instead of doing intersection calculations between the ray and every object in the scene, we can now trace the ray from subregion to subregion in the subdivision of occupied space. For each subregion that the ray passes through, there will only be a small number of objects (typically one or two) with which it could intersect. Provided that we can rapidly find the node in the octree that corresponds to a subregion that a ray is passing through, we have immediate access to the objects that are on, or close to, the path of the ray. Intersection calculations need only be done for these objects. If space has been subdivided to a level where each subregion contains only one or two objects, then the number of intersection tests required for a region is small and does not tend to increase with the complexity of the scene.

8.5.3 Tracking a ray using an octree

In order to use the space subdivision to determine which objects are close to a ray, we must determine which subregion of space the ray passes through. This involves tracking the ray into and out of each subregion in its path. The main operation required during this process is that of finding the node in the octree, and hence the region in space, that corresponds to a point (x, y, z).

The overall tracking process starts by detecting the region that corresponds to the start point of the ray. The ray is tested for intersection with any objects that lie in this region and, if there are any intersections, then the first one encountered is the one required for the ray. If there are no intersections in the initial region, then the ray must be tracked into the next region through which it passes. This is done by calculating the intersection of the ray with the boundaries of the region and thus calculating the point at which the ray leaves the region. A point on the ray a short distance into the next region is then used to find the node in the octree that corresponds to the next region. Any objects in this region are then tested for intersections with the ray. The process is repeated as the ray tracks from region to region until an intersection with an object is found or until the ray leaves occupied space.

The simplest approach to finding the node in the octree that corresponds to a point (x, y, z) is to use a data structure representation of the octree to guide the search for the node. Starting at the top of the tree, a simple comparison of coordinates will determine which child node represents the subregion that contains the point (x, y, z). The subregion, corresponding to the child node, may itself have been subdivided and another coordinate comparison will determine which of its children represents the smaller subregion that contains (x, y, z). The search proceeds down the tree until a terminal node is reached. The maximum number of nodes traversed during this search will be equal to the maximum depth of the tree. Even for a fairly fine subdivision of occupied space, the search length will be short. For example, if the space is subdivided at a resolution of $1024 \times 1024 \times 1024$, then the octree will have depth of 10 $(= \log_8 (1024 \times 1024 \times 1024))$.

So far we have described a simple approach to the use of an octree representation of space occupancy to speed up the process of tracking a ray. Two variations of this basic approach are described by Glassner (1984) and Fujimoto *et al.* (1986). Glassner describes an alternative method for finding the node in the octree corresponding to a point (x, y, z). In fact, he does not store the structure of the octree explicitly, but accesses information about the voxels via a hash table that contains an entry for each voxel. The hash table is accessed using a code number calculated from the (x, y, z) coordinates of a point. The overall ray tracking process proceeds as described in our basic method.

In Fujimoto *et al.* (1986) an alternative approach to tracking the ray through the voxels in the octree is described. This method eliminates floating-point multiplications and divisions. To understand the method it is convenient to start by ignoring the octree representation. We first describe a simple data structure representation of a space subdivision called SEADS (spatially enumerated auxiliary data structure). This involves dividing all of occupied space into equally sized voxels regardless of occupancy by objects. The three-dimensional grid obtained in this way is analogous to that obtained by the subdivision of a two-dimensional graphics screen into pixels. Because regions are subdivided regardless of occupancy by objects, a SEADS subdivision generates many more voxels than the octree subdivision described earlier. It thus involves 'unnecessary' demands for storage space. However, the use of a SEADS enables very fast tracking of rays from region to region. The tracking algorithm used is an extension of the DDA (digital differential analyser) algorithm used in two-dimensional graphics for selecting the sequence of pixels that represent a straight line between two given end-points. The DDA algorithm used in two-dimensional graphics selects a subset of the pixels passed through by a line, but the algorithm can easily be modified to find all the pixels touching the line. Fujimoto *et al.* (1986) describe how this algorithm can be extended into three-dimensional space and used to track a ray through a SEADS three-dimensional grid. The advantage of the '3D-DDA' is that it does not involve floating-point multiplication and division. The only operations involved are addition, subtraction and comparison, the main operation being integer addition on voxel coordinates.

The heavy space overheads of the complete SEADS structure can be avoided by returning to an octree representation of the space subdivision. The 3D-DDA algorithm can be modified so that a ray is tracked through the voxels by traversing the octree. In the octree, a set of eight nodes with a common parent node represents a block of eight adjacent cubic regions, forming a $2 \times 2 \times 2$ grid. When a ray is tracked from one region to another within this set, the 3D-DDA algorithm can be used without alteration. If a ray enters a region that is not represented by a terminal node in the tree, but is further subdivided, then the subregion that is entered is found by moving down the tree. The child node required at each level of descent can be discovered by adjusting the control variables of the DDA from the level above. If the 3D-DDA algorithm tracks a ray out of the $2 \times 2 \times 2$ region currently being traversed, then the octree must be traversed upwards to the parent node representing the complete region. The 3D-DDA algorithm then continues at this level, tracking the ray within the set of eight regions containing the parent region. The upward and downward traversals of the tree involve multiplication and division of the DDA control variables by 2, but this is a cheap operation.

8.6 Data structures for ray tracing: BSP trees

8.6.1 BSP trees

Kaplan (1985) describes a technique called 'space tracing'. This again utilizes a subdivision of occupied space to take advantage of spatial coherence in improving ray tracing performance. The auxiliary structure used to represent the subdivision is essentially an octree, but the precise data structure representation used to index the octree differs from those described previously. It is termed a binary space partitioning tree, or BSP tree.

Figure 8.8 demonstrates the idea in two dimensions. It contains a one-level subdivision of a square region together with the one-level

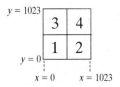

Quadtree

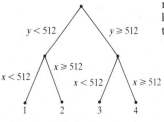

BSP tree

Figure 8.8
Quadtree and BSP tree representations of a one-level subdivision of a two-dimensional region.

quadtree representation and the corresponding BSP tree. A simple extension to three dimensions enables an octree to be coded as a BSP tree. Each non-terminal node in the BSP tree represents a single partitioning plane that divides occupied space into two. A terminal node represents a region that is not further subdivided and would contain pointers to data structure representations of the objects intersecting that region (again typically one or two).

A BSP tree would be used in ray tracing in just the same way as in the basic octree technique described earlier. To track a ray into a new region, a point (x, y, z) in that region is generated. The node in the tree corresponding to this point is found by checking the point (x, y, z) against the plane equation at each node and following the appropriate branch at each node. The ray is then checked for intersection with any objects in the region represented by the terminal node of the BSP tree that is found by this search.

8.6.2 Adaptive subdivision with a BSP tree

When a BSP tree is used to represent a subdivision of space into cubic cells, it exhibits no significant advantage over a direct data structure encoding of the octree. However, nothing said above requires that the subdivision should be into cubic cells. In fact the idea of a BSP tree was originally introduced in Fuchs (1980) where the planes used to subdivide space could be at any orientation. In Fuchs (1980) the BSP structure was used as an aid to sorting the planes in a scene into a back-to-front ordering consistent with a given view point. The planes used to subdivide space were the planes defined by the polygons constituting the scene. These planes could lie at any orientation.

In ray tracing, it is convenient if the partitioning planes lie at right-angles to the axes as this simplifies the test to see on which side of a plane a point lies. However, a scheme where the position of the partitioning planes depends on the distribution of the objects within occupied space has certain advantages.

Objects will often be unevenly distributed throughout occupied space. This is particularly the case when the 'objects' are actually patches used to approximate the surfaces of real objects. A single real object will be represented by a large cluster of patches in space and there will be relatively large regions of empty space between objects.

We can easily illustrate the idea of adaptive partitioning in two dimensions and give some idea of why it is advantageous. Figures 8.9 and 8.10 show two alternative partitions of a region containing 16 objects

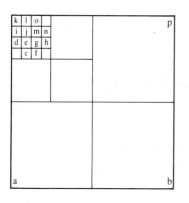

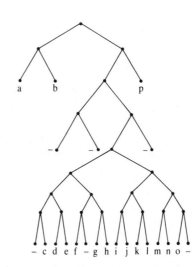

Figure 8.9
Straightforward
subdivision of a
two-dimensional scene
containing 'objects' a–p
unevenly distributed
throughout the scene.
The search path length
in the tree for most
objects is 8.

labelled a–p. These objects are rather unevenly distributed throughout this region. In Figure 8.9, a straightforward quadtree subdivision has been used and this has been represented by a BSP tree. The maximum depth of this tree is eight, and this would be the maximum length of search required to identify the region in which a given point lies.

In Figure 8.10, adaptive partitioning has been used. At each step, a partitioning line has been chosen that divides the current region in such a way that the region contains equal numbers of objects on either side of the line. This results in a more balanced BSP tree in which the maximum search length is four.

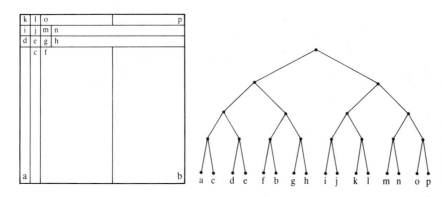

Figure 8.10
Adaptive BSP
subdivision of a
two-dimensional scene
with unevenly distributed
objects. The maximum
search path length in the
BSP tree is reduced to 4.

197

Projects, notes and suggestions

8.1 Adaptive depth control

Modify the naive ray tracing program of the last chapter to incorporate adaptive depth control. A preliminary version could use a single reflection and a single refraction coefficient at each interface in implementing the decision whether or not to terminate the trace. A final version would require three coefficients of each type at each interface, and the decision as to whether or not to continue the trace would depend on the maximum of the three attenuation factors for a ray.

8.2 Bounding volumes (*)

Create a simple scene that consists of a small number of separate clusters of objects (all spheres, say) where the clusters have differing shapes. Select an appropriate bounding volume for each cluster (a sphere, a cylinder or a box) and incorporate bounding volume tests in the intersection calculations for your ray tracer. This will involve the implementation of a hierarchical data structure where each bounding volume contains references to the data structures for the objects it contains. This could be extended to a hierarchical structure of bounding volumes where the bounding volumes themselves are contained in larger bounding volumes.

8.3 Objects defined by implicit quadric equations

Implement intersection tests for objects represented implicitly by quadric equations. (These equations were presented in Project 1.6.) Develop a system of bounding volumes that can be used to accelerate the intersection tests for these objects.

8.4 Intersection tests for patch models (*)

Implement a system of bounding volumes for objects whose surfaces are represented by a set of bicubic patches as described in Chapter 6. The bounding volume for an individual patch should be a box constructed such that its faces are parallel to the axes of the world coordinate system. Its extent can be calculated from the maxima and minima of the x, y and z coordinates of the control points for the patch. If a ray intersects the bounding volume for a patch, the patch is subdivided as described in Chapter 6, the bounding box for each of the subdivisions is calculated and the intersection test repeated for the subdivisions. This subdivision process is repeated until the patch is smaller than some accuracy requirement.

8.5 First-hit speed up (*)

The calculations for the intersections of the first level rays in a ray tracer can be accelerated by the use of standard rendering algorithms. For example, a modification of the Z-buffer algorithm can be used to generate the object visible at each pixel in the viewing plane from a given view point (Weghorst *et al.*, 1984). Incorporate this extension in your ray tracer.

8.6   Spatial coherence (*)

Implement one of the spatial coherence schemes described. A preliminary version could use a simple uniform subdivision of space into fairly large voxels. Each voxel would have an associated list of the objects that it contains. Tracing a ray would involve tracking it from one voxel to another. Intersection tests would be carried out only for objects in the voxels traversed by the ray.

Now implement a 3D-DDA algorithm (Fujimoto *et al.*, 1986) for tracking a ray through the voxels in your uniform subdivision. Finally, incorporate an octree representation of your scene and modify the DDA algorithm to deal with the problem of moving from the current voxel into a larger or a smaller voxel.

CHAPTER NINE

Diffuse Illumination and the Development of the Radiosity Method

The major image synthesis methods in current use are the Phong reflection model and ray tracing. Simple reflection models are visually characterized by their limitations and this is generally due to the fact that such models only attend to one aspect of light–object interaction – the reflection of incident light, due to a light source, from a surface. Dissatisfaction with the resulting 'plastic model floating in free space' look leads naturally to ad hoc *'add ons'; techniques such as shadows and texture mapping were grafted onto basic reflection models.*

Ray tracing is an elegant technique that uses the same basic theoretical method for reflection, refraction and shadows. Although often described as a global illumination method, it is pointed out in Chapter 7 that it only attends to one aspect of global illumination – specular reflection and refraction – and this accounts for the distinct ray-traced signature of images produced by this method. This is because to trace diffuse interaction would involve spawning a very large number of rays at each ray–surface intersection. Radiosity provides a solution to diffuse interaction, but at the expense of dividing the environment into largish elements (over which the illumination is constant). This approach cannot cope with sharp specular reflections and essentially we have two global solutions: ray tracing that deals with global specular reflection and radiosity which deals with global diffuse reflection.

The radiosity method was developed to account for the interaction of diffuse light between elements in a scene. The method is excellent for generating scenes of interior environments, which are mostly collections of non-specular objects; and the method has produced realistic looking interiors, resulting in a shift in synthesized images towards global realism, rather than scenes as collections of non-interacting, separately synthesized objects. In simple 'non-interacting' reflection models, diffuse interaction is simulated by using an ambient term, normally a constant.

The radiosity method was developed at Cornell University in 1984 (Goral et al., 1984) and most of the development work since then has been carried out at Cornell. A radiosity-based approach is reported in Nishita and Nakame (1985), again applied to room interiors. This is a less general approach than the Cornell method that integrates explicit shadow determination with the overall solution.

Radiosity is a method whose processor demands are at least as heavy as ray tracing and this is no doubt one of the reasons for its lack of dissemination throughout the computer graphics community. As with ray tracing, after the initial establishment of the method, recent research has concentrated on developing algorithmic enhancements that make the method more practical, and on integrating other reflection phenomena such as specular reflection into the method.

Although the term 'realistic' is a much-overused adjective in computer graphics, it is indisputable that radiosity has produced the most realistic and impressive images to date.

9.1 Radiosity theory

The radiosity method was developed in radiative heat transfer (see, for example, Siegel and Howell, 1984) to account for heat transfer between elements in furnaces or on a spacecraft. It is a conservation of energy or energy equilibrium approach, providing a solution for the radiosity of all surfaces within an enclosure. The energy input to the system is from those surfaces that act as emitters. In fact, a light source is treated like any other surface in the algorithm except that it possesses an initial (non-zero) radiosity. The radiosity solution provides for previously unmodelled diffuse light phenomena such as 'colour bleeding' from one surface to another, shading within shadow envelopes and penumbrae along shadow boundaries. Greenberg *et al.* (1986) give a startling illustration of colour bleeding and demonstrates the inability of conventional methods, such as ray tracing, to cope with this phenomenon.

The radiosity method is an object space algorithm, solving for the intensity at discrete points or surface patches within an environment and not for pixels in an image plane projection. The solution is thus independent of viewer position. This complete solution is then injected into a renderer that computes a particular view. This phase of the method does not require much computation and different views are easily obtained from the general solution. The method is based on the assumption that all surfaces are perfect diffusers or ideal lambertian surfaces.

Radiosity, B, is defined as the energy per unit area leaving a surface patch per unit time and is the sum of the emitted and the reflected energy:

$$B_i \, dA_i = E_i \, dA_i + R_i \int_j B_j F_{ji} \, dA_j$$

where the reflected energy is given by the reflectivity of patch i multiplied by that fraction of the radiosity of patch j, given by the form factor F_{ji}, that determines the fraction of the energy leaving patch j which arrives at patch i. The integral is over all patches j in the environment. R_i is the fraction of the incident light that is reflected from the surface in all directions. R_i is related, but not equal, to the diffuse reflection coefficient used in Chapters 2 and 3.

The reciprocity relationship (Siegel and Howell, 1984) gives:

$$F_{ij} A_i = F_{ji} A_j$$

and division by dA_i gives:

$$B_i = E_i + R_i \int_j B_j F_{ij}$$

For a discrete environment the integral is replaced by a sum and constant radiosity is assumed over small discrete patches, giving:

$$B_i = E_i + R_i \sum_{j=1}^{n} B_j F_{ij}$$

Such an equation exists for each surface patch in the enclosure and the complete environment produces a set of n simultaneous equations of the form:

$$\begin{bmatrix} 1 - R_1 F_{11} & -R_1 F_{12} & \cdots & -R_1 F_{1n} \\ -R_2 F_{21} & 1 - R_2 F_{22} & \cdots & -R_2 F_{2n} \\ \cdot & \cdot & & \cdot \\ \cdot & \cdot & & \cdot \\ \cdot & \cdot & & \cdot \\ -R_n F_{n1} & -R_n F_{n2} & \cdots & 1 - R_n F_{nn} \end{bmatrix} \begin{bmatrix} B_1 \\ B_2 \\ \cdot \\ \cdot \\ \cdot \\ B_n \end{bmatrix} = \begin{bmatrix} E_1 \\ E_2 \\ \cdot \\ \cdot \\ \cdot \\ E_n \end{bmatrix} \qquad \textbf{(9.1)}$$

The E_i are non-zero only at those surfaces that provide illumination and these terms represent the input illumination to the system. The R_i are known or can be calculated and the F_{ij} are a function of the geometry of

Figure 9.1
Form factor geometry for
two patches *i* and *j*.
(After Goral *et al.*
(1984).)

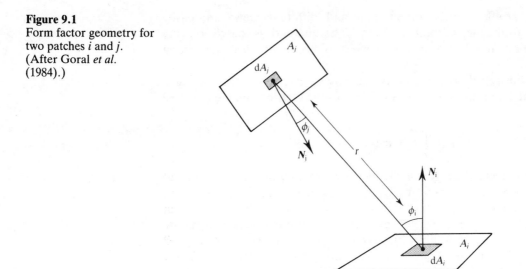

the environment. The reflectivities are wavelength-dependent terms and
Equation 9.1 should be regarded as a monochromatic solution, a
complete solution being obtained by solving for however many colour
bands are being considered. We can note at this stage that $F_{ii} = 0$ for a
plane or convex surface – none of the radiation leaving the surface will
strike itself. Also, from the definition of the form factor the sum of any
row of form factors is unity.

Since the form factors are a function only of the geometry of the
system they are computed once only. Solution of this set of equations
produces a single value for each patch and this information is then input
to a standard Gouraud renderer to give an interpolated solution across all
patches.

The method is bound by the time taken to calculate the form
factors expressing the radiative exchange between two surface patches A_i
and A_j. This depends on their relative orientation and the distance
between them and is given by the radiative energy leaving surface A_i that
strikes A_j directly, divided by the radiative energy leaving surface A_i in all
directions in the hemispherical space surrounding A_i. That is,

$$F_{A_iA_j} = F_{ij} = \frac{1}{A_i} \int_{A_i} \int_{A_j} \frac{\cos\phi_i \cos\phi_j}{\pi r^2} \, dA_j \, dA_i$$

where the geometric conventions are illustrated in Figure 9.1. In any
practical environment A_j may be wholly or partially invisible from A_i and
the integral needs to be multiplied by an occluding factor H which is a

binary function that depends on whether the differential area dA_i can see dA_j or not. This double integral is difficult to solve except for specific shapes.

Form factor is one of a number of similar terms (others include 'diffuse view factor', 'shape factor' and 'angle factor') used to characterize the effects of the geometry of two surfaces on the radiative exchange between them.

9.2 Form factor determination

A numerical method of evaluating form factors was developed in 1985 (Cohen and Greenberg, 1985) and this is known as the hemicube method. The patch-to-patch form factor can be approximated by the differential area to finite area equation

$$F_{ij} \approx F_{dA_iA_j} = \int_{A_j} \frac{\cos \phi_i \cos \phi_j}{\pi r^2} \, dA_j$$

where we are now considering the form factor between the elemental area dA_i and the finite area A_j. dA_i is positioned at the centre point of patch i, the average position of patch i with respect to patch j. The veracity of this approximation depends on the area of the two patches compared with the distance, r, between them. We can thus set up an elemental area on patch i which has as its view of the environment a hemisphere surrounding the patch and use projections onto this hemisphere to evaluate the form factor.

To evaluate this integral a 'hemicube' method was developed which enables the form factors to be calculated for complex multi-object environments. A hemicube is used to approximate the hemisphere because flat projection planes are computationally less expensive. The hemicube is constructed around the centre of each patch with the hemicube Z axis and the patch normal coincident (Figure 9.2). The faces of the hemicube are divided into pixels – a somewhat confusing use of the term since we are operating in object space. Every other patch in the environment is projected onto this hemicube. Two patches that project onto the same pixel can have their depth compared and the further patch rejected, since it cannot be seen from the receiving patch. This approach is analogous to a Z-buffer algorithm except that there is no interest in intensities at this stage. The hemicube algorithm only facilitates the calculation of the form factors that are subsequently used in calculating diffuse intensities and an 'item buffer' is maintained indicating which patch is seen at each pixel on the hemicube.

Figure 9.2
Evaluating the form
factor F_{ij} by projecting
patch j onto a hemicube
centred on patch i. (After
Cohen and Greenberg
(1985).)

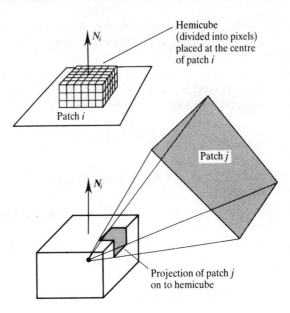

The contribution of each pixel defines a delta form factor – an approximation to

$$F_{dA_i\ dA_j} = \frac{\cos \phi_i \cos \phi_j}{\pi r^2}$$

the differential to differential area form factor, and summing over the hemicube gives the differential area to finite area for each patch j. Performing this operation for all patches gives a row of N form factors in Equation 9.1. The hemicube operation is repeated for all patches, each calculation providing a row in Equation 9.1.

The contribution of each pixel in the hemicube to the form factor is a function both of the patches that project onto the pixel and its position in the hemicube and

$$F_{ij} = \sum_q \Delta F_q$$

where ΔF_q is the form factor associated with the pixel q and where the summation is over the values of q such that patch j projects on to pixel q (Figure 9.3). Thus the evaluation of a form factor reduces to summing the delta form factors for the pixels that occupy the projection of the path on

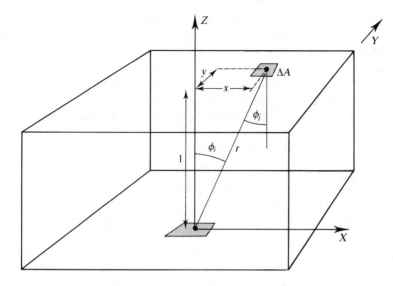

Figure 9.3
Geometry of delta form
factors for a pixel ΔA on
top of the hemicube.
(After Cohen and
Greenberg (1985).)

to the hemicube. This operation is based on the fact that patches which have the same projection on to a hemisphere (or hemicube) have the same form factor. The delta form factors for each pixel in the cube can be precalculated and stored in a look-up table. For example, for a pixel positioned on the top surface of the hemicube

$$\Delta F_q = \frac{1}{\pi(x^2 + y^2 + 1)^2} \Delta A$$

This derives (Figure 9.3) from:

$$r = (x^2 + y^2 + 1)^{1/2}$$
$$\cos \phi_i = \cos \phi_j$$
$$= \frac{1}{(x^2 + y^2 + 1)^{1/2}}$$
$$\Delta F_q = \frac{\cos \phi_i \cos \phi_j}{\pi r^2} \Delta A$$

similarly, for a pixel positioned on the side of the hemicube:

$$\Delta F_q = \frac{z}{\pi(y^2 + z^2 + 1)^2} \Delta A$$

Equation 9.1 possesses certain properties (fully described in Cohen and Greenberg (1985)) that can be exploited to give an efficient Gauss–Seidel iterative solution (see Projects, notes and suggestions at the end of this chapter) and the final centre patch radiosities are injected into a bilinear interpolation scheme to provide a continuous shaded solution for the environment.

The method can be summarized in the following stages:

(1)   computation of the form factors, F_{ij};

(2)   solving the radiosity matrix equation;

(3)   rendering by injecting the results of stage (2) into a bilinear interpolation scheme;

(4)   repeating stages (2) and (3) for the colour bands of interest.

Form factors are a function only of the environment and are calculated once only and can be re-used in stage (2) for different reflectivities, colour bands and light source values. Thus a solution can be obtained for the same environment with, for example, some light sources turned off. The solution produced by stage (2) is a view-independent solution and if a different view is required then only stage (3) is repeated.

Stage (2) implies the computation of a view-independent rendered version of the solution to the radiosity equation which supplies a single value, a radiosity, for each patch in the environment. From these values vertex radiosities are calculated and these vertex radiosities are used in the bilinear interpolation scheme to provide a final image. A depth buffer algorithm is used at this stage to evaluate the visibility of each patch at each pixel on the screen. (This stage should not be confused with the hemicube operation that has to evaluate interpatch visibility during the computation of form factors.)

A number of factors make the general application of the basic radiosity method somewhat difficult. The coding complexity is high and the method requires extensive computing resources.

The time taken to complete the form factor calculation depends on the square of the number of patches. A hemicube calculation is performed for every patch (onto which all other patches are projected). The overall calculation time thus depends on the complexity of the environment and the accuracy of the solution, as determined by the hemicube resolution. Although diffuse illumination changes only slowly across a surface, aliasing can be caused by too low a hemicube resolution and accuracy is required at shadow boundaries. Storage requirements are also a function of the number of patches required. All these factors mean that there is an upward limit on the complexity of the scenes that can be handled by the radiosity method.

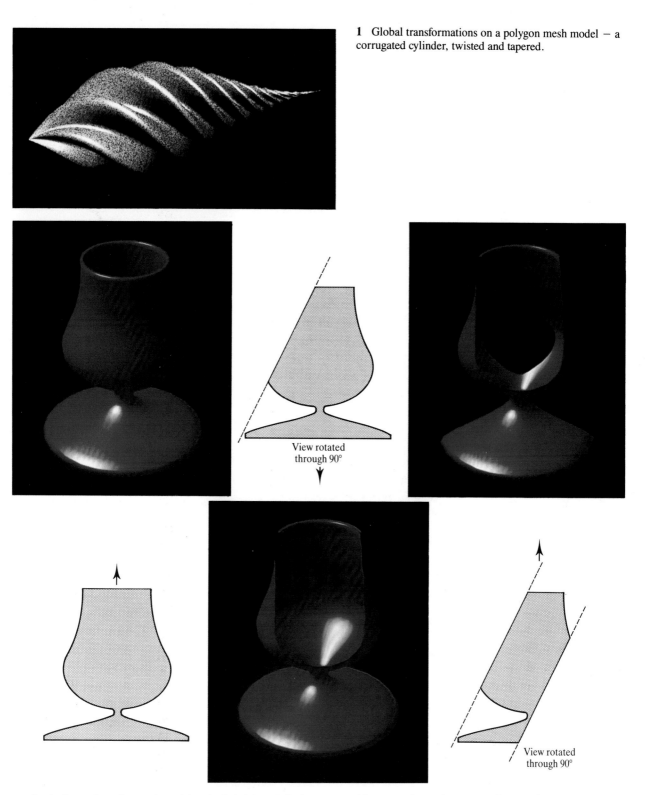

1 Global transformations on a polygon mesh model — a corrugated cylinder, twisted and tapered.

View rotated through 90°

View rotated through 90°

2 A view volume interacting with a shaded object. Bringing near and far planes into coincidence with an object; *(centre)* near plane coincides; *(right)* both planes coincide with the object.

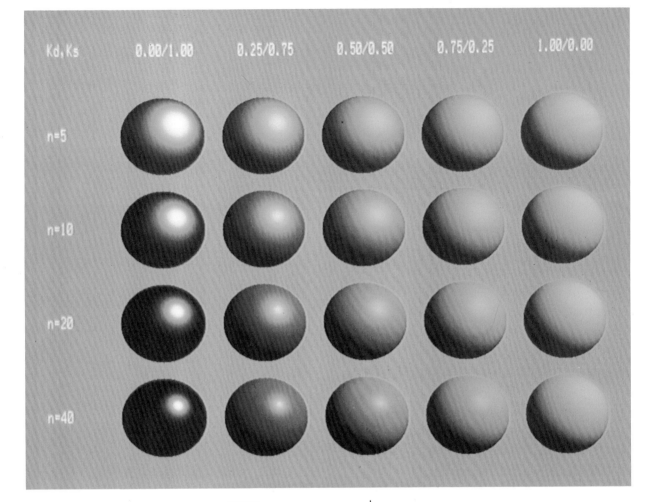

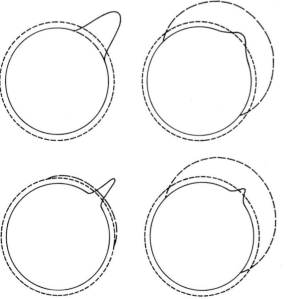

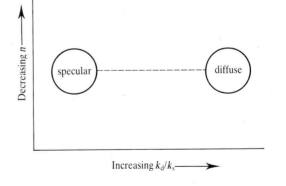

3 *(Top and above)* The twenty spheres example (after an illustration by Roy Hall). *(left)* Slices through the specular bump showing the variation in magnitude of the diffuse, specular and ambient components over the surface of each of the following spheres: top row, spheres 1 and 4; bottom row, spheres 1 and 4.

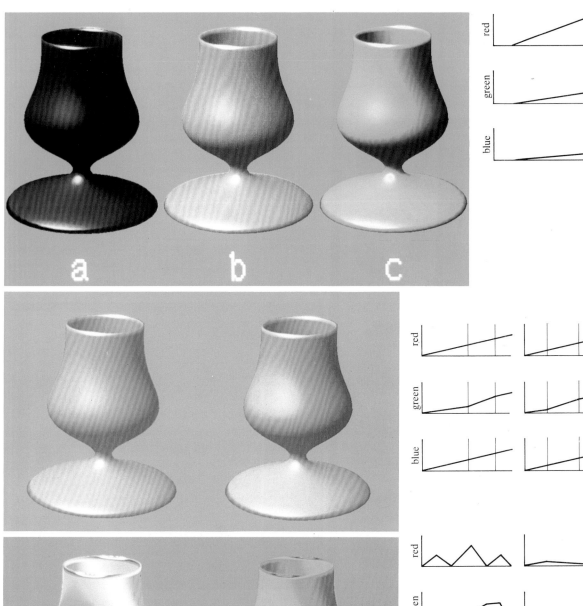

4 Using LUT profiles to control the colour and the degree of specularity of an object. *(top)* All objects have a similar profile, copper (object a) is shown. *(centre)* Varying the position of the blend region. *(bottom)* Special effects.

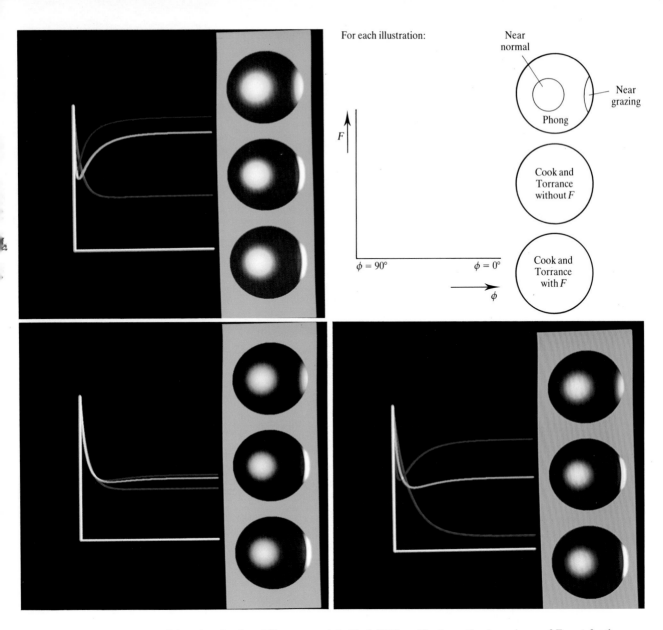

For each illustration:

Near normal

Near grazing

Phong

Cook and Torrance without F

Cook and Torrance with F

F

$\phi = 90°$ $\phi = 0°$

ϕ

5   The Cook and Torrance model used to simulate different materials. Each RGB profile shows the dependence of F on ϕ for the material: *(top left)* gold; *(bottom left)* silver; *(bottom right)* copper.

6 The Utah teapot and shading options. Note the visibility of piecewise linearities along silhouette edges since this representation contains only 512 polygons. *(top left)* Wireframe plus vertex normals. *(top right)* Constant shaded polygons. *(bottom left)* Gouraud shading. *(bottom right)* Phong shading.

7 Parametric patch rendering at different levels of uniform subdivision (128, 512, 2048 and 8192 polygons).

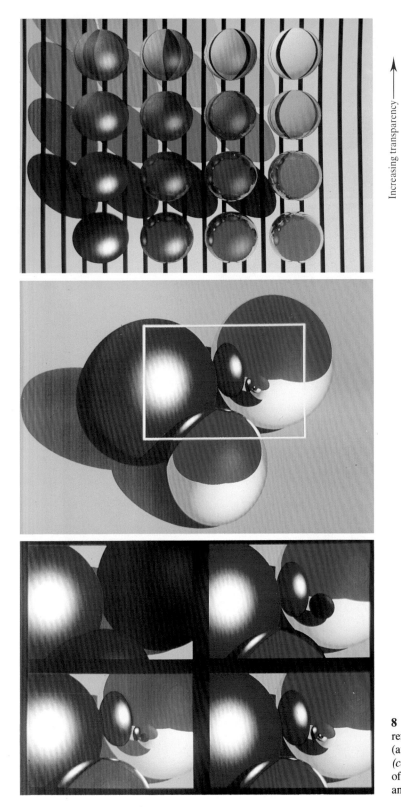

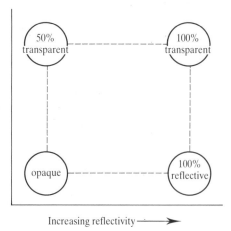

8 Ray tracing spheres. *(top)* Reflective and refractive spheres against a striped background (after an illustration by Apollo Computers). *(centre)* Ray tracing to a depth of 6. *(bottom)* Part of the above image traced to a depth of 1, 2, 3 and 4.

9 Radiosity illustrations. *(top)* Dutch interior, after Vermeer. This image was inspired by the work of the 17th century Dutch painter, Jan Vermeer, whose sensitivity to the interplay of light and surfaces helped to give his painting a dramatic effect. The radiosity method was used to compute the global diffuse illumination during a view-independent preprocess. After the view was determined, a Z-buffer based algorithm similar to distributed ray tracing was used to compute the specular reflection on the marble floor. (Courtesy of John Wallace. © 1987 by Cornell University, Program of Computer Graphics). *(bottom)* Simulated steel mill. The image was created using a modified version of the hemicube radiosity algorithm, computed on a VAX 8700 and displayed on a Hewlett-Packard Renaissance Display. The environment consists of approximately 55 000 elements, and is one of the most complex environments computed to date. (Courtesy of Stuart Feldman and John Wallace, Program of Computer Graphics, Cornell University).

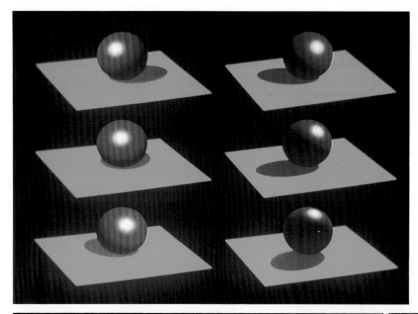

10 Varying light source position in a shadow algorithm.

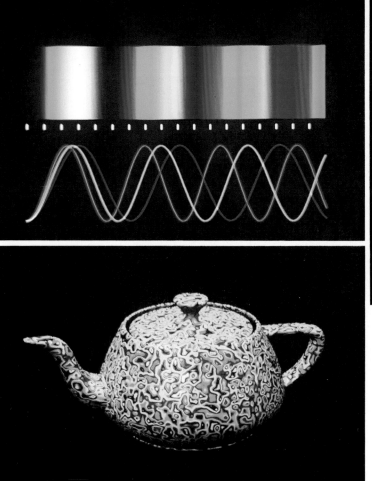

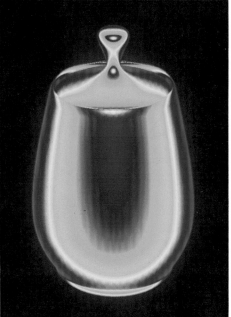

11 Thin film interference used as a texture method. *(above left)* Newton's colours due to the interference of a light wave with a thin film. *(above)* One-dimensional texture mapping: using thin film interference to render an object. *(left)* Thin film interference produced by modulating the depth of the film on the surface.

12 Surfaces modulated by three-dimensional texture fields. *(left)* Cube of cubes: the centre point of each cube is used to obtain a colour from the RGB cube. *(below)* Wood grain: harmonic functions (Fourier synthesis). *(centre)* Marble texture: equivalent to harmonic function plus noise. *(bottom)* Using a three-dimensional noise function.

13 Two-dimensional texture mapping methods. *(top)* Recursive teapots: conventional two-dimensional texture wrapping using mip-map filtering. *(bottom)* Bump mapping (courtesy of J. Blinn).

14 Recursively generated tree shapes. *(top)* Two runs of the program using the same 'skeletal' parameters. *(bottom)* Two runs of the program using 'bushy' parameters.

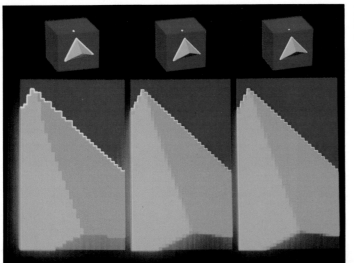

15 Supersampling and filtering. Top row: full size images. Bottom row: × 10 images, from left to right: an unfiltered image; a 3 × 3 filter; a 5 × 5 filter.

16 *(Left)* A frame from *Luxo Jr.* produced by John Lasseter, Bill Reeves, Eben Ostby and Sam Leffler; © 1986 Pixar; Luxo™ is a trademark of Jak Jacobson Industries. The film was animated by a keyframe animation system with procedural animation assistance, and frames were rendered with multiple light sources and procedural texturing techniques. *(below)* This frame from *Luxo Jr.* exhibits motion blur as described in Chapter Thirteen.

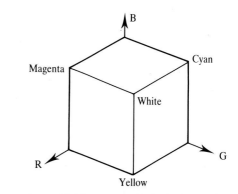

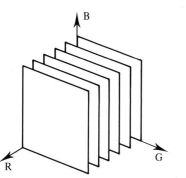

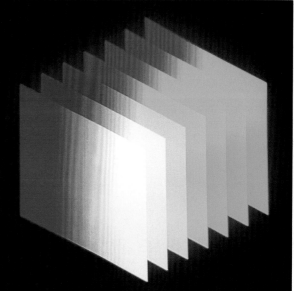

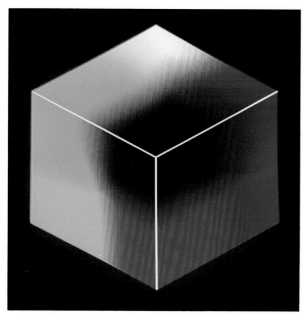

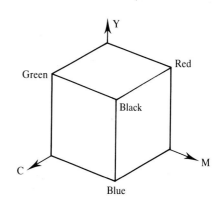

17 *(Top)* The RGB cube. *(centre)* Planes in the RGB cube parallel to the BG plane. *(bottom)* The CMY cube.

18 HSV and HLS colour models.

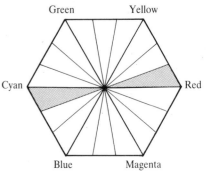

(a) HSV colour model: slices through the Value axis at 20° intervals.

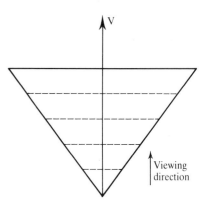

(b) HSV colour model: slices of constant V.

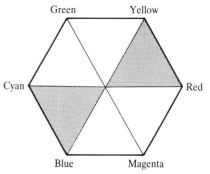

(c) HLS colour model: three slices through the L axis at 60° intervals.

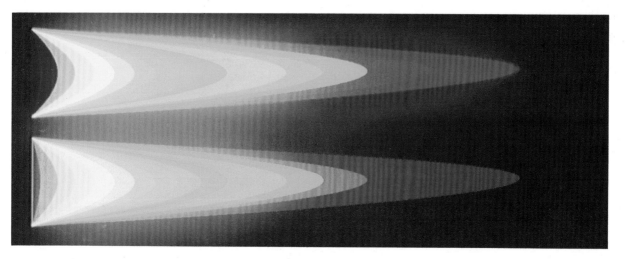

19 Colour mapping. Upper (0, 0.5, 1) to (240, 0.5, 1) in HLS;
Lower; tilting the plane of the interpolation path, (0, 0.7, 1) to (240, 0.3, 1) in HLS.

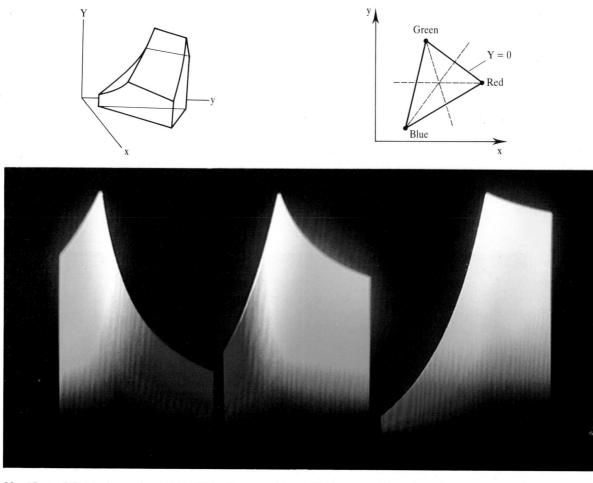

20 *(Centre left)* Monitor gamut solid in 1931 xyY space; *(above)* Three cross-sections through the solid in CIE xyY space;
(centre right) The position of the cross-sections on the plane Y=O.

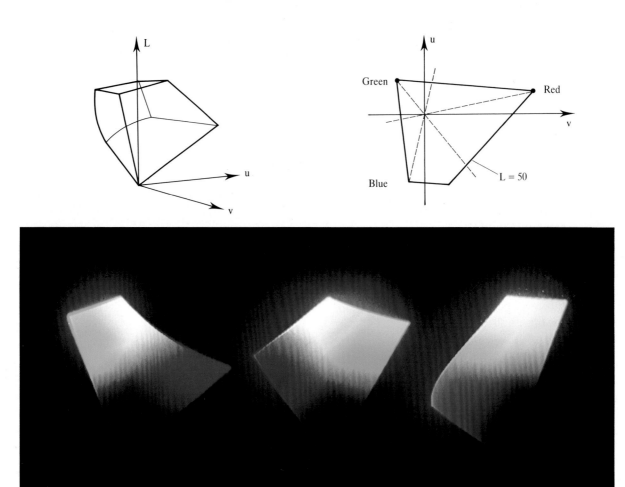

21 *(Top left)* Monitor gamut solid in L*u*v* space; *(above)* Three cross-sections through the solid in L*u*v* space; *(top right)* The position of the cross-sections in a plane of constant L.

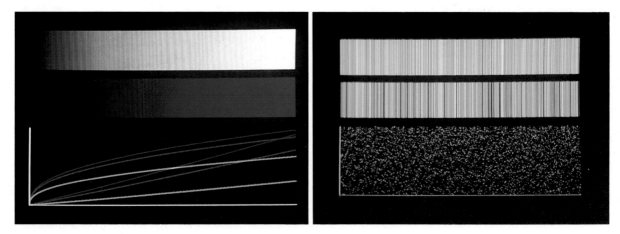

22 Gamma correction showing contrast and chromaticity shift. The top bar in each illustration is gamma corrected. *(left)* Colour ramp showing a chromaticity shift. *(right)* Random colours showing a contrast shift.

9.3 Further development of the radiosity method

9.3.1 Increasing the accuracy of the solution

Most of the computation in the radiosity method is taken up by the calculation of the form factors and the size of the problem is a function of the number of patches squared. The quality of the image is a function of the size of the patches and it is pointed out in Cohen *et al.* (1986) that in regions of the environment, such as shadow boundaries, that exhibit a high radiosity gradient the patches should be subdivided. Thus the Cornell radiosity method can be seen as a general approach that devotes processing resources according to the image context. In contrast, the approach taken by Nishita and Nakamae (1985) is to determine or 'predetect' penumbrae and umbrae explicitly, using a shadow volume algorithm, and then to merge this information with a standard radiosity solution.

Cohen *et al.* (1986) develop a technique called substructuring and the idea is to generate an accurate solution for the radiosity of a point from the 'global' radiosities obtained from the initial 'coarse' patch computation.

The basis of the method is contained in the original differential area to finite area approximation to the finite area form factor, where it was assumed that:

$$F_{A_iA_j} \approx F_{dA_iA_j}$$

If a patch is subdivided into elements or subpatches then we can evaluate a set of form factors for each of the elements to each of the N patches. This increases the number of form factors from $N \times N$ to $M \times N$, where M is the total number of elements created, and naturally increases the time spent in form factor calculation. Patches that need to be divided into elements are revealed by examining the graduation of the coarse patch solution. The previously calculated (coarse) patch solution is retained and the fine element radiosities are then obtained from this solution using:

$$B_{iq} = E_q + R_q \sum_{j=1}^{N} B_j F_{(iq)j} \qquad \textbf{(9.2)}$$

where B_{iq} is the radiosity of element q, B_j is the radiosity of patch j and $F_{(iq)j}$ is the element q to patch j form factor.

In other words, as far as the radiosity solution is concerned, the cumulative effect of elements of a subdivided patch is identical to that of the undivided patch; or, subdividing a patch into elements does not affect the amount of light that is reflected by the patch. So after determining a solution for patches, the radiosity within a patch is solved independently among patches. In doing this Equation 9.2 assumes that only the patch in question has been subdivided into elements – all other patches are undivided.

The process of computing the form factors and evaluating the radiosity solution now expands into three steps:

(1)   evaluating a radiosity solution using the patch to patch form factors;

(2)   subdividing selected patches into elements and calculating $M \times N$ element to patch form factors;

(3)   determining the element radiosities from patch radiosities in the subdivided areas.

Thus the radiosity solution phase of the computation remains constant. The method is distinguished from simply subdividing the environment into smaller patches. This strategy would result in $M \times M$ new form factors (rather than $M \times N$) and an $M \times M$ system of equations.

Subdivision of patches into elements is carried out adaptively. The areas that require subdivision are not known before a solution is obtained. These areas are obtained from an initial solution and are then subject to a form factor subdivision. The previous form factor matrix is still valid and the radiosity solution is not recomputed. Only parts of the form factor determination are further discretized and this is then used in the third phase (determination of the element radiosities from the coarse patch solution). This process is repeated until it converges to the desired degree of accuracy. Thus image quality is improved in areas that require more accurate treatment.

In the same paper (Cohen *et al.*, 1986), details are given on merging texture mapping with the radiosity solution. This involves retaining the idea of a patch having constant radiosity over its extent, calculating the radiosity solution and then texture mapping during the rendering phase.

For a pixel the texture mapping is computed by:

$$B_{\text{pixel}} = B_{\text{average}} \frac{R_{\text{pixel}}}{R_{\text{average}}}$$

where B_{pixel} is the final radiosity of a pixel, B_{average} is the radiosity derived from the element radiosity solution, R_{pixel} is the reflectivity given by the texture map for the pixel and R_{average} is the average reflectivity of the texture map. Cohen points out that this technique enables the contribution from, say, a painting to the illumination of the environment to be the same as if it were one average colour.

9.3.2 Hybrid radiosity and ray tracing

The standard radiosity method, as described above, provides a solution for the interaction of diffuse surfaces in a closed environment. If the radiosity method is to become a standard image synthesis technique, then it must include the modelling of specular phenomena. Wallace *et al.* (1987) do this by incorporating ray tracing and splitting the method into a two-pass approach.

The radiosity method was first extended to include specular interaction by Immel *et al.* (1986) who incorporated a bidirectional reflectivity function into the basic radiosity equation and adopted a view-independent solution to specular interreflection. However, this approach results in massive computational overheads for anything but simple scenes, because in a view-independent solution, although the diffuse illumination changes relatively slowly over a surface, fine subdivision is required for specular interaction.

In Wallace's two-pass aproach, the first pass is the computation of a view-independent solution – an enhanced radiosity solution. The philosophy of the technique is outlined in Figure 7.15 and is based on what Wallace describes as the four 'mechanisms' of illumination. These define the nature of the interaction between two surfaces and include diffuse-to-diffuse, specular-to-diffuse, diffuse-to-specular and specular-to-specular interaction.

The two components of the two-pass view-independent–view-dependent approach are termed the preprocess and the postprocess. The preprocess is enhanced to include diffuse transmission (translucency) and specular-to-diffuse transport. The basic radiosity method – using a hemicube for the form factor determination – is then employed.

Translucency is implemented by using a hemicube on the back as well as the front of the surface, allowing backward as well as forward form factors to be calculated. Specular-to-diffuse transport can occur when, for example, two diffuse patches 'see' each other via an intermediate specularly reflecting surface, and this phenomenon is taken into account by using an extra form factor for such patches. This process determines the intensity of the diffuse component due to the diffuse-to-specular, specular-to-specular and specular-to-diffuse interactions and it results in a view-independent solution that incorporates these mechanisms. Specular surfaces are restricted to perfect mirrors and the extra paths are taken into account by extra form factors which are calculated by considering a virtual environment (Figure 9.4). The environment is expanded in this way and the normal radiosity equation is enhanced with the extra form factors from the virtual environment. This is the disadvantage of the method. Since the form factor calculations always predominate, introducing extra or virtual environments substantially increases the computation time.

Figure 9.4
C is a perfect mirror and a path for diffuse interaction between patch A and B via C can be modelled by constructing a virtual patch B'.

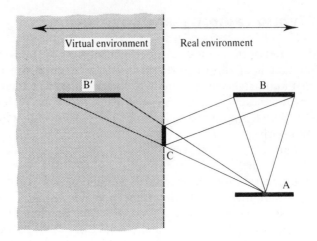

Thus, in the preprocess, or view-independent solution, specular transport is accounted for, but only to the extent necessary to calculate the diffuse component accurately. The postprocess computes a view-dependent solution from the preprocess results and the fact that a view-dependent approach is taken means that it is possible to calculate the global specular reflection and global specular transmission using a ray tracing approach. The ray tracing method adopted is similar to distributed ray tracing (see Chapter 7). The bump in the specular reflectivity function is simulated by using a reflection frustum and the infinitely thin specular beam of a naive ray tracer is avoided. The reflection frustum samples the 'important' incoming directions (that is, important as far as specular reflection is concerned). Incoming diffuse intensities that contribute to each reflection frustum are calculated by linear interpolation from the view-independent or preprocess patch vertex intensities.

Figure 9.5
Specular interaction: the incoming diffuse component due to patch j is obtained by sampling across its projection onto the plane of the reflection frustum.

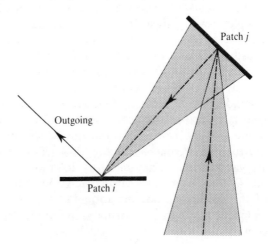

The reflection frustum is implemented geometrically as a square pyramid, whose end face is divided into $n \times n$ 'pixels' (Figure 9.5). The incoming intensities that stream through each pixel can then be summed to simulate the specular spread and also be subjected to a weighting function that simulates the shape of the specular spread. Wallace limits the amount of the work that has to be done at this stage by limiting the recursive depth over which the process operates and also by reducing the pixel resolution of the end face of the reflection frustum as a function of trace depth.

9.3.3 Progressive refinement

It was mentioned above that, unlike other major image synthesis techniques, the radiosity method has not, to date, been taken up by the computer graphics community, as a result presumably of the extremely large computational overheads of the method. In a paper published in 1988, Cohen *et al.* address this problem and develop an important technique called progressive refinement.

The general goal of progressive or adaptive refinement can be taken up by any slow image synthesis technique and it attempts to find a compromise between the competing demands of interactivity and image quality. A synthesis method that provides adaptive refinement would present an initial quickly rendered image to the user. This image is then progressively refined in a 'graceful' way. Cohen defines this as a progression towards higher quality, greater realism etc. in a way that is automatic, continuous and not distracting to the user.

The radiosity method is particularly suited to this approach – the spatial resolution of the image remaining constant, while the illumination calculations are refined. This contrasts with the the options in ray tracing where the only simple refinement process that does not involve losing previously calculated information is to increase progressively the two-dimensional spatial resolution.

The two major problems in the radiosity method are the storage costs and the calculation of the form factors. Cohen points out that for an environment of 50×10^3 patches, even though the resulting square matrix of form factors may be 90% sparse (many patches cannot see each other), this still requires 10^9 bytes of storage (at four bytes per form factor).

Both the requirements of progressive refinement and the elimination of precalculation and storage of the form factors are met by an ingenious restructuring of the basic radiosity algorithm. The stages in the progressive refinement are obtained by displaying the results as the iterative solution progresses. The solution is restructured and the hemicube evaluation order is optimized so that the convergence is 'visually graceful'. This restructuring enables the radiosity of all patches to be updated at each step in the solution, rather than having a step providing an update to the current approximation for a single patch. Maximum visual difference between steps in the solution can be achieved by processing patches according to their energy contribution to the environment. The radiosity method is particularly suited to a progressive refinement approach because it computes a view-independent solution. Viewing this solution (by rendering from a particular view point) can proceed independently as the radiosity solution progresses.

In the conventional application of the Gauss–Seidel method to solving the radiosity equation, a single iteration evaluates an improved estimate of the radiosity for each patch i using:

$$B_i = \ E_i + R_i \ \sum_{j=1}^{n} B_j F_{ij}$$

This is an estimate of the radiosity of patch i based on the current estimate of all other patches. Cohen likens this process to 'gathering'. The radiosity of patch i is evaluated by gathering in all the incoming contributions for all patches in the environment. If this solution is displayed for each step, then during the first Gauss–Seidel iteration an approximate solution appears slowly for one patch at a time.

Cohen 'reverses' this process in the following way. A single term from the above summation determines the contribution to the radiosity of patch i due to that from patch j:

$$B_i \text{ due to } B_j = R_i B_j F_{ij}$$

This relationship can be reversed by using the reciprocity relationship:

$$B_j \text{ due to } B_i = R_j B_i F_{ij} \ A_i / A_j$$

and this is true for all patches j. This relationship can be used to determine the contribution to each patch j in the environment from the single patch i. This is termed 'shooting', where a single radiosity (patch i) shoots light into the environment and the radiosities of all patches j are updated simultaneously. Note that the form factors, F_{ij}, used to determine the contribution of patch i to all other patches in the environment are the form factors obtained from the hemicube positioned at patch i. This fact means that the first complete update (of all the radiosities in the environment) is obtained from 'on the fly' form factor computations. Thus an initial approximation to the *complete* scene can appear when only the first row of form factors has been calculated. This elminates high start-up or precalculation costs.

Steps in the process can be displayed in a progressive refinement sequence if we add ΔB_j to each patch j in the iteration sequence. This is accomplished as follows:

```
repeat
    for {each patch i} do
        {position a hemicube on
        patch i and calculate form
        factors Fij (for the first iteration)}
        for {each patch j (j ≠ i)} do
            ΔRad := Ri ΔBi Fij Ai/Aj
            ΔBj   := ΔBj + ΔRad
            Bj    := Bj + ΔRad

    ΔBi := 0
until convergence
```

This process is repeated until convergence is achieved. This is carried out by subdividing patches and examining the radiosity gradient between neighbouring elements. All radiosities B_i and ΔB_i are initially set either to zero or to their emission values. As this process is repeated for each patch i the solution is displayed and at each step the radiosities for each patch i are updated.

If the output from the algorithm is displayed without further elaboration, then a scene, initially dark, gradually becomes lighter as the incremental radiosities are added to each patch. Cohen optimizes the 'visual convergence' of this process by sorting the order in which the patches are processed according to the amount of energy that they are likely to radiate. This means, for example, that emitting patches, or light sources, should be treated first. This gives an early well-lit solution. The next patches to be processed are those that received most light from the light sources and so on. It is pointed out by Cohen that, by using this ordering scheme, the solution proceeds in a way that approximates the propagation of light through an environment. In reality, for a light source such as sunlight streaming through a window, most of the ambient light comes from the first bounce of the light from the surfaces in the room. Although this produces a better visual sequence than an unsorted process, the solution still progresses from a dark scene to a fully illuminated scene. To overcome this effect an ambient light term is added to the intermediate radiosities. This term is used only to enhance the display and is not part of the solution. The value of the ambient term is based on the current estimate of the radiosities of all patches in the environment and, as the solution proceeds and becomes 'better lit', the ambient contribution is decreased.

Thus the final solution is based on:

(1) the 'shooting' method of solving the radiosity equation, where incremental radiosity additions are made to all patches j due to patch i;

(2) using a sorting method to determine the order in which the patches i are selected;

(3) adding a (decreasing) ambient term to illuminate early iterations.

Two images generated by the Program of Computer Graphics, Cornell University are shown in Plate 9.

Projects, notes and suggestions

9.1 Radiosity implementation (*)

Using an environment complexity consistent with your computing resources, develop a radiosity system. Note that each polygon/patch must have an emission value (zero except for light sources) and a reflectivity for each colour band in the solution. Also note that the final part of the process – computing a view from the view-independent solution, can use an adapted Z-buffer renderer of Chapter 5.

Develop an animated sequence from the solution that is a 'walk' through the scene.

From the point of view of development and testing it may be useful to implement the progressive refinement method.

A short note on the Gauss–Seidel method

Cohen and Greenberg (1985) point out that the Gauss–Seidel method is guaranteed to converge rapidly for equation sets such as Equation 9.1. The sum of any row of form factors is by definition less than unity and each form factor is multiplied by a reflectivity of less than unity. The sum of the row terms in Equation 9.1 (excluding the main diagonal term) is thus less than unity. The main diagonal term is always unity ($F_{ii} = 0$ for all i) and these conditions guarantee fast convergence.

The Gauss–Seidel method is an extension to the following iterative method. Given a system of linear equations:

$$\mathbf{Ax} = \mathbf{E}$$

such as Equation 9.1, we can rewrite equations for $x_1, x_2, \ldots, x_i$ in the form:

$$x_1 = \frac{E_1 - a_{12}x_2 - a_{13}x_3 - \ldots - a_{1n}x_n}{a_{11}}$$

which leads to the iteration:

$$x_1^{(k+1)} = \frac{E_1 - a_{12}x_2^{(k)} - \ldots - a_{1n}x_n^{(k)}}{a_{11}}$$

In general:

$$x_i^{(k+1)} = \frac{E_i - a_{i1}x_1^{(k)} - \ldots - a_{i,i-1}x_{i-1}^{(k)} - a_{i,i+1}x_{i+1}^{(k)} - \ldots - a_{in}x_n^{(k)}}{a_{ii}} \tag{9.3}$$

This formula can be used in an iteration procedure:

(1) Choose an initial approximation, say,

$$x_i^{(0)} = \frac{E_i}{a_{ii}}$$

for $i = 1, 2, \ldots, n$, where E_i is non-zero for emitting surfaces or light sources.

(2) Determine the next iterate

$$x_i^{(k+1)} \text{ from } x_i^{(k)}$$

using Equation 9.3.

(3) If $| x_i^{(k+1)} - x_i^{(k)} | <$ a threshold, for $i = 1, 2, \ldots, n$, then stop the iteration, otherwise return to step (2).

This is known as Jacobi iteration. The Gauss–Seidel method improves on the convergence of this method by modifying Equation 9.3 to use the latest available information. When the new iterate $x_i^{(k+1)}$ is being calculated, new values $x_1^{(k+1)}$, $x_2^{(k+1)}, \ldots, x_{i-1}^{(k+1)}$ have already been calculated and Equation 9.3 is modified to:

$$x_i^{(k+1)} = \frac{E_i - a_{i1}x_1^{(k+1)} - \ldots - a_{i,i-1}x_{i-1}^{(k+1)} - a_{i,i+1}x_{i+1}^{(k)} - \ldots - a_{in}x_n^{(k)}}{a_{ii}} \tag{9.4}$$

Note that when $i = 1$ the right-hand side of the equation contains terms with superscript k only, and Equation 9.4 reduces to Equation 9.3. When $i = n$ the right-hand side contains terms with superscript $k + 1$ only.

Convergence of the Gauss–Seidel method can be improved by the following method. Having produced a new value $x_i'^{(k+1)}$, a better value is given by a weighted average of the old and new values:

$$x_i^{(k+1)} = rx_i'^{(k+1)} + (1 - r) x_i^{(k)}$$

where r (>0) is an arbitrary relaxation factor independent of k and i. Cohen *et al.* (1988) report that a relaxation factor of 1.1 works for most environments.

CHAPTER TEN

Further Realism: Shadows, Texture and Environment Mapping

Shadow generation and texture mapping are two common additions to simple shading that attempt to increase the realism of three-dimensional shaded objects. Both elaborations are implemented by a variety of ad hoc *algorithms and, with the exception of shadow computation in ray tracing, neither area has been incorporated in a theoretical reflection–illumination model. Unlike shading, no particular technique predominates and the choice of a suitable method, particularly with texture algorithms, is motivated by the desired visual effect. Shadow algorithms are distinguished both by the method used and the type of shadow produced. The methods used in texture algorithms are so diverse that they can only really be categorized according to the end effect. Although some overview of both areas will be given, this chapter will concentrate on the implementation of methods that have gained some popularity.*

10.1 Shadows

10.1.1 The functions of shadows

Shadows are an important, and somewhat neglected, addition to the repertoire of techniques used to visualize three-dimensional objects in computer graphics. Simple shadows (see Section 10.1.3) can be used to dissolve the perceptual effect of objects floating above the ground and they are far less expensive to compute and are more necessary for simple

219

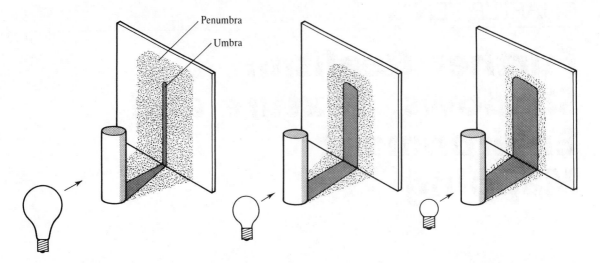

Figure 10.1
Umbra–penumbra
dependence on the size
of the light source.

images than, for example, the accurate modelling of ambient illumination.

Plate 10 demonstrates this effect, where the shadows appear to serve two functions. Firstly, they 'anchor' the spheres to the green planes, negating the computer graphics 'look' of objects floating in space; secondly, they emphasize the changing direction of the light source.

Shadows vary tremendously as a function of the lighting environment. They can be hard edged or soft edged and contain both an umbra and a penumbra area. The relative size of the umbra–penumbra is a function of the size and the shape of the light source and its distance from the object (Figure 10.1). The umbra is that part of a shadow that is completely cut off from the light source, whereas the penumbra is an area that receives some light from the source. A penumbra surrounds an umbra and there is always a gradual change in intensity from a penumbra to an umbra. In computer graphics, if we are not modelling illumination sources, then we usually consider point light sources at large distances, and assume in the simplest case that objects produce umbrae with sharp edges. This is still only an approximation. Even although light from a large distance produces almost parallel rays, there is still light behind the object as a result of diffraction and the shadow grades off. This effect also varies over the distance a shadow is thrown. These effects, that determine the quality of a shadow, enable us to infer information concerning the nature of the light source and they are clearly important to us as human beings perceiving a three-dimensional environment. For example, the shadows that we see outdoors depend on the time of day and whether the sky is overcast or not.

So far we have only talked about single primary sources. Once we have multiple sources all at different intensities and reflecting surfaces (that can be treated as secondary sources) then shadows become part of the global illumination problem, and indeed an elegant, but extremely expensive, method for shadow generation is given as part of a simple ray tracing algorithm in Chapter 7.

10.1.2 Computer graphics and shadows

A number of aspects of shadows are exploited in the computer generation of the phenomenon. These are now discussed.

- No shadows are seen if the view point is coincident with the (single) light source. An equivalent form of this statement is that shadows can be considered to be areas hidden from the light source, implying that modified hidden surface algorithms can be used to solve the shadow problem.

- If the light sources are point sources then there is no penumbra to calculate.

- For static scenes shadows are fixed and do not change as the view point changes. If the relative positions of objects and light sources change, the shadows have to be recalculated. This places a high overhead on three-dimensional animation where shadows are important for depth and movement perception.

Because of the high computational overheads, shadows have been regarded in much the same way as texture mapping – as a quality add-on. They have not been viewed as a necessity and compared with shading algorithms there has been little consideration of the quality of shadows. Most shadow generation algorithms produce hard edge point light source shadows.

With the exception of shadow generation in ray tracing programs, all algorithms deal only with polygon mesh models.

10.1.3 Simple shadows on a ground plane

An extremely simple method of generating shadows is reported by Blinn (1988). It suffices for single-object scenes throwing shadows on a flat ground plane. The method simply involves drawing the projection of the object on the ground plane. It is thus restricted to single-object scenes, or multi-object scenes where objects are sufficiently isolated so as not to cast shadows on each other. The ground plane projection is easily obtained from a linear transformation and the projected polygon can be scanned into a Z-buffer as part of an initialization procedure at an appropriate (dark) intensity.

Figure 10.2
Ground plane shadows
for single objects.

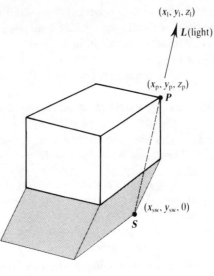

If the usual illumination approximation is made – single point source at an infinite distance – then we have parallel light rays in a direction $L = (x_1, y_1, z_1)$ as shown in Figure 10.2. Any point on the object $P = (x_p, y_p, z_p)$ will cast a shadow at $S = (x_{sw}, y_{sw}, 0)$. Considering the geometry in the figure, we have:

$$S = P - \alpha L$$

and, given that $z_{sw} = 0$, we have:

$$0 = z_p - \alpha z_1$$
$$\alpha = z_p / z_1$$

and

$$x_{sw} = x_p - (z_p/z_1)x_1$$
$$y_{sw} = y_p - (z_p/z_1)y_1$$

As a homogeneous transformation this is

$$[x_{sw}\ y_{sw}\ 0\ 1] = [x_p\ y_p\ z_p\ 1] \begin{bmatrix} 1 & 0 & 0 & 0 \\ 0 & 1 & 0 & 0 \\ -x_1/x_1 & -y_1/z_1 & 0 & 0 \\ 0 & 0 & 0 & 1 \end{bmatrix}$$

Note from this that it is just as easy to generate shadows on a vertical back or side plane. Blinn (1988) also shows how to extend this idea to handle light sources that are at a finite distance from the object.

This type of approximate shadow (on a flat ground plane) is beloved by traditional animators and its use certainly enhances movement in three-dimensional computer animation.

10.1.4 Shadow algorithms

Unlike hidden surface removal algorithms, where one or two algorithms now predominate and other methods are only used in special cases, no popular candidate has emerged as the top shadow algorithm. In fact shadow computation is a rather neglected area of computer graphics. What follows, therefore, is a brief description of four major approaches. Shadow generation in ray tracing is separately described in Chapter 7.

Shadow algorithms: projecting polygons–scan line

This approach was developed by Appel (1968) and Bouknight and Kelley (1970). Adding shadows to a scan line algorithm requires a preprocessing stage that builds up a secondary data structure which links all polygons that may shadow a given polygon. Shadow pairs – a polygon together with the polygon that it can possibly shadow – are detected by projecting all polygons onto a sphere centred at the light source. Polygon pairs that cannot interact are detected and discarded. This is an important step because for a scene containing n polygons the number of possible projected shadows is $n(n-1)$.

The algorithm processes the secondary data structure simultaneously with a normal scan conversion process to determine whether any shadows fall on the polygon that generated the visible scan line segment under consideration. If no shadow polygon(s) exist then the scan line algorithm proceeds as normal. If shadow polygon(s) exist then there are three possibilities:

(1)   The shadow polygon does not cover the generated scan line segment and the situation is identical to an algorithm without shadows.

(2)   Shadow polygon(s) completely cover the visible scan line segment and the scan conversion process proceeds but the pixel intensity is modulated by an amount that depends on the number of shadows that are covering the segment. For a single light source the segment is either in shadow or not.

(3)   A shadow polygon partially covers the visible scan line segment. In this case the segment is subdivided and the process is applied recursively until a solution is obtained.

Figure 10.3
Polygons that receive a shadow from another polygon are linked in a secondary data structure. Scan line segments are now delineated by both view point projection boundaries and shadow boundaries.

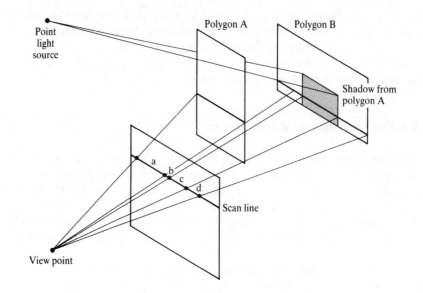

A representation of these possibilities is shown in Figure 10.3. These are, in order along the scan line:

- Polygon A is visible; therefore it is rendered.
- Polygon B is visible and is rendered.
- Polygon B is shadowed by polygon A and is rendered at an appropriately reduced intensity.
- Polygon B is visible and is rendered.

Shadow algorithms: shadow volumes

The shadow volume approach was originally developed by Crow (1977) and subsequently extended by others. In particular, Brotman and Badler (1984) used the idea as a basis for generating 'soft' shadows – that is, shadows produced by a distributed light source.

A shadow volume is the invisible volume of space swept out by the shadow of an object. It is the infinite volume defined by lines emanating from a point light source through vertices in the object. Figure 10.4 conveys the idea of a shadow volume. A finite shadow volume is obtained by considering the intersection of the infinite volume with the view volume. The shadow volume is computed by first evaluating the contour edge of the object, as seen from the light source. Planes defined by the light source and the contour edges define the bounding surface of the shadow volume. This scheme can be integrated into a number of hidden surface removal algorithms and the polygons that define the shadow volume are processed with the object polygons except that they are

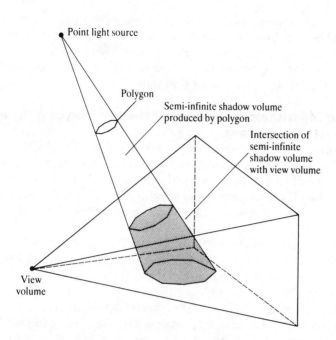

Figure 10.4
Finite shadow volume
defined by a polygon, a
point light source and a
view volume.

considered invisible. A distinction is made between 'front-facing'
polygons and 'back-facing' polygons and the relationship between shadow
polygons labelled in this way and object polygons is examined. A point
on an object is deemed to be in shadow if it is behind a front-facing
shadow polygon and in front of a back-facing polygon, that is if it is
contained within a shadow volume.

As it stands the algorithm is most easily integrated with a depth
priority hidden surface removal algorithm. Brotman and Badler use an
enhanced Z-buffer algorithm and this approach has two significant
advantages:

(1)   the benefits of the Z-buffer rendering approach are retained, and

(2)   their method is able to compute soft shadows or umbra–penumbra
       effects.

The price to be paid for using a shadow volume approach in conjunction
with a Z-buffer is memory cost. The Z-buffer has to be extended such
that each pixel location is a record of five fields. As shadow polygons are
'rendered' they modify counters in a pixel record and a decision can be
made as to whether a point is in shadow or not.

Soft shadows are computed by modelling distributed light sources
as arrays of point sources and linearly combining computations due to
each point source.

The original shadow volume approach places heavy constraints on the database environment; the most serious restriction is that objects must be convex polyhedrons. Bergeron (1986) developed a general version of Crow's algorithm that overcomes these restrictions and allows concave objects and penetrating polygons.

Shadow algorithms: derivation of shadow polygons from light source transformations

This approach was developed by Atherton and Weiler (1978) and relies on the fact that applying hidden surface removal to a view from the light source produces polygons or parts of polygons that are in shadow. It also relies on the object space polygon clipping algorithm (to produce shadow polygons that are parts of existing polygons) of Weiler and Atherton (1977).

A claimed advantage of this approach is that it operates in object space. This means that it is possible to extract numerical information on shadows from the algorithm. This finds applications, for example, in architectural CAD.

The algorithm enhances the object data structure with shadow polygons to produce a 'complete shadow data file'. This can then be used to produce any view of the object with shadows. It is thus a good approach in generating animated sequences where the virtual camera changes position, but the relative positions of the object and the light source remain unchanged. Referring to Figure 10.5, the first step in the algorithm is to apply a transformation such that the object or scene is viewed from the light source position. Hidden surface removal then

Figure 10.5
Deriving shadow polygons from light source transformations.

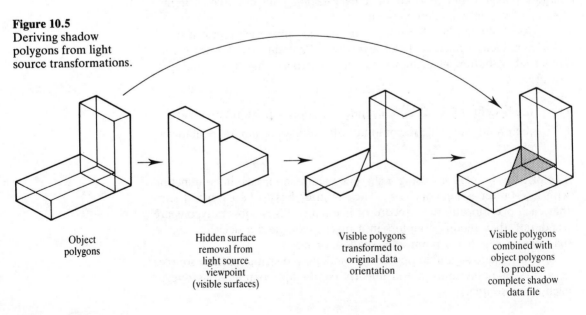

Object polygons

Hidden surface removal from light source viewpoint (visible surfaces)

Visible polygons transformed to original data orientation

Visible polygons combined with object polygons to produce complete shadow data file produces visible polygons, that is polygons that are visible to the light source and are therefore not in shadow. This polygon set can then be combined with the original object polygons, provided that both data sets are transformed to the same orientation. The process of combining these sets results in a complete shadow data file – the original polygon set enhanced by shadow polygons for a particular light source. Transforming the database to the required view point and applying hidden surface removal will then result in an image with shadows.

Shadow algorithms: shadow Z-buffer

Possibly the simplest approach to the shadow computation, and one that is easily integrated into a Z-buffer based renderer is the shadow Z-buffer developed by Williams (1978). This technique requires a separate shadow Z-buffer for each light source and in its basic form is only suitable for a scene illuminated by a single light source. Alternatively, a single-shadow Z-buffer could be used for many light sources and the algorithm executed for each light source, but this would be somewhat inefficient and slow.

The algorithm is a two-step process. A scene is 'rendered' and depth information stored into the shadow Z-buffer using the light source as a view point. No intensities are calculated. This computes a 'depth image' from the light source of these polygons that are visible to the light source.

The second step is to render the scene using a Z-buffer algorithm. This process is enhanced as follows. If a point is visible, a coordinate transformation is used to map (x, y, z), the coordinates of the point in three-dimensional screen space (from the view point), to (x', y', z'), the coordinates of the point in screen space from the light point. If z' is greater than the value stored in the shadow Z-buffer for that point, then a surface is nearer to the light source than the point under consideration and the point is in shadow, and thus a shadow 'intensity' is used; otherwise the point is rendered as normal.

10.2 Texture

10.2.1 Introduction to texture

Texture mapping was one of the first developments towards making images of three-dimensional objects more interesting and apparently more complex. The original motivation for texture mapping was to diminish the 'shiny plastic' effects produced by using the simple Phong reflection model and to enable different objects to exhibit different surface properties (apart from the trivial distinction of colour).

In a sense the term texture is somewhat misleading; with the exception of bump mapping (Blinn, 1978b; see Section 10.2.9), which gives the impression of actual surface perturbation, the normal semantics associated with the term texture, most methods modulate the colour of a surface using repeating motifs or a frame-grabbed image. Textures on real objects usually exhibit both surface and colour modulation – the bark on a tree or the texture of a woven fabric, for example.

There are three major considerations in texture mapping:

(1)   What attribute or parameter of the model or object is to be modulated to produce the desired textural effect?

(2)   How is the texture mapping to be carried out? Given that a texture is defined in a texture domain and an object exists as world space data, we need to define a mapping between these domains.

(3)   Texture mapping requires special anti-aliasing treatment because it tends to produce worse aliasing artefacts than other techniques associated with image synthesis.

These three considerations are dealt with in order.

10.2.2 Object attributes modulated for texture

In a review paper Heckbert (1986) categorizes the parameters that can be modulated to provide a textural impression. A modified version of this categorization is as follows:

- Surface colour (diffuse reflection coefficient(s)):
  This is the most commonly used parameter for texture mapping and involves, for example, in a simple reflection model, modulating the diffuse coefficient. The first example of this was Catmull (1974).

- Specular and diffuse reflection (environment mapping):
  This method is now known as environment mapping and has come to be regarded as a separate technique rather than as a category of texture mapping. It is described in Section 10.3 and was first developed by Blinn and Newell (1976).

- Normal vector perturbation:
  This is an elegant device, developed again by Blinn (1978b) that 'tricks' a simple reflection model into producing what appears to be a perturbed surface.
  An extension to this technique is given in Kajiya (1985) which Kajiya calls 'frame mapping'. In this method a 'frame bundle' rather than just a normal vector is perturbed. A frame bundle for a surface is a local coordinate system given by the tangent, binormal and normal to the surface. Kajiya points out that

this approach allows a mapping of the directionality of surface features such as hair and cloth.

- Specularity:
  Although this effect was reported by Blinn (1978b) (yet again) it does not seem to have been used to any great extent. The attribute modulated is the surface roughness function in the Cook–Torrance reflection model (Chapter 3). An example of a surface with variable shininess is an object painted with textured paint.

- Transparency:
  An example of the modulation of transparency is given in Gardener (1985). This particular example is interesting in that it is not strictly a method of applying texture to an object but a method of generating a complete object – a cloud – using a mathematical texture function to modulate the transparency of an ellipsoid. A real-life example of this case is chemically etched glass.

One can further distinguish among these methods by noting that all the methods except environment mapping 'cement' a texture onto the object and the texture then becomes a 'permanent' part of the object, invariable under object transformations and viewing conditions. Environment mapping, in contrast, depends on where the object is placed in an environment and this is a further justification for considering environment mapping as a technique distinct from texture mapping.

10.2.3 Texture mapping: general

Texture mapping is the process of transforming a texture onto the surface of a three-dimensional object. The possibilities of texture mapping are summarized in Figure 10.6, where it is indicated that the texture domain can be one dimensional, two dimensional or three dimensional. Although two-dimensional texture domains are the most popular (they can be

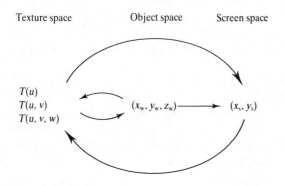

Figure 10.6
Possible texture mappings.

229

Figure 10.7
In general the inverse mapping from screen space to texture space produces a curvilinear quadrilateral.

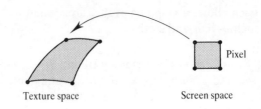

Texture space   Screen space

constructed, for example, from frame-grabbed images, thus offering an infinite variety of texture patterns), mapping from one-dimensional or three-dimensional domains is generally considerably easier.

Figure 10.6 shows that two major implementations are possible:

(1)   mapping from texture space to object space (usually a two-dimensional to three-dimensional transformation) and then performing the viewing projection to screen space;

(2)   mapping directly from texture to screen space (usually a two-dimensional to two-dimensional transformation).

Most attention has been paid to the second method and an inverse mapping is commonly employed, where the screen space is uniformly sampled and the inverse or pre-image of a pixel in texture space is formed. The area thus produced in the texture domain is then sampled and filtered and a texture value returned to the pixel. Filtering methods, dealt with below, are easier to implement for inverse mapping.

The difficulties that occur in texture mapping arise from the situation shown in Figure 10.7. The transformation from the screen domain to the texture domain is non-linear and in general this results in a pixel 'pre-image' that is a curvilinear quadrilateral whose shape varies as the pixel position changes.

As well as the aliasing artefacts that occur, specifying a mapping for a polygon mesh object or non-parametric object is difficult. One-dimensional and three-dimensional texture domains have the advantage that the mapping is trivial, but the textural effects that can be obtained are generally much more restricted than in two-dimensional texture domains where any two-dimensional image can be used as a texture pattern.

In the following sections techniques utilizing one-dimensional, three-dimensional and finally two-dimensional texture domains are described. A single example technique is given for the one-dimensional and three-dimensional cases, and the remainder of the material on texture is devoted to techniques employing a two-dimensional texture domain. This reflects the current popularity of usage in computer graphics.

10.2.4 A one-dimensional texture domain technique

This technique modulates the diffuse coefficients as a function of ϕ, the angle between the light direction vector L and the surface normal N. It can be used to simulate thin film interference – the physical phenomenon that produces colour changes in, for example, a soap film on a bubble or an oil film on the surface of water. As shown in Figure 10.8 colour changes occur in thin films because of interference between the wave reflected from the thin film surface and the wave reflected from the surface covered by the thin film. Incident white light has components subtracted from it, if the interference, for particular wavelengths, is destructive. It can be shown (Nassau, 1983) that the wavelength at which cancellation occurs is a function of the refractive index, η, of the film, its thickness d and the angle of incidence of the incoming light, ϕ.

Plate 11 (top left) shows the degree of cancellation or reinforcement for red, green and blue light. The horizontal axis, known as 'retardation', R, is a linear function $2\eta d \cos \theta$. θ is the angle of refraction between paths a and b (Figures 10.8 and 3.6) and is related to ϕ by Snell's law:

$$\eta = \sin \phi / \sin \theta$$

The vertical axis shows the reflection interference intensity ($0 =$ cancellation and $1 =$ reinforcement). The combination of these colours gives an approximation to Newton's interference colour sequence, shown below the cancellation–reinforcement functions. The functions shown are:

$$
\begin{aligned}
r &= \left[1 - \cos \left(\frac{2\pi R}{\lambda_r} \right) \right] \times 0.5 \\
g &= \left[1 - \cos \left(\frac{2\pi R}{\lambda_g} \right) \right] \times 0.5 \\
b &= \left[1 - \cos \left(\frac{2\pi R}{\lambda_b} \right) \right] \times 0.5
\end{aligned}
\tag{10.1}
$$

The nice thing about this method is that two of these three variables can be made a constant and varying the third means that the texture is in effect a function of one variable. For example, we can make the refractive index and thickness a constant and vary the diffuse colour as a function of ϕ. ϕ is the angle between L and N – the angle of incidence – from which θ and R are obtained and used in Equations 10.1 to index a colour.

Note that this method does not strictly conform to our model of mapping from a texture domain to an object domain; rather, the angle

Figure 10.8
Ray e is formed by
interference between d
reflected from surface 1
and ray a (refracted and
reflected from surface 2
and refracted again).

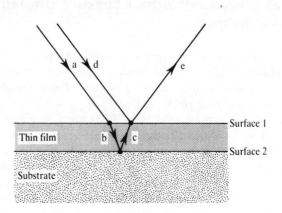

that L makes with the surface normal is used to control the surface colour
and this depends on the position of the object with respect to the light
source.

Plate 11 (top right) shows an object rendered using exactly this
technique. Plate 11 (bottom) shows the effect that can be obtained by
enhancing this technique by perturbing the depth of the thin film at the
same time.

10.2.5 Three-dimensional texture domain techniques

Another method that neatly circumvents the mapping problem is to
employ a three-dimensional field. We can imagine that a texture value
exists everywhere in the object domain. Ignoring object scale problems
(the texture 'size' will not vary as the size of the object changes) we can
then say that, given a point on the surface of an object (x_w, y_w, z_w), its
texture is given by the identity mapping: $T(x_w, y_w, z_w)$. This is equivalent
to sculpting or carving an object out of a solid block of material. The
colour of the object is determined by the intersection of its surface with
the predefined three-dimensional texture field of the block. This method
was reported simultaneously in Perlin (1985) and Peachey (1985) wherein
the term 'solid texturing' was coined.

A fairly obvious requirement of this technique is that the three-
dimensional texture field is obtained by procedural generation. Storing a
complete three-dimensional field would be prohibitively expensive in
memory requirements. Thus the coordinates (x_w, y_w, z_w) are used to index
a procedure that defines the three-dimensional texture field for that point.

A significant advantage of the elimination of the mapping problem
is that objects of arbitrary complexity can receive a texture on their

surface in a 'coherent' fashion. No discontinuities occur when the texture appears on the object.

An interesting possibility occurs when using this technique in an animated sequence. The correct approach is to subject the texture field to the same transformations as the object such that the texture remains static on the surface of the object. However, the 'incorrect' approach – moving the object through a static texture field – can produce unique effects.

An 'easy' example of this technique is shown in Plate 12. Here 125 cubes are shaded and the colour of each cube is obtained by an identity mapping between (x_w, y_w, z_w), the coordinate of a reference vertex on each cube, and the corresponding point $RGB(x_w, y_w, z_w)$ in an RGB cube defined over the domain of the object (see Chapter 14 for further details on the RGB cube).

Two further examples of this technique demonstrate the idea. Firstly, wood grain can be simulated by a set of concentric cylinders, whose reference axis is, in general, tilted with respect to one of the reference axes of the object. This approach is shown in Plate 12 where the three-dimensional texture field is a set of functionally defined concentric cylinders modulated with a harmonic function. The procedure given in Program 10.1 returns a colour (r, g, b) given texture space coordinates (u, v, w). This is obtained by taking the world or object space coordinate (x_w, y_w, z_w) and subjecting it to a linear transformation:

$$(u, v, w) = \text{Tilt}(x_w, y_w, z_w)$$

which defines a particular orientation between the texture field and the object.

The texture field is a modular function of *radius*. For strict concentric cylinders:

$radius := sqrt(sqr(u) + sqr(w))$

To apply a sinusoidal perturbation we have:

$radius := radius + 2*sin(20*angle)$

Finally, we apply a small twist along the axis of the cylinder

$radius := radius + 2*sin(20*angle + v/150)$

An extension of this basic idea is to use a general three-dimensional noise function to perturb the basic field, rather than to use a context-dependent perturbation, as we did for the wood grain. This approach is now well established in three-dimensional computer graphics because visually it works well. An example of marble texture is shown in Plate 12. The texture field in this case is a set of alternating black,

Program 10.1 A procedure for representing wood grain.

```
procedure wood_grain(u, v, w: real; var r, g, b: real);

   var radius, angle: real;
       grain: integer;

begin
   radius := sqrt(sqr(u) + sqr(w));
   if w = 0 then angle := pi/2
   else angle := arctan(u, w);
   {arctan evaluates arctan (u/w), but uses quadrant information to return a
    value in the range 0 . . 2π}
   radius := radius + 2*sin(20*angle + v/150);
   grain := round(radius) mod 60;
   if grain < 40 then
      begin
         r := r_light;
         g := g_light;
         b := b_light;
      end else
      begin
         r := r_dark;
         g := g_dark;
         b := b_dark;
      end;
end   {of wood_grain};
```

grey, white and grey slabs. A three-dimensional noise function, fully described in Chapter 11, is used to modulate the basic black–grey stripes to give an impression of turbulent flow. In the procedure shown in Program 10.2, *width* defines the overall width (in object space) of a full cycle of marble texture (that is from dark to light). *dd* is used to define the relative widths of the different coloured stripes (that is, four bands [0 . . 3], [4 . . 8], [9 . . 11] and [12 . . 16]).

Another way of looking at this particular example is that it is the combination of two procedurally defined texture fields. One field consists of the low frequency black, grey and white slabs, the other is a three-dimensional noise function.

The final example (see Plate 12) uses a similar technique but the amplitude of the three-dimensional noise perturbation is increased to such an extent that the marble effect is destroyed. These two examples show the power of the method in being able to generate visually different effects from the same procedural basis.

Program 10.2 A procedure for representing marble.

```
procedure marble(u, v, w: real; var r, g, b: real);

    const
        width = 0.02;

    var
        d, dd: real;
        i: real;

begin
    d := (u + 15000)*width + 7*noise(u/100, v/200, w/200);
    dd := trunc(d) mod 17;
    if dd < 4 then
        i := 0.7 + 0.2*noise(u/70, v/50, w/50)
    else
        if (dd < 9) or (dd >= 12) then
        begin
            d := abs(d − trunc(d/17)*17 − 10.5)*0.1538462;
            i := 0.4 + 0.3*d + 0.2*noise(u/100, v/100, w/100);
        end
        else
            i := 0.2 + 0.2*noise(u/100, v/100, w/100);
    r := 0.9*i;
    g := 0.8*i;
    b := 0.6*i;
end   {marble};
```

10.2.6   Two-dimensional texture domain techniques

One of the major problems in two-dimensional texture domain techniques is the difficulty of mapping a two-dimensional image onto a three-dimensional object surface. In general, a 'wallpapering' technique, where the texture image is glued to the surface, will not work because of the topological constraints, and the texture image has to be cut or distorted. The problem becomes more acute with polygon mesh models, where polygons are only defined at their vertices. A tedious and labour-intensive way of dealing with this problem is actually to predistort the texture domain so that a fit is possible.

10.2.7 Two-dimensional texture domain techniques: mapping onto bicubic parametric patches

The first use of texture in computer graphics was a method developed by Catmull (1974). This technique is applied to bicubic parametric patch models; the algorithm subdivides a surface patch in object space, and at the same time executes a corresponding subdivision in texture space. The idea is that the patch subdivision proceeds until it covers a single pixel (a standard patch subdivision approach described in detail in Chapter 6). When the patch subdivision process terminates the required texture value(s) for the pixel is (are) obtained from the area enclosed by the current level of subdivision in the texture domain. This is a straight-forward technique that is easily implemented as an extension to a bicubic patch renderer. A variation of this method has been used recently by Cook *et al.* (1987) where object surfaces are subdivided into 'micropoly-gons' and flat shaded with values from a corresponding subdivision in texture space.

An example of this technique is shown in Plate 13. Here each patch on the teapot causes subdivision of a single texture map, which is itself a rendered version of the teapot. For each patch, the *u, v* values from the parameter space subdivision are used to index the texture map whose *u, v* values also vary between 0 and 1. This scheme is easily altered to, say, map four patches into the entire texture domain by using a scale factor of two in the *u, v* mapping.

Problems that occur in two-dimensional texture mapping onto polygon mesh definitions are now dealt with.

10.2.8 Two-dimensional texture domain techniques: mapping onto polygon mesh models

We need to overcome two difficulties with two-dimensional texture domain mapping onto polygon mesh models. Firstly, the interior of polygons, defined only by their vertices, needs to be parametrized so that a mapping can be derived for all interior points. If the object is made up of planar surfaces, for example extruded characters, then, depending on the nature of the pattern, discontinuities in texture may not matter. However, if the object is made up of curved surfaces, the problem of wrapping or warping the texture onto the polygon mesh surface has to be dealt with.

Parametrization techniques are fully described by Heckbert (1986) who points out that the easiest polygon to parametrize is a triangle. For

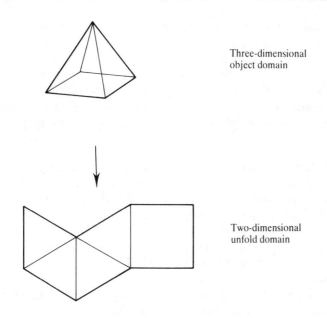

Three-dimensional
object domain

Figure 10.9
'Unfolding' a polygon
mesh object.

Two-dimensional
unfold domain

any point on the object (x, y, z) there is a linear relationship with u and v:

$$(x, y, z) = (A_k u + B_k v + C_k, \ A_y u + B_y v + C_y, \ A_z u + B_z v + C_z)$$

For polygons with more than three vertices a non-linear transformation is required and given this fact, together with the topological problems of mapping all the vertices from the complete polygon mesh, it is doubtful whether this straightforward mathematical approach is viable.

Two empirical methods that overcome both the topological problems and the parametrization difficulties are now described.

Polygon mesh texture mapping: unfolding the polygon mesh
A technique developed by Samek *et al.* (1986) reduces the dimensionality of the polygon mesh object from three to two by 'unfolding' adjacent polygons into a two-dimensional folding plane. This process is shown in Figure 10.9 for a four-sided pyramid. The texture space is then easily projected onto the object in the unfold plane and the algorithm in this way effectively maps each vertex in every polygon to an appropriate (u, v) coordinate in texture space.

Unfolding is performed by pivoting each polygon in the object about the edge with its neighbour. Because the unfolding process depends on polygonal adjacencies, a restriction of the method is that the object must be a single surface topologically. It should be clear from Figure 10.9 that there are possible discontinuities in texture across polygon boundaries.

Polygonal adjacency information must be set up in a data structure

237

and the algorithm unfolds polygon n by firstly finding the angle between polygon n and polygon $n - 1$ (the last transformed polygon). This angle is incorporated in a transformation that pivots polygon n about the common edge between it and polygon $n - 1$ so that both polygons now lie in the unfold plane. The original common edge relationship between polygon n and polygon $n - 1$ is maintained in the unfold plane by concatenating polygon n's pivot matrix with the unfolding transform of polygon $n - 1$.

Polygon mesh texture mapping: two-part mapping

Two-part texture mapping is a recently developed technique that overcomes the mapping problem by using an 'easy' intermediate surface onto which the texture is initially projected. Introduced by Bier and Sloan (1986), it is a method that will map two-dimensional texture onto unconstrained polygon mesh models. The method can also be used to implement environment mapping and is thus a method that unifies texture mapping and environment mapping. The texture is projected onto the surface in a way that depends only on the geometry of the object, known as a 'target' object, and not on its parametrization.

The basis of the method is as follows:

(1)   The first stage is a mapping from two-dimensional texture space to a simple three-dimensional intermediate surface such as a cylinder:

$$T(u, v) \rightarrow T'(x_i, y_i, z_i)$$

This is known as the S mapping.

(2)   A second stage maps the three-dimensional texture pattern onto the object surface:

$$T'(x_i, y_i, z_i) \rightarrow O(x, y, z)$$

This is referred to as the O mapping.

These combined operations can distort the texture pattern onto the object in a 'natural' way; for example, one variation of the method is a 'shrinkwrap' mapping, where the planar texture pattern shrinks onto the object in the manner suggested by the eponym.

For the S mapping Bier and Sloan describe four intermediate surfaces: a plane at any orientation, the curved surface of a cylinder, the faces of a cube and the surface of a sphere. Although it makes no difference mathematically, it is useful to consider that $T(u, v)$ is mapped onto the interior surfaces of these objects. For example, consider the cylinder. Given a parametric definition of the curved surface of a cylinder as a set of points (θ, h) we have:

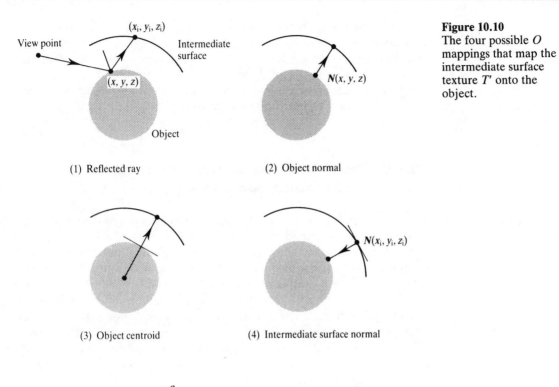

Figure 10.10
The four possible O
mappings that map the
intermediate surface
texture T' onto the
object.

(1) Reflected ray

(2) Object normal

(3) Object centroid

(4) Intermediate surface normal

$$S_{\text{cylinder}}: \quad (u, v) \rightarrow (\frac{c}{r}u + \theta_0, \ dv + h_0)$$

where c and d are scaling factors and θ_0 and h_0 position the texture on the cylinder of radius r. The inverse is

$$S^{-1}_{\text{cylinder}}: \quad (\theta, h) \rightarrow (\frac{r}{c}(\theta - \theta_0), \ \frac{1}{d}(h - h_0))$$

Various possibilities occur for the O mapping where the texture values for $O(x, y, z)$ are obtained from $T'(x_i, y_i, z_i)$, and these are best considered from a ray tracing point of view. The four O mappings are shown in Figure 10.10 and are:

- the intersection of the reflected view ray with the intermediate surface, T' (this is in fact environment mapping);
- the intersection of the surface normal at (x, y, z) with T';
- the intersection of a line through (x, y, z) and the object centroid with T';
- the intersection of the line from (x, y, z) to T' whose orientation is given by the surface normal at (x_i, y_i, z_i).

239

Excluding the first, which is concerned with environment mapping (rather than mapping texture onto a surface), we have three O mappings and four S mappings giving a total of 12 possible combinations. Bier and Sloan state that only five of these combinations are useful. For example, they give the name 'shrinkwrap' to the combination of cylinder S mapping with intermediate surface normal O mapping.

10.2.9 Two-dimensional texture domain techniques: bump mapping

This is an important technique because it simulates a wrinkled or dimpled surface rather than modulating the colour of a flat surface. Apparent surface perturbations are produced by 'tricking' the reflection model with a jittered surface normal. Its single disadvantage is that the surface perturbations do not appear on the silhouette edge. Blinn (1978b) first noted that 'the effect of wrinkles on the perceived intensity is primarily due to their effect on the direction of the surface normal (and thus the light reflected) rather than their effect on the position of the surface'. This observation led to the development of a technique, known as bump mapping, that jitters the surface normal N by a perturbation vector D prior to its use in intensity calculations:

$$N' = N + D$$

N' is derived from a texture function in the following way. If $O(u, v)$ is a parametrized function representing an object surface where $O(u, v)$ is the position vector for a point on the surface, then

$$N = \frac{\partial O}{\partial u} \times \frac{\partial O}{\partial v}$$

is the normal at a point on the surface. (The partial derivatives lie in the tangent plane to the surface and their cross-products define the surface normal.) $T(u, v)$ is a two-dimensional texture function known as a bump map. This function is the source texture function that is used to control the perturbation of the original surface normal. The relationship between D and $T(u, v)$ is now derived.

First we use $T(u, v)$ to add a small increment to O:

$$O'(u, v) = O(u, v) + T(u, v) \frac{N}{|N|}$$

This displaces a surface point in the direction of its surface normal. The normal vector to the perturbed surface is given by taking the cross-products of the partial derivatives of O':

$$N'(u, v) = \frac{\partial O'}{\partial u} \times \frac{\partial O'}{\partial v}$$

$$\frac{\partial O'}{\partial u} = \frac{\partial O}{\partial u} + \frac{\partial T}{\partial u} \frac{N}{|N|} + T \frac{\partial}{\partial u} \left(\frac{N}{|N|} \right)$$

$$\frac{\partial O'}{\partial v} = \frac{\partial O}{\partial v} + \frac{\partial T}{\partial v} \frac{N}{|N|} + T \frac{\partial}{\partial v} \left(\frac{N}{|N|} \right)$$

If T is small (that is, the height of the surface irregularities is small compared with the spatial extent of the surface) the last term in each equation can be ignored, and

$$N'(u, v) = \frac{\partial O}{\partial u} \times \frac{\partial O}{\partial v} + \frac{\partial T}{\partial u} \frac{N \times \partial O/\partial v}{|N|}$$

$$+ \frac{\partial T}{\partial v} \frac{N \times \partial O/\partial u}{|N|}$$

$$+ \frac{\partial T}{\partial u} \frac{\partial T}{\partial v} \left(\frac{N \times N}{|N|^2} \right)$$

The first term is just the normal to the unperturbed surface and the last term is always zero, so we have

$$N'(u, v) = N + \frac{\partial T}{\partial u} \frac{N \times \partial O/\partial v}{|N|}$$

$$+ \frac{\partial T}{\partial v} \frac{N \times \partial O/\partial u}{|N|}$$

or

$$N' = N + D$$

The process is normally implemented by precalculation in a look-up table. A graphic representation of the process is shown in Figure 10.11 for a function of a single parameter interacting with a one-dimensional bump map. Plate 13 shows two objects produced by the method.

Finally, one of the problems with the technique occurs when objects are scaled. If the object is scaled by a factor of 2, the normal

Figure 10.11
A one-dimensional example of the stages involved in bump mapping (after Blinn (1978b)).

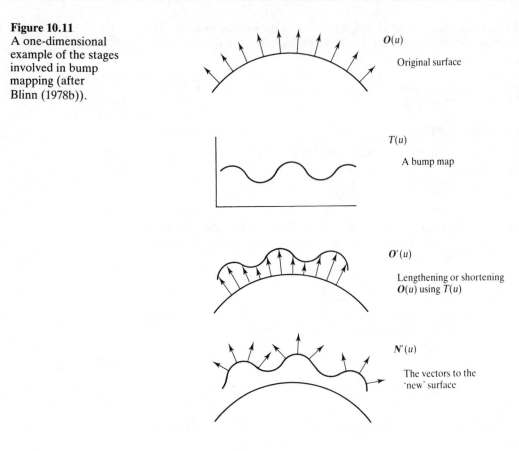

$O(u)$

Original surface

$T(u)$

A bump map

$O'(u)$

Lengthening or shortening $O(u)$ using $T(u)$

$N'(u)$

The vectors to the 'new' surface

vector length is scaled by a factor of 4 and the perturbation amount is only scaled by 2. The effect of this is that as the object is scaled up the wrinkles are flattened out.

10.2.10 Anti-aliasing and texture mapping

Aliasing artefacts are extremely problematic in texture mapping. Artefacts are highly noticeable, particularly in texture that exhibits coherence or periodicity, and originates from point sampling (see Chapter 12 for a more theoretical discussion on general anti-aliasing techniques). For example, unless inverse mapping is accurately performed then neither the shape nor the area of the mapped pixel area in the texture domain is known. Accurate mapping produces, in general, a curvilinear quadrilateral. In extreme cases point sampling without filtering will lead to extreme errors. A large number, perhaps thousands, of texels (an

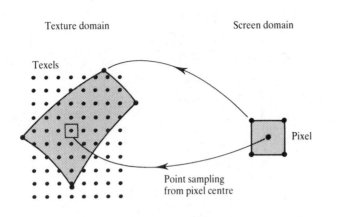

Figure 10.12
The many texels to one
pixel problem in texture
mapping.

Texture domain

Screen domain

Texels

Pixel

Point sampling
from pixel centre

element that is the smallest square area in the texture domain) will map
into a single pixel (Figure 10.12). This case can arise when a number of
texels map onto a surface, but the projection of the surface in screen
space is small, either because of its depth or because of its orientation
with respect to the viewing direction.

A number of points arise from these considerations. Correct
filtering of non-linearly mapped areas requires space-variant filters, that is
filters whose shape and area change as they move across the texture
domain. Because of the prominence of aliasing artefacts that arise from
texture mapping, it is important to address the aliasing problem
'correctly'. Approximate general anti-aliasing solutions, such as supersampling, may not be effective.

10.2.11 Approximations to space-variant filters

There are a number of empirical approaches to the space variant filtering
problem. In the previously mentioned subdivision patch renderer,
Catmull (1974) computes an unweighted average of the texels corresponding to a screen pixel. The shape of the area mapped in the texture
domain is deemed to be a quadrilateral. Blinn and Newell (1976) use a
similar approach involving a pyramid weighting function with the pyramid
distorted to fit the approximating quadrilateral.

Feibush *et al.* (1980) and Gangnet *et al.* (1982) also describe
empirical approaches to space variant filtering.

A method that is claimed to be both economical and accurate is the
elliptical weighted average (EWA) filter proposed by Greene and
Heckbert (1986). The basis of this method is to approximate square pixel
areas in screen space with a circle. The reason for this is that the inverse

Figure 10.13
'Iso-Q' contours in the texture domain. (After Greene.)

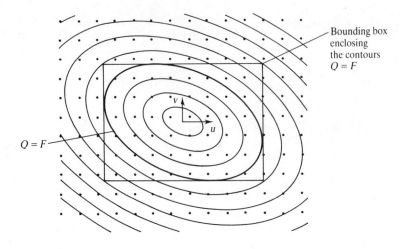

Bounding box enclosing the contours $Q = F$

$Q = F$

mapping of a circle is always an ellipse. Even though the size, eccentricity and orientation of the ellipse change, the shape is invariant and this fact is exploited in the method. The filter function, circularly symmetric in screen space, is warped into an ellipse in texture space, where it is a quadratic function:

$$Q(u, v) = Au^2 + Buv + Cv^2$$

This function is shown in Figure 10.13 as a set of 'iso-Q' contours. The algorithm is as follows:

(1)　The partials ($\partial u/\partial x$, $\partial v/\partial x$) and ($\partial u/\partial y$, $\partial v/\partial y$) are used to compute the parameters of the ellipse that corresponds to the circular pixel. These partials are computed from the texture mapping and generally measure the dynamic rate of change of u and v in texture space with respect to x and y in screen space.

$$A = v_x^2 + v_y^2$$
$$B = -2\,(u_x v_x + u_y v_y)$$
$$C = u_x^2 + u_y^2$$

where u_x and v_y are the above partials.

(2)　The ellipse is then enclosed in a bounding box.

(3)　This space is scanned and Q is efficiently evaluated using finite differences. Points satisfying:

$$Q(u, v) < F \text{ for some threshold } F$$

where $F = (u_x v_y - u_y v_x)^2$, are used to index a look-up table that stores a filter function which may, for example, be a Gaussian or sinc function. Q therefore serves to provide inclusion testing and an index function for the prestored look-up table. This method is claimed to be twice as fast as methods of similar quality.

10.2.12 Prefiltering techniques

The computational cost of the previously discussed filtering techniques is always some function of the area of the inverse mapped pixel in texture space. Using such methods in a context where, for example, large texture areas are mapped into small screen areas is costly. Prefiltering techniques are approaches where cost does not grow in proportion to mapped texture area.

An elegant prefiltering technique that has achieved some popularity is Williams (1983) 'mip-mapping' scheme. Instead of a texture domain comprising a single image, Williams uses many images, all derived by averaging down the original image to successively lower resolutions. Each image in the sequence is at exactly half the resolution of the previous. A possible texture domain layout is shown in Figure 10.14 and is effectively a three-dimensional database with a third parameter, D, used to select the particular image resolution required. Plate 13 (top right) shows a mip-

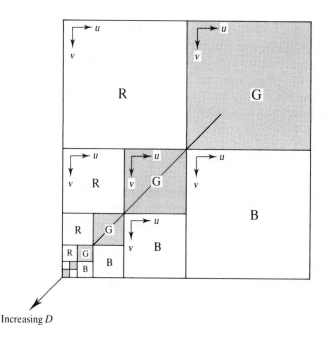

Increasing D

Figure 10.14
Organization of a prefiltered mip-mapped texture domain.

245

Figure 10.15
A representation of filtering errors that occur when a square, rectangle and suitably oriented ellipse are used to approximate a quadrilateral area in the texture domain. (After Heckbert.)

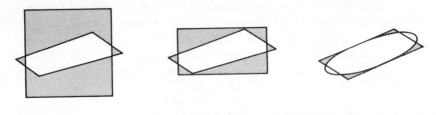

map that was used in conjunction with Catmull's mapping method, described previously, to produce Plate 13 (top left).

The term 'mip' is derived from *multum in parvo* or many things in a small place. In a low resolution version of the image each texel represents the average of a number of texels. By a suitable choice of D, an image at appropriate resolution is selected and the filtering cost remains constant – the many texels to one pixel cost problem being avoided. In this way the original texture is filtered and, to avoid discontinuities between the images at varying resolutions, different levels are also blended. Blending between levels occurs when D is selected. The images are discontinuous in resolution but D is a continuous parameter. Linear interpolation is carried out from the two nearest levels.

Williams selects D from:

$$D = \max_- \text{ of } \left[\left(\left(\frac{\partial u}{\partial x} \right)^2 + \left(\frac{\partial v}{\partial x} \right)^2 \right)^{1/2}, \left(\left(\frac{\partial u}{\partial y} \right)^2 + \left(\frac{\partial v}{\partial y} \right)^2 \right)^{1/2} \right]$$

This method of prefiltering is equivalent to approximating a texture quadrilateral with a square. Figure 10.15, based on an illustration by Heckbert, graphically highlights the approximation implicit in this technique, and compares this method with the more accurate methods described in the previous section. Anti-aliasing is always a compromise.

Another implication of square filtering is that it presupposes that the required compression is symmetric. Since, in this scheme, the addressing is based on the axis of maximum compression, for surfaces that curve away from the viewer fuzziness may result (although Williams claims that in animated sequences where areas collapse into long thin edges the quality of the mapping is not noticeably degraded).

Crow (1984) proposes a generalization of Williams technique that uses a single table from which a virtually continuous range of texture densities can be drawn. It is pointed out by Crow that his method is equivalent to mip-mapping where each texture intensity is replaced by a value representing the sum of the intensities of all texels contained in the rectangle defined by the texel of interest. This table is sampled in four places for any rectangle and a sum of texel intensities found from a sum and two differences taken from the table.

Mip-mapping can also be extended into a three-dimensional domain and used as a filtering method for three-dimensional or solid textures. This approach is, however, somewhat limiting because the power of three-dimensional textures is that they are generally a procedural technique that do not require prefiltered maps to be precalculated and stored prior to mapping.

10.2.13 Anti-aliasing and three-dimensional texture mapping

We have seen that the use of a three-dimensional texture field produces convincing texture and eliminates many of the difficulties associated with two-dimensional mapping methods. An associated advantage, that emerges from the procedural nature of the method, is that points can be calculated at any level of detail. Effectively the texture field can be sampled as finely or as coarsely as required. This compares advantageously with precalculated or fixed two-dimensional maps, which either have to be stored at different levels of detail (mip-mapping) or with which careful anti-aliasing has to be employed. Simple anti-aliasing techniques such as supersampling are easily extended to three-dimensional texture fields and the aliasing problems that occur with two-dimensional texture mapping (that are a function of the mapping itself) are avoided. Anti-aliasing three-dimensional texture fields is discussed in detail in Peachey (1988). Peachey points out that it is often possible with procedurally generated textures to integrate anti-aliasing into the generation method by averaging the texture field over a spherical region of appropriate diameter, rather than point sampling the function.

10.3 Environment mapping

This term refers to the process of reflecting the surrounding environment in a shiny object. It tends to be classified as a texture technique, although it is distinguished from 'normal' texture mapping in that the pattern seen on an object is a function of the view vector V. A particular detail in the environment will move across the object as V changes. Environment mapping can also be considered as a simplification of ray tracing, where only the reflected ray is traced and the process is terminated at a depth of two.

The principle of the technique is shown in Figure 10.16. For a perfect mirror object the view ray V is reflected from the surface of the object, giving a reflected view ray:

$$V_r = V + 2N \cos \theta$$

Figure 10.16
Environment mapping:
using the reflected view
ray V_r to index an
environment map.

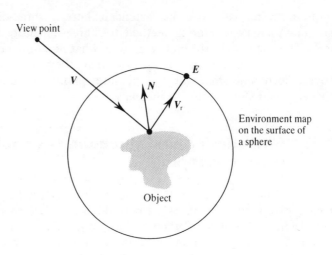

View point

V

N

E

V_r

Environment map
on the surface of
a sphere

Object

where θ is the angle between the surface normal N and V. The intersection of this ray with a surface, such as the interior of a sphere that
contains an image of the environment to be reflected in the object, gives
the shading attributes for the point O on the object surface.

In practice four rays through the pixel point define a reflection
'cone' with a quadrilateral cross-section (Figure 10.17). The region that
subtends the environment map is then filtered to give a single shading
attribute for the pixel.

Environment maps are usually prefiltered and transformed into
two-dimensional images. Here we are effectively reducing a three-

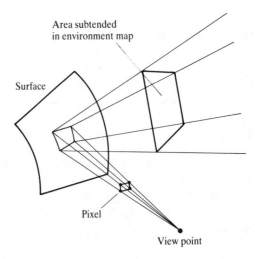

Area subtended
in environment map

Surface

Pixel

View point

Figure 10.17
Reflection 'cone'
subtends a quadrilateral
area in the environment
map.

dimensional problem to a two-dimensional one. This reduction is precomputed and stored as an environment map. The illumination as seen from a point on an object surface is then given by a single indexing operation into the map rather than as a three-dimensional object space calculation – as in ray tracing. Environment mapping can also be seen as a technique that extends the limited illumination possibilities in the n (small integer) point light source Phong shading technique. An environment can be viewed as an infinity of light sources and a map can represent any arbitrary geometry of light sources such as an indoor or outdoor scene. From this point of view geometrically distributed light sources such as strip lights are just rectangles of high intensity white values in the environment map.

The first use of environment mapping was by Blinn and Newell (1976) wherein the sphere interior technique was used and a latitude–longitude map created. The practical difficulty with this approach is in the production of the environment map. Predistorting an environment to fit the interior surface of a sphere is difficult. Another disadvantage of this technique is that it is only geometrically accurate for small objects based on the centre of the sphere. As the object size becomes large with respect to the environment sphere, or the object is positioned a long way from this centre, the geometric distortion increases.

Using the reflected view vector, V_r, it is a simple matter to index into a latitude–longitude environment map. If $E(i, j)$ $(0 \leqslant i \leqslant 1, 0 \leqslant i \leqslant 1)$ is a point on the map and the reflected view vector is:

$$V_r = (V_{rx}, V_{ry}, V_{rz})$$

then

$$i = \frac{1}{2}\left[1 + \frac{1}{\pi}\tan^{-1}(V_{rx}/V_{rz})\right]$$
$$j = 0.5 + 0.5V_{ry}$$

Recent developments in environment mapping (see, for example, Miller and Hoffman (1984) and Greene (1984)) treat the environment as a set of two-dimensional projections. Using the interior of a cube as an environment map is more convenient than using a sphere. It means, for example, that a map can be created from a real environment by photographing or frame grabbing the environment in six directions using a flat field lens with a 90° view field. Alternatively, six views of a simulated environment can be generated by a rendering system. Miller and Hoffman use the cube projection as an intermediate step in creating a single latitude–longitude map. The trade-off between using a latitude–

longitude map and a six-component cube map are concerned with the nature of the shapes that are projected by the reflection cone in each domain. These are fully discussed by Greene.

Greene points out that, although environment mapping is a less versatile technique than ray tracing, it eliminates certain ray tracing problems. It is far less expensive, handles diffuse illumination 'correctly', and can use texture filtering to overcome the ray tracing aliasing artefacts that arise from point sampling. In particular, diffuse and specular surface illumination is found by prefiltering regions of two-dimensional diffuse and specular environment maps. Integration over a two-dimensional environment map projection, rather than over a three-dimensional environment (which is what anti-aliasing operations in ray tracing do), can produce gross errors, but Greene points out that 'the subjective quality of reality cues produced by environment mapping may be superior to those produced by a naive ray tracer'. An obvious disadvantage of environment mapping is that an object will not normally be able to contain reflections of itself, since the object will not appear in the environment map.

The above discussion applies to specular illumination environment maps. Miller and Hoffman have shown how to create a diffuse illumination environment map. The shading attributes obtained for a point on the surface then consist of both a diffuse and a specular component and the diffuse component gives an approximate solution to the global interaction of diffuse light that is not catered for in ray tracing. The specular–diffuse surface attributes or coefficients then select the proportion of the contribution from each map. A perfect diffuse surface would only have a contribution from the diffuse map and a perfect mirror object would only access the specular map:

$$I = k_d D(N) + k_s S(V_r)$$

where D is the contribution from the diffuse map, indexed by the surface normal, and S is the contribution from the specular map, indexed by the reflected view vector.

A diffuse environment map is effectively a highly blurred version of the specular environment map. It is created by convolving an illumination map with a Lambert's law cosine function. Each point on the diffuse map is a weighted sum of all illumination on the surface of a hemisphere centred at that point. The diffuse map is indexed by the surface normal N. A useful attribute of the diffuse map is that it contains no high frequency components and can thus be stored at extremely low resolution.

Projects, notes and suggestions

10.1 Shadows on side or ground planes

Implement Blinn's method of projecting shadows onto a ground plane for planes parallel to the x_w, y_w plane, the x_w, z_w plane and the y_w, z_w plane. Develop the technique to calculate 'perspective' shadows for local light sources. Here we have:

$$S = P - \alpha(P - L)$$

10.2 Shadow Z-buffer

Implement the shadow Z-buffer algorithm described in the text.

10.3 Shadow algorithm investigation

The disadvantages of most shadow algorithms that deal with polygon mesh models is that their geometric coding complexity is high and they can only generate hard-edged shadows. An expensive, but simple, method is to use shadow feelers (see Chapter 7) and to apply them to polygon mesh objects. Experiment with this idea. Note that shadow feeler rays on the interior of polygons can be interpolated from vertex values. Can this method be adapted to model fuzzy shadows, and if so how?

How can intersection testing be optimized if the constraint that shadow feelers either intersect one object or none is made?

What is wrong with the idea of saying that a polygon does not contain a shadow if none of the vertex shadow feelers intersects an object (and conversely that it does have a shadow if any of its vertex shadow feelers do intersect)?

10.4 Texture mapping for bicubic patches

Implement a simple two-dimensional texture mapping technique for bicubic patches using subdivision. Extend the method to include mip-mapping as a filtering technique.

10.5 Two-part texture mapping (*)

Using an appropriate test pattern such as a grid, implement the two part texture mapping scheme described in Chapter 10. Bier and Sloan (1986) state that only five out of the twelve intermediate/O mappings are appropriate. Find these mappings and investigate their properties.

10.6 Solid texture

Implement the three-dimensional or solid texture method and investigate the efficacy of the following methods of solid texture definition:

- Concentric cylinders perturbed in various ways.
- A 'bubble' texture formed by placing spheres of random radii at random locations.
- The three-dimensional noise function (Chapter 11).
- Three-dimensional Fourier synthesis (Chapter 11).
- A distorted colour solid such as the RGB cube that has undergone a linear or non-linear transformation.
- A two-dimensional texture function repeated along one axis. Say, for example, we have a frame-grabbed image $T(u, v)$; we could use this to generate a three-dimensional texture field as follows:

$$O(x_w, y_w, z_w) = T(x_w, y_w)$$

10.7 Texture anti-aliasing

Compare the efficacy of the two texture anti-aliasing methods described in the text; mip-mapping (Wilhems, 1987) and EWA filtering (Greene and Heckbert, 1986).

10.8 Environment mapping (*)

Implement an environment mapping scheme using any predeveloped ray tracing software to trace V rays from each pixel into the environment.

You can build an environment map for a simulated interior by rendering the interior six times from the point of view of the object that is to be mapped, that is six viewing planes on the faces of a cube that surround the object.

How can light sources be incorporated into the environment map?

10.9 Environment mapping and anti-aliasing

Anti-aliasing operations in environment mapping are just as important as they are in texture mapping. If a surface has a high curvature, adjacent pixels in the viewplane can produce reflected view vectors that map into non-adjacent pixels in the environment maps. An obvious solution is to find the area subtended by the rays through each pixel corner (Figure 10.17) and to obtain an average value. Implement this scheme.

A short note on diffuse and specular tables

Miller and Hoffman (1984) generalize environment mapping to include specular and diffuse reflection tables. Tables are precomputed, reducing the mapping process to table look up indexed by the surface normal N and V_r, the reflected view vector. These tables are dependent on the properties of specific objects and this specificity is one of the disadvantages of the method. This work is also reported in Greene and Heckbert (1986).

Miller and Hoffman start with a simulated or photographed environment map on six faces of a cube. This they refer to as an illumination table. It is from this basic map that the diffuse and specular tables are precomputed. These tables are essentially two-dimensional look-up tables. They are indexed by vectors that are converted into a two-dimensional form (for example, by converting into polar coordinates, or into a point on the surface of the enclosing cube).

To create the diffuse table the illumination map is convolved with a Lambert's law cosine function. The diffuse map is given by:

$$D(N) = \sum_L I(L) \; \text{Area}(L) \; f_d(N \cdot L)$$

where, for a particular value of N, L ranges over all possible directions into the illumination table $I(L)$, Area is the angular area subtended by sampling with L and f_d is the diffuse convolution function. Miller and Hoffman give the following examples of this convention for f_d:

- Lambertian reflection: k_d is the diffuse reflection coefficient and

$$f_d(N \cdot L) = \begin{cases} k_d \, (N \cdot L) & \text{for } N \cdot L > 0 \\ 0 & \text{for } N \cdot L \leq 0 \end{cases}$$

- Light sources:

$$f_d(N \cdot L) = k_d \text{ for all } N \cdot L$$

From this it can be seen that the diffuse table is a blurred version of the illumination map that is to be indexed by N, the surface normal, and this scheme reduces finding diffuse illumination to a single table look up. The diffuse table is computed and stored at very low resolution (by definition it contains no high frequency components). Miller and Hoffman quote 36×72 pixels (equivalent to Gouraud-shaded spheres with facets at every $5°$).

The specular table indexed by V_r is given by:

$$S(V_r) = \sum_L I(L) \; \text{Area}(L) \; f_s(V_r \cdot L)$$

where f_s is the specular convolution function, for example

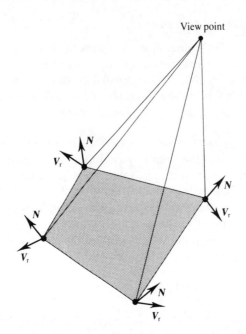

Figure 10.18 Vertex normals and vertex reflected view vectors are calculated for each vertex in the model and then interpolated.

$$f_s(V_r \cdot L) = k_s(V_r \cdot L)^n$$

In this case, by raising $V_r \cdot L$ to a power, there is no weighting given to elements where V_r and L are more than a few degrees apart, giving the effect of near-mirror-like reflections with a small amount of scattering. This is similar to the way the specular term is evaluated in Phong shading.

10.10 Environment mapping – diffuse and specular tables

Compute diffuse and specular tables as outlined above and with a ray tracing scheme use V_r to index the specular table and N to index the diffuse table.

10.11 Environment mapping – polygon mesh objects

Implement the diffuse and specular table approach for polygon mesh objects using a conventional renderer. Do this by calculating a vertex normal (as in Phong shading) and using this normal to calculate a V_r for each vertex (Figure 10.18). During scan conversion both the vertex normals and the V_r are interpolated in the usual way. This gives for each pixel in each polygon an interpolated N and V_r to index the diffuse and specular table respectively.

CHAPTER ELEVEN

Functionally Based Modelling

This chapter looks at the idea of generating objects or structures procedurally. This is an important area in computer graphics, and is the only practical way in which certain scenes can be generated. For example, trees in a forest landscape can only be sensibly generated procedurally. An example of procedural generation that we have already touched on is the definition of a three-dimensional texture field. Precalculation and storage of a texture field would be expensive and the texture is calculated at rendering time from a procedure.

In this chapter we present three general techniques that have found considerable application in three-dimensional computer graphics. These are:

(1)   deterministic or non-stochastic functions (mainly harmonic functions) that have been used in terrain generation,

(2)   stochastic functions that have been used in generating such phenomena as terrain, fire and turbulence, and

(3)   a combination of (1) and (2) that has been used, for example, in water or wave models.

These techniques are used to modulate an attribute of an existing object (as in, for example, the marble texture described in Chapter 10) or the function may itself produce an object as in the particle system now described.

Functional modelling came to be used in computer graphics more or less simultaneously by a number of practitioners all of whom were interested in producing apparently complex images without having to set up that complexity in large polygon mesh based systems. The term database amplification was coined to reflect the fact that highly detailed complex images could be produced from a 'small formula'. The general technique is clearly applicable to simulating natural phenomena, where complexity is mediated by some degree of self-similarity.

11.1 Particle systems

An example of a functional scheme that produces an object description is Reeves' particle modelling system (Reeves, 1983). Here the modelling of the object and the process of rendering merge into a single functional approach. This technique is used to model phenomena that Reeves calls fuzzy objects and includes, for example, fire, cloud and water. Reeves' particle systems are inextricably bound up with animation and, although static objects can be developed using this technique, the process is most impressive when modelling time-varying phenomena, such as fire.

An object is represented by a cloud of elementary particles each of which is born, evolves in space and dies or extinguishes, all at different times. Individual particles move in three-dimensional space and change such attributes as colour, transparency and size as a function of time.

Both the global behaviour of a particle cloud and the detailed behaviour of individual particles are derived from various functions. For example, the number of particles generated at a particular time t can be derived from:

$$N_t = M_t + \text{Random}(r)V_t$$

where M_t is the mean number of particles in the population, $\text{Random}(r)$ is a pseudo-random variable and V_t is the variance of the population.

The same approach can be used to determine values for initial parameters that may describe, for example, the ejection of a particle from a point. The parameters used by Reeves are:

- initial position,
- initial velocity (both speed and direction),
- initial size,
- initial colour,
- initial transparency,
- shape, and
- lifetime.

The movement of individual particles is then scripted using these parameters as a function of time. Reeves used precisely such a system in *Star Trek II* to generate a transformation (of a dead planet into a live planet) by moving a wall of fire across a planet's surface.

11.2 Fractal systems

Fractal geometry is a term coined by Benoit Mandelbrot (Mandelbrot 1977, 1982). The term was used to describe the attributes of certain natural phenomena, for example, coastlines. A coastline viewed at any level of detail – at microscopic level, at a level where individual rocks can be seen or at 'geographical' level – tends to exhibit the same level of jaggedness; a kind of statistical self-similarity. Fractal geometry provides a description for certain aspects of this ubiquitous phenomenon in nature and its tendency towards self-similarity. This is illustrated conceptually in Plate 14, which was generated by a simple recursive routine (Program 11.1) that basically draws *n*-ary trees. Such parameters as branch angle and length are randomly perturbed. (Since this simple program uses lines to simulate three-dimensional primitives we are up against the same problem we had in Chapter 1 with respect to using standard or non-standard two-dimensional line drawing utilities. The non-standard utilities used in the program are *Colour*, *Move_to* and *line_to*.) Plate 14 (top) shows two executions of the same procedure using a binary tree rule. The other two illustrations were produced by introducing more than two branches at each node. It can be seen from these examples that realism could be increased by making the diameter of the branches vary as a function of depth, introducing, say, bending due to wind and utilizing the third spatial dimension. The branching scheme is easily extended into the third dimension by using two angles at a branch – an azimuth and elevation angle. An impressive example of this kind of approach is given in 'The Mighty Maple' (Bloomenthal, 1985), where the tree model is three dimensional and texture mapping is employed to model the bark on the branches.

In three-dimensional computer graphics, fractal techniques have been used to generate terrain models and the easiest techniques involve subdividing the facets of the objects that consist of triangles or quadrilaterals. A recursive subdivision procedure is applied to each facet, to a required depth or level of detail, and a convincing terrain model results. Subdivision in this context means taking the mid-point along the edge between two vertices and perturbing it along a line normal to the edge. The result of this is to subdivide the original facets into a large number of smaller facets, each having a random orientation in three-dimensional space about the original facet orientation. The initial global shape of the object is retained to an extent that depends on the

Program 11.1 Recursive routine for drawing binary trees.

```
procedure tree(x, y: real; angle, branchfan, height: real;
                heightfactor, anglefactor: real;
                branchdensity, depth: integer);
const pi = 3.142;
var i, xint, yint: integer; xinc, yinc, start, theta: real;
begin
  xint := round(x); yint := round(y);
  if depth = 0 then
  begin   { draw a 'leaf' }
    Colour(green);
    Move_to(xint − 2,yint); Line_to(xint + 2, yint);
    Move_to(xint, yint − 4); Line_to(xint, yint + 4)
  end
  else
  begin
    start := angle − branchfan/2;
    theta := branchfan/branchdensity;
    if depth <=2 then heightfactor := heightfactor/2;
    xinc := height*cos(angle/180*pi);
    yinc := height*sin(angle/180*pi);
    angle := start;
    Colour(red);
    Move_to(xint, yint); Line_to(round(x + xinc), round(y + yinc));
    for i := 1 to branchdensity + 1 do
    begin
      tree(x + xinc, y + yinc,
        angle/2 + sign(angle)*random(round(abs(angle)) + 1),
        branchfan*anglefactor,
        height*heightfactor/2 + random(round(height*heightfactor) + 1),
        heightfactor, anglefactor, branchdensity, depth − 1);
      angle := angle + theta
    end
  end
end;
```

perturbation at the subdivision and a planar four-sided pyramid might turn into a 'Mont Blanc' shaped object.

Most subdivision algorithms are based on a formulation by Fournier *et al.* (1982) that recursively subdivides a single line segment. This algorithm was developed as an alternative to more mathematically correct, but expensive, procedures suggested by Mandelbrot. It uses self-similarity and conditional expectation properties of fractional Brownian motion to give an estimate of the increment of the stochastic process. The

Program 11.2 Recursive subdivision of a line.

```
procedure fractal(t1, f1, t2, f2, resolution, roughness: real);

var r, tmid, fmid: real;

begin
  if (sqr(t2 − t1) + sqr(f2 − f1)) < sqr(resolution) then
    begin
      Move_to(round(t1), round(f1));
      Line_to(round(t2), round(f2))
    end
  else
  begin
    r := rand (−1, +1);
    tmid := (t1 + t2)/2 − roughness*(f2 − f1)*r;
    fmid := (f1 + f2)/2 + roughness*(t2 − t1)*r;
    fractal(t1, f1, tmid, fmid, resolution, roughness);
    fractal(tmid, fmid, t2, f2, resolution, roughness)
  end
end;
```

process is also Gaussian and the only parameters needed to describe a Gaussian distribution are the mean (conditional expectation) and the variance.

The procedure shown in Program 11.2 recursively subdivides a line $(t1, f1)$, $(t2, f2)$ generating a scalar displacement of the mid-point of the line in a direction normal to the line (Figure 11.1).

To extend this procedure to, say, triangles or quadrilaterals in three-dimensional space, we treat each edge in turn, generating a

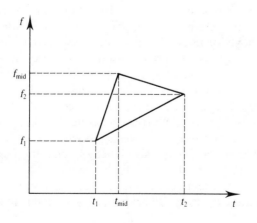

Figure 11.1
Line segment
subdivision.

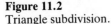

Figure 11.2
Triangle subdivision.

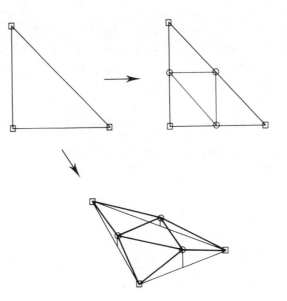

displacement along a mid-point vector that is normal to the plane of the original facet (Figure 11.2). Using this technique we can take a smooth pyramid, say, made of large triangular faces and turn it into a rugged mountain.

Fournier categorizes two problems in this method – internal and external consistency. Internal consistency requires that the shape generated should be the same whatever the orientation in which it is generated, and that coarser details should remain the same if the shape is replotted at greater resolution. To satisfy the first requirement, the Gaussian randoms generated must not be a function of the position of the points, but should be unique to the point itself. An invariant point identifier needs to be associated with each point. This problem can be solved in terrain generation by giving each point a key value used to index a Gaussian random number. A hash function can be used to map the two keys of the end-points of a line to a key value for the mid-point. Scale requirements of internal consistency means that the same random numbers must always be generated in the same order at a given level of subdivision.

External consistency is harder to maintain. Within the mesh of triangles every triangle shares each of its sides with another; thus the same random displacements must be generated for corresponding points of different connecting triangles. This is already solved by using the key value of each point and the hash function, but another problem still exists, that of the direction of the displacement.

If the displacements are along the surface normal of the polygon under consideration, then adjacent polygons which have different normals (as is, by definition, always the case) will have their mid-points displaced into different positions. This causes gaps to open up. A solution is to displace the mid-point along the average of the normals to all the polygons that contain it but this problem occurs at every level of recursion and is consequently very expensive to implement. Also, this technique would create an unsatisfactory skyline because the displacements are not constrained to one direction. A better skyline is obtained by making all the displacements of points internal to the original polygon in a direction normal to the plane of the original polygon. This cheaper technique solves all problems relating to different surface normals, and the gaps created by them. Now surface normals need not be created at each level of recursion and the algorithm is considerably cheaper because of this.

Another two points are worth mentioning. Firstly, note that polygons should be constant shaded without calculating vertex normals – discontinuities between polygons should not be smoothed out. Secondly, consider colour. The usual global colour scheme uses a height-dependent mapping. In detail, the colour assigned to a mid-point is one of its end-point's colours. Which one is chosen is determined by a boolean random which is indexed by the key value of the mid-point. Once again this must be accessed in this way to maintain consistency, which is just as important for colour as it is for position.

11.3 Functions suitable for three-dimensional texture

11.3.1 The three-dimensional *noise* function

The two common bases used in three-dimensional texture synthesis are harmonic functions and random functions. Useful effects such as marble are easily achieved by combining both.

The foundation of stochastically based solid texture, discussed in Chapter 10, is a pseudo-random noise function that is indexed by a three-dimensional point or vector. The nature and design of such a function was proposed by Perlin (1985) who introduced a function called *noise*. Perlin points out that the function was designed to have the following properties:

- statistical invariance under rotation,
- a narrow bandpass limit in frequency (it has no visible features larger or smaller than a certain range), and
- statistical invariance under translation.

noise has a pseudo-random value for points defined with integral *x, y, z* coordinates – the integer lattice. For all other points in the space the value of *noise* is determined by interpolation from the values on the integer lattice. The necessity for this approach can be seen by imagining the result of simply returning a pseudo-random number for every (floating point) three-dimensional vector input to the function. The procedure shown in Program 11.3 is a simple implementation of *noise*.

Program 11.3 A simple implementation of *noise*.

```
procedure initialise_noise;

  var
    x, y, z, xx, yy, zz: nrange;

begin
  {set up the noise lattice}
  for x := 0 to max_noise do
    for y := 0 to max_noise do
      for z := 0 to max_noise do
      begin
        noise_table[x, y, z] := round(random(1)*10000);
        if x = max_noise then xx := 0 else xx := x;
        if y = max_noise then yy := 0 else yy := y;
        if z = max_noise then zz := 0 else zz := z;
        noise_table[x, y, z] := noise_table[xx, yy, zz]
      end;
end   {initialise_noise};

function frac(r: real): real;

begin
  frac := r − trunc(r);
end {frac};

function noise(x, y, z: real): real;

  var
    ix, iy, iz: integer;
    ox, oy, oz: real;
    n: integer;
    n00, n01, n10, n11: real;
    n0, n1: real;
```

```
begin
    {offset x, y, z to ensure they are positive}
    x := x + 15000; y := y + 15000; z := z + 15000;

    {find lattice coordinates and real offsets}
    ix := trunc(x) mod max_noise;
    iy := trunc(y) mod max_noise;
    iz := trunc(z) mod max_noise;
    ox := frac(x); oy := frac(y); oz := frac(z);

    {interpolate to get noise value at (ix + ox, iy + oy, iz + oz)}

    n := noise_table[ix, iy, iz];
    n00 := n + ox*(noise_table[ix + 1, iy, iz] − n);
    n := noise_table[ix, iy, iz + 1];
    n01 := n + ox*(noise_table[ix + 1, iy, iz + 1] − n);
    n := noise_table[ix, iy + 1, iz];
    n10 := n + ox*(noise_table[ix + 1, iy + 1, iz] − n);
    n := noise_table[ix, iy + 1, iz + 1];
    n11 := n + ox*(noise_table[ix + 1, iy + 1, iz + 1] − n);

    n0 := n00 + oy*(n10 − n00);
    n1 := n01 + oy*(n11 − n01);
    noise := (n0 + oz*(n1 − n0))*0.0001;
end    {noise};
```

Perlin uses this *noise* function in a variety of contexts to modulate the colour and perturb the normal of three-dimensional objects. One of the most effective applications of *noise* developed by Perlin is a synthetic turbulence function used to model a solar corona. Plate 9 was generated using this technique as discussed in Chapter 10.

11.3.2 Fourier synthesis

Fourier synthesis can be used as a basis for many natural phenomena including water and terrain. It appears to have been first used in computer graphics to simulate terrain in flight simulators (Schachter 1980, 1983). In this application two-dimensional cosine functions are used simply to modulate the colour of a flat plane in perspective, to provide economical texturing for depth cues.

Gardener (1984, 1985) has used three-dimensional and two-dimensional Fourier synthesis to model clouds, trees and terrain, and points out that the approach is powerful enough to model both 'micro' features – such as leaves on trees and wrinkles on terrain – as well 'macro' features – the clustering of trees and the major topography of hills.

Building a three-dimensional texture field using Fourier synthesis means generating parameters which specify the amplitude, frequency and phase of sinusoids. These are then linearly combined to produce a function in which, by careful choice of the design parameters, the underlying periodicities may be masked or hidden. Gardener uses a three-dimensional function $G(X, Y, Z)$ to model the amorphous shape of trees and clouds, modulating the surface intensity and the transparency of the ellipsoids. The parameter scheme evolved by Gardener (1988) is:

$$G(X, Y, Z) = \sum_{i=1}^{n} C_i[\cos(\omega_{x_i} X + \phi_{x_i}) + A_0]$$

$$\times \sum_{i=1}^{n} C_i[\cos(\omega_{y_i} Y + \phi_{y_i}) + A_0] \qquad \textbf{(11.1)}$$

$$\times \sum_{i=1}^{n} C_i[\cos(\omega_{z_i} Z + \phi_{z_i}) + A_0]$$

where n is a value between 4 and 7, and $C_{i+1} \approx 0.707 C_i$. C_1 is chosen such that $G(X, Y, Z) \leqslant 1$. The initial values of ω specify the underlying or base frequencies such as the rolling of hills in a terrain.

ϕ_{x_i}, ϕ_{y_i} and ϕ_{z_i} are phase shifts into which a random component can be built. A_0 is the basic offset providing contrast control.

A complete study of the way in which these parameters are varied to provide convincing natural texture is to be found in Gardener (1988).

Projects, notes and suggestions

11.1 Trees

Extend Program 11.1 so that it produces a tree in three-dimensional space, as suggested in the text.

11.2 Fractal terrains

Develop the recursive subdivision procedure (Program 11.2) so that it generates a terrain in three-dimensional space using the technique suggested in the text.

11.3 Spectral terrains

Use a two-dimensional version of Equation 11.1 to generate a terrain. Do this by using $G(X, Y)$ to specify elevation values at each point on a regular grid. This then defines a polygon mesh structure that can be rendered by a conventional renderer. Note how simple and effective control is available over the ruggedness of the terrain by controlling spatial frequency and amplitude parameters. Can this approach, which is far simpler than subdivision, produce the same visual effects as the fractal technique?

11.4 Animated spectral terrain

Produce an animated film, where a coherent perturbation of a suitable shape, that is (say) parallel to one of the coordinate axes moves through the terrain. Various possibilities exist; for example, the size of the perturbation can increase or decrease as it travels, or a central perturbation could move outwards.

11.5 Simple wave models

Using the 'perturbed grid' of the previous two projects use a single travelling sinusoid, around a single disturbance, to simulate an object being dropped in water. Modulate the amplitude as a function of time such that the ripples die as they spread. A more elaborate wave model is to be found in Fournier (1986).

11.6 Three-dimensional modulation of surfaces

Use Equation 11.1 to modulate the surface of any convenient model; for example, displace the vertices of an approximately spherical object an amount specified by Equation 11.1 along a line from the centre of the object to the vertex (note that the easiest way to implement this method is to use a full Z-buffer renderer).

11.7 Landscapes (*)

Integrate all the above techniques into a landscape generation system using a full Z-buffer to solve the compositing problems.

Gardener in (1984) gives details on models for the placement and distribution of, for example, trees in a complex landscape.

11.8 Particle systems

Design a particle system that will generate a system to model fireworks. This is best demonstrated using an animated sequence. Variables include different shaped explosions, different ejection angles, different trajectories and the colour of the particle changing as a function of time.

CHAPTER TWELVE

Anti-aliasing Techniques

This chapter is a general approach to aliasing in computer graphics and gives an informal theoretical background to the problem. Context-dependent techniques for ray tracing and texture mapping are presented in Chapters 7 and 10. Texture mapping, for example, requires a specialized anti-aliasing approach and, with most texture methods, space variant filtering techniques are required. Temporal anti-aliasing is discussed in Chapter 7 (distributed ray tracing) and Chapter 13 (animation).

The fundamental cause of aliasing in computer graphics is the creation of images by a regular sampling process in the space (and in the case of animation the time) domain. The sampling process is a result of the nature of the display device, which in raster graphics is a finite array of pixels of a certain size. The final stage in the generation of an image is the calculation of intensities for each pixel. This always involves mapping an intensity, $I(x, y)$ in a continuous two-dimensional image space (that is a projection from continuous three-dimensional image space) to a pixel in discrete image display space. This mapping, usually produced by an incremental shading algorithm (where a new intensity $I + \delta I$ is calculated for a new position $X + \delta X$) is equivalent to sampling continuous two-dimensional image space with an array of discrete sample points based, say, at the centre of each pixel. This view, of image synthesis as a sampling process, is important in anti-aliasing because it enables us to use signal processing theory as a theoretical base. However, it is important to bear in mind that, unlike for example, image processing, we cannot view computer graphics practically as consisting of two separate phases where a continuous image is generated then sampled. In computer graphics image generation and sampling is a single process.

Figure 12.1
Common aliasing
artefacts.

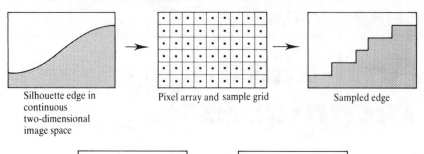

Silhouette edge in
continuous
two-dimensional
image space

Pixel array and sample grid

Sampled edge

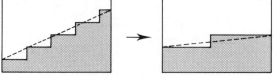

Jagged edge patterns change depending on line orientation

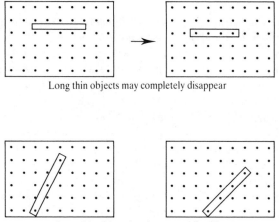

Long thin objects may completely disappear

Long thin objects break up unpredictably

The most familiar manifestation of aliasing is jagged silhouette edges (Figure 12.1). A silhouette edge is the boundary of a polygon, or any surface unit, that exhibits a high contrast over its background. (In general, contrast means light and dark areas of the same colour. Aliasing is not as noticeable when the silhouette edge and the background have the same luminance but different colours – the eye is more sensitive to luminance contrasts than colour contrasts.)

Another aliasing artefact occurs when small objects, whose spatial extent is less than the area of a pixel, are rendered or not depending on whether they are intersected by a sample point. A long thin object may break up depending on its orientation with respect to the sample array (Figure 12.1).

These artefacts can be particularly troublesome in animated sequences. Jagged edges 'crawl' and small objects may appear and disappear ('scintillate'). Such changes are intolerable in flight simulators, for example, where the point of the animated sequence is to instruct the pilot to react to subtle changes in the image.

A particularly degenerate manifestation of aliasing occurs when texture is used on surfaces subject to a perspective transformation. The texture in the distance breaks up and produces highly noticeable low frequency aliases and moiré interference patterns. Again this has to be eliminated from flight simulators where texture patterns are used as a cheap method of enhancing reality and imparting depth cues.

12.1   Aliasing artefacts and Fourier theory

Anti-aliasing methods are easy to understand algorithmically and the simplest solution is easy to implement. Their theoretical base, which is best dealt with in the Fourier domain, is more difficult. This section assumes a rudimentary appreciation of Fourier theory but it can easily be skipped. The standard methods used in anti-aliasing can be treated informally – the mechanics of the algorithms impart a reasonable appreciation of the process.

An important theorem – the sampling theorem – relates the resolution of the sampling grid to the nature of the image, or more specifically to the spatial frequencies in the image. (See Oppenheim and Shafer (1975) for a detailed treatment of digital signal processing.) It is intuitively obvious that the busier, or more detailed, the image is, the finer the sampling grid has to be to capture this detail. The sampling theorem is best treated for functions of a single variable and is as follows:

> A continuous function of a single variable can be completely represented by a set of samples made at equally spaced intervals. The intervals between such samples must be at less than half the period of the highest frequency component in the function.

For example, if we consider a single sinusoidal function of x, it is easily seen that if the relationship between the sampling frequency and the function is as shown in Figure 12.2(a) then no information is lost. The

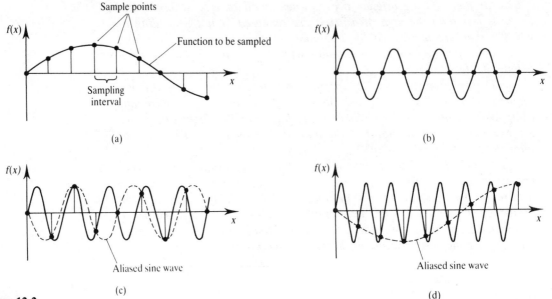

Figure 12.2
Space domain
representation of the
sampling of a sine wave:
(a) sampling interval is
less than one-half the
period of the sine wave;
(b) sampling interval is
equal to one-half the
period of the sine wave;
(c) sampling interval is
greater than one-half the
period of the sine wave;
(d) sampling interval is
much greater than one-
half the period of the sine
wave.

sampling frequency in this case is greater than twice the frequency of the sinusoid. If the sampling frequency is equal to twice the sine wave frequency (Figure 12.2(b)) then the samples can coincide with the sine wave zero crossings as shown, and no information can be recovered from the samples concerning the sine wave. When the sampling frequency is less than twice that of the sine wave (Figures 12.2(c) and 12.2(d)) then the information contained in the samples implies sine waves (shown by the dotted lines) at lower frequencies than the function being sampled. These lower frequencies are known as aliases and this explains the derivation of the term.

The situation can be generalized by considering these cases in the frequency domain for an $f(x)$ containing information that is not a pure sine wave. We now have an $f(x)$ that is any general variation in x and may, for example, represent the continuous variation in intensity along a segment of a scan line. The frequency spectrum of $f(x)$ will exhibit some 'envelope' (Figure 12.3(a)) whose limit is the highest frequency component in $f(x)$; say, f_{max}. The frequency spectrum of a sampling function (Figure 12.3(b)) is a series of lines, theoretically extending to infinity, separated by the interval f_s (the sampling frequency). Sampling in the space domain involves multiplying $f(x)$ by the sampling function. The equivalent process in the frequency domain is convolution and the frequency spectrum of the sampling function is convolved with that of $f(x)$ to produce the frequency spectrum shown in Figure 12.3(c) – the spectrum of the sampled version of $f(x)$. This sampled function is then

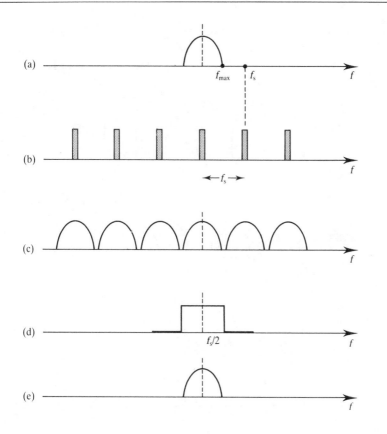

Figure 12.3
Frequency domain
representation of the
sampling process when
$f_s > 2f_{max}$: (a) frequency
spectrum of $f(x)$;
(b) frequency spectrum
of the sampling function;
(c) frequency spectrum of
the sampled function
(convolution of (a) and
(b)); (d) ideal
reconstruction filter;
(e) reconstructed $f(x)$.

multiplied by a reconstructing filter to reproduce or display the original function. A good example of this process, in the time domain, is a modern telephone network. In its simplest form this involves sampling a speech waveform, encoding and transmitting digital versions of each sample over a communications channel, then reconstructing the original signal from the decoded samples by using a reconstructing filter.

The equivalent process considered in the space domain is multiplication of the original function with the sampled function, followed by convolution of the sampled version of the function with a reconstructing filter.

Now in the above example the condition:

$$f_s > 2f_{max}$$

is true. In the second example (Figure 12.4) we show the same two processes of convolution and multiplication but this time we have:

$$f_s < 2f_{max}$$

Figure 12.4
Frequency domain
representation of the
sampling process when
$f_s < 2f_{max}$: (a) frequency
spectrum of $f(x)$;
(b) frequency spectrum
of the sampling function;
(c) frequency spectrum of
the sampled function;
(d) ideal reconstructing
filter; (e) distorted $f(x)$.

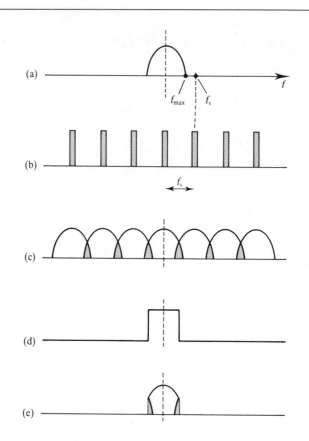

Incidentally, $f_s/2$ is known as the Nyquist limit. Here the envelopes representing the information in $f(x)$, overlap. It is as if the spectrum has 'folded' over a line defined by the Nyquist limit. This folding is an information destroying process; high frequencies (detail in images) are lost and appear as interference (aliases) in low frequency regions.

In a situation where the sampling frequency is fixed (this is mostly the case, for example, in applications where $f(x)$ is a function of time) aliasing can be prevented by an anti-aliasing filter. The function being sampled is filtered, prior to sampling, by a low pass filter whose cut-off frequency corresponds to the Nyquist limit. That is, all components in $f(x)$ whose frequency is greater than $f_s/2$ are eliminated.

How does this theory relate to computer graphics? In computer graphics terms, $f(x)$ is a segment along a scan line. The sampling function has a frequency of 1 cycle per pixel (that is, we sample the information at the centre of each pixel). If we then convert these samples for display, by passing each pixel value through a D/A converter, this is equivalent to using a box-shaped reconstruction filter.

Another point we have to consider is that we now have images which are functions of two spatial variables and a two-dimensional sampling grid. The sampling theorem extends to two-dimensional frequencies or spatial frequencies. The two-dimensional frequency spectrum of a graphics image in the continuous generation domain is theoretically infinite. Sampling and reconstructing in computer graphics is the process of calculation of a value at the centre of a pixel and then assigning that value to the entire spatial extent of that pixel.

Aliasing artefacts in computer graphics can be reduced by increasing the frequency of the sampling grid (that is, increasing the spatial resolution of the pixel array). There are two drawbacks to this approach: the obvious one that there is both an economic and a technical limit to increasing the spatial resolution of the display (not to mention the computational limits on the cost of the image generation process) and, since the frequency spectrum of computer graphics images can extend to infinity, increasing the sampling frequency does not necessarily solve the problem. If, for example, we applied the increased resolution approach to coherent texture in perspective, we would simply shift the aliasing effects up the spatial frequency spectrum.

There are two major established methods for removing/reducing aliasing artefacts in computer graphics. The most popular approach is loosely known as supersampling or postfiltering. The second, less common, method is to approximate a two-dimensional anti-aliasing filter and to perform the equivalent operation to removing spatial frequencies above the Nyquist limit. This is sometimes confusingly called prefiltering. A computer graphics image cannot be prefiltered because it does not exist until it is sampled. The term prefiltering is used to signify that the algorithm is equivalent in effect, but not in implementation, to an anti-aliasing prefilter. A third method, recently developed, is known as stochastic sampling. These three methods are now described.

12.2 Supersampling or postfiltering

This method is theoretically a three-stage process with the second and third stages in practice combined. The stages are:

(1) The continuous image generation domain is sampled at n times the display resolution. In practice this means the image is generated using an image synthesis technique at n times the display resolution.

(2) This sampled image is then low pass filtered at the Nyquist limit of the display device, and,

(3) The filtered image is re-sampled at the device resolution.

This method works well with most computer graphics images and is easily

Table 12.1 Bartlett windows used in postfiltering a supersampled image.

3 × 3			5 × 5					7 × 7						
1	2	1	1	2	3	2	1	1	2	3	4	3	2	1
2	4	2	2	4	6	4	2	2	4	6	8	6	4	2
1	2	1	3	6	9	6	3	3	6	9	12	9	6	3
			2	4	6	4	2	4	8	12	16	12	8	4
			1	2	3	2	1	3	6	9	12	9	6	3
								2	4	6	8	6	4	2
								1	2	3	4	3	2	1

integrated into a Z-buffer algorithm. It does not work with images whose spectrum energy does not fall off with increasing frequency. (As we have already mentioned, supersampling is not, in general, a theoretically correct method of anti-aliasing.) Texture rendered in perspective is the common example of an image that does not exhibit a falling spectrum with increasing spatial frequency.

Supersampling methods differ trivially in the value of n and the shape of the filter used. For, say, a medium resolution image of 512×512 it is usually considered adequate to supersample at 2048×2048 ($n = 4$). The high resolution image can be reduced to the final 512×512 form by averaging and this is equivalent to convolving with a box filter. Better results can be obtained using a shaped filter, a filter whose values vary over the extent of its kernel. There is a considerable body of knowledge on the optimum shape of filters with respect to the nature of the information that they operate on (see, for example, Oppenheim and Shafer (1975)). Most of this work is in digital signal processing and has been carried out with functions of a single variable $f(t)$. Computer graphics has unique problems that are not addressed by conventional digital signal processing techniques. For example, space-variant filters are required in texture mapping. Here both the weights of the filter kernel and its shape have to change.

To return to supersampling and shaped filters; Crow (1981) used a Bartlett window, three of which are shown in Table 12.1, to reconstruct display resolution samples from a supersampled image. Digital convolution is easy to understand and implement but is computationally expensive. A window is centred on a supersample and a weighted sum of products is obtained by multiplying each supersample by the corresponding weight in the filter. The weights can be adjusted to implement different filter kernels. Ignoring edge effects, the digital convolution proceeds by moving the window through n supersamples and computing the next weighted sum of products. Using a 3×3 window means that nine supersamples are involved in the final pixel computation. However, using the 7×7 window means a computation of 49 integer multiplications. The implication of the computation overheads is obvious. For example, reducing a 2048×2048 supersampled image to 512×512, with a 7×7

filter kernel, requires $512 \times 512 \times 49$ multiplications and additions. Each group of images in Plate 15 consists of an original and two enlargements. The middle and right-hand group are anti-aliased using 3×3 and 5×5 reconstructing filters.

An inevitable side effect of filtering is blurring. This occurs because information is integrated from a number of neighbouring pixels. This means that the choice of the spatial extent of the filter is a compromise. A wide filter has a lower cut-off frequency and will be better at reducing aliasing artefacts. It will, however, blur the image more than a narrower filter which will exhibit a higher cut-off frequency and be more expensive to implement.

Finally, the disadvantages of the technique should be noted. Supersampling is not a suitable method for dealing with very small objects. Also, it is a 'global' method – the computation is not context dependent. A scene that exhibited a few large area polygons would be subject to the same computational overheads as one with a large number of small area polygons (see, for example, Chapter 7 for a description of a method where the anti-aliasing 'effort' is a function of the spatial complexity of the image). The memory requirements are large if the method is to be used with a Z-buffer. The supersampled version of the image has to be created and stored before the filtering process can be applied. This increases the storage requirements of the Z-buffer by a factor of n^2, making it essentially a virtual memory technique.

12.3 Prefiltering or area sampling techniques

The originator of this technique was Catmull (1978). Although Catmull's original algorithm is prohibitively expensive, it has spawned a number of more practical successors.

The algorithm essentially performs subpixel geometry in the continuous image generation domain and returns for each pixel an intensity which is computed by using the areas of visible subpixel fragments as weights in an intensity sum (Figure 12.5). This is equivalent to convolving the image with a box filter and using the value of the convolution integral at a single point as the final pixel value. (Note that the width of the filter is less than ideal and a wider filter using information from neighbouring regions would give a lower cut-off frequency.) Another way of looking at the method is to say that it is an area sampling method. All the area of subpixel fragments is taken into account (as opposed to simply increasing the spatial resolution of the sampling grid).

Catmull's method is incorporated in a scan line renderer. It proceeds by dividing the continuous image generation domain into square pixel extents. An intensity for each square is computed by clipping polygons against the square pixel boundary. If polygon fragments overlap within a square they are sorted in z and clipped against each other to produce visible fragments. A final intensity is computed by multiplying

Figure 12.5
Polygons are clipped
against pixel edges and
each other to yield a set
of visible fragments.

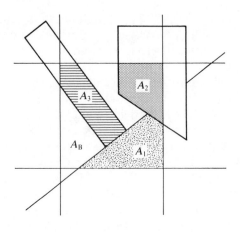

Intensity = $I_1A_1 + I_2A_2 + I_3A_3 + I_BA_B$

the shade of a polygon by the area of its visible fragment and summing.

The origin of the severe computational overheads inherent in this method is obvious. The original method was so expensive that it was only used in two-dimensional animation applications involving a few largish polygons. Here most pixels are completely covered by a polygon and the recursive clipping process of polygon fragment against polygon fragment is not entered.

Recent developments have involved approximating the subpixel fragments with bit masks (Carpenter, 1984; Fiume and Fournier, 1983). Carpenter (1984) uses this approach with a Z-buffer to produce a technique known as the A-buffer (anti-aliased, area averaged, accumulator buffer). The significant advantage of this approach is that floating point geometry calculations are avoided. Coverage and area weighting is accomplished by using bitwise logical operators between the bit patterns or masks representing polygon fragments. It is an efficient area sampling technique, where the processing per pixel square will depend on the number of visible fragments.

Another efficient approach to area sampling, due to Abram and Westover (1983), precomputes contributions to the convolution integral and stores these in look-up tables indexed by the polygon fragments. The method is based on the fact that the way in which a polygon covers a pixel can be approximated by a limited number of cases. The algorithm is embedded in a scan line renderer. The convolution is not restricted to one pixel extent but more correctly extends over, say, a 3×3 area. Pixels act as accumulators whose final value is correct when all fragments that can influence its value have been taken into account.

Consider a 3×3 pixel area and a 3×3 filter kernel (Figure 12.6) A single visible fragment in the centre pixel will contribute to the

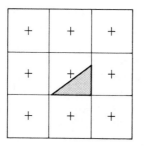

Figure 12.6
A single fragment in the centre pixel will cause contributions to filtering on each of the nine squares.

convolution integral when the filter is centred on each of the nine squares. The nine contributions that such a fragment makes can be precomputed and stored in a look-up table. The two main stages in the process are:

(1)   Find the visible fragments and identify or categorize their shape.

(2)   Index a precomputed look-up table which gives the nine contributions for each shape. A single multiplication of the fragment's intensity by the precomputed contribution weighting gives the desired result.

Abram assumes that the shapes fall into one of seven categories:

- There is no fragment in the pixel.
- The fragment completely covers the pixel.
- The fragment is trapezoidal and splits the pixel along opposite edges.
- The fragment is triangular and splits the pixel along adjacent edges.
- The complement of the previous category (a pentagonal fragment).
- The fragment is an odd shape that can be described by the difference of two or more of the previous types.
- The fragment cannot be easily defined by these simple types.

12.4   A mathematical comparison

We can generalize and compare the above two methods from a more rigorous viewpoint. The filtering or convolution operation can be defined as:

$$s(i, j) = \iint I(i + x, j + y) \, F(x, y) \, \mathrm{d}x \, \mathrm{d}y \qquad \textbf{(12.1)}$$

277

where $s(i, j)$ is a single sample from a continuous two-dimensional image I, and $F(x, y)$ is a filter kernel. The integration is performed by placing the filter kernel at (i, j) and integrating over the extent of the filter. This equation is evaluated for all (i, j).

First consider supersampling. This method is used with point sampling algorithms such as the Z-buffer or ray tracing. I has already been reduced to samples or supersamples and the above integral can only be approximated. We do not have available a continuous image I to sample and this approximation to the continuous integral expresses the deficiency of the technique mathematically. We can increase the 'integrity' of the approximation by increasing the number of super-samples, but this has serious consequences for the rendering costs.

The second method, sub-pixel geometry, in contrast, solves Equation 12.1 directly but uses a poor filter kernel F. The renderer 'retains' a continuous image I by performing subpixel geometry. This I is convolved with F to produce the required samples but F is only a single pixel wide, and consequently its frequency cut-off is high and its ability to deal with high frequency artefacts is less than that of a filter with a wider kernel.

To sum up we have: in the first method I has already been sampled and we attempt to diminish this by increasing the number of the samples; in the second method I is continuous but the algorithmic constraints of the method restrict F to an area of one pixel.

12.5 Stochastic sampling

This method is used by Cook (Cook *et al.*, 1984; Cook, 1986) both to solve the aliasing problem and to model fuzzy phenomena in distributed ray tracing. The method has also been investigated in Abrams and Westover (1985) and Dippe and Wold (1985). Its relevance to ray tracing is discussed in Chapter 7.

A reference to the receptor organization in the human eye is given in Cook (1986). Cook points out that the human eye contains an array of non-uniformly distributed photoreceptors, and that this is the reason that the eye does not produce its own aliasing artefacts. Photoreceptor cells in the fovea are tightly packed and the lens acts as an anti-aliasing filter. However, in the region outside the fovea, the spatial density of the cells is much lower and in this region the cells are non-uniformly distributed. A detailed description of these factors is given by Williams and Collier (1983).

The basis of the method is to perturb the position of the sampling points. High frequency information above the Nyquist limit is then mapped into noise. Aliasing artefacts are traded for noise. The distribution from which the perturbations are selected determines the spectral character of the noise, and the frequency of the information

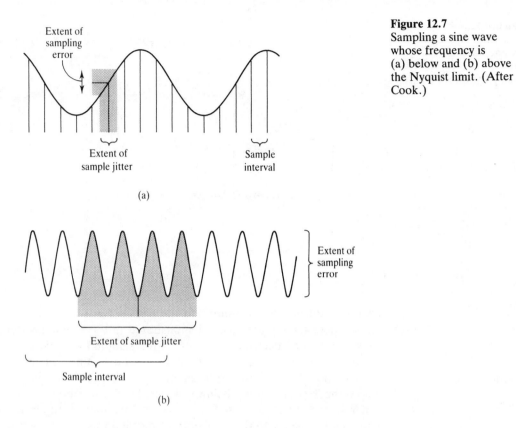

Extent of
sampling
error

Extent of
sample jitter

Sample
interval

(a)

Extent of
sampling
error

Extent of sample jitter

Sample interval

(b)

Figure 12.7
Sampling a sine wave
whose frequency is
(a) below and (b) above
the Nyquist limit. (After
Cook.)

being sampled (relative to the sampling frequency) determines the energy
of the noise. The method can be seen as a two-stage process:

(1)   Sample the image using a sampling grid where the (x, y) position of
each sampling point has been subjected to a random perturbation.

(2)   Use these sample values with a reconstruction filter to determine
the pixel intensities to which the unperturbed sample positions
correspond.

The basis of the method is demonstrated in Figure 12.7 which is based on
Cook's illustration in Cook (1986). In Figure 12.7(a) a sine wave with a
frequency below the Nyquist limit is sampled. Jittering or perturbing the
samples over the region shown introduces a corresponding error in the
sample amplitude. The information is thus sampled and a level of noise is
introduced into the spectrum of the samples. In Figure 12.7(b) a sine
wave with a frequency above the Nyquist limit is sampled. Here the
perturbation results in an almost random value for the amplitude. Thus,
where uniform sampling would produce an alias for this sine wave, we

279

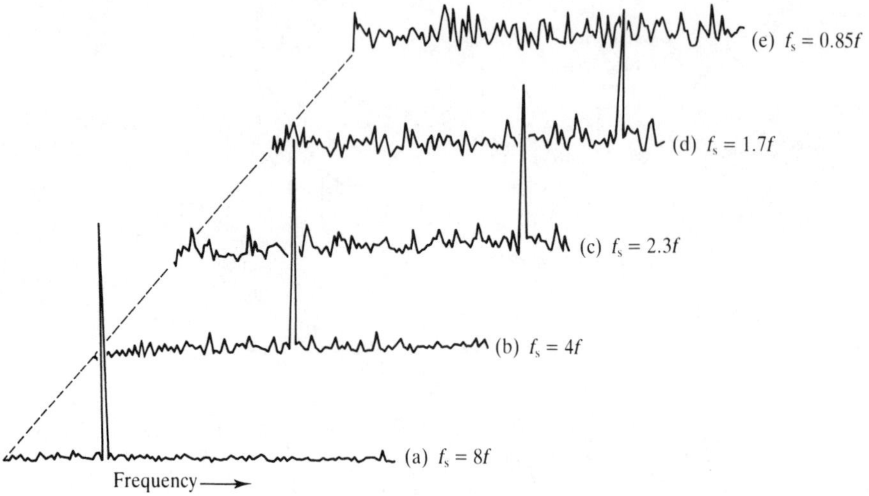

Figure 12.8
Varying the frequency of
a sine wave (f) with
respect to a perturbed
sampling frequency (f_s).

(e) $f_s = 0.85f$

(d) $f_s = 1.7f$

(c) $f_s = 2.3f$

(b) $f_s = 4f$

(a) $f_s = 8f$

Frequency ⟶

have introduced instead noise and the alias is traded off against noise.

These factors are easily demonstrated in the frequency domain by considering the spectrum of a sine wave sampled by this method and again varying the frequency about the Nyquist limit. Figures 12.8(a), 12.8(b) and 12.8(c) show the frequency spectrum of single sine waves (all below the Nyquist limit) being sampled by this method. Note that, in general, the noise amplitude will be a function of the ratio of the sampling frequency to the frequency of the sine wave being sampled. The further the frequency is below the Nyquist limit, the lower will be the amplitude of the noise added to the sample. Figure 12.8(d) shows the spectrum for a sine wave with frequency above the Nyquist limit. The original information is now lost and an aliased frequency appears but is attenuated. The attenuation is dependent on how far the sine wave is above the Nyquist limit. Figure 12.8(e) shows no perceptible spike but the noise amplitude is increased. The perturbation can range in x over a minimum of half a cycle (where the sine wave frequency is at the Nyquist limit) and will in general range over a number of complete cycles. If the range encompasses an exact number of cycles then, for white noise jitter, the probability of sampling each part of the sine wave tends to be equal and the energy in the samples appears as white noise. A mathematical treatment of the attenuation due to white noise jitter and Gaussian jitter is given in Balakrishnan (1962).

One of the problems of this method is that it is only easily incorporated into methods where the image synthesis uses an incoherent sampling method. This is certainly the case in ray tracing, where rays are spawned in the continuous object space domain, and are in effect samples in this space. They can easily be jittered. In 'standard' image synthesis

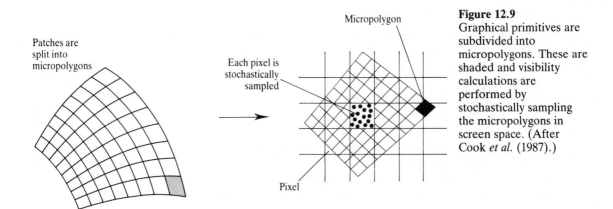

Patches are
split into
micropolygons

Each pixel is
stochastically
sampled

Micropolygon

Pixel

Figure 12.9
Graphical primitives are
subdivided into
micropolygons. These are
shaded and visibility
calculations are
performed by
stochastically sampling
the micropolygons in
screen space. (After
Cook *et al.* (1987).)

methods, using say interpolative shading in the context of a Z-buffer or
scan line algorithm, introducing jitter presents much more of a difficulty.
The algorithms are founded on uniform incremental methods in screen
space and would require substantial modification to have the effect of
two-dimensional sampling perturbation. Although such algorithms are
equivalent to image generation in a continuous domain succeeded by two-
dimensional sampling, in practice the sampling and generation phases are
not easily unmeshed.

A major rendering system, called REYES (Cook *et al.*, 1987) does,
however, integrate a Z-buffer based method with stochastic sampling.
This works by dividing initial primitives, such as bicubic parametric
patches, into (flat) 'micropolygons' (of approximate dimension in screen
space of half a pixel). All shading and visibility calculations operate on
micropolygons. Shading occurs prior to visibility calculations and is
constant over a micropolygon. The micropolygons are then stochastically
sampled from screen space, the Z value of each sample point is calculated
by interpolation and the visible sample hits are filtered to produce pixel
intensities (Figure 12.9). Thus shading is carried out at micropolygon
level and visibility calculations at the stochastic sampling level.

This method ignores the coherence approach of 'classical' rendering methods, by splitting objects into micropolygons. It is most suitable
for objects consisting of bicubic parametric patches because they can be
easily subdivided.

Projects, notes and suggestions

Some of the projects for this chapter include the use of Fourier theory. This is
extremely useful in gaining an understanding of the basis of aliasing and the efficacy
of the various cures. We include a short note on Fourier transforms at this point.

A short note on Fourier transforms

The discrete Fourier transform (DFT) is an approximation to the continuous Fourier integral:

$$F(\omega) = \int_{-\infty}^{\infty} x(t) \exp(-j2\pi\omega t) \, dt$$

The discrete transform is used when a set of sample function values, $x(i)$, are available at equally spaced intervals $i = 0, 1, 2, ..., N-1$. The DFT converts the given values into the sum of a discrete number of sine waves whose frequencies are numbered $u = 0, 1, 2, ..., N-1$, and whose amplitudes are given by:

$$F(u) = \frac{1}{N} \sum_{i=0}^{N-1} x(i) \exp\left(-j2\pi u \, \frac{i}{N}\right)$$

This expression can be implemented directly as a slow DFT. (More usually a fast Fourier transform (FFT) would be used to compute a DFT.) The above DFT can be expressed as:

$$F(u) = \frac{1}{N} \sum_{i=0}^{N-1} x(i) \cos\left(2\pi u \, \frac{i}{N}\right) - \frac{j}{N} \sum_{i=0}^{N-1} x(i) \sin\left(2\pi u \, \frac{i}{N}\right)$$

and this form is easily implemented in a program. This will give a cosine and a sine transform respectively for the complex-valued function $F(u)$. The amplitude spectrum is what is required for the projects and this is given by the sum of the squares of the cosine and the sine transform.

12.1 Supersampling

Examine the efficacy of supersampling using a magnified test image (see, for example, Plate 15). Experiment with the degree of supersampling and with box and shaped filters of various widths.

12.2 Texture artefacts

Produce a 'problematic' texture, say a checkerboard pattern in perspective coming to a point at the top of the screen. Select a number of scan lines for increasing values of y_s and produce a Fourier transform of the intensity variation along a scan line. Correlate the information in the frequency spectra with the Nyquist limit of the device and the onset of aliasing artefacts on the screen.

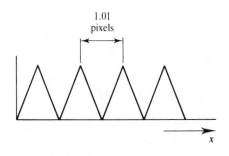

1.01
pixels

x

Figure 12.10   A one-dimensional test pattern to be used in Project 12.3.

12.3   Fourier domain and filtering

Generate a description of an 'impossible' one-dimensional test pattern, such as a set of triangles slightly wider than 1 pixel (Figure 12.10). Produce the following plots.

- Space domain

  (1a)   the original function $f(x)$;
  (2a)   the sampled function (that is, the values of $f(x)$ at pixel centres);
  (3a)   the sampled function convolved with a box filter one pixel wide.

Note that (3a) is an approximation to the output that will appear on the screen. There is a final degradation process that rounds the edges in (3a) owing to the defocusing or smearing effect of the electron beam in the CRT.

- Frequency domain

  (1b)   an amplitude spectrum of $f(x)$;
  (2b)   an amplitude spectrum of the sampled version of $f(x)$;
  (3b)   an amplitude spectrum of the filter;
  (4b)   the product of (2b) and (3b), which is the amplitude spectrum of the sampled signal after filtering.

Note the difference between (4b) and (1b). Relate this difference to the appearance of aliasing artefacts in (2a) and (3a).

Repeat the above procedure using a test pattern where the width of the triangles is now increased to 10 pixels and compare the results.

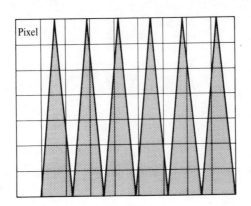

Figure 12.11 A two-dimensional test pattern to be used in Project 12.4.

12.4 Stochastic sampling

This project is based on work reported in Cook (1986). Use the triangles in the previous project as a two-dimensional test pattern (Figure 12.11) of bright triangles on a dark background over a spatial extent of, say, 100×100 pixels. Sample this pattern using one sample per pixel and a 3×3 filter kernel to reconstruct a rendered pattern on the screen.

Repeat this process but this time jitter the samples in x and y. Compare the results. Finally, increase the sampling rate and produce two further images using 16 uniform samples per pixel and 16 jittered samples per pixel.

CHAPTER THIRTEEN

Three-dimensional Animation

It is a curious fact that, at the moment, almost all three-dimensional computer animation is produced for the entertainment or advertising industry. Flight and military simulators are major exceptions to this, but apart from some efforts in animating scientific phenomena, most productions end up on the TV screen. This situation is beginning to change with the emphasis on scientific applications (see the discussion of ViSC below).

This is all the more curious when the artistic constraints of three-dimensional animation are considered. Compared with traditional animation, the computer animator has far fewer artistic degrees of freedom, and great efforts have to be devoted to extracting as much novelty and variety from the simple device of rigid objects moving with respect to one another. However you look at it, in the end it is some kind of variation on tumbling logos and virtual cameras choreographed with exotic zoom sequences. Undoubtedly the major research effort in computer graphics has been devoted to more and more realistic image synthesis and three-dimensional animation has been attracted and fossilized by the high commercial rewards of the entertainments industry.

It is interesting to note that one of the main attributes of three-dimensional computer animation, the precise shading of three-dimensional objects, is completely absent from traditional animation. In Disney's productions the characters are flat shaded and the illusion of movement through three-dimensional space is carried by the fluidity of the characters, the imaginative use of perspective in the background and the choreography of the virtual camera. The first traditional animation to feature shaded characters and objects to any extent is Who Framed Roger Rabbit?, *animated by Richard Williams. This film makes a feature of integating live action with animated characters, and the complexity of the interaction is assisted by employing shading in the animated parts.*

Memorable three-dimensional computer animation productions are few in number, but recently notable productions have emerged from the major animation system manufacturers. A landmark film is Luxo Jr. *(John Lasseter, Pixar, 1986). Apart from being extremely successful artistically, the film contains many messages for would-be computer animators. The success of this particular film is due entirely to the ability of Lasseter to invest a degree of 'Disney-type' characterization in a rigid but articulated object – an anglepoise lamp. A frame from this film is shown in Plate 16.*

This feature was the first serious attempt to invoke the well-known principles of traditional animation in three-dimensional computer animation. Although this is not necessarily the way computer animation should go, it highlights the main drawback of TV commercials and title sequences – their sterility and sameness. In fact, animation in the context of computers, as far as the current state of the art is concerned, is a misuse of the word. 'Animation' means to give life or character to, and computer animation is mostly restricted to giving 'movement' to rigid bodies.

It is evident that there is a place for three-dimensional computer animation in engineering simulation and scientific visualization (ViSC) just as (static) computer graphics is already universally used in these fields. Already high quality colour three-dimensional graphics is used to visualize and provide insight into complex phenomena characterized by massive datasets, such as fluid behaviour in liquids and gases, and three-dimensional computer animation will eventually provide a powerful tool for the investigation of dynamic phenomena.

Examples of three-dimensional animation in ViSC have recently emerged but their extreme diversity and small numbers emphasize the newness of the field. It is probable that the eventual mainstream application of computer animation will be ViSC. In a recent panel (McCormick et al., 1987), ViSC was defined as follows:

> *Visualization transforms the symbolic into the geometric, enabling researchers to observe their simulations and computations. Visualization offers a method for seeing the unseen. It enriches the process of scientific discovery and fosters profound and unexpected insights. In many fields it is already revolutionizing the way scientists do science.*
>
> *Visualization embraces both image understanding and image synthesis. That is, visualization is a tool both for interpreting image data fed into a computer, and for*

generating images from complex multidimensional data sets. It studies those mechanisms in humans and computers which allow them in concert to perceive, use and communicate visual information. Visualization unifies the largely independent but convergent fields of:

> *Computer graphics*
> *Image processing*
> *Computer vision*
> *CAD*
> *Signal processing*
> *User interface studies*

One of the major applications of ViSC that involves three-dimensional computer animation is computational fluid dynamics. This refers to the numerical solution of the partial differential equations of fluid flow. Animation of such phenomena as shock waves, vortices, shear layers and wakes, all of which depend on time, is of major importance. The variety of productions that can be loosely inserted in the ViSC category can be shown by describing a few examples.

Blinn's Mechanical Universe *(Blinn, 1987) is a large-scale project running to 7.5 hours of screen time. Simulating physical phenomena, Blinn uses a mixture of two-dimensional and three-dimensional animation to produce arresting sequences of such diverse phenomena as molecular dynamics and general relativity. In what must be the longest computer animation production, Blinn demonstrates how to use computer animation tools in both the visualization and the explanation of environments that have no 'real visualization' – the world of molecules and universes.*

As well as being a visual implementation or passive reflection of scientific phenomena, three-dimensional computer animation can provide a testbed for scientific investigation. Reynolds (1987) simulates flocking behaviour in birds and fishes. In this intriguing study each simulated member of the flock is an independent actor that navigates 'according to its local perception of the dynamic environment, the laws of simulated physics that rule its motion, and a set of behaviours programmed into it by the animator'. It is evident that the investigation of flocking dynamics, as a function of individual and aggregate behaviour, would not be possible without the investigator being able to view the final animation of the flock.

In the following sections a brief overview of the methods used to produce three-dimensional computer animation is given. Animation interfaces are extremely varied, reflecting the diverse requirements of the productions. The central paradox is that they should be sufficiently high level to buffer an animator from detailed programming intervention. This, however, inevitably restricts the freedom of the animator, locking him into the objects and choreography permitted by the interface.

Production of an animated film sequence encompasses three topics:

(1)   the modelling of the three-dimensional objects,

(2)   scripting their motion and/or the motion of a virtual camera, and

(3)   rendering the frames in the sequence.

The considerations involved in the first and third topics are no different from those of static images and the remainder of this chapter deals with the second subject.

13.1   Approaches: three-dimensional key frame systems

Three-dimensional key frame systems are the most popular type of animation system in use today. They were developed as a logical extension to the traditional key frame approach – a method that was dictated by the large manual overheads of traditional production, where skilled animators define 'key frames' in a sequence, leaving the production of the 'in-between' frames to a group of less skilled animators called in-betweeners.

In three-dimensional computer animation this system is commonly used for animating rigid bodies. An animator specifies the position and perhaps the attitude of the body at certain instants – key frames – and the system interpolates a path and evaluates the in-between frames. If the scene is not too complex, or if the objects are displayed as wireframes, then this process can occur in real time and the animator can interactively respecify a key frame, or decide on the next in the sequence, while continually viewing a loop of the results. A simple example of this process is shown in Figure 13.1. This example uses cubic polynomial splines as the interpolating method which gives first- and second-order continuity through the data points (velocity and acceleration respectively) and this implies a smooth motion sequence. For the data in the table the polynomial spline, shown as three univariate functions, was produced.

Key position number	Time (s)	Position x	y	z
1	0.0	−3000	0	2000
2	1.0	−2000	−2000	3000
3	2.0	0	−3000	2000
4	5.0	2600	1400	−2200
5	8.0	3000	3000	−3000

Figure 13.1
Cubic polynomial splines fitted through the given data.

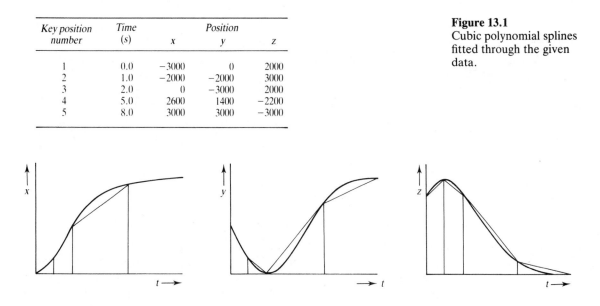

The polynomial splines can then be sampled at equal intervals to give the positional information required for the in-between frames. This idea is commonly extended to allow the animator to edit the three position–time polynomials graphically.

13.1.1 Key frame systems: kinetic control

In key frame systems it is extremely useful to be able to control the kinetic (velocity and acceleration) characteristics independently of the positional information in the key frames. Kinetic control implies varying the number of in-between frames, which causes an object to move faster or slower without its start and final positions being changed.

Steketee and Badler (1985) describe a double interpolant method that provides convenient kinetic control and continuity of acceleration (second-order continuity). This is accomplished by defining two interpolants that provide the basis of a key frame interface. The kinetic interpolant is a function that relates key frames to time and the position interpolant relates position (x, y, z) to key frame. The kinetic interpolant controls the timing of the key frames but contains no information on the actual motion of the object, the position interpolant specifies the position of the object and contains no information on the timing of the key frames. Both interpolants are B-splines. B-splines are a good choice for

289

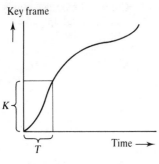

Kinetic interpolant
(user edits)

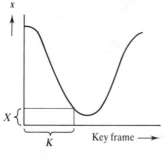

Position interpolant
(user edits)

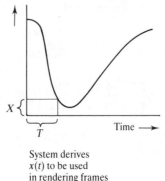

System derives
$x(t)$ to be used
in rendering frames

Figure 13.2
The double-interpolant
method.

animation interfaces because the curves can be changed and this change localized to a small region (see Chapter 6 for details on B-splines). A function relating position to time is derived from both of these and this function drives the final animation sequence. Note that although three functions $x(k_f)$, $y(k_f)$ and $z(k_f)$ would be used to represent position, a single one-dimensional function, $k_f(t)$, represents the kinetic interpolant and controls the timing of all three motion parameters. A representation of the process is shown in Figure 13.2.

From these considerations it can be seen that the major problem in key frame systems is how to provide an interface that allows a four-dimensional function to be edited. An interface that supplies four graphs (functions of a single variable) seems difficult to use, even if the animation is continually being looped in another viewport.

Shelley and Greenberg (1982) define a more elaborate interface. A path for a moving object, in effect a three-dimensional view of the four-dimensional position–time function, is defined interactively as a three-dimensional curve through the environment. Time is measured along the curve. The kinetic characteristic is represented as a vertical offset from the spatial path. This elaborate, intuitively appealing interface seems ideally suited for interactively determining the motion of a single object through a number of static objects. The static objects assist the interpretation of the kinetic information in the representation. Perhaps pseudo-colour is a better way to represent kinetic information superimposed on a spatial curve.

Finally, note that effective choreography of the virtual camera is one of the most powerful effects in computer animation. Generally it can be treated like any other object in the scene and choreographed using spline interpolants. However, as well as controlling the position of the view point, other parameters (for example, tilt, centre of interest in virtual camera terms) of a viewing system need to be controlled.

13.1.2 Keyframe systems: rotation

Although translation is easily used in a key frame system, a problem is posed with rotation. Rotation is normally specified by a nine-component rotation matrix and the problem arises because the components are not independent. Interpolating components independently between key values would result in in-betweens in which the object would undergo deformations. Even if Euler angles are used (specifying rotation as a composite of three successive rotations about axes fixed in the object called yaw, pitch and roll) the in-betweening will try to produce twisting about each axis simultaneously.

A solution suggested by Shoemake (1985) is to use quaternions to specify rotation. Using a quaternion to represent rotation is based on Euler's theorem which states that any displacement of a body with a single point fixed can be represented by a single rotation about some axis. Thus a quaternion contains four components, a three component vector and an angle or scalar:

$$w + xi + yj + zk$$

It can be interpreted as an algebraic quantity, a point in four-dimensional space or as a scalar plus a three-dimensional vector.

Shoemake describes how to use quaternions in a key frame system for rotation and suggests an approach whereby a conventional interface (Euler angles, say) is used and the information is transformed into a quaternion representation. Interpolation can then take place, and the results transformed back and used to produce in-betweens.

13.2 Approaches: parametric systems

Parametric systems are similar to key frame interpolation, but the nature of the information given at key frames tends to be more complex and consists of parameters that control the subsequent behaviour of the object, rather than just position, say.

Parameters are injected at key frames and may be interpolated to provide a set of parameters for each in-between frame. An example of such a system is *em* (Hanrahan and Sturman, 1985). Such systems are more elaborate than simple key frames and allow more complex object behaviour between key frames. Another advantage of this approach is that interaction can be far more powerful.

Hanrahan's system models inputs as variables whose numerical values are derived from physical interface devices. For example,

$$dx \mathrel{+}= wheelx$$
$$dy \mathrel{+}= wheely$$
$$spin \mathrel{+}= 10*joyz$$

are assignment statements where the left-hand sides are a parameter of the model of the object that is being animated and the right-hand sides are input variables or functions of them. An interactive loop can then be set up whereby the animator controls the behaviour of the object in the in-between frames by using input devices.

Consider, for example, an object that is to spin at a varying rate while translating between two positions. This would be a tedious problem with a basic interactive keyframe system. It would be easily scripted using the programming language approach described in Section 13.3, but alterations in the spinning mode depend on an edit and recompile mode. If the spin is parametrized then interaction of the sequence is possible with spin parameters input from a suitable device. The power of the system depends on the ability of the animator to parametrize the behaviour of the object.

13.3 Approaches: programmed animation and scripting systems

In this approach an animator writes a program to produce a sequence. The program is either written in a standard high level language, and the animation produced through a graphical interface, or it is written in a specially designed animation scripting system.

The disadvantages of this approach are obvious. The sequence cannot be seen until the program is written. Animation effects are reflected in high level constructs such as **for** loops and this distance between the 'script' and the effect is anti-intuitive. Skilled programming expertise is obviously required to build up an animated sequence from, say, Pascal or FORTRAN facilities, and the quality of the animation depends on the ability of the animator–programmer to bridge the gap between the programming constructs and their visual effect.

An obvious development of this algorithmic approach is to develop animation languages or to provide extensive animation facilities in a general-purpose computer language. The program that produces the animation is generally known as a script. An example of this approach is Reynolds' Actor Script Animation System (ASAS) (Reynolds, 1982). The script in the animation language still retains its analogy to a program, with the normal advantages of this approach: the ability to edit a sequence and to provide a progressive refinement facility, the ability to accumulate expertise by building up library facilities, the ability to tackle progressively more complex problems by using accumulated expertise (bootstrapping). As well as these advantages an animation language will reduce the conceptual distance between a program and script and its effect, and should be accessible to animators who are not necessarily skilled programmers.

ASAS contains all the normal structured programming facilities, such as loops, conditionals and typed data structures. It can be considered to be an extension to LISP or a system that is implemented in LISP. In this respect, while it can be said that a would-be animator need not necessarily be a skilled programmer, certainly skills must be developed in ASAS to write a script, and LISP conventions are not easy for a novice.

ASAS is an environment that allows geometric objects, operations on these objects and **animate** blocks that allow **actors** to be 'directed'. Reynolds uses the term **actor** which he describes as a chunk of code that will be executed once each frame. An actor is responsible for a visible element in an animation sequence and the code chunk will contain all values and computations which relate to that object. Control over parallel actor processes is possible by message passing. Scenes in a production sequence are analogized by **animate** blocks which constitute the coarse structure of the action.

The following example from Reynolds (1982) is a script that contains one **animate** block. This block starts two similar **actors**, a green spinning cube and a blue spinning cube at different times. Both **actors** then run until the end of the block.

```
(script spinning-cubes

        (local: (runtime 96)
                (midpoint(half runtime)))

        (animate (cue (at 0)
                 (start(spin-cube-actor green)))

                 (cue (at midpoint)
                 (start (spin-cube-actor blue)))

                 (cue (at runtime)
                     (cut))))
```

A unique object called a **newton** is available. Reynolds describes this as an animated numeric object. These can be used anywhere a numeric value is used, but their value is updated between frames. A **newton** data structure can store any complete sequence that may, for example, be any function such as a quadratic or cubic curve.

A similar programming approach, but using a Pascal-type basis, is given in Magnenat-Thalmann and Thalmann (1985). Again, the philosophy is to provide a convenient animation-based programming environment that enables a director to write a script. One of the major ways that this is done is to provide 'animated basic types'. This is a generalized extension of the previously described newton.

As well as applying this concept to scalar types such as integer and real, Magnenat-Thalmann and Thalmann introduce animated extended types such as vector. Starting and stopping values and motion laws can be incorporated in the type declaration and vectors subsequently referred to in the program or script by using a single variable name.

An example taken from Magnenat-Thalmann and Thalmann (1985) serves to illustrate the philosophy of this approach. The language is called CINEMIRA.

```
type TVEC = animated VECTOR;
            val ≪ 0, 10, 4 ≫ .. UNLIMITED;
            time 10..13;
            law ≪ 0, 10, 14 ≫ + ≪ 3, 0, 0 ≫ *(CLOCK − 10);
            end;
var VEC: TVEC;
```

Here a vector is defined that starts at time 10 and moves with a constant speed ≪3, 0, 0≫ from the point ≪0, 10, 4≫ and stops at time 13.

Camera choreography is also implemented in the type declarations. Although this approach is completely general and places no restrictions on the use of computer facilities, it can be seen that a user has to be rather well versed in programming in structured languages.

Recognizing this fact, Magnenat-Thalmann and Thalmann developed an artist-oriented system that produces code in CINEMIRA. This is called ANIMEDIT and using this facility an animator can specify a complete script without programming in CINEMIRA. The system is interactive, and, together with the freedom from having to use structured programming constructs, this makes it accessible to artists in a way that exploits their creativity.

ANIMEDIT thus combines the advantages of an animation-based system with the freedom of 'pure' interactive systems. The approach is a formal reflection of the work methods adopted by many commercial animation houses, who employ both animators for their creativity and programmers to create new tools for the animator to use.

The ANIMEDIT system contains eight operational modes:

- Variable mode: this mode allows the animator to create extended variables, with motion laws etc. It is not made clear in Magnenat-Thalmann and Thalmann (1985) exactly how a (computer-unskilled) animator can set these up.

- Object mode: this mode sets up the system's modelling capabilities and allows the animator to create objects and operate on their attributes.

- Decor mode: similar to the previous mode, it facilitates the building of backgrounds etc.

- Actor mode: in this mode the animator defines actors (animated objects) together with the transformations to which they have to be subjected.

- Camera mode: this is similar to the actor mode as far as movement is concerned. (Clearly the camera cannot take attributes such as colour.)

- Light mode: position and colour of light sources can be defined together with their motion.

- Animation mode: this mode directs the action, starting and stopping actors, cameras etc.

- Control mode: this controls entry to other modes.

The point of this edit system is fairly obvious. These eight modes, it has been decided, are the creative states that an animator requires to control detailed, but low level, graphic utilities that will produce an animated sequence that is near to the designer's intentions.

13.4 Approaches: simulated or model-driven systems

An unfortunate confusion has arisen over the use of the term 'parameter' in computer animation. We shall reserve its use to describe interactive systems (see above) where the parameters in the model are connected to the user interface.

Another major type of computer animation, sometimes described as parametric, involves using the mathematical equations that model or specify motion for a particular phenomenon to drive the animation. A system is simulated or scripted by a mathematical model. This type of animation finds applications in engineering – particularly the simulation of machines – where both the kinematics and the motion are constrained by the physical design of the machine.

One of the problems of key frame systems, or kinematic systems where the animator specifies positions and angles as a function of time, is that they are low level and make the animator independently control aspects of the behaviour of objects that are dynamically interdependent. Simulation (rather than animation) attempts to exploit this inter-dependence.

The principle of this type of animation is now explained for rigid bodies. Full implementation details are beyond the scope of this text and the reader should refer to the references given.

We can start by considering particles and Newton's second law:

$$\boldsymbol{F} = M\boldsymbol{a}$$
$$= M\, \mathrm{d}\boldsymbol{P}/\mathrm{d}t^2 \tag{13.1}$$

where $\boldsymbol{F}$ is a three-dimensional force vector acting on a particle of mass m and $\boldsymbol{P}$ is the position of the particle in three-dimensional space.

A simulator supplies a force and mass and integrates the above equation to solve for position. Euler's method can be used to obtain a new position $\boldsymbol{P}_{i+1}$ at time $t + \delta t$ from:

$$\boldsymbol{P}_{i+1} = \boldsymbol{P}_i + \boldsymbol{v}_i\,\delta t + \tfrac{1}{2}\,\boldsymbol{a}_i\,\delta t^2$$

where $\boldsymbol{v}_i$ and $\boldsymbol{a}_i$ are velocity and acceleration. The accuracy of Euler's method is a function of the time step δt. Wilhems (1987) points out, in a useful distillation of dynamics relevant to computer animation–simulation, that the accuracy of this numerical approximation can be increased by using the Runge–Kutta method.

Possibly the first application of this technique was in Reeves' particle method (Chapter 11). Here individual particles could be scripted from equations describing their trajectory in three-dimensional space and the overall effect was to model a 'fuzzy' object by using a sufficiently large number of particles.

In computer simulation we are generally going to be interested in bodies rather than particles and this complicates things considerably and adds to the computing expense. Either non-particle masses can be dealt with on the basis that they are rigid and their shape does not change (see, for example, Hahn (1988)) or elasticity theory can be used to model bodies that deform under, say, collision (Terzopoulos and Fleischer, 1988; Terzopoulos and Witkin, 1988; Terzopoulos et al., 1987).

The motion of rigid bodies can be represented by the sum of two motions. First we consider two coordinate systems: a fixed system and a moving system embedded in the body and participating in its motion. The latter is conveniently positioned at the centre of mass of the body. An infinitesimal displacement used in an integral model can then be described as a translation of the body from its position at time t to its position at time $t + \delta t$, together with a rotation about its centre of mass which orients the body about the final position of its centre of mass. This makes a rigid body a system with six degrees of freedom.

The Euler method can be used to describe the motion and this results in six equations. Three are the equations of motion for the translational component:

$$F = Ma$$

as before and three are the rotational equations of motion relating angular acceleration and mass to torque (the rotational analogue of the above equation). This model is controlled by the simulator supplying both a force and a torque.

Mass distribution is described by moments of inertia about each axis in the coordinate system embedded in the body:

$$I_x = \sum m(y^2 + z^2)$$
$$I_y = \sum m(x^2 + z^2)$$
$$I_z = \sum m(x^2 + y^2)$$

This considers the rigid body to be a system of particles each of mass m. Examples of moments of inertia for symmetric homogeneous rigid bodies are:

- A sphere of radius R:

$$I_x = I_y = I_z = \tfrac{2}{5}MR^2$$

  where $M = \sum m$ is the mass of the body.

- A cylinder of radius R and height h:

$$I_x = I_y = \tfrac{1}{4}M(R^2 + \tfrac{1}{3}h^2)$$
$$I_z = \tfrac{1}{2}MR^2$$

  where the z axis is along the axis of the cylinder.

- A box of sides a, b and c:

$$I_x = \tfrac{1}{12}M(a^2 + b^2)$$
$$I_y = \tfrac{1}{12}M(a^2 + c^2)$$
$$I_z = \tfrac{1}{12}M(b^2 + c^2)$$

  where the axes x, y and z are along the sides c, b and a respectively. This is useful in computer animation because in certain applications a bounding box is a sufficient approximation to a body, as far as the equations of motion are concerned.

These simple objects are symmetrical, that is their mass is arranged symmetrically around a centre of mass.

The six equations of motion for a symmetrical rigid body are completed by the three rotational equations of motion:

$$N_x = I_x \dot{\omega}_x + (I_z - I_y)\omega_y\omega_z$$
$$N_y = I_y \dot{\omega}_y + (I_x - I_z)\omega_x\omega_z \qquad (13.2)$$
$$N_z = I_z \dot{\omega}_z + (I_y - I_x)\omega_x\omega_y$$

where N is the torque acting on the body, ω is the angular velocity with respect to the local frame of reference, and the equations are specified in a local coordinate system embedded in the body, whose axes are the principal axes of inertia. Equations 13.1 and 13.2 are combined into a single set of six equations by transforming:

$$F = Ma$$

into the moving coordinate system fixed to the body:

$$F_x = M(\dot{v}_x + \omega_y v_z - \omega_z v_y)$$
$$F_y = M(\dot{v}_y + \omega_z v_x - \omega_x v_z)$$
$$F_z = M(\dot{v}_z + \omega_x v_y - \omega_y v_x)$$

A simulator supplies an applied force F that is assumed to operate at the centre of mass and a torque vector N. The equations can be solved for v and ω. Full details on converting between coordinate frames and the formulae for non-symmetric bodies is given in Wilhems (1987).

The above theory only provides a basis for a computer simulation. An interesting or useful animation sequence is likely to include objects interacting with other objects and/or the environment.

Realistic animation of complex or non-symmetric rigid bodies is dealt with by Hahn (1988). Here dynamic interaction between rigid bodies is simulated using the appropriate Newtonian dynamics. The focus of this study is to remove the scripting of rigid body interaction from the animator's artistic judgement and to give it over to the underlying mathematics.

In Hahn's system objects to be simulated are given physical characteristics, such as shape, density, coefficient of restitution, coefficient of friction etc. These properties are used to calculate attributes such as total mass, centre of mass and moments of inertia.

At any instant an object possesses a velocity (linear and angular), a position and orientation. This dynamic state at time t is used to solve for the dynamic state at time $t + \delta t$, where δt is the time between frames. (Initial states may be scripted.) The new frame calculation involves two separate processes. Firstly, the objects are moved using general equations of motion of rigid bodies under external forces and torque and the properties of the object. Secondly, the objects are checked for collision and impact dynamics is used to calculate the behaviour of the object after collision.

The novel aspect of this work is the nature of the collision detection (the simulation deals with polygon mesh objects of arbitrary complexity, rather than simple analytical or symmetric objects) and the use of impact dynamics to solve the problem of the complex interaction involved. Collisions are also dealt with in Moore and Wilhems (1988). Hahn uses a hierarchical bounding box scheme to aid collision detection. Because collisions may occur between t and $t + \delta t$, objects may exist in a penetrating state and have to be 'backed up' to the collision point. Impact dynamics is a solution method where two bodies have deemed to have acted on each other with a certain impulse over a short period of time. A solution is obtained using this approach and the conservation of linear and angular momenta.

One of the major implications of this work is that rigid bodies can be made far more complex than would otherwise be the case if they were being 'normally scripted'. An example given by Hahn is a four-legged bench tumbling down a set of stairs.

Terzopoulos and co-workers (Terzopoulos and Fleischer, 1988; Terzopoulos and Witkin, 1988; Terzopoulos et al., 1987) simulate the interaction of non-rigid objects in a physical environment. Using the dynamics of non-rigid bodies they have simulated realistic motion arising from the interaction of deformable models with forces, ambient media and impenetrable objects.

The implications of both these studies in engineering testing or a simulation of real testing are evident. Just as in flight simulation, where situations can be created that would be hazardous in reality, simulation of testing can no doubt widen the horizon of investigation, lower its cost and increase its flexibility.

Other less general examples are given by Fournier (1986) who models ocean waves and Weil (1986) wherein free-hanging cloth is simulated.

A novel example of simulated animation is to be found in Waters (1987). Certain facial muscle processes are parametrized to create the animation of facial expression. The faces are polygon mesh representations derived from a photographic technique and the muscle models are used to control features such as the lips, eyebrows, eyelids and jaw rotation. These are driven from the muscle models to produce simulations of such emotions as happiness, fear, anger, disgust and surprise.

Finally, camera movement can also be scripted from a simulation system. The basic movement of a camera tracking an object can be extracted from the object movement. A reference point on the object can be sampled every n frames. These positions can then be interpolated using a key frame system for the camera. This has the advantage that the camera will generally execute smooth motion despite any frame-to-frame motion complexity of the object.

299

13.5 Temporal anti-aliasing

Temporal aliasing artefacts arise from undersampling in the time domain. An animated sequence, whether considered as a three-dimensional or a two-dimensional time-varying sequence, is a set of samples at equal intervals in time.

The most obvious temporal aliasing artefact arises from 'periodic' motion and the familiar example is a rotating wheel that can appear to be stationery, or even rotate backwards, depending on the relationship between the sampling frequency and the rotational frequency. Other artefacts arise from the nature of the generation of frames that are to constitute a sequence. Simple animation sequences are like snapshots taken with an infinitely short exposure time. The process is analogous to ignoring spatial aliasing in static image generation and sampling with a fixed two-dimensional grid.

A mathematical statement of the problem is obtained by extending Equation 12.1 as follows:

$$s(i, j, T) = \iiint I(i + x, j + y, T + t) \, F(x, y, t) \, \mathrm{d}x \, \mathrm{d}y \, \mathrm{d}t$$

where the integral must now be solved or approximated for i, j and T, the frame time. This implies solving the visibility problem as a function of time and filtering. Herein lies the potential expense of the method – generating extra frames that are then filtered to provide a single anti-aliased image. As with spatial anti-aliasing two approaches are possible: a supersampling approach (which is an approximate solution in time just as it was in space) and some algorithmic approximation to the continuous approach.

The easiest solution for spatial anti-aliasing – supersampling and reconstructing using a filter – is also the easiest to apply in the time domain. To do this more frames are generated than are finally required – supersampling is applied in the time domain. Consecutive frames at the supersample rate are then averaged or filtered to provide a normal frame rate sequence. For fast moving objects this will cause 'motion blur' and the process is exactly the same as a moving object blurring on film owing to the finite exposure time of the camera shutter. This approach was used by Korein and Badler (1983). Fast moving objects in an animation sequence appear slightly blurred in the direction of their motion and this blurring effect reduces the jerkiness that may otherwise be perceived by a viewer. It is interesting to note that, in traditional cel animation, animators use 'speed streaks' to simulate this blur.

Although time domain supersampling is in principle an 'easy' technique, it does require that, for the sake of efficiency, it is only applied to moving detail in the frames. It should be applied only where necessary and this requires knowledge of the degree and nature of individual object movement. This is equivalent in the time domain to the philosophy adopted by Mitchell (1987) in the space domain, where adaptive supersampling was applied depending on the nature of the image.

A problem arises out of this method if objects are thin in the direction of motion. Rather than appearing as a blur, a moving object appears in anti-aliased frames as a sequence of objects, a problem termed the 'spaghetti' effect by cel animators. Korein and Badler discuss this problem and suggest solutions.

One of the solutions is contained in a different approach to the problem, termed a continuous algorithm to distinguish it from the supersampling solution. In this algorithm, each moving object is assigned a continuous object space transformation function, which enables areas that moving objects cover to be determined. The area–intensity projected by visible objects onto a pixel over the subintervals in the continuous temporal interval between two frames can then be determined and a filtered pixel intensity solution obtained.

Korein and Badler also point out the desirability and difficulty of integrating spatial and temporal anti-aliasing. Other approaches to temporal anti-aliasing can be found in the lens and aperture camera model of Potmesil and Chakravarty (1983) and in the use of distributed ray tracing in Cook *et al.* (1984).

In Cook's method (Cook *et al.*, 1984) the temporal dimension is accorded the same status as any other dimension in the distributed ray tracing model (see Chapter 7) and rays are distributed in time as well as space. This confers the same economical benefits in the time domain as does distributed ray tracing in the space domain. An example, a frame from *Luxo Jr.*, generated using this method is shown in Plate 16.

Projects, notes and suggestions

Various simple animation projects are distributed throughout the text and we shall restrict ourselves here to specifying a single project that involves a simple study of human articulated movement. It is a comprehensive study that combines many elements of three-dimensional animation; notably the design of a scripting system using forward kinematics, specification of kinematics, key framing and the design of an articulated structure.

13.1 Large animation project (*)

Design an animation system that will accept an English word and produce a script which will control a simple articulated model of the human hand executing an American Sign Language (ASL) gesture.

The project can be undertaken at almost any level of difficulty ranging from stick figure implementation of finger spelling (see below) up to a general implementation of ASL together with realistic modelling of the hand and complex gestural dymamics that signers use.

Notes on the animation project

ASL consists of various gestures and movements of the arms and hands, in order to convey the normal ideas and objects that can be expressed in English. For example, the sign for 'drive' is to place the hands in a 'steering wheel configuration' and to move them from side to side. (Any instruction manual in ASL will give a dictionary of gestures.) ASL is an excellent study for a scripted animation system because it supplies a formal specification for a large proportion of all the gestures possible with the hands and forearm (with, of course, one notable exception).

A subset of ASL is finger spelling, used when no sign for a word exists. Finger spelling is a technique whereby each of the 26 letters of the alphabet are portrayed in some way by one or other of the hands. The project can initially be developed for finger spelling and then extended to sign words.

There is a large literature, mainly connected with robotics, on the animation of articulated structures, but this is mainly to do with goal-directed motion. This means that, given a particular position and orientation, how is this going to be achieved?

This project is different in that it is driven by a script – a set of linear transformations that control the movement of the finger and thumbs to produce the gesture corresponding to the sign. This is known as a forward kinematics system.

There are a number of aspects to the project:

(1) *Modelling*

This can be as basic or as elaborate as desired. In Figure 13.3 cylinders and spheres have been used to model the fingers. The palm has been completely omitted.

(2) *Script compilation*

This requires the production of a script that controls the animated model. Points that you may consider are:

- Can the gestures in ASL be organized into a hierarchy around a subset of gestures that are common to more than one sign?
- The hand model itself is hierarchical and this should be exploited.

(3) *In-betweening considerations*

All gestures should be 'eased in' and 'eased out' by using an appropriate kinetic interpolant to accelerate into a movement and decelerate out of it.
Try the cubic:

$$d = 3t^2 - 2t^3$$

where t is the frame number in the sequence of frames and d gives a fractional value that determines an angular movement.

All finger-spelling gestures (with the exception of 'J' and 'Z') can be

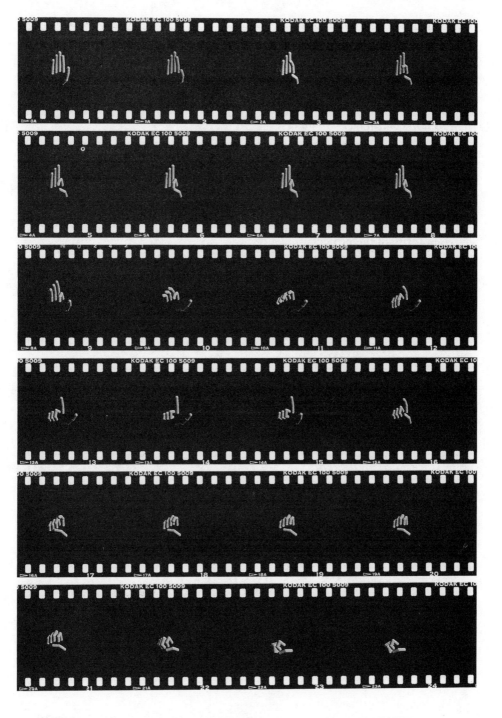

Figure 13.3 Twenty-four frames from a sequence that spells 'FLEX'.

defined as a set of rotations and the number of frames generated should be a function of the maximum angular movement of any finger.

Spelling consecutive letters means that the start position for letter n is the final position of letter $n - 1$ and this specifies the key frames in any sequence. Is this the way in which practitioners of ASL actually execute a finger spelling sequence?

(4) *Position control and dynamics*

In a simple system you must choose letters that do not cause fingers to collide and move through each other; for example, Figure 13.3 shows frames from the sequence 'FLEX' deliberately chosen to avoid this. An easy way to deal with this problem in finger spelling is to set up a 26×26 table that returns either 'no clash' or points to a suitable intermediate position. (Collision detection and avoidance, in general, represent a substantial increase in the complexity of the project.)

How are the movements of separate fingers to be synchronized? Each digit will generally move through a different set of angles. The questions are:

- Do all digits start at the same time?
- Do all digits stop at the same time?
- Do digits start at the same time and finish in their 'own' time depending on their angular travel?

These considerations will affect the final appearance of the animation far more than any shortcomings in the physical modelling.

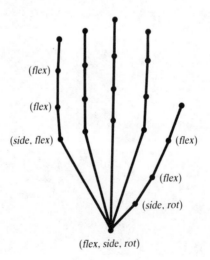

Figure 13.4 An articulated structure for the human hand.

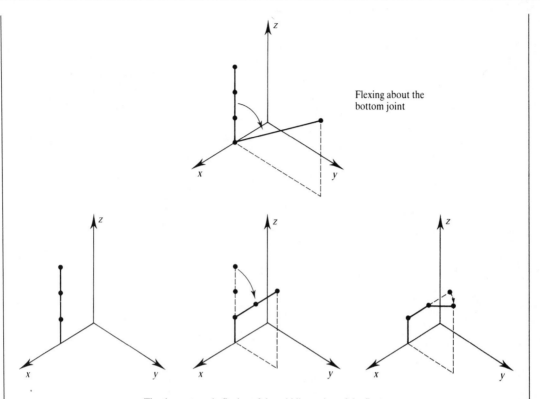

The three stages in flexing of the middle section of the finger

Figure 13.5 Flexing scheme used for fingers.

(5)   *Articulated structure for fingers*

A suggested articulated structure is shown in Figure 13.4. A subset of the
movements *flex*, *side* and *rot* are associated with each joint and this works
quite well. For a finger, *flex* is constrained nested rotation (Figure 13.5) in a
y–z plane about the x axis, and *side* is constrained rotation about the y axis. In
a simple system *rot* can be rotation about the z axis. For example, the angle
set for an 'A' is shown in Figure 13.6.

flex for a thumb is not quite as simple and this requires some
investigation. Consider that the thumb generally moves in a conical volume;
the degree of *flex* about the top and middle joints can be independent of any
other movement and occurs at some angle to the plane of finger flexing. The
bottom joint undergoes sideral and rotational motion.

Technically the finger joints are hinge joints, the wrist is a ball-and-
socket joint and the thumb is a saddle joint.

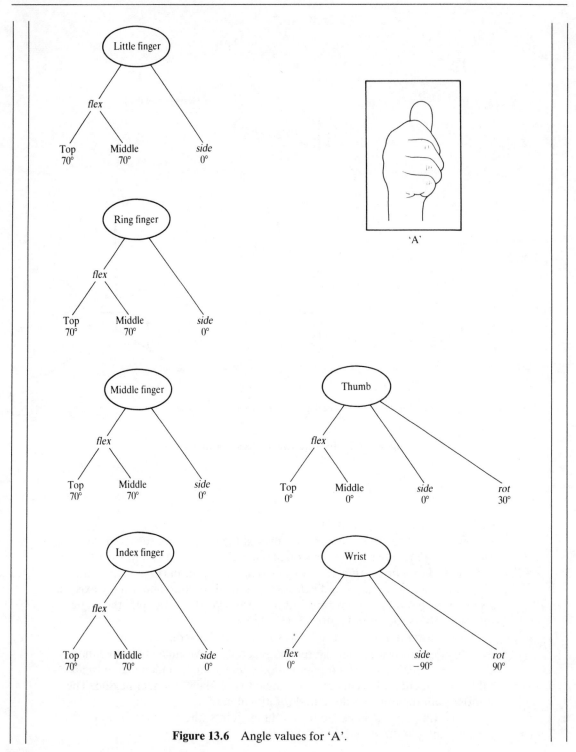

Figure 13.6 Angle values for 'A'.

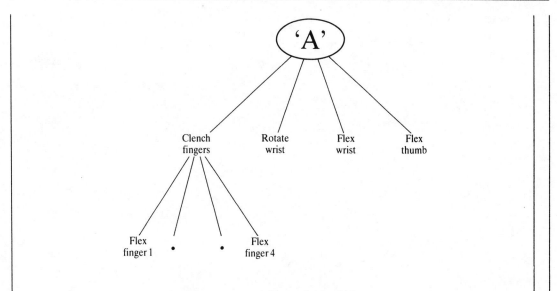

Figure 13.7 A hierarchy for 'A'.

(6) *Storing signs*

Movements for all letters can be organized into a hierarchy reflecting the fact that signs use a set of common movements; for example, a wrist rotation of 90° followed by a flexing of all fingers around the middle joint of 45°. An appropriate hierarchy for 'A' is shown in Figure 13.7.

This should be enough information to get you started.

CHAPTER FOURTEEN

Colour Science and Computer Graphics

This chapter is an introduction to those aspects of colour science pertinent to computer graphics. Colour is a much underrated topic in computer graphics, presumably because it is only recently that 24-bit systems have become widely available. Three main topics are dealt with. Firstly monitor or device gamut models are introduced. These are hardware-oriented models that describe the colour that is produced on the device in terms of those values input directly to the device. Other hardware-oriented models are television transmission definitions. They describe the way in which colour is encoded for transmission down a television channel. A knowledge of such models is important to workers who produce images that are to be sent over such channels.

This chapter only deals briefly with those aspects of colour science important to computer graphics. A comprehensive general treatment of colour science is to be found in Wyszecki and Stiles (1967) and Hunt (1975). For aspects pertaining to television, and hence computer graphics monitors, see Neal (1973), Wentworth (1955), Wintringham (1951) and Sproson (1983).

The common device gamut model is the RGB system. This specifies a colour in terms of the values of the red, green and blue signals that are used to drive the monitor. It is difficult to specify colours, and colour changes, in this system and the RGB model is often front ended by a user interface model. The purpose of user interface models is to facilitate the specification of colours using more intuitive parameters.

A proportion of the chapter is devoted to perceivable or standard colour models. (The range or gamut of display devices is, for reasons that will become clear later, always less than the gamut of colours perceivable by human beings). There are international standards for describing colours. These are extremely important because they provide a language of communication for colours. New areas of computer graphics demand the production of standard colours on computer graphics monitors and a study of perceivable colour models is becoming increasingly important. For example, an architect may wish to render the interior of a room accurately, given surfaces defined by standard colours and lit by standard illuminants.

Human beings react to colour stimuli in a number of ways. There is a straightforward psychophysical reaction that enables us to perceive light as a colour sensation. Except for people who suffer from colour blindness this reaction is approximately the same for everyone. There are loose physiological reactions to colour: most people deem the reds and purples to be warm colours and blues to be cold. There are cultural and religious associations pertaining to colour, particularly when combined with symbols. In the creation of that icon of the corporate state – the company logo – colour is usually an integral part of the design. Technological societies make heavy use of colour. Complex natural phenomena and human-made systems are often explained in textbooks and other educational media by using coloured diagrams. Colour is used in such diagrams to enhance certain areas, to distinguish areas from neighbours and to aid the perception of connectivity. The London underground railway map is a good example of the effective and elegant use of colour and stylization.

In computer graphics a large number of colours are normally available to the programmer. Graphics terminals now have at least 256 colours (usually selected from a larger palette) and up to 16 million for a 24-bit system. To be able to use these colours effectively, and to produce a colour display that is optimal for a particular application, a reasonable understanding of the way in which colours can be designated and specified is required. (Note that it is highly unlikely that any colour monitor could display 16 million colours perceptibly different to the human eye. The reason for the emergence of the 24-bit system is to give an 8 bit × 8 bit × 8 bit RGB colour space for shading. This is fully discussed below.) Firstly let us look at the major application areas in computer graphics that use colour. We can identify, possibly, three separate areas. Consideration of these three areas demonstrates the need for a sound understanding of the way in which colour is designated and specified.

14.1 Applications of colour in computer graphics

14.1.1 Abstractions created by the programmer

This is the most familiar and common area of computer graphics. Although it does not directly form part of three-dimensional rendering there are certain overlaps (particularly if the three-dimensional scene is a functional abstraction such as a machine part in CAD), and it is useful to digress briefly and discuss this topic. It can use a minimum of colour resources and such models are in frequent use on machines large and small. The humble bar chart and histogram, displaying data that is a function of a single variable, is an obvious example. In interactive CAD systems we may have a complex menu showing primitives available and operations on these primitives. The design of both simple static displays of single line images, and complex displays in an interactive graphics system, benefits from a knowledge of the effective use of colour. In such systems colour can be used to highlight particular items on the screen, to rank items in a hierarchy, to set up logical or connectivity relationships between items, to aid legibility and to enhance the appeal of a display. Often colour is used dynamically, for example as a flashing colour for urgent highlighting or to animate flow along a pathway. How then are we to be guided in the selection of colours? A detailed discussion of this topic is to be found in Murch (1983). Two global principles are worth mentioning here.

Firstly, strict economy should always be exercised in the use of colours. This is a principle that equally applies to three-dimensional rendering. Even though with modern systems hundreds, thousands or millions of colours may be available to a programmer, colours used to indicate different functions, items or logical relationships should be limited to less than ten. Although colours can be used to highlight logical relationships, flow and so on, they cannot overcome the limitation that human beings can only absorb a certain amount of information at any instant. As the number of available colours on the display increases, their distinctiveness is reduced and the complexity of the display increases, counteracting the initial reason for using colours.

The second overriding principle is that colours should be ranked. Some colours are more distinctive than others and this hierarchy must be taken into account when assigning colours to areas in the display. A connected consideration here is contrast. The actual colour we perceive depends on background or surrounding colour as well as the nature of the foreground colour.

14.1.2 The synthesis of three-dimensional scenes

In the special case of image synthesis, or the creation of three-dimensional objects or scenes to some degree of realism, the variation of colour within an object is controlled by a shader. A shading model, however, only controls the variation of colour within a single object. In multi-object scenes, colour guidelines may still be of paramount importance. We may even have to use these controls in a single object to make the structure of the object understandable. In CAD, we may have a complex object such as a part made up of several subassemblies. Although the part may be manufactured, finally, in a single colour, it can be displayed with the subassemblies shaded in different colours.

14.1.3 Modelling of non-visual data

Many important application areas involve the display of non-visual data superimposed on, or in some way combined with, visual structure. The difference between this and programmer-created abstractions is that usually the data is collected from the physical world. Colour is usually combined with shape to display the data in physical conjunction with the object to which the data relates. This is one of the most powerful application areas of computer graphics, and gives us, in effect, visualizations that we have never seen before. One of these is medical imagery, where X-ray tomography or ultrasonic scanning will produce a two-dimensional array or cross-section of intensity values. These are then displayed using colour to represent intensity. In the case of X-ray tomography the data intensity is related to the X-ray absorption, which is proportional to tissue density. Mapping these values into colour gives a visualization of the organs under examination in terms of the X-ray absorption coefficients. As boundaries between tissue of different density exhibit different absorption coefficients, the colours in the display that are assigned to these differing values, providing a colour map of a cross-section through that part of the body under examination.

Another common example is earth resources satellite imagery where colours are used to represent reflectance from the non-visual part of the spectrum, for example the response from an infrared scanner. Such data can also be combined with non-geographical or economic data to provide thematic maps.

Stress data in structures can be collected from transducers and these values superimposed on the outline of a structure. This may be a two-dimensional section or a three-dimensional model. In all of these cases it is important that the mapping between the data values and the colour scale is such that the resulting display properly reflects the nature of the variation in the data.

14.2 Monitor models

14.2.1 The RGB model

The RGB model is the standard monitor gamut model. A computer graphics monitor is driven by three (R, G, B) intensity signals, where $(0, 0, 0)$ is the colour black and $(1, 1, 1)$ is white. Between these two extremes a range of intensities is available, typically 256 for each colour in a 24 bits per pixel system.

The RGB colour space can be represented as a cube (Figure 14.1 and Plate 17). The main diagonal of the cube (from the origin to the point $(1, 1, 1)$) is an achromatic line or gray scale. This colour solid represents all the colours available on the monitor.

Three important points need to be made concerning the RGB model:

(1)   The RGB cube may differ from monitor to monitor depending on the physical characteristics of the phosphors. In other words, colours are defined by a numeric triple that is particular to the monitor used. The point (r, g, b) will in general produce slightly different colours on different monitors.

(2)   The RGB cube represents a subset of the colours perceivable by the human visual system.

(3)   The RGB cube is not a perceptually uniform colour space. Uniform intervals along any straight line in the space will not produce colours that are uniformly different as far as the human

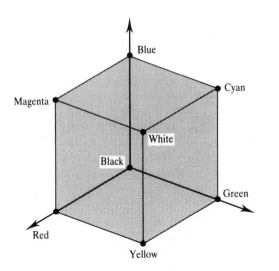

Figure 14.1
The RGB colour solid (compare with Plate 17).

313

visual system is concerned. This is particularly true for low intensities. In a 24-bit system, for example, 256 steps are possible along each axis. Depending on the region of the cube addressed, it may be that as many as 20 to 30 steps are required to produce a perceivable difference.

All of these points are taken up in detail later.

Plate 17 shows two representations of the RGB cube. These were produced on a 24-bit system and it can be seen that, with 256 discrete values along each axis, there are no visible boundaries between adjacent colours. The colour space of such a system is, therefore, visually continuous.

14.2.2 The CMY model

The relationship between the CMY and RGB models is easily seen by comparing Plate 17 (top) with 17 (bottom) and Figure 14.1 with Figure 14.2. Cyan, magenta and yellow are the complements of red, green and blue. White light is now at the origin of the colour solid, with black as the value $(1, 1, 1)$.

The CMY model is important in hardcopy devices such as ink jet plotters that allow mixing of colours and it may be used to drive such a device from a HSV or HLS model (see below) in the same way that the RGB model is used to control a colour monitor.

Cyan, magenta and yellow are called subtractive primaries because their effect is to subtract colour from white light. A piece of white paper

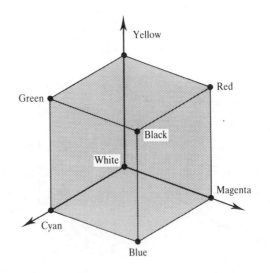

Figure 14.2
The CMY colour solid (compare with Plate 17).

reflects white light and the effect of depositing a yellow ink is to remove the blue, leaving the green and red components of the reflected light. Similarly cyan (blue and green) removes red from the white spectrum. In contrast, mixing colours by controlling the intensity of phosphor dots on a monitor screen is the production of colour by an additive mechanism. In general the colour which is the complement of the CMY colour is subtracted from the reflected light. The relationship between the CMY and RGB model is given by:

$$\begin{bmatrix} C \\ M \\ Y \end{bmatrix} = \begin{bmatrix} 1 \\ 1 \\ 1 \end{bmatrix} - \begin{bmatrix} R \\ G \\ B \end{bmatrix}$$

and

$$\begin{bmatrix} R \\ G \\ B \end{bmatrix} = \begin{bmatrix} 1 \\ 1 \\ 1 \end{bmatrix} - \begin{bmatrix} C \\ M \\ Y \end{bmatrix}$$

The disadvantages listed for the RGB model also apply to the CMY model. The two general disadvantages of these hardware models are:

(1)   It is difficult, without considerable experience, to work in such spaces. Specifying particular colours and directions to alter a colour (that is, how to brighten it or to make it more brownish for example) is not intuitive.

(2)   A colour C is identified only by the model label or the value of the three parameters (R, G, B). It is of no direct relevance to any colour standard and the same values of (R, G, B) may produce a different colour on another system.

14.3   Television transmission spaces

14.3.1   YIQ space

The YIQ system is the colour primary system adopted by the NTSC for colour television broadcasting. The YIQ colour solid is formed by a linear transformation of the RGB cube. Its purpose is to exploit certain characteristics of the human visual system to maximize the use of a fixed bandwidth and to provide compatibility with black-and-white television. This originally meant the need for black-and-white receivers to continue working when colour was introduced.

A large proportion of computer graphics, particularly animation, is produced for television and a knowledge of the attributes, particularly the limitations, of the YIQ system is important when rendering for TV.

The RGB to YIQ transformation is given by:

$$Y = 0.299R + 0.587G + 0.114B$$
$$I = 0.74(R - Y) - 0.27(B - Y)$$
$$Q = 0.48(R - Y) + 0.41(B - Y)$$

Y is known as luminance, and is the only component that is used by a black-and-white receiver. I and Q (the letters relate to the modulation method used to encode a carrier signal) are formed from the red difference component $(R - Y)$ and the blue difference component $(B - Y)$. These difference components are small for dark colours and colours of low saturation. These components are known as chrominance. Thus the luminance information is expressed by Y and the chrominance components carry colour information. Expressing a colour as a luminance component (Y) and two colour components is similar to the specification method used by the CIE (Section 14.6).

In matrix form the YIQ transformation is expressed more succinctly as:

$$\begin{bmatrix} Y \\ I \\ Q \end{bmatrix} = \begin{bmatrix} 0.299 & 0.587 & 0.114 \\ 0.596 & -0.274 & -0.322 \\ 0.212 & -0.523 & 0.311 \end{bmatrix} \begin{bmatrix} R \\ G \\ B \end{bmatrix}$$

and the inverse of this matrix gives the reverse transform:

$$\begin{bmatrix} R \\ G \\ B \end{bmatrix} = \begin{bmatrix} 1 & 0.956 & 0.621 \\ 1 & -0.272 & -0.647 \\ 1 & -1.105 & 1.702 \end{bmatrix} \begin{bmatrix} Y \\ I \\ Q \end{bmatrix}$$

The main characteristic of the NTSC system is that the chrominance signals are transmitted at a much reduced bandwidth compared with the luminance signal. This strategy is based on certain aspects of the human visual system; principally that the eye is more sensitive to changes in luminance than it is to colour changes of very small regions.

The Y signal is transmitted at a bandwidth of 4.2 MHz, the I channel bandwidth is 1.3 MHz and the Q channel is restricted to 0.7 MHz. The received image can thus be considered to be made up of three component images with unbalanced spatial resolution. The Y image is at full video resolution of 220 Hz per scan line but the spatial resolutions of the I and Q images are reduced by factors of approximately 4 and 6 respectively. (Incidentally, this effect is easily seen on a colour television receiver by turning the colour off so that a black-and-white picture is seen. If the colour is now restored, it can be seen that the onset of colour appears to 'smear' the edges of the image.) This implies that spatial resolutions greater than 440 pixels are degraded by the YIQ conversion.

The effect of a transmission channel degradation on colour can easily be simulated on a computer graphics monitor by transforming the RGB colour of each pixel into the YIQ representation, filtering the I and Q values (to simulate bandwidth reduction), transforming back into the RGB domain and displaying the results. If the image is rendered at video resolution, then this means leaving the Y value unchanged and subjecting the I and Q values to a bandwidth reduction factor of, say, 4 and 6 respectively. This is done by applying one-dimensional filters to scan line segments. The filters should be 4 and 6 pixels wide. Finally the Y'I'Q' representation is transformed back to RGB. The whole process can be summarized:

(1)   RGB $\rightarrow$ YIQ;
(2)   YIQ $\rightarrow$ YI'Q' (limit the spatial resolution of the I and Q values over a scan line segment);
(3)   YI'Q' $\rightarrow$ R'B'G';
(4)   display R'G'B'.

A detailed discussion of the practical problems of rendering for the NTSC video standard is given in Chuang (1985).

14.3.2 YUV colour space

The YUV colour space is the PAL (European) transmission standard. In this system the weighting coefficients used for the Y signal are the same as the NTSC system. U and V are given by:

$$U = 0.493(B - Y)$$
$$V = 0.877(R - Y)$$

Thus the forward transformation into YUV space is:

$$\begin{bmatrix} Y \\ U \\ V \end{bmatrix} = \begin{bmatrix} 0.299 & 0.587 & 0.114 \\ -0.147 & -0.289 & 0.437 \\ 0.615 & -0.515 & -0.100 \end{bmatrix} \begin{bmatrix} R \\ G \\ B \end{bmatrix}$$

and the inverse of this matrix gives the reverse transform as before:

$$\begin{bmatrix} R \\ G \\ B \end{bmatrix} = \begin{bmatrix} 1 & 0 & 1.140 \\ 1 & -0.394 & -0.581 \\ 1 & 2.028 & 0 \end{bmatrix} \begin{bmatrix} Y \\ U \\ V \end{bmatrix}$$

The PAL system occupies a higher bandwidth than the NTSC and more bandwidth is available for the chrominance signals. The Y bandwidth is 5.5 MHz and the U and V bandwidths are equal at 1.9 MHz. Chroma cross-talk (see Chuang (1985)) is eliminated in the PAL system.

It is important to note that we have assumed that the above transformations are linear functions of R, G and B. In fact, in practice, YIQ and YUV are functions of gamma-corrected R, G and B and the transformations used are thus non-linear. Gamma correction is discussed in some detail in Section 14.6.5.

Incidentally it is worth noting that some computer graphics hardware designed specifically for television uses a YUV representation rather than an RGB representation. Currently a prominent 'paintbox' system uses a YUV representation where the U and V images are stored at half the resolution of the Y image. Recommendation 601 of the CCIR ('Encoding parameters of digital television for studios') recommends that the spatial sampling frequency of the YUV components should be in the ratio 4:2:2 and that each Y value should be coded to a resolution of 8 bits. This implies that a full-colour image for television YUV systems uses the equivalent memory of 16 bits per pixel compared with the computer graphics 'standard' of 24 bits per pixel.

14.4   Colour models

14.4.1   The HSV single hexcone model

The hue–saturation–value (HSV) or single hexcone model was proposed by Smith (1978). It can be employed in any context where a user requires control or selection of a colour or colours on an aesthetic or similar basis. It enables control over the range or gamut of an RGB monitor using the perceptually based variables hue, saturation and value. This means that a user interface can be constructed where the effect of varying one of the three qualities is easily predictable. A task, such as making colour X brighter, paler or more yellow, is far easier when these perceptual variables are employed, than having to decide on what combinations of RGB changes are required.

The HSV model is based on polar coordinates rather than cartesians and H is specified in degrees in the range (0°–360°). One of the first colour systems based on a polar coordinates and perceptual parameters was that due to Munsell (1946). His colour notation system was first published in 1905 and is still in use today. Munsell called his perceptual variables hue, chroma and value and we can do no better than reproduce his definitions for these. Chroma is related to saturation – the term that appears to be preferred in computer graphics.

Munsell's definitions are:

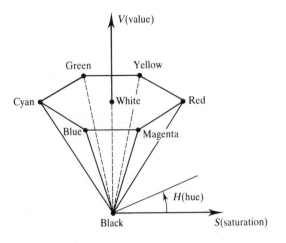

Figure 14.3
HSV single hexcone
colour solid.

- Hue: It is that quality by which we distinguish one colour family from another, as red from yellow, or green from blue or purple.

- Chroma: It is that quality of colour by which we distinguish a strong colour from a weak one; the degree of departure of a colour sensation from that of a white or gray; the intensity of a distinctive hue; colour intensity.

- Value: It is that quality by which we distinguish a light colour from a dark one.

Smith's model relates to the way in which artists mix colours. Referring to the difficulty of imagining the relative amounts of R, G and B required to produce a single colour, he says:

> Try this mixing technique by mentally varying RGB to obtain pink or brown. It is not unusual to have difficulty.
> . . . the following (HSV) model mimics the way an artist mixes paint on his palette: he chooses a pure hue, or pigment and lightens it to a **tint** of that hue by adding white, or darkens it to a **shade** of that hue by adding black, or in general obtains a **tone** of that hue by adding some mixture of white and black or gray.

In the HSV model varying H corresponds to selecting a colour. Decreasing S (desaturating the colour) corresponds to adding white. Decreasing V corresponds to adding black. Figure 14.3 shows the HSV single hexcone colour solid and Plate 18(a) is a further aid to its interpretation showing slices through the achromatic axis. The right-hand half of each slice is the plane of constant H and the left-hand half that of $H + 180°$. The title of Smith's paper, 'Colour gamut transform pairs',

319

Figure 14.4
The RGB cube and a
subcube sharing the
achromatic diagonal.

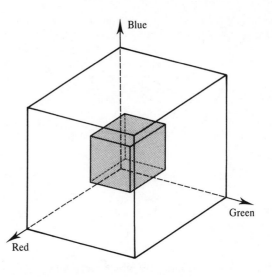

refers to the formulae required to convert from a system such as HSV to RGB and vice versa. Conversion to RGB to drive the monitor would be required in an interface that allowed a user to work in HSV space. Similarly the reverse would be required if the interface allowed existing values on the screen to be interrogated. A user may require the HSV values of a colour that has been generated earlier or that has been produced by another process.

A procedure that converts HSV to RGB is given in Program 14.1. Note that the transform is not affine and straight lines in HSV space do not transform into straight lines in RGB space and vice versa. This is important when colour interpolation is used.

The derivation of the transform is easily understood by considering a geometric interpretation of the hexcone. If the RGB cube is projected along its main diagonal onto a plane normal to that diagonal, then a hexagonal disc results.

The following correspondence is then established between the six RGB vertices and the six points of the hexcone in the HSV model.

RGB		HSV
(100)	red	$(0, 1, 1)$
(110)	yellow	$(60, 1, 1)$
(010)	green	$(120, 1, 1)$
(011)	cyan	$(180, 1, 1)$
(001)	blue	$(240, 1, 1)$
(101)	magenta	$(300, 1, 1)$

where H is measured in degrees. This hexagonal disc is the plane containing $V = 1$ in the hexcone model. For each value along the main

Program 14.1   Transformations from RGB to HSV and from HSV to RGB.

```
procedure RGB_to_HSV(R, G, B: real; var H, S, V: real);

  const undefined = maxint;

  function max_of(Red, Green, Blue: real): real;
    var max: real;

    begin
      if Red > Green then max := Red else max := Green;
      if Blue > max then max := Blue;
      max_of := max;
    end;

  function min_of(Red, Green, Blue: real): real;
    var min: real;

    begin
      if Red < Green then min := Red else min := Green;
      if Blue < min then min := Blue;
      min_of := min;
    end;

  var max_value, min_value, diff, r_dist, g_dist, b_dist: real;

  begin
    max_value := max_of(R, G, B);
    min_value := min_of(R, G, B);
    diff := max_value − min_value;
    V := max_value;
    if max_value <> 0 then S := diff/max_value else S := 0;
    if S = 0 then H := undefined
    else begin
            r_dist := (max_value − R)/diff;
            g_dist := (max_value − G)/diff;
            b_dist := (max_value − B)/diff;
            if R = max_value then H := b_dist − g_dist
            else if G = max_value
                    then H := 2 + r_dist − b_dist
                  else if B = max_value
                          then h := 4 + g_dist − r_dist;
            H := h*60;
            if H < 0 then H := H + 360;
         end;
  end;


procedure HSV_to_RGB(H, S, V: real; var R, G, B: real);
```

```
        var f, p, q, t: real; i: integer;

    begin
      if s = 0 then begin
                R := V; G := V; B := V;
             end
      else begin
             if H = 360 then H := 0;
             H := H/60;
             i := TRUNC(h);
             f := H − i;
             p := V*(1 − S);
             q := V*(1 − (S*f));
             t := V*(1 − (S*(1 − f)));
             case i of
                0: begin R := V; G := t; B := p; end;
                1: begin R := q; G := V; B := p; end;
                2: begin R := p; G := V; B := t; end;
                3: begin R := p; G := q; B := V; end;
                4: begin R := t; G := p; B := V; end;
                5: begin R := V; G := p; B := q; end;
             end;
          end;
    end;
```

diagonal in the RGB cube (increasing blackness) a contained subcube is defined (Figure 14.4). Each subcube defines a hexagonal disc. The stack of all hexagonal discs makes up the HSV colour solid. Plate 18(b) shows the discs overlaid. The reverse transform (RGB to HSV) is also given in Program 14.1.

14.4.2 The HLS model

The HLS model is closely related to the HSV model. It is based on the Ostwald colour system (Ostwald, 1931) and is used by the graphics hardware manufacturer Tektronix. It can be considered a deformation of the HSV solid with the V axis 'pulled' upwards to form a double hexcone (Figure 14.5). Tektronix uses a double cone and the hexcone form is given in Foley and Van Dam (1982) for consistency with the HSV model.

The central axis is now termed L (lightness) and hue is again

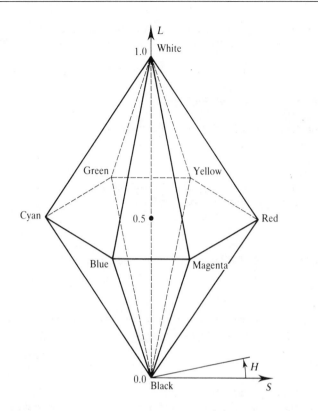

Figure 14.5
Double hexcone HLS
colour model.

measured circumferentially in degrees around the hexcone. The colour white in this model now has the same 'geometric status' as black, that is a single point. Because of this it is an intuitively more satisfying model. The HLS model is as easy to use as the HSV model. However, the plane of saturated hues now occurs at $L = 0.5$ and this is given as a disadvantage (in Foley and Van Dam (1982)) when the model is used as a software interface for colour selection.

Plate 18(c) shows slices through the L axis at 120° intervals. As in Plate 18(a) these are planes of two value hues (H and $H + 180°$). The pair of procedures required to convert values between HLS space and RGB space is given in Program 14.2.

Finally, it should be stated that both the HSV and the HLS models are only convenient ways of specifying a colour or movement of a colour in a space related to the RGB monitor domain. They do not completely agree with the psychophysics of colour spaces. In particular the models imply that maximum saturation ($V = 1$ or $L = 0.5$) occurs at the same point for all colours. This is not consistent with the fact that there are certain colours of high luminance (yellows) and other colours that achieve maximum saturation at relatively low lightness levels (blues). Also, the

323

Program 14.2 Transformations from RGB to HLS and from HLS to RGB.

```
procedure RGB_to_HLS(R, G, B: real; var H, L, S: real);

const undefined = maxint;

function max_of(Red, Green, Blue: real): real;
  var max: real;

  begin
    if Red > Green then max := Red else max := Green;
    if Blue > max then max := Blue;
    max_of := max;
  end;

function min_of(Red, Green, Blue: real): real;
var min: real;

begin
  if Red < Green then min := Red else min := Green;
  if Blue < min then min := Blue;
  min_of := min;
end;

const small_value = 0.0000001;
var max_value, min_value, diff, r_dist, g_dist, b_dist: real;

begin
  max_value := max_of(R, G, B); min_value := min_of(R, G, B);
  diff := max_value − min_value;
  L := (max_value + min_value)/2;
  if ABS(diff) < small_value then
    begin
      S := 0; H := undefined;
    end
  else begin
        if L <= 0.5 then S := diff/(max_value + min_value)
        else S := diff/(2 − max_value − min_value);
        r_dist := (max_value − R)/diff;
        g_dist := (max_value − G)/diff;
        b_dist := (max_value − B)/diff;
        if R = max_value then H := b_dist − g_dist
        else if G = max_value then h := 2 + r_dist − b_dist
            else if B = max_value then H := 4 + g_dist − r_dist;
        H := H*60;
        if H < 0 then H := H + 360;
      end;
end;
```

```
procedure HLS_to_RGB(H, L, S: real; var R, G, B: real);

    var p1, p2: real;

    function RGB(q1, q2, hue: real): real;
        begin
            if hue > 360 then hue := hue − 360;
            if hue < 0    then hue := hue + 360;
            if hue < 60   then RGB := q1 + (q2 − q1)*hue/60
            else if hue < 180 then RGB := q2
                else if hue < 240
                        then RGB := q1 + (q2 − q1)*(240 − hue)/60
                        else RGB := q1;
        end;

    begin
        if L <= 0.5 then p2 := L*(1 + S)
        else p2 := L + S − L*S;
        p1 := 2*L − p2;
        if S = 0 then begin
                        R := L; G := L; B := L;
                    end
        else        begin
                        R := RGB(p1, p2, H + 120);
                        G := RGB(p1, p2, H);
                        B := RGB(p1, p2, H − 120);
                    end;
    end;
```

transformations do not eliminate the problems of non-uniform perceptual steps. In fact these transformations introduce a further confusion. For example, the HLS parameters are not always perceptually independent. A user may perceive a change in one parameter, for example lightness, when it is another, say hue, that has actually been changed. This problem is further discussed in Section 14.6.6 where an interface that is based on perceptual measurements is examined.

14.4.3 User interface programs

The HLS or HSV models are convenient to use in an interface program, that will allow a user to select a colour. Two-dimensional slices through a colour solid can be used as the basis of user interfaces, in the simplest case, for the free selection of a single colour. Of course, usually the selection of a colour will be bound by context-dependent constraints, but selecting a single colour could be determined in, for example, the HLS model by allowing the user to control HLS values through a suitable input device.

Two extreme models are possible. Firstly, a single block of colour could be controlled by H, L and S potentiometers. Secondly, a user could walk through a colour solid, or have consecutive slices displayed under control of a single potentiometer. An H potentiometer would control consecutive rhombii, where L and S vary over a two-valued region of H. In such displays it is usual to divide the planes into small regions, each of a constant colour, with explicit boundaries between colour patches in black or gray.

14.4.4 Colour interpolation

Colour interpolation means choosing a path C in a colour space, where C is a straight line or otherwise. This path defines a set of colours along its length that can be indexed by the attribute to be represented by the colour.

Gouraud shading, introduced earlier, is an example of linear interpolation in RGB space. It is instructive to examine Gouraud shading in terms of colour interpolation. Gouraud shading involves calculating vertex intensities and using these to interpolate along a scan line. Two intensity sets (I_{r1}, I_{g1}, I_{b1}) and (I_{r2}, I_{g2}, I_{b2}) are calculated. The intensity between these two points is given by:

$$I = dI_1 + (1 - d)I_2$$

The path defined by this linear interpolation is a straight line through (I_{r1}, I_{g1}, I_{b1}) and (I_{r2}, I_{g2}, I_{b2}). The intensity:

$$I = (I_r^2 + I_g^2 + I_b^2)^{1/2}$$

changes but the relative weights of R, G and B remain unchanged. For example:

$$\frac{I_{r1}}{(I_{r1}^2 + I_{g1}^2 + I_{b1}^2)^{1/2}} = \frac{I_{r2}}{(I_{r2}^2 + I_{g2}^2 + I_{b2}^2)^{1/2}}$$

This path in RGB space corresponds to a line in HSV space of unchanging H and S. Thus in HSV space Gouraud shading corresponds to a line of constant S in a plane of constant H. For example, $(0.6, 0.4, 0.2)$ to $(0.15, 0.1, 0.05)$ in RGB space corresponds to a path $(60, 0.66, 0.6)$ to

(60, 0.66, 0.15) in HSV space. Gouraud shading is linear interpolation in a colour space along a path that constrains colour changes to changes in intensity.

A simple example of colour interpolation that uses non-linear interpolation is the weighting of the colour of an object according to its distance from the viewer. This is a common approach in flight simulation, where distant objects blend into the horizon colour because of atmospheric haze. Such effects are important in flight simulators to enhance depth perception.

A possible scheme to simulate atmospheric haze is to choose a linear path in, say, HSV space from the object colour to a horizon colour. There may be a number of objects in the scene, all of different 'start' colours, and these would define a number of paths C converging on the horizon colour. The colour of the object would be chosen from its path to the horizon colour according to its depth. This selected colour could then be used in a Gouraud shading scheme (provided that the depth extent of the object is small compared with the depth dimension of the scene). The object would then be rendered at a varying intensity of a single colour (according to the shading interpolation) but this single colour used by the shader will vary according to depth.

In the case of atmospheric haze a non-linear depth interpolation is used to select a colour from C:

$$C_d = C_s \exp(-fd) + C_h[1 - \exp(-fd)]$$

where d is the depth, C_d is the depth-weighted colour used by the Gouraud shader, C_s is the start colour of the object from the object database, C_h is the horizon colour and f is a fading constant.

Finally, Foley and Van Dam (1982) point out that if interpolation is carried out between any two colours (rather than the special case of Gouraud interpolation) then a different set of interpolants will be produced depending on whether the interpolation is carried out in RGB space or HSV space. This is because, in general, a straight line in RGB space does not transform to a straight line in HSV space.

Pseudo-colour enhancement

Pseudo-colour enhancement is a common application of colour interpolation. A pseudo-colour mapping can be selected from a colour solid by an interpolation in the space of the colour solid.

Pseudo-colour enhancement is often used to display a function of two variables. It attempts to give a visualization of a function $f(x, y)$ by enhancing the perceptibility of the value of f and (possibly) the shape of f over the domain of (x, y) by making the 'iso-f' contours visible. The purpose of pseudo-colour enhancement, sometimes called false colour enhancement, is to increase the perceptibility of (usually non-visual) data.

Generally it is used in applications where displaying $f(x, y)$ as a shaded three-dimensional solid would be inappropriate or expensive.

It is commonly used in a large number of diverse practical applications; for example, in medical imaging. Here the data may be tomographic X-rays, the output from an ultrasonic scanner or the data from an infrared sensor. In all of these cases the idea is to give an immediate and recognizable display of two-dimensional numeric data such that the underlying structure of the organ producing the X-ray absorption coefficients, the ultrasonic reflections or the infrared emission is seen.

Pseudo-colour enhancement grew with colour display technology and the reasons for its popularity and success are fairly obvious. Three-dimensional data that would otherwise have to be presented in such a form as a gray scale mapping or a contour map is viewed in the expanded perceptual space of the human colour vision system. Small changes in the intensity of the function being represented are immediately noticeable. This is both the advantage and the danger of the technique. Changes that are too small to be seen in a gray scale version will be visible if they span a colour boundary. The disadvantage is that such boundaries give rise to false contours.

To most people the most familiar manifestation of pseudo-colour enhancement is a geographic terrain map, where the height above sea level is indicated by a colour. This is an old application of pseudo-colour enhancement and pre-dates computer graphics by at least 300 years. Colours are chosen traditionally with green representing low heights. Heights from 0 to 1000 m may be represented by lightening shades of green through to yellow. Darkening shades of brown may represent the range 1000 to 3000 m. Above 3000 m there is usually two shades of purple, and white is reserved for 6000 m and above. Looking through an atlas will confirm the following points:

(1) The number of shades employed tends to remain constant. The upper ranges are expanded or contracted to fit the variation of the region covered by the map. The number of colours used in any map is always kept to between, say, six and ten.

(2) The boundaries between regions lying in different height ranges are always apparent – because adjacent colours are sufficiently contrasty and because boundaries are usually explicitly plotted with a thin blue line.

(3) The colour choice has an associated physical basis – green for grass, brown then purple for high land then white for snow.

This is a good example in that it covers most of the points that are important when choosing a colour scale in pseudo-colour enhancement.

The general process of pseudo-colour enhancement involves transforming a data set (usually non-visual) by using its value to index a colour range or scale. If $C(r)$ is the colour range and $f(x, y)$ the dataset then $C[kf(x, y)]$ is the colour at (x, y). $C(r)$ is either continuous in r or a stepped piecewise linear function. The function C is a path through part of a colour solid.

Now consider the three observations from the terrain map example. The first point is that the number of colours used must be kept to a minimum if a good quantitive impression is to be obtained of the variation of f over the domain of (x, y). This is related to the second consideration – the explicit display of false contours, the boundaries between adjacent colours in the range C. These are called false contours because they are discontinuities which do not exist in the original data and are a consequence of the range boundaries if a stepped function is chosen for C. Whether the contours aid interpretation or not depends on the context. In a terrain map they are certainly desirable. The closeness of the contours gives an impression of the rate of change of height in a region. There may be contexts where the false contours should not be displayed. In such a case a continuous C should be chosen. To use another geographic example, it may be undesirable to highlight false contours in a population density map. It may be that apparent directional rates of change of population are not significant and do not correlate with geographical features.

Plate 19 illustrates some of the practical considerations. An $f(x, y)$ is displayed in each of the cases with the maximum value of $f(x, y)$ at the left-hand side. $f(x, y)$ decreases linearly along the centre of the band – the function is half of an elliptically shaped cone. A linearly decreasing function like this is a worst case for pseudo-colour enhancement because adjacent colours in $f(x, y)$ are always going to be adjacent colours from C.

The most common C is the rainbow scale, with red used to represent high or hot and blue used for low intensity or cold. This scale is popular because it is familiar. In the upper illustration the scale is produced by 15 linear steps around the H (hue) edge of the HLS solid, that is from $(0, 0.5, 1)$ to $(240, 0.5, 1)$. The number of steps chosen has a marked effect on the appearance of $f(x, y)$. The fewer the steps chosen, the more visible are the false contours. The smaller the steps the more the visibility of the contours tends to decrease. However, as can be seen from the upper illustration, the use of 15 steps produces variable visibility of the contours. In the green region the contrast between neighbouring colours is so low that the contours are invisible. This is because equal angular steps along the circumferential interpolation path in HLS space do not result in equal perceptual steps. The situation can be improved by tilting the plane of the interpolation path and using a C from $(0, 0.7, 1)$ to $(240, 0.3, 1)$ as in the lower illustration. This tilts the path out of the plane of the maximum saturation colours. This is in line with one of the ten 'commandments' proposed by Murch (1983). This paper deals with the appropriate selection of colours when they are being used to convey information in diagrams and other abstractions. This text deals mostly with using colour to synthesize reality in shaded solids and such considerations are outside its scope but some areas naturally overlap. Murch's first rule is: avoid the simultaneous display of highly saturated spectrally extreme colours. This rule is certainly broken by the standard rainbow mapping which is garish. This garishness can be reduced and at the same time the green contrast enhanced, by tilting the path of C as described.

A more formal approach to procuring a C that consists of equal perceptual steps is given in Meyer and Greenberg (1980). This consists of selecting C from a perceptually uniform colour scale such as the Munsell or Optical Society of America (OSA) scale. This is a more difficult approach because it requires calibration of the monitor to ensure that the colours displayed are accurate renditions of the required standard colours. Further details of such schemes are given below.

14.4.5 The use of standard colour models

An increasingly important aspect of computer graphics is the generation, on a monitor, of standard colours and the ability to reproduce a colour sensation defined as a spectral energy distribution. Standard colour models give a specification for every colour sensation that is perceivable by the human visual system.

There are many reasons why we may wish to do this. Firstly, reality; certain application areas may require the ability to reproduce standard colours accurately. One has already been mentioned – rendering the interior of a room which may be subject to different lighting conditions. The effect of subtle changes in the nature and position of light sources may have to be simulated and the varying nature of daylight taken into account. The reaction of surfaces to such varying illumination may have to be rendered to a high degree of accuracy. The characteristics of such surfaces may themselves be defined in terms of standard paints or dyes. Chapter 9 deals with the radiosity method which models the illumination in an internal environment to a high degree of accuracy. Such a system could certainly be used in conjunction with a standard colour model.

The visualization of putative products in CAD applications may require a high degree of colour accuracy. One possible example is car design, where colour and its fashionable temporal variations are of such stylistic importance.

The second important point is communication. Given a standard colour system, paint and textile manufacturers, as well as computer graphics workers, can unambiguously communicate a colour specification. Communication is also possible between media, where a standard specification system is used. An artist may produce a particular set of colours, on a computer graphics monitor, that is finally to be produced as a paint, dye or ink.

Finally, reproducibility; a colour produced on one graphics monitor may have to be reproduced exactly, at a later time, or on a different monitor or graphics system. All of these considerations require the use of a standard colorimetric system and its implementation in a graphics system.

14.5 Basic colorimetry concepts

The sensation of colour is a complex phenomenon that depends on the nature of the stimulus and the response characteristics of the human visual system. Most colours that we perceive in real life result from the incidence of white light on a surface. A green surface reflects green light and absorbs light at all other wavelengths. There is not, however, a single colour that we would describe as green but a continuum of colours.

There are two main ways in which colours are described or measured. The first is to use a set of standard colours or charts to designate a colour. Various systems exist for the organization of such charts. Possibly the best known is the Munsell colour specification system (Munsell, 1946). In such systems colours are organized in three-dimensional space and charts are published that are slices through the resulting colour solid. All such colour order systems are attempts to find a natural method, or plan, of organizing colours in three-dimensions such that the user of the system has an intuitive appreciation of the form of the space. Stated another way: given all the perceivable colours as small elemental solids, a colour order system uses these as pieces of a three-dimensional jigsaw to build up a colour solid. This solid (or charts that comprise slices through it) can then be used by artists, designers or anyone concerned with using colour in a methodical manner.

The Munsell colour system was devised in 1905 by Albert H. Munsell and exists in the form of a book of charts. The three dimensions proposed by Munsell are hue, value and chroma. His definitions of these dimensions are reproduced in Section 14.4.1. Each of these dimensions is divided into perceptually equal steps. Hues are divided into 100 steps, values into 10 steps and chroma into 16 steps. The Munsell solid is not regular but is a distorted spherical shape. Unlike the HLS and HSV models the Munsell system incorporates the true nature of the colour solid (for example, high lightness yellows and low lightness blues). The coordinate system on which the colour ordering is based is best thought of

Figure 14.6
The cylindrical coordinate system of the Munsell colour space.

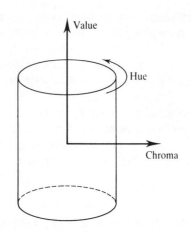

as a cylindrical system (Figure 14.6). Hue is measured in 100 equal steps around around the circumference, chroma is measured along a radial line and value along the long axis of the cylinder. Slicing the solid along any diameter gives a chart of constant Munsell hue, with variation in chroma along any horizontal set and variation in value along any vertical set. The vertical set at the centre of the system, and forming the axis of the cylinder, consists of the achromatic colours going from black to white. It is a distorted form of the HLS model with the distortions being due to the fact that the steps are of equal perceptual value and also that perceivable colours exist outside the monitor gamut.

The second common way of specifying a colour is the CIE (Commission Internationale L'Eclairage) system. This is an objective or numeric system based originally on colour matching experiments. It embraces the human eye response and uses a system that can be related to wavelength. It is based on the classical tristimulus theory of human colour perception. At this point it is worth noting that this is only one theory of colour vision. Other theories exist and in particular Land (1977) disputes the tristimulus theory stating:

> 'If the nature of the responses of the photoreceptors in the retina of the eye even approximated what most of us were taught in school, functioning primarily as intensity-level meters with peaks in three different parts of the spectrum, we would be continually confusing one colour with another.'

However, the tristimulus theory is widely accepted in colour science because it fits in with the method of measuring the human response to a colour – matching a colour to the weighted sum of red, green and blue components.

332

14.5.1 Designating a colour by using three primaries

As a preliminary to the description of the CIE system we shall look at how a colour sensation can be matched by a weighted sum of three primary colours. Also in this section we shall describe how such measurements relate to the spectrophotometric or physical measurement of coloured light.

Most colours can be matched by the additive mixture of three fixed or primary colours. More accurately, we say that a normal observer can match the effect of a colour stimulus by combining light from three primary sources in appropriate proportions. This fact, known as the trichromatic generalization theory, has been known for about 200 years and is demonstrated by an experiment due to Grassman in 1835. The set-up is shown in Figure 14.7. Light from a test lamp is viewed by an observer, and matched by controlling the proportion of light radiating from red, green and blue lights. The values (r, g, b) so obtained are known as the tristimulus values. We can then define the colour as a point or vector in the linear RGB space of the primary sources:

$$C = rR + gG + bB$$

The scalars (r, g, b) are known as the tristimulus values with respect to the RGB primaries. If different primaries are used, then in general different tristimulus values would be obtained when matching a colour. Tristimulus values are always defined with respect to a primary set. A primary colour set is any set of three colours, such that none of the primaries can be matched by a mixture of the other two. There are, however, other considerations involved in the choice of the primary colour set. We can

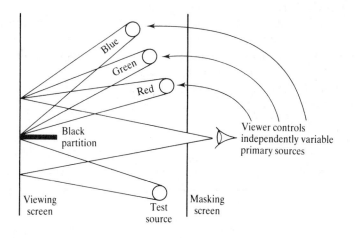

Figure 14.7
Schematic diagram for Grassman's experiment.

333

Figure 14.8
A light source, in general, exhibits a spectral energy distribution with radiant energy throughout the visual range.

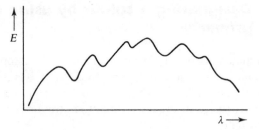

note at this stage that the RGB set is disadvantageous in this respect: we cannot define mixtures that will reproduce the complete set of perceivable colours. The gamut or range of the RGB set is a subset of all the colours that a human being with normal colour vision will perceive. This is a point that we shall return to later.

A question that immediately arises is: how does this trichromatic generalization relate to the physical reality of radiant energy as a measurable quantity? A light source, or colour stimulus, of whatever form, can be quantified as a spectral power distribution (Figure 14.8). Such a distribution would be obtained from a spectrophotometer that measures radiant energy as a function of wavelength. The spectral power envelope precisely describes, in physical terms, the nature of the stimulus. The shape of such a distribution can be categorized by three parameters. Firstly we can define a dominant wavelength – that wavelength at which the distribution peaks. Secondly we can make reference to the spectral power distribution for equal energy white light, which has a uniform distribution, and that for monochromatic light, whose distribution is a single line (Figure 14.9). We can say that white light has 0% purity and monochromatic light has 100% purity. Thus the 'peakier' the distribution the more pure the colour stimulus or the closer it approaches that of a monochromatic source. Finally we can define the energy, which is the area under the curve.

The connection between this model and the the tristimulus model is made by stating that a colour stimulus C is made up of a certain continuum of elemental monochromatic components $C(\lambda)$ where:

$$C = \int_{\lambda} C(\lambda)\, d\lambda$$

Figure 14.9
The spectral energy distribution for equal energy white light and a monochromatic source.

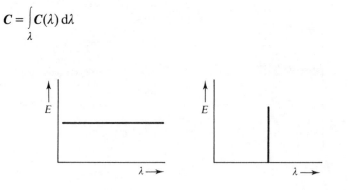

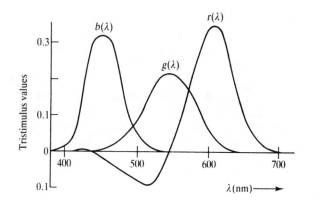

Figure 14.10
The colour matching
functions $r(\lambda)$, $g(\lambda)$ and
$b(\lambda)$.

This means that the sensation produced by the colour stimulus C, is the additive mixture of the elemental monochromatic components $C(\lambda)\,d\lambda$. We can then say that:

$$r = \int_{\lambda} R(\lambda)\,d\lambda$$

$$g = \int_{\lambda} G(\lambda)\,d\lambda$$

$$b = \int_{\lambda} B(\lambda)\,d\lambda$$

where $R(\lambda)\,d\lambda$, $G(\lambda)\,d\lambda$ and $B(\lambda)\,d\lambda$ are the tristimulus values of the monochromatic element $C(\lambda)\,d\lambda$ and (r, g, b) are those of C. We relate $R(\lambda)$, $G(\lambda)$ and $B(\lambda)$ to the spectral distribution of C as follows:

$$r = \int_{\lambda} P(\lambda)r(\lambda)\,d\lambda$$

$$g = \int_{\lambda} P(\lambda)g(\lambda)\,d\lambda \qquad\qquad \textbf{(14.1)}$$

$$b = \int_{\lambda} P(\lambda)b(\lambda)\,d\lambda$$

$r(\lambda)$, $g(\lambda)$ and $b(\lambda)$ are three functions of wavelength referred to as colour matching functions (Figure 14.10). Equation 14.1 expresses the relationship between the (r, g, b) values and the spectral power distribution $P(\lambda)$ of a colour stimulus. Colour matching functions specify the variation of tristimulus values with wavelength for equal energy monochromatic stimuli. (The reason for the negative-going excursion in Figure 14.10 is discussed in Section 14.6.) Units for the tristimulus values are chosen such that an equal amount of the primaries matches a particular white – usually equal energy white.

Now given that we can categorize a colour stimulus, or a particular spectral power distribution, by the three components (r, g, b), how can we reproduce such a stimulus on a computer graphics monitor from a computer program? In terms of colour, a monitor consists of three luminous sources (the red, green and blue phosphors). Each of these has a characteristic spectral power distribution unique to the particular phosphors used and driving a (calibrated) monitor with the (r, g, b) components of C will produce a light whose spectral power distribution will not, in general, match that of C. The answer to this is given by a stronger form of the trichromatic generalization. Two colours C_1 and C_2 match, even though their spectral power distributions, P_1 and P_2 are different, if:

$$\int_\lambda P_1(\lambda) r(\lambda) \, d\lambda = \int_\lambda P_2(\lambda) r(\lambda) \, d\lambda$$

$$\int_\lambda P_1(\lambda) g(\lambda) \, d\lambda = \int_\lambda P_2(\lambda) g(\lambda) \, d\lambda$$

$$\int_\lambda P_1(\lambda) b(\lambda) \, d\lambda = \int_\lambda P_2(\lambda) b(\lambda) \, d\lambda$$

That is, if:

$$r_1 = r_2$$
$$g_1 = g_2$$
$$b_1 = b_2$$

then the colours match despite the difference in P_1 and P_2. This is called a metameric match. (An isomeric match is where $P_1 = P_2$.) Given a colour stimulus (r, g, b) we can reproduce a metameric match on a computer graphics monitor provided that the above condition is true. The fact that the resulting spectral power distribution of the patch of light radiated from a phosphor triad will not necessarily match the spectral power distribution of the colour stimulus being modelled does not matter. This is the basis for the reproduction of standard colours on a monitor.

14.5.2 Basic physiological aspects

The designation of a colour by three primaries fits in with one of the major theories of human colour vision. The initial stimulus in human colour perception comes from densely packed receptors in the retina known as cones. These contain chemicals known as photopigments whose response depends on the wavelength of light incident on them. Three types of photopigments are found in cones and these are known colloquially as the red, green and blue photopigments. Their relative sensitivity is shown in Figure 14.11. One photopigment (blue) has a peak response at 445 nm and does not respond to light of wavelength greater than 520 nm. The green and red photopigments actually respond to light of all visible wavelengths but are maximally sensitive to 535 nm and

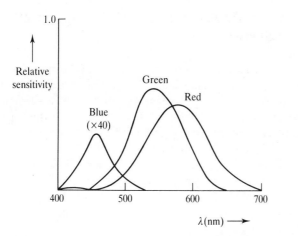

Figure 14.11
The relative sensitivity of
retinal photopigments.

575 nm respectively. Note that even the so-called red photopigment has a peak sensitivity at a wavelength of 575 nm, which is yellow.

The overall sensitivity of these photoreceptors as a function of wavelength is given by the sum of the three characteristics (Figure 14.12). This is known as the luminous efficiency characteristic and it is used to relate brightness to luminance: a scale in which the energy of the light is modulated by the sensitivity of the eye to light of different wavelengths. The luminous efficiency curve is maximally sensitive at 555 nm and least sensitive as the wavelength approaches the blue and red regions. This means, for example, that reds and blues must be of a greater intensity than greens to be perceived as equal intensity.

The luminance Y of a spectral power distribution is defined as:

$$Y = \int_{\lambda} P(\lambda)V(\lambda)\,d\lambda$$

where $V(\lambda)$ is the luminous efficiency characteristic.

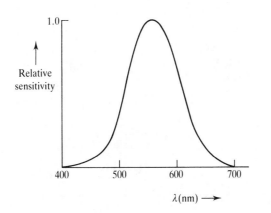

Figure 14.12
The luminous efficiency
characteristic.

337

14.5.3 Specification of a colour by chromaticity coordinates

Often it is useful to specify a colour in terms of the fractional contribution of the (r, g, b) tristimulus values, rather than their absolute level. For example, in computer graphics, the orientation of a surface may change with respect to the observer. The shape of the spectral power distribution, characterizing the reflected light from the surface, remains unchanged. The envelope simply moves up and down. The proportion of r, g and b required to match this distribution will remain the same.

We define chromaticity coordinates as:

$$r_f = r/(r + g + b)$$
$$g_f = g/(r + g + b)$$
$$b_f = b/(r + g + b)$$

and we need only specify any pair of chromaticity coordinates – the third is determined from:

$$r_f + g_f + b_f = 1$$

If the data in the colour matching functions is converted on a wavelength-to-wavelength basis to chromaticity coordinates, and the values of r_f and g_f (say) plotted on a chromaticity diagram, then Figure 14.13 results. This gives a characteristically shaped locus for the monochromatic or spectral colours. The points $(1, 0)$, $(0, 1)$ and $(0, 0)$ on the diagram intersect this locus at the wavelengths 700, 546 and 435.8 nm – the wavelengths of the primaries on which Figure 14.13 is based.

At this stage it is useful to state a further aspect of the trichromatic

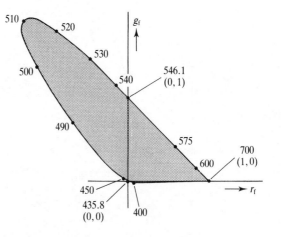

Figure 14.13
r_f, g_f chromaticity diagram showing the spectrum locus from 400 to 700 nm.

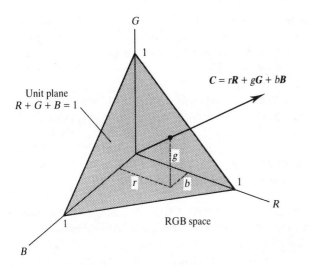

RGB space

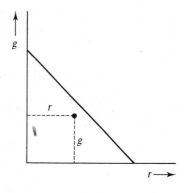

Chromaticity diagram (RG plane)

Figure 14.14
The geometric relationship between the chromaticity diagram and RGB space.

generalization theory. This is: if a colour C_1 is matched by tristimulus values (r_1, g_1, b_1) and a colour C_2 by (r_2, g_2, b_2) then:

$C_1 + C_2$ is matched by $(r_1 + r_2, g_1 + g_2, b_1 + b_2)$

This is known as the law of additive mixture. For example:

$$C_1 = rR + gG + bB$$
$$C_2 = 2rR + 2gG + 2bB$$
$$C_3 = 3rR + 3gG + 3bB$$

are three points in RGB space lying on the line from $(0, 0, 0)$ to $(3r, 3g, 3b)$. The additive mixture of two identical colour stimuli results in a vector of the same direction but twice the length of the vector representing the original stimulus. We say that the direction of the vector represents colour quality (specifically chromaticity) and the length of the vector relates to luminance. The chromaticity coordinates of a colour constitute the point (in RGB space) of intersection of the vector C with the unit plane and the chromaticity diagram is the projection of this model onto, for example, the R–G plane (Figure 14.14). This gives a geometric interpretation of the expression of a colour as a pair of chromaticity coordinates.

14.6 The CIE standard

This is an internationally accepted standard (or standard data set) that is used in the specification of colour. It can be used as a basis from which other colour systems can be compared. In computer graphics it provides a means for displaying standard colours on a particular monitor (because the monitor characteristics are defined with CIE metrics). It also provides a link between colour systems. The production of, for example, Munsell colours on a graphics monitor would proceed via two transformations: Munsell to CIE and CIE to monitor RGB.

In the CIE system a colour is expressed as the triple representing a point in CIE XYZ space. These values are the tristimulus values based on the CIE primaries. More commonly the triple (x, y, Y) is used, where Y is the tristimulus value of the second primary and (x, y) are chromaticity coordinates. In many contexts Y is ignored and a colour is designated only by a pair of chromaticity coordinates as discussed in the previous section.

At this stage it should be pointed out that, for reasons discussed below, The CIE XYZ primaries are non-real or imaginary colours. X is a reddish primary that has a higher saturation than any real red colour. Y is similarly a supersaturated green, having the same wavelength as green and Z is a supersaturated blue primary of the same hue or wavelength as blue.

In 1931 the CIE standard observer was defined. This is an observer whose colour matching properties are defined (from carefully collected and normalized data) to be those of an ideal or average normal trichromat (a person with normal trichromatic colour vision). The colour matching properties of this standard observer are defined as a set of trimulus values, with respect to the CIE primaries, tabulated at wavelength intervals of 5 nm. The data was defined originally with respect to three real primaries, RGB. Given that any set of trimulus values can be transformed into any other set, the CIE transformed this RGB set into the CIE set based on non-real primaries. Consequently the XYZ values for a standard observer can be interpreted as the amount of each of the three CIE primary stimuli that would have to be mixed for a colour match if the CIE observer was able to use the non-real primaries rather than RGB primaries.

The reason for the choice of supersaturated non-real primaries is the desire to avoid negative weights for the tristimulus values as suggested by Figure 14.10. This shows the tristimulus functions based on RGB primaries and shows that some colours cannot be obtained without a negative proportion of one primary. The appearance of the negative weights in the tables was deemed to be inconvenient at a time when computation tools were not as ubiquitous as they are now. The CIE matching functions are shown in Figure 14.15. The non-real CIE primaries are used to define all visible colours using positive weights or tristimulus values. Other factors influence the choice of the particular values for the transformation. In particular the X and Z primaries are contained in the plane of zero luminance (the alychne) and the Y primary is normal to this plane. In addition the shape of the Y matching function

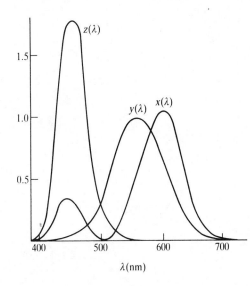

Figure 14.15
The CIE matching
functions.

is set to the luminous efficiency characteristic. Thus we have a system where two of the primaries have zero luminance, the luminance component being described by the other. This simplifies luminance calculations. Note that the integration of the matching functions and a flat spectral curve results in equal values of XYZ.

14.6.1 Derivation of the CIE primaries

It is easy to see how the CIE primaries are defined by using an rg chromaticity diagram. Three steps are involved. Firstly the line of zero luminance, on which the X and Z primaries are located, can be plotted. Zero luminance is defined as:

$$0 = 0.177R + 0.812G + 0.0106B$$

these values being obtained from the luminous efficiency curve for the RGB primaries. Given that:

$$b_f = 1 - r_f - g_f$$

we have:

$$g_f = -0.207r_f - 0.0132$$

This line is drawn on the chromaticity diagram. A tangential line is then drawn on the spectrum locus at 504 nm and the third line is obtained by

Figure 14.16
Construction of the CIE
primaries.

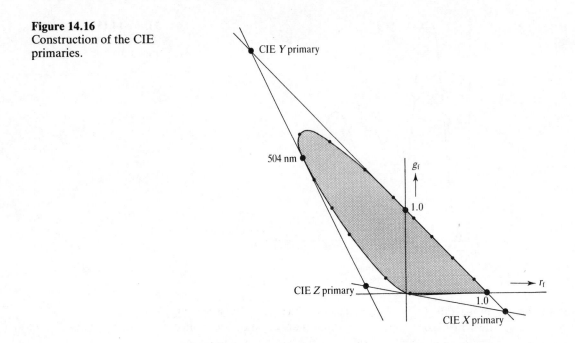

extending the long wavelength end of the locus, which is a straight line
for wavelengths greater than 570 nm.(These choices have to do with
minimizing the number of primaries required to represent a colour and
maximizing the area occupied by colours on the chromaticity diagram.)
The intersection of these three lines defines the CIE XYZ primaries
(Figure 14.16). If this diagram is then replotted with these lines as
orthogonal axes then the CIE chromaticity diagram results (Figure
14.17).

The effect of this transformation on the RGB primaries is:

$$(r_f, g_f, b_f) \rightarrow (x, y, z)$$

R (700 nm): $(1, 0, 0) \rightarrow (0.735, 0.265, 0)$

G (546 nm): $(0, 1, 0) \rightarrow (0.273, 0.717, 0.009)$

B (435.8 nm): $(0, 0, 1) \rightarrow (0.167, 0.009, 0.825)$

E (equal energy white):
  $(0.333, 0.333, 0.333) \rightarrow (0.333, 0.333, 0.333)$

14.6.2 The chromaticity diagram and its uses

The wing-shaped CIE chromaticity diagram (Figure 14.17) is extensively
used in colour science. It encompasses all the perceivable colours in two-
dimensional space by ignoring the luminance Y. The locus of the spectral

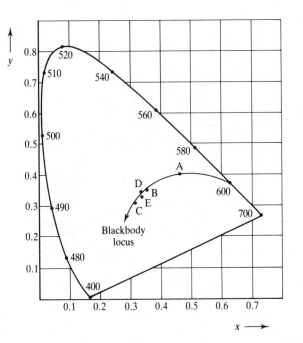

Figure 14.17
The CIE chromaticity
diagram.

colours is formed by the curved line from blue (400 nm) to red (700 nm). The straight line between the end points is known as the purple or magenta line. Along this line are located the saturated purples or magentas. These are colours whose perceivable sensation cannot be produced by any single monochromatic stimulus, and which cannot be isolated from daylight.

Also shown on the diagram are various CIE standard illuminants together with E (equal energy white). These have the following chromaticity coordinates:

Illuminant   *Chromaticity coordinates*

A (0.448, 0.408)
B (0.349, 0.352)
C (0.310, 0.316)
D_{65} (0.313, 0.329)

These are located on, or near, a curve of increasing temperature called the blackbody locus. This is the locus of the colour of a blackbody radiator as it is heated above 1000 K. Thus illuminant A is redder than illuminant C. Illuminant B approximates noon sunlight and illuminant C overcast light at noon. Illuminant D_{65} is used as an alignment white for many computer graphics monitors. Such standard illuminants can be used as illuminant colours when a scene is illuminated in computer graphics.

343

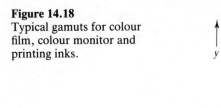

Figure 14.18
Typical gamuts for colour film, colour monitor and printing inks.

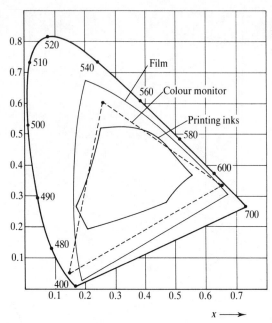

The interaction of the surface in the scene (defined by the spectral reflectance distribution) can be accurately calculated. This aspect is further discussed below.

There are a number of uses of the CIE chromaticity diagram. Firstly, it can be used to compare the gamut of various display devices. This is important in computer graphics when an image is eventually to be reproduced on a number of different devices. Figure 14.18 shows a CIE chromaticity diagram with the gamut of a typical computer graphics monitor together with the gamut for modern printing inks. The printing ink gamut is enclosed within the monitor gamut, which is itself enclosed by the gamut for colour film. This means that some colours attainable on film are not reproducible on a computer graphics monitor, and certain colours on a monitor cannot be reproduced by printing. The gamuts of display devices and reproduction techniques are always contained by the gamut of perceivable colours – the saturated or spectral colours being the most difficult to reproduce. However, this is not generally a problem because spectral and near-spectral colours do not tend to occur naturally. It is the relative spread of device gamuts that is important rather than the size of any gamut with respect to the visual gamut. (A more useful comparison of monitor and film gamuts, that includes the dimension luminance, is given in Section 14.6.6.)

The monitor gamut is a triangle because it specifies all those colours that can be additively mixed from three coloured lights – the

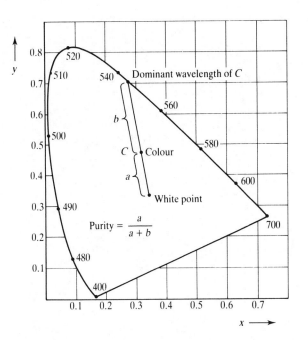

Figure 14.19
The dominant
wavelength and purity of
a colour are determined
by drawing a line through
the white point and the
colour to intersect the
boundary.

display RGB phosphors. The triangular monitor gamut in CIE xy space is to be found in most texts dealing with colour science in computer graphics, but it is somewhat misleading. The triangle is actually a projection, with the vertices formed from three CIE xyY points, where each 'phosphor vertex' has a different luminous value. Plate 20 shows three slices through the solid monitor gamut in CIE xyY space.

The chromaticity coordinates of these phosphors are always available from the monitor manufacturer (or the tube manufacturer). These vary slightly according to the phosphor; for example, long persistence phosphors, used in monitors for an interlaced display, have different characteristics from normal phosphors. Each vertex is always away from the saturated boundaries because each phosphor emits a band of wavelengths. The red phosphor is usually nearest to the boundary.

The chromaticity diagram can be used to translate the chromaticity coordinates into the duple dominant wavelength and purity. If a line is extended from the white point through the colour C to intersect the spectral locus, then that intersection gives the dominant wavelength of C. The purity of the colour specifies the amount of white light that it contains. Spectral colours are 100% pure and white light is 0% pure. The ratio $a/(a + b)$ in Figure 14.19 gives the purity of colour C.

The effect of mixing colours is easily predicted using chromaticity coordinates. If a colour is to be produced from a mixture of two other colours, then all of those colours on a line connecting the colours can be

345

Figure 14.20
The gamuts of two- and
three-colour additive
mixtures.

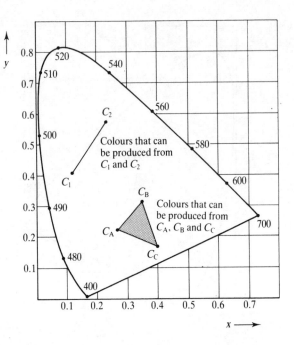

produced (Figure 14.20). If a colour is to be created from the additive
mixture of three colours then the triangle formed by these colours on the
chromaticity diagram defines the gamut of available colours. To mix two
colours C_1 and C_2 their CIE XYZ values must be summed:

$$C_{12} = C_1 + C_2$$
$$= (X_1 + X_2, \; Y_1 + Y_2, \; Z_1 + Z_2)$$
$$= (X_{12}, \; Y_{12}, \; Z_{12})$$

The relationship between the (X, Y, Z) values and the (x, y, Y) representation is given by:

$$X = x(Y/x) \qquad Y = Y \qquad Z = (1 - x - y)(Y/y)$$

Thus to specify an addition as a function of the chromaticity coordinates
we have:

$$x_{12} = \frac{(x_1 k_1 + x_2 k_2)}{(k_1 + k_2)}$$

Similarly

$$y_{12} = \frac{(y_1 k_1 + y_2 k_2)}{(k_1 + k_2)}$$

14.6.3 CIE xyY colour solid for a computer graphics monitor

It is useful to gain a conceptual understanding of the CIE xyY space, or that subset of the space that contains the gamut of a computer graphics monitor. The CIE colour solid for lights and fluorescent objects is formed by extruding the (x, y) chromaticity diagram along the Y axis. Planes of constant Y all contain identically shaped chromaticity diagrams. For non-fluorescent objects the situation is somewhat different. Here we are characterizing transmitted light that has been subject to selective absorption, and only certain regions of the wing-shaped chromaticity diagram exist as the luminance is increased. The chromaticity diagram shrinks around the white axis and at $Y = 1$ the diagram reduces to a single point. (For $Y = 1$ the only colour that can be produced is white.) The shape of the (x, y, Y) solid is defined for reflective objects by the MacAdam limits (MacAdam, 1981). These are the solid boundaries in planes of constant luminance. The CIE (x, y, Y) colour solid for a computer graphics monitor is a subset of the CIE solid for coloured lights.

The monitor solid in CIE XYZ space is a rectangular parallelepiped but the non-linear transformation into (x, y, Y) space results in a six-sided solid made up of curved surfaces. Three slices through this space are shown in Plate 20. These show the solid and its outline, in a plane through and perpendicular to the blue–yellow, red–cyan and green–magenta lines in the (x, y) plane. These lines are shown in Figure 14.21 which also shows the outline of the solid in planes of constant Y.

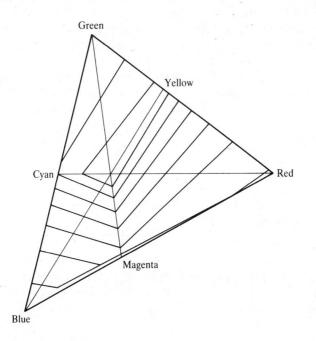

Figure 14.21
Boundaries of planes of constant Y and red–cyan, blue–yellow and green–magenta lines.

Return now to Figure 14.18. The full lines show the gamuts of film in the same plane. From this it can be seen that the differences are significant in certain areas. In the yellow and cyan regions, film is capable of greater saturation than the monitor but at lower luminance. In the red and green regions the monitor is capable of higher saturation at higher luminance. Clearly these considerations are important if colour work is to be accurately reproduced on film.

Of course the colour plate version of Figure 14.18 cannot possibly show the correct variations in the regions where film gamut is contained within a monitor gamut. Film has been used to record the slices and this image has been further subject to a printing process. Thus some regions of the colour plate have been subject to two gamut reductions.

14.6.4   CIE to monitor RGB transformation

Earlier we discussed the potential advantages that standard colour spaces such as the CIE system have for computer graphics. Using CIE space, for example, means that we must be able to transform a point in CIE space into monitor RGB space using a transformation:

$$\begin{bmatrix} R \\ G \\ B \end{bmatrix} = \begin{bmatrix} x_1 & x_2 & x_3 \\ y_1 & y_2 & y_3 \\ z_1 & z_2 & z_3 \end{bmatrix} \begin{bmatrix} X \\ Y \\ Z \end{bmatrix}$$

Any colour specified by a spectral distribution can be displayed accurately on a calibrated RGB monitor, by first obtaining its XYZ value (multiplying the spectral distribution by the CIE XYZ matching functions) and then using this transformation. The coefficients of the transformation matrix are determined from knowledge of the orientation of the RGB axes with respect to the CIE XYZ axes and from the coordinates of a single point in both systems. The former is obtained from the chromaticity coordinates of the monitor phosphors and the latter is the so-called alignment white. For example, the chromaticity coordinates of the monitor used in this text (a long persistence type suitable for interlaced systems) are:

	x	y
Red	0.620	0.330
Green	0.210	0.685
Blue	0.150	0.063

It is easier to consider the transformation from RGB to CIE XYZ space and to derive the required CIE XYZ to RGB coefficient matrix from the inverse of this. That is:

$$(XYZ_{CIE}) = T(RGB)$$
$$(RGB) = T^{-1}(XYZ_{CIE})$$

Assuming that the outputs from the phosphors are linearly related to the RGB voltages (see next section), we have:

$$\begin{bmatrix} X \\ Y \\ Z \end{bmatrix} = \begin{bmatrix} X_r & X_g & X_b \\ Y_r & Y_g & Y_b \\ Z_r & Z_g & Z_b \end{bmatrix} \begin{bmatrix} R \\ G \\ B \end{bmatrix}$$

where (X_r, X_g, X_b) are the tristimulus values required to produce a unit amount of the R primary, (Y_r, Y_g, Y_b) are the tristimulus values to produce a unit amount of the G primary etc. We define:

$$\begin{bmatrix} D_r \\ D_g \\ D_b \end{bmatrix} = \begin{bmatrix} X_r + Y_r + Z_r \\ X_g + Y_g + Z_g \\ X_b + Y_b + Z_b \end{bmatrix}$$

and write the previous equation as:

$$\begin{bmatrix} X \\ Y \\ Z \end{bmatrix} = \begin{bmatrix} D_r x_r & D_g x_g & D_b x_b \\ D_r y_r & D_g y_g & D_g y_b \\ D_r z_r & D_g z_g & D_b z_b \end{bmatrix} \begin{bmatrix} R \\ G \\ B \end{bmatrix}$$

where:

$$x_r = X_r/D_r \qquad y_r = Y_r/D_r \qquad z_r = Z_r/D_r \quad \text{etc.}$$

Writing the coefficients as a product of two matrices we have:

$$\begin{bmatrix} X \\ Y \\ Z \end{bmatrix} = \begin{bmatrix} x_r & x_g & x_b \\ y_r & y_g & y_b \\ z_r & z_g & z_b \end{bmatrix} \begin{bmatrix} D_r & 0 & 0 \\ 0 & D_g & 0 \\ 0 & 0 & D_b \end{bmatrix} \begin{bmatrix} R \\ G \\ B \end{bmatrix} \qquad \textbf{(14.2)}$$

where the first matrix is the chromaticity coordinates of the monitor phosphor. We now specify that equal RGB voltages of $(1, 1, 1)$ should produce the alignment white:

$$\begin{bmatrix} X_w \\ Y_w \\ Z_w \end{bmatrix} = \begin{bmatrix} x_r & x_g & x_b \\ y_r & y_g & y_b \\ z_r & z_g & z_b \end{bmatrix} \begin{bmatrix} D_r \\ D_g \\ D_b \end{bmatrix}$$

For example, with D_{65} we have:

$$x_w = 0.313 \qquad y_w = 0.329 \qquad z_w = 0.358$$

and scaling the white point to give unit luminance yields

$$X_w = 0.951 \qquad Y_w = 1.0 \qquad Z_w = 1.089$$

Using the above monitor chromaticities gives:

$$\begin{bmatrix} X \\ Y \\ Z \end{bmatrix} = \begin{bmatrix} 0.584 & 0.188 & 0.179 \\ 0.311 & 0.614 & 0.075 \\ 0.047 & 0.103 & 0.939 \end{bmatrix} \begin{bmatrix} R \\ G \\ B \end{bmatrix}$$

Inverting the coefficient matrix gives:

$$\begin{bmatrix} R \\ G \\ B \end{bmatrix} = \begin{bmatrix} 2.043 & -0.568 & -0.344 \\ -1.035 & 1.939 & 0.042 \\ 0.011 & -0.184 & 1.078 \end{bmatrix} \begin{bmatrix} X \\ Y \\ Z \end{bmatrix}$$

14.6.5 Monitor calibration and gamma correction

All of the foregoing discussion has implicitly assumed that there is a linear relationship between the actual RGB values input to a monitor and the intensity produced on the screen. This is not the case. The red intensity, for example, produced on a monitor screen by an input value of R_i is:

$$R_m = (R_i)^{\gamma_r}$$

where γ_r is normally in the range 2.3–2.8. If γ_r, γ_g and γ_b are known then so-called gamma correction can be applied to R_i:

$$R_i' = k(R_i)^{1/\gamma_r}$$

An inexpensive method for determining γ is given in Cowan (1983). This correction is easily incorporated in a video lookup table. There is a further discussion of the implementation of compensation tables in Catmull (1979). Note that the price paid for implementing gamma correction in a look-up table is a reduction in the dynamic range. For example, if k is chosen such that 0 maps to 0 and 255 to 255 then 256 intensity levels are reduced to 167 for a gamma of 2.7. This can cause banding and it is better to perform the correction in floating point arithmetic and then to round.

The difference that gamma correction makes is shown in Plate 22, where the top band is corrected. (The RGB graphs show the components that constitute each strip.) Note that there is a general intensity change; the lower intensities are lifted, resulting in practice in a reduction in contrast. There is also a chromaticity shift. This is because, in general, the chromaticity of the uncorrected colours is wrong. Consider, for example, the RGB triple $(0, 255, 127)$. If this is left uncorrected, the red and green components remain the same but the blue is lifted by the monitor gamma and a chromaticity shift results. We can only make this observation relative to the uncorrected strip. It does not imply that we cannot generate an identical display (to the uncorrected one) by using gamma correction.

Apart from second-order effects, such as gun independence (fully discussed in Cowan (1983)), calibrating a monitor to reproduce CIE colours depends on the following important factors. Monitor controls must be finally adjusted against actual colour samples and fixed. Viewing conditions, particularly ambient illumination, must be stabilized. Finally, note that the characteristics of a monitor may change from day to day and effect the calibration.

14.6.6 CIE LUV space

The 1931 CIE (x, y, Y) space, with its peculiarly shaped colour solid, is inconvenient in computer graphics. We can retain the original advantages of CIE space (direct relationship with standard colour systems, an unambiguous specification language for colour communication etc.) and gain two more significant advantages by working in CIE LUV space. These advantages are:

(1) CIE LUV space is a perceptually uniform space (approximately) and can be used to advantage in colour interpolation (see Section 14.4.4).

(2) The CIE LUV colour solid can be described in a cylindrical coordinate system and is similar, in this respect, to the HLS double hexcone model. It is thus amenable to incorporation in a user interface.

Both these advantages together with the original advantages of 1931 CIE space make this colour space extremely important to computer graphics practitioners engaged in serious colour work.

The 1931 CIE x–y chromaticity diagram has a significant disadvantage. Equally noticeable colour changes are not represented by uniform distances in (x, y) space. Perceptually equal changes are shortest in the violet region and longest in the green region. A transformation, accepted by the CIE in 1960, distorts the (x, y) space to correct this:

$$u = 2x/(6y - x + 1.5)$$
$$v = 3y/(6y - x + 1.5)$$

A more recent adoption (1974) defines (u', v') space as:

$$u' = 2x/(6y - x + 1.5)$$
$$v' = 4.5y/(6y - x + 1.5)$$

Y remains unchanged. Finally, this space is subject to a further transformation to define 1976 CIE LUV space. This transformation makes two adjustments. Firstly, it centres the achromatic axis on the point (0, 0). Secondly, zero luminance ($L^* = 0$) now becomes a single point. The L*u*v* definition is:

$$L^* = 116(Y/Y_w)^{1/3} - 16$$
$$u^* = 13L^*(u' - u_w')$$
$$v^* = 13L^*(v' - v_w')$$

where u', v' and Y are the coordinates of the colour in (u', v', Y) space and u_w, v_w and Y_w are the coordinates of the white point in this space. Three slices through this space are shown in Plate 21. From these illustrations it can be seen that the solid is a distorted double cone. This is not unlike the HLS model and we can thus define H, L and S parameters for this model and use these in a user interface if required. The definitions are:

$$H \text{ (hue)} = \arctan(v^*/u^*)$$
$$L \text{ (lightness)} = L^* \tag{14.2}$$
$$S \text{ (saturation)} = (u^* + v^*)^{1/2}$$

H is known as the CIE 1976 uv hue angle and L is the CIE 1976 psychometric lightness. S is the CIE 1976 uv chroma. Strictly speaking saturation must be defined in terms of luminance and the CIE 1976 psychometric saturation is defined as:

$$S_{uv} = \frac{\text{CIE 1976 uv chroma}}{L^*}$$
$$= \frac{(u^{*2} + v^{*2})^{1/2}}{L^*}$$

A further development of this philosophy is the Tektronix HVC system (Taylor, 1988). This is based approximately on the CIE LUV space using an H (hue) axis (0–360°), a V (value) axis (0–100) and a C (chroma) axis (0–100). It combines the interface advantages of the HLS model with the perceptually based measurements of the CIE space used and eliminates some of the problems of the HLS space that were discussed above.

14.7 Realistic rendering and reflection models

Reflection models produce an intensity for the light reflected from an object. This depends on the many factors discussed in earlier chapters. An aspect of reflection models, necessarily postponed until now, is the accurate reproduction of the colour of reflected light. The standard method adopted in computer graphics is to work with three intensity equations and to use these to drive an RGB monitor. This approach is fine for most computer graphics applications, where accurate colour modelling is not required. It is only in fairly specialized applications that it is important to render the precise colour of the light reflected from an object. For example, applications programs in the paint, dyeing or textile industry may demand high colour accuracy.

Apart from deficiencies that arise from undersampling, Hall (1986a) points out that performing computations in RGB colour space results in distortions. He gives an example of light reflecting from a perfect mirror. Using the primaries for a typical monitor and an NTSC white point, the reflectivities of the mirror at RGB values are 1.103, 0,970 and 0.822 and for, say, a D_{65} light source are 0.956, 1.019 and 0.898. Multiplying these triples gives a resultant RGB for reflected light that differs substantially from the light source colour. This is because $(R, G, B) = (1, 1, 1)$ specifies a monitor white point rather than the reflectivity of a perfect mirror.

Consider first the deficiencies of the three-colour approach. The characteristics of illuminants, the reflectivity of objects and the transmittivity of transparent objects are all wavelength-dependent functions. Hall and Greenberg (1983) point out that modelling such characteristics by three-point samples can lead to colour aliasing artefacts. These errors can be amplified in ray tracing programs because they accumulate in successive multiplications.

The solution to both these problems is to perform all computations in wavelength or spectral space, then transform for image storage into CIE XYZ space by using the matching functions to reduce the resulting spectral distribution of reflected intensity to an XYZ triple. This can then be transformed into any monitor RGB space. Sampling methodologies for spectral domain calculations are given in Hall and Greenberg (1983).

The obvious practical question is: how many spectral samples should be involved in the integral product of the tristimulus matching functions with the illuminant distribution? In Hall and Greenberg (1983) an experiment is described where a test environment, consisting of two overlapping filters, is illuminated by a D_{65} illuminant. A control image is generated by calculating light transmitted through the filters at 1 nm intervals. This is compared with images generated using three RGB samples and nine spectral samples. It is shown that the three-sample method generated significant colour artefacts, but the nine-sample method closely approximated the correct intensity function. Hall and Greenberg claim that, although the time spent in intensity calculations is substantially increased, the total computation time over the three-sample RGB approach is only 2%. However, it is not made clear to what 'total computation time' refers. The geometric calculation time is substantially different between a Phong model and ray tracing.

Glassner (1984) generates ray-traced images using 16 spectral samples. No formal justification is given for this. Also, in this paper the images that are generated are 'normal' computer graphics abstractions that do not really justify such a high colour accuracy.

Finally, note that if computations are carried out in the spectral domain using real illuminant spectral distributions in conjunction with real object reflectivity functions, then there is no guarantee that when the results are reduced to monitor RGB values, that these will be in the range $(0,0,0) \leqslant (R, G, B) \leqslant (1,1,1)$. Values outside of this range have to be limited in some way. It is an open question as to whether it is better to clamp to 0 and 1 or to adopt some other strategy as maintaining hue or dominant wavelength and desaturate until the calculated colour lies within the monitor range. This topic is discussed in detail in Hall (1983a).

Projects, notes and suggestions

14.1 HSV interface

Write a program that provides a user interface for an HSV model for Project 2.5.

14.2 Television colour solids

Produce a representation of YIQ and YUV space using a suitable set of cross-sections.

14.3 Pseudo-colour enhancement

Write an interface that will allow a naive user to select different colour mappings for the pseudo-colour enhancement of an appropriate function (this could be done by, for example, controlling the tilt of a plane containing a path in HSV space).

Choose a particular mapping in HSV space and compare this with an image generated from an 'identical' mapping using CIE HLS parameters (Equation 14.2). In each case use regular increments along the path.

Investigate perceptual differences between the images (and numeric differences by examining pixel values) as a function of the position of the path in the colour spaces.

14.4   CIE–RGB transformation

Determine the CIE–RGB transformation for your equipment and implement gamma correction.

14.5   Colour space sampling

Investigate the effects of the common procedure in computer graphics of performing calculations at three fixed wavelengths in RGB space.

Here you could refer to the methodology employed by Hall and Greenberg (1983) who generated a test environment consisting of two overlapping filters and compared variations along an appropriate scan line from images that were computed from:

- three samples in CIE XYZ space;
- three samples in RGB space;
- nine spectral samples;
- a control image (generated from samples at 1 nm intervals).

Of what relevance is undersampling in colour space to three-dimensional computer graphics?

APPENDIX A

Viewing Transformation for a Simple Four-parameter Viewing System

This appendix derives the matrix, $\mathbf{T}_{\text{view}}$, that transforms points in the world coordinate system to points in the view coordinate system for the simple fourparameter viewing system described in Chapter 1. The material is produced, not primarily to derive the result, but as a useful educational exercise in manipulating three-dimensional linear transformations.

The viewing transformation, $\mathbf{T}_{\text{view}}$, transforms points in the world coordinate system into the view coordinate system:

$$[x_v \; y_v \; z_v \; 1] = [x_w \; y_w \; z_w \; 1] \; \mathbf{T}_{\text{view}}$$

A view point (Figure A.1) is given as a set of three coordinates specifying the view point in the world coordinate system. An object described in the world coordinate

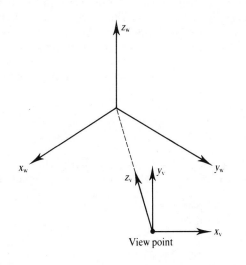

Figure A.1
World and view coordinate systems.

357

Figure A.2
Spherical coordinates
enable a simple interface
for the four-parameter
viewing system.

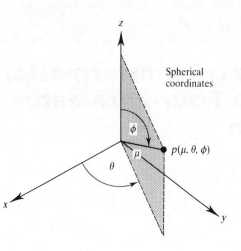

system is viewed from this point along a certain direction. In the view coordinate system, the z axis points towards the world system origin and the x axis is parallel to the x–y plane of the world system. We shall adopt a left-handed convention for the view coordinate system. In the view coordinate system the x and y axes match the axes of the display system and the z_v direction is away from the view point (into the display screen). World coordinates are normally right-handed systems so that in the computation of a net transformation matrix for the viewing transformation we would include a conversion to a left-handed system.

We can now specify the net transformation matrix as a series of translations and rotations that take us from the world coordinate system into the view coordinate system, given a particular view point.

These steps will be given as separate transformation matrices and the net transformation matrix resulting from the product will simply be stated.

In this simple system the viewing transformation is best specified using spherical instead of cartesian coordinates. We specify a view point in spherical coordinates by giving a distance from the origin μ and two angles, θ and ϕ, as shown in Figure A.2.

These are related to the view point's cartesian coordinates as follows:

$$T_x = \mu \sin \phi \cos \theta$$
$$T_y = \mu \sin \phi \sin \theta$$
$$T_z = \mu \cos \phi$$

Another fact we require in this derivation is that to change the origin of a system from $(0, 0, 0, 1)$ to $(T_x, T_y, T_z, 1)$ we use the transformation:

$$\begin{bmatrix} 1 & 0 & 0 & 0 \\ 0 & 1 & 0 & 0 \\ 0 & 0 & 1 & 0 \\ -T_x & -T_y & -T_z & 1 \end{bmatrix}$$

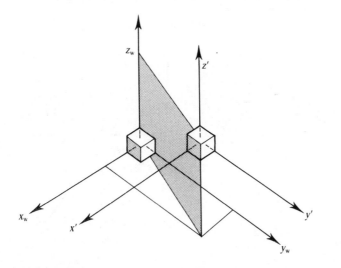

Note that this is the inverse of the transformation that would take a point from $(0, 0, 0, 1)$ to $(T_x, T_y, T_z, 1)$.

The four transformations required to take the object from a world coordinate system into a view coordinate system are:

(1)   Translate the world coordinate system to (T_x, T_y, T_z), the position of the view point. All three axes remain parallel to their counterparts in the world system. The cube in Figure A.3 is not an object that is being transformed but is intended to enhance an interpretation of the axes. Using spherical coordinate values for T_x, T_y, and T_z the transformation is:

$$
\mathbf{T}_1 = \begin{bmatrix}
1 & 0 & 0 & 0 \\
0 & 1 & 0 & 0 \\
0 & 0 & 1 & 0 \\
-\mu \cos\theta \sin\phi & -\mu \sin\theta \sin\phi & -\mu \cos\phi & 1
\end{bmatrix}
$$

(2)   The next step is to rotate the coordinate system through $90° - \theta$ in a clockwise direction about the z' axis. The rotation matrices defined in Chapter 1 were for counterclockwise rotation relative to a coordinate system. The transformation matrix for a clockwise rotation of the coordinate system is the same as that for a counterclockwise rotation of a point relative to the coordinate system. The x'' axis is now normal to the plane containing μ, (Figure A.4).

$$
\mathbf{T}_2 = \begin{bmatrix}
\sin\theta & \cos\theta & 0 & 0 \\
-\cos\theta & \sin\theta & 0 & 0 \\
0 & 0 & 1 & 0 \\
0 & 0 & 0 & 1
\end{bmatrix}
$$

Figure A.4
Transformation 2.

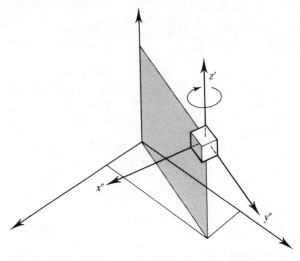

(3)   The next step is to rotate the coordinate system through $180° - \phi$ counterclockwise about the x' axis. This makes the z''' axis pass through the origin of the world coordinate system (Figure A.5).

$$\mathbf{T}_3 = \begin{bmatrix} 1 & 0 & 0 & 0 \\ 0 & -\cos\phi & -\sin\phi & 0 \\ 0 & \sin\phi & -\cos\phi & 0 \\ 0 & 0 & 0 & 1 \end{bmatrix}$$

(4)   Finally we convert to a left-handed system as described above.

$$\mathbf{T}_4 = \begin{bmatrix} -1 & 0 & 0 & 0 \\ 0 & 1 & 0 & 0 \\ 0 & 0 & 1 & 0 \\ 0 & 0 & 0 & 1 \end{bmatrix}$$

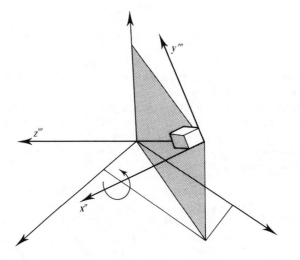

Figure A.5
Transformation 3.

Multiplying these together gives the net transformation matrix required for the viewing transformation.

$$\mathbf{T}_{\text{view}} = [\mathbf{T}_1\ \mathbf{T}_2\ \mathbf{T}_3\ \mathbf{T}_4] \begin{bmatrix} -\sin\theta & -\cos\theta\cos\phi & -\cos\theta\sin\phi & 0 \\ \cos\theta & -\sin\theta\cos\phi & -\sin\theta\sin\phi & 0 \\ 0 & \sin\phi & -\cos\phi & 0 \\ 0 & 0 & \mu & 1 \end{bmatrix}$$

where

$$[x_v\, y_v\, z_v\, 1] = [x_w\, y_w\, z_w\, 1]\mathbf{T}_{\text{view}}$$

APPENDIX B

A Wireframe System

B.1 Introduction

This appendix presents a complete program (Program B.1) that sets up a data structure for objects and draws a wireframe projection of these objects in two-dimensional screen space. The data structure used is more complicated than it need be for wireframes, because the program is subsequently used by procedures that perform shading (Appendix C).

The appendix is intended to provide further study of the material given in Chapter 1, particularly with regard to implementation details and the relationship between data structures and graphical programming techniques. The program is written in a way that hopefully facilitates this. Machine-dependent material is inevitably embedded (SunCore system) but apart from this single, rather large, program, other examples in the text are machine independent.

The general approach to wireframe drawing used in the program is:

(1) Set up the parameters of a general viewing system.

(2) Use three-dimensional line-drawing utilities:

$$move\_to3D(x, y, z)$$
$$line\_to3D(x, y, z)$$

or use the GKS-3D/PHIGS utility:

$$polyline3(\ )$$

to draw the wireframe object.

The alternative approach to wireframe drawing mentioned in Chapter 1 is:

(1) Implement your own viewing system.

(2)   Use two-dimensional line-drawing utilities:

$$move\_to(x, y)$$
$$line\_to(x, y)$$

or use the GKS (two-dimensional) utility:

$$polyline(\ )$$

that operate on screen coordinates output from the user-implemented transformations described in Chapter 1. This approach has to be used on a graphics system that does not have three-dimensional utilities.

B.2   Data structure

This section is not for the faint hearted but its worth a glance if you are using the program. Implementers will find a detailed study of this section useful. Early mistakes in the design of a data structure are usually left and can have tedious consequences. The data structure has the following attributes:

(1)   It is a hierarchical object, surface, polygon scheme as outlined in Chapter 1.

(2)   Vertex details are stored once only and different polygons can share the same vertex. However, this does not apply if the vertices are shared by two surfaces. Here a shared vertex is stored for each surface.

(3)   Polygon normals are stored (for culling) and vertex normals are stored (for shading).

A scene is composed of a number of objects and stored in the data structure as a list of objects. The pointer to the start of the list is *ObjectHead* (Figure B.1). The fields of an object record have self-explanatory names; for example, *Transform* is a transformation matrix that will be used to transform the object (rotate, scale and so on).

An object is constructed from a number of surfaces, the first of which is pointed to by the field *SurfaceHead* in the object cell. Again they are stored in a list as shown in Figure B.1. Each surface is represented by a mesh of polygons. The field *NoofPolygons* in a surface cell tells us how many polygons there are in the list pointed to by the field *PolygonHead*. Each polygon cell contains space to store a normal and a boolean culled flag.

A polygon is defined using a set of vertices. They are listed in a defined order (counterclockwise with respect to viewing from the outside of the object). This order is needed to obtain the correct normal direction when calculating the polygon normal.

Each vertex list cell (Figure B.1) points to a vertex record (using the field *Vertex*) where the details of a vertex are stored. This enables adjacent polygons to share a vertex and vertices to be stored only once (unless they happen to be shared by adjacent surfaces). Thus many polygons can point to the same vertex record.

The vertex details for a particular object are stored as a list pointed to by a field labelled *VertexHead* in the object cell. This simplifies transformation operations, since the vertices to be transformed are now directly accessible at the top level of the data structure.

In order to calculate a vertex normal, the surrounding polygon normals are averaged. Therefore, a list of the polygons that share a vertex must be recorded. This list is pointed to by the field *Polygons* within a vertex cell.

To build the data structure we need a scene file. An example is:

```
1                     { 1 = perspective 0 = parallel }
−7000                 { view distance }
10000                 { perspective distance }
−0.7 −0.4 −0.3        { viewplane normal }
  0.0   0.0   1.0     { view up vector }
0                     { draw vertex normals 0 = false 1 = true}

4                     { no. of objects }

cube.obj
  0.4   0.4   0.4     { scale }
  0.0   0.0   0.0     { rotate }
  0.5   1.7 −0.6      { translate }
F.obj
  1.0   1.0   1.0
  0.0   0.0   0.0
  1.7 −0.4   0.0
cube.obj
  0.2   0.2   1.0
  0.0   0.0   0.0
  0.0   1.7   0.8
cylinder.obj
  0.9   0.9   1.0
  0.0   0.0   0.0
  0.0   0.0   0.0
```

This structure is as follows:

> viewing information
>
> number of objects
>
> for each object
>> object data filename
>> object transformations

In the above example there are four objects in the scene with data defined in three files. The transformations to be carried out on an object are read into the

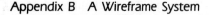

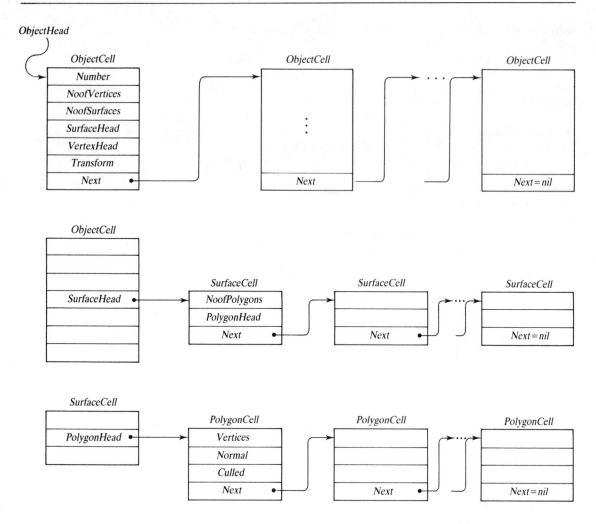

program and a net transformation matrix is constructed. This is then stored in the *Transform* field of an object cell.

An object data file is structured as follows:

Number of vertices, number of polygons, number of surfaces.

Vertex information
  vertex number, x, y, z

Polygon information
  polygon number, surface number, number of vertices, list of vertex numbers.

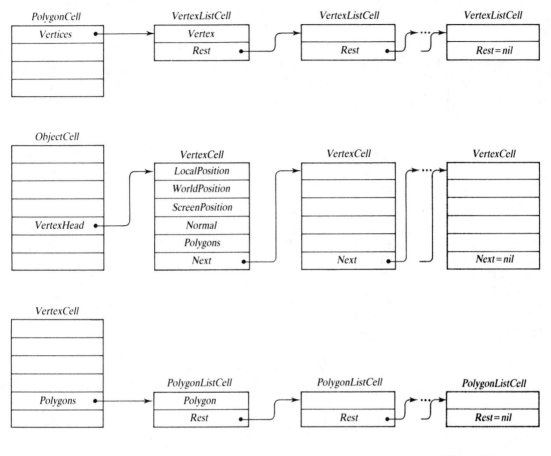

Figure B.1
The data strucure.

We can now look at a practical example of the complete data structure for a single simple object (Figure B.2). It may seem that, for such a simple object, the information content of the data structure is somewhat high, but in practice objects may have hundreds or thousands of polygons and an economical representation becomes a necessity. Also, bear in mind that the structure is enhanced with shading requirements.

Although it may seem more expensive to use pointers, rather than array indexing, the use of arrays is inflexible with regard to the size of the scene that can be stored in a data structure. With a pointer structure the data structure 'automatically' expands and contracts to fit the specified scene.

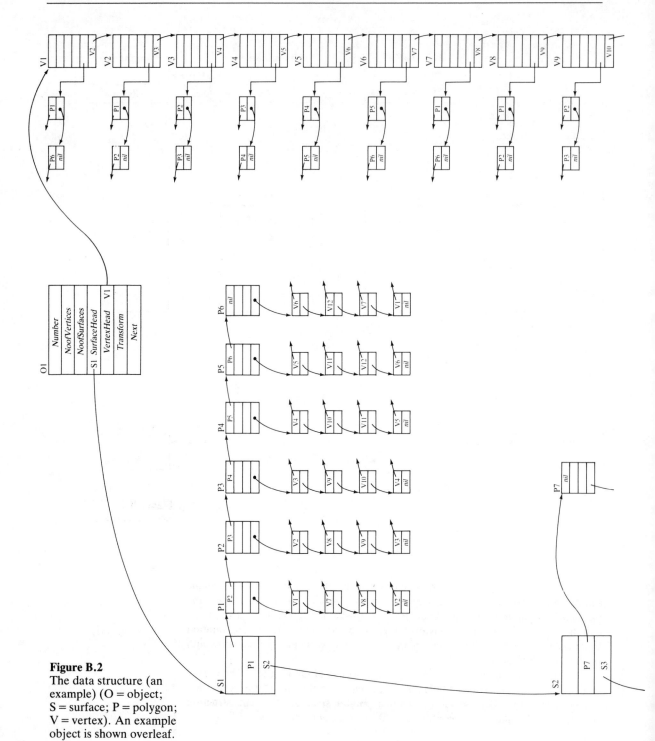

Figure B.2
The data structure (an example) (O = object; S = surface; P = polygon; V = vertex). An example object is shown overleaf.

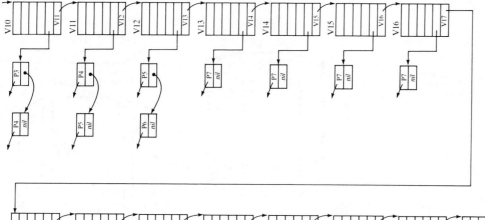

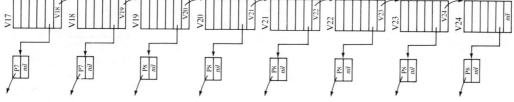

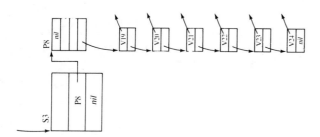

Figure B.2 (*contd*)   A cylinder

Vertices 1–12

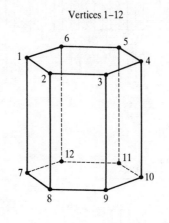

(Top) surface 2 polygon 7

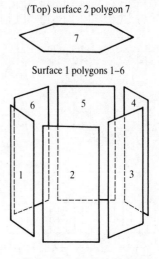

Surface 1 polygons 1–6

(Bottom) surface 3 polygon 8

Data file

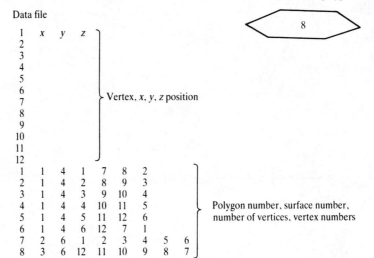

	x	y	z					
1								
2								
3								
4								
5								
6								
7								
8								
9								
10								
11								
12								

Vertex, *x*, *y*, *z* position

1	1	4	1	7	8	2		
2	1	4	2	8	9	3		
3	1	4	3	9	10	4		
4	1	4	4	10	11	5		
5	1	4	5	11	12	6		
6	1	4	6	12	7	1		
7	2	6	1	2	3	4	5	6
8	3	6	12	11	10	9	8	7

Polygon number, surface number, number of vertices, vertex numbers

B.3   Program

Firstly, system-dependent parts are appropriately covered in gray. These are mainly to do with initialization and will have an equivalent in your system. In order of execution the main procedures are:

- *ReadScene*: this reads a scene specification as described in the data structure section.

- *TransformObject*: for each object, this procedure takes the net transformation matrix stored in the field *Transform* of an object cell and multiplies the vertices pointed to by the field *VertexHead* by this matrix. This transforms the vertices which define the object from their 'local positions' to their 'world positions', both values being stored in the vertex cell.

- *CalculateNormals*: this procedure calculates both the polygon normals and the vertex normals for all objects in the scene.

- *CullObjectPolygons*: this applies the culling procedure to object polygons, 'marking' the data structure appropriately.

- *DrawObject*: is a hierarchical procedure already described in Chapter 1. It finally uses:

$$MoveTo3D(x, y, z)$$
$$LineTo3D(x, y, z)$$

which are themselves defined using system dependent utilities.

Program B.1   A wireframe drawing program.

```
program SimpleWireFrame(input, output);

const
    MaxVertices = 2000;

type
    Vector = record x, y, z: real; end;
    Matrices = array [0..3, 0..3] of real;
    String32 = packed array [1..32] of char;

    ObjectPtr = ^ObjectCell;
    SurfacePtr = ^SurfaceCell;
    PolygonPtr = ^PolygonCell;
    PolygonList = ^PolygonListCell;
    VertexPtr = ^VertexCell;
    VertexList = ^VertexListCell;

    VertexListCell = record
                        Vertex: VertexPtr;
                        Rest: VertexList;
                     end;
```

```
PolygonListCell = record
                    Polygon: PolygonPtr;
                    Rest: PolygonList;
                end;
ObjectCell = record
                Number: integer;
                NoofVertices, NoofSurfaces: integer;
                SurfaceHead: SurfacePtr;
                VertexHead: VertexPtr;
                Transform: Matrices;
                Next: ObjectPtr;
            end;
SurfaceCell = record
                NoofPolygons: integer;
                PolygonHead: PolygonPtr;
                Next: SurfacePtr;
            end;
PolygonCell = record
                Vertices: VertexList;
                Normal: Vector;
                Culled: boolean;
                Next: PolygonPtr;
            end;
VertexCell = record
                LocalPosition,
                WorldPosition,
                ScreenPosition,
                Normal: Vector;
                Polygons: PolygonList;
                Next: VertexPtr;
            end;
Windows = record
                x0, x1, y0, y1: real;
            end;
ViewPorts = record
                x0, x1, y0, y1, z0, z1: real;
            end;


var
    ObjectHead,
    Object                : ObjectPtr;
    ViewReferencePoint    : Vector;
    ViewPlaneNormal       : Vector;
    ViewDistance          : real;
    FrontDistance         : real;
    BackDistance          : real;
    ProjectionType        : integer;
    ProjectionVector      : Vector;
    TheWindow             : Windows;
    ViewUpVector          : Vector;
    TheViewPort           : ViewPorts;
    ProjectionDistance,
    ViewPlaneDistance     : real;
```

372

```
DisplayScreen          : vwsurf;    { a record containing information about the
                                      output screen }
DrawVertexNormals: boolean;


function radian(x: real): real;
const
  pi = 3.1415926536;
begin
  radian := x*pi/180;
end   { radian };


function Magnitude(a: Vector): real;
begin
  with a do Magnitude := sqrt(sqr(x) + sqr(y) + sqr(z))
end   { Magnitude };


procedure Normalise(a: Vector; var b: Vector);
var denom, r: real;
begin
  denom := Magnitude(a);
  if denom = 0.0 then b := a
  else
  begin
    r := 1.0/denom;
    b.x := a.x*r;
    b.y := a.y*r;
    b.z := a.z*r;
  end;
end   { Normalise };


function DotProduct(a, b: Vector): real;
begin
  DotProduct := a.x*b.x + a.y*b.y + a.z*b.z;
end   { DotProduct };


procedure ReturnIdentityMatrix(var m: Matrices);
var
  i, j: integer;
begin
  for i := 0 to 3 do
    for j := 0 to 3 do
      if i = j then m[i, j] := 1.0
      else m[i, j] := 0.0;
end   { ReturnIdentityMatrix };


procedure ReturnZeroMatrix(var m: Matrices);
var
  i, j: integer;
begin
  for i := 0 to 3 do
    for j := 0 to 3 do
      m[i, j] := 0.0;
end   { ReturnZeroMatrix };
```

373

```
procedure MatrixMult(m1, m2: Matrices; var m: Matrices);
var
  i, j, element: integer;
begin
  ReturnZeroMatrix(m);
  for i := 0 to 3 do
    for j := 0 to 3 do
      for element := 0 to 3 do
        m[i, j] := m[i, j] + m1[i, element]*m2[element, j];
end   { MatrixMult };


procedure MatrixVector(m: Matrices; v: Vector; var mv: Vector);
begin
  with v do
  begin
    mv.x := m[0, 0]*x + m[0, 1]*y + m[0, 2]*z + m[0, 3];
    mv.y := m[1, 0]*x + m[1, 1]*y + m[1, 2]*z + m[1, 3];
    mv.z := m[2, 0]*x + m[2, 1]*y + m[2, 2]*z + m[2, 3];
  end;
end   { MatrixVector };


procedure WriteMatrix(m: Matrices);
var
  i, j: integer;
begin
  for i := 0 to 3 do
  begin
    for j := 0 to 3 do
      write(m[i, j]:10:3);
    writeln;
  end;
  writeln;
end   { WriteMatrix };


procedure Initialisation;
var
  f: integer;
  tstr: vsurfst;
begin
  tstr := ' ';
  DisplayScreen.screenname := tstr;
  DisplayScreen.windowname := tstr;
  DisplayScreen.windowfd := 0;
  DisplayScreen.dd := pasloc(pixwindd);
  DisplayScreen.instance := 0;
  DisplayScreen.cmapsize := 0;
  DisplayScreen.cmapname := tstr;
  DisplayScreen.flags := 0;
  f := initializecore(BASIC, NOINPUT, THREED);
  f := initializevwsurf(DisplayScreen, CORE_FALSE);
  f := selectvwsurf(DisplayScreen);
  f := CreateRetainSeg(1);   { creates a segment on the current vwsurf }
```

```
ProjectionDistance := 10000.0;
with ViewReferencePoint do
begin
  x := 0.0; y := 0.0; z := 0.0;
end;
with ViewPlaneNormal do
begin
  x := -0.7; y := -0.4; z := -0.3;
end;
ViewDistance := -6000.0;
FrontDistance := 0.0;
BackDistance := 1.0;
ProjectionType := PARALLEL;
with ProjectionVector do
begin
  x := 0.0; y := 0.0; z := 1.0;
end;
with TheWindow do
begin
  x0 := -1.0; x1 := 1.0; y0 := -0.75; y1 := 0.75;
end;
with ViewUpVector do
begin
  x := 0.0; y := 0.0; z := 1.0;
end;
with TheViewPort do
begin
  x0 := 0.0; x1 := 1.0;
  y0 := 0.0; y1 := 0.75;
  z0 := 0.0; z1 := 1.0;
end;
DrawVertexNormals := false;
end   { Initialisation };

procedure SetUpViewingParameters(var SceneF: text);
var
  f, tempint: integer;
  tvpn: real;
begin
  readln(SceneF, tempint);
  if tempint = 0 then ProjectionType := PARALLEL
  else ProjectionType := PERSPECTIVE;
  readln(SceneF, ViewDistance);
  readln(SceneF, ProjectionDistance);
  with ViewPlaneNormal do readln(SceneF, x, y, z);
  with ViewUpVector do readln(SceneF, x, y, z);
  readln(SceneF, tempint);
  if tempint = 1 then DrawVertexNormals := true
  else DrawVertexNormals := false;
  with ViewPlaneNormal do
  begin
    tvpn := -ProjectionDistance/sqrt(sqr(x) + sqr(y) + sqr(z));
    ProjectionVector.x := x*tvpn;
```

```
                    ProjectionVector.y := y*tvpn;
                    ProjectionVector.z := z*tvpn;
                  end;
                f := setviewplanedist(ViewDistance);
                with ViewPlaneNormal do
                  f := setviewplanenorm(x, y, z);
                with ViewUpVector do
                  f := setviewup3(x, y, z);
                with ProjectionVector do
                  f := setprojection(ProjectionType, x, y, z);
                with TheWindow do
                  f := setwindow(x0, x1, y0, y1);
              end   { SetUpViewingParameters };


procedure ReadObject(FileName: String32; var Object: ObjectPtr);
var
  VertexMapArray: array[1..MaxVertices] of VertexPtr;
  SMapArray: array[1..MaxVertices] of integer;
  ObjF: text;

  procedure ReadVertices(NoofVertices: integer;
                              var VertexHead: VertexPtr);
  var
    vno, n: integer;
  begin
    for vno := 1 to NoofVertices do
    begin
      SMapArray[vno] := 0;
      new(VertexMapArray[vno]);
      with VertexMapArray[vno]^ do
      begin
        with LocalPosition do readln(ObjF, n, x, y, z);
        Polygons := nil;
      end;
    end;
    for vno := 1 to NoofVertices − 1 do
      VertexMapArray[vno]^.Next := VertexMapArray[vno + 1];
    VertexHead := VertexMapArray[1];
    VertexMapArray[NoofVertices]^.Next := nil;
  end   { ReadVertices };

  procedure ReadSurfaces(NoofSurfaces: integer;
                              var SurfaceHead: SurfacePtr;
                              var NoofVertices: integer;
                              var VertexHead: VertexPtr);
  var
    sno: integer;
    Surface: SurfacePtr;

    procedure ReadPolygons(sno, NoofPolygons: integer;
                                var PolygonHead: PolygonPtr;
                                var NoofVertices: integer;
                                var VertexHead: VertexPtr);
```

```pascal
var
  pno: integer;
  PolyP: PolygonPtr;

procedure ReadPolygon(sno: integer;
                      PolyP: PolygonPtr;
                      var NoofVertices: integer;
                      var VertexHead: VertexPtr);
var
  vno, NoofVerts, VertexNumber: integer;
  VertL: VertexList;
  tvptr: VertexPtr;

  procedure AddPolyToPolyList(PolyP: PolygonPtr;
                              var PolyL: PolygonList);
  begin
    if PolyL = nil then
    begin
      new(PolyL);
      PolyL^.Polygon := PolyP;
      PolyL^.Rest := nil;
    end
    else AddPolyToPolyList(PolyP, PolyL^.Rest);
  end  { AddPolyToPolyList };

begin  { ReadPolygon }
  with PolyP^ do
  begin
    Vertices := nil;
    read(ObjF, NoofVerts);
    for vno := 1 to NoofVerts do
    begin
      if Vertices = nil then
      begin
        new(VertL);
        Vertices := VertL;
      end
      else
      begin
        new(VertL^.Rest);
        VertL := VertL^.Rest;
      end;
      read(ObjF, VertexNumber);
      if SMapArray[VertexNumber] = 0 then
        SMapArray[VertexNumber] := sno
      else if SMapArray[VertexNumber] <> sno then
      begin
        NoofVertices := NoofVertices + 1;
        SMapArray[VertexNumber] := sno;
        new(tvptr);
        tvptr^ := VertexMapArray[VertexNumber]^;
        tvptr^.Polygons := nil;
        tvptr^.Next := VertexHead;
        VertexHead := tvptr;
        VertexMapArray[VertexNumber] := tvptr;
      end;
```

377

```
                        VertL^.Vertex := VertexMapArray[VertexNumber];
                        AddPolyToPolyList(PolyP, VertL^.Vertex^.Polygons);
                    end;
                end;
                VertL^.Rest := nil;
            end   { ReadPolygon };

        begin   { ReadPolygons }
            PolygonHead := nil;
            for pno := 1 to NoofPolygons do
            begin
                if PolygonHead = nil then
                begin
                    new(PolyP);
                    PolygonHead := PolyP;
                end
                else
                begin
                    new(PolyP^.Next);
                    PolyP := PolyP^.Next;
                end;
                ReadPolygon(sno, PolyP, NoofVertices, VertexHead);
            end;
            PolyP^.Next := nil;
        end   { ReadPolygons };

    begin   { ReadSurfaces }
        SurfaceHead := nil;
        for sno := 1 to NoofSurfaces do
        begin
            if SurfaceHead = nil then
            begin
                new(Surface);
                SurfaceHead := Surface;
            end
            else
            begin
                new(Surface^.Next);
                Surface := Surface^.Next;
            end;
            with Surface^ do
            begin
                readln(ObjF, NoofPolygons);
                ReadPolygons(sno, NoofPolygons, PolygonHead,
                             NoofVertices, VertexHead);
            end;
        end;
        Surface^.Next := nil;
    end   { ReadSurfaces };
```

```
begin { ReadObject }
  new(Object);
  Object^.next := ObjectHead;
  ObjectHead := Object;
  reset(ObjF, FileName);
  with ObjectHead^ do
  begin
    readln(ObjF, NoofVertices);
    writeln('NoofVertices:', NoofVertices: 6);
    ReadVertices(NoofVertices, VertexHead);
    readln(ObjF, NoofSurfaces);
    writeln('NoofSurfaces:', NoofSurfaces: 6);
    ReadSurfaces(NoofSurfaces, SurfaceHead, NoofVertices, VertexHead);
    writeln('NoofVertices:', NoofVertices:6);
  end;
end   { ReadObject };

procedure ReadXforms(var XformF: text; Object: ObjectPtr);
var
  x, y, z: real;
  sm, rm, tm: Matrices;

  procedure ReturnScaleMatrix(var m: Matrices; x, y, z: real);
  begin
    ReturnIdentityMatrix(m);
    m[0, 0] := x;
    m[1, 1] := y;
    m[2, 2] := z;
  end;  { ReturnScaleMatrix };

  procedure ReturnRotateMatrix(var m: Matrices; x, y, z: real);
  var
    mx, my, mz: Matrices;
  begin
    x := radian(x);
    y := radian(y);
    z := radian(z);
    ReturnIdentityMatrix(mz);
    mz[0, 0] := cos(z); mz[0, 1] := -sin(z);
    mz[1, 0] := sin(z); mz[1, 1] := cos(z);
    ReturnIdentityMatrix(my);
    my[0, 0] := cos(y); my[0, 2] := sin(y);
    my[2, 0] := -sin(y); my[2, 2] := cos(y);
    ReturnIdentityMatrix(mx);
    mx[1, 1] := cos(x); mx[1, 2] := -sin(x);
    mx[2, 1] := sin(x); mx[2, 2] := cos(x);
    MatrixMult(my, mx, m);
    MatrixMult(mz, m, m);
  end    { ReturnRotateMatrix };
```

379

```
    procedure ReturnTranslateMatrix(var m: Matrices; x, y, z: real);
    begin
      ReturnIdentityMatrix(m);
      m[0, 3] := x;
      m[1, 3] := y;
      m[2, 3] := z;
    end   { ReturnTranslateMatrix };

begin   { ReadXforms }
  readln(XformF, x, y, z);
  ReturnScaleMatrix(sm, x, y, z);
  readln(XformF, x, y, z);
  ReturnRotateMatrix(rm, x, y, z);
  readln(XformF, x, y, z);
  ReturnTranslateMatrix(tm, x, y, z);
  with Object^ do
  begin
    MatrixMult(rm, sm, Transform);
    MatrixMult(tm, Transform, Transform);
  end;
end   { ReadXforms };

procedure ReadScene(fname: String32);
var
  SceneF: text;
  i, NoofObjects: integer;
  ObjName: String32;
  Object: ObjectPtr;
begin
  reset(SceneF, fname);
  SetUpViewingParameters(SceneF);
  readln(SceneF, NoofObjects);
  for i := 1 to NoofObjects do
  begin
    readln(SceneF, ObjName);
    writeln; write('Reading object:');
    writeln(ObjName); writeln;
    ReadObject(ObjName, Object);
    ReadXforms(SceneF, Object);
  end;
end   { ReadScene };

procedure TransformObject(Object: ObjectPtr);
var
  Vertex: VertexPtr;
begin
  with Object^ do
  begin
    Vertex := VertexHead;
    while Vertex <> nil do
```

```
  begin
    with Vertex^ do
      MatrixVector(Transform, LocalPosition, WorldPosition);
    Vertex := Vertex^.Next;
    end;
  end;
end   { TransformObject };

procedure CalculateNormals(Object: ObjectPtr);

  procedure CalculatePolygonNormals(Object: ObjectPtr);
  var
    Surface: SurfacePtr;
    Polygon: PolygonPtr;

    procedure CalculateNormal(Polygon: PolygonPtr);
    var
      VList: VertexList;
      wp1, wp2, wp3: Vector;
      Success: boolean;

      procedure CalcNorm(wp1, wp2, wp3: Vector;
                         var n: Vector;
                         var Success: boolean);
      const
        AlmostZero = 1E-5;
      var
        a, b: Vector;
      begin
        with a do
        begin
          x := wp2.x − wp1.x;
          y := wp2.y − wp1.y;
          z := wp2.z − wp1.z;
        end;
        with b do
        begin
          x := wp3.x − wp2.x;
          y := wp3.y − wp2.y;
          z := wp3.z − wp2.z;
        end;
        with n do
        begin
          x := a.y*b.z − a.z*b.y;
          y := a.z*b.x − a.x*b.z;
          z := a.x*b.y − a.y*b.x;
          Success := abs(x) + abs(y) + abs(z) > AlmostZero;
        end;
      end   { CalcNorm };
```

```
begin { CalculateNormal }
  with Polygon^ do
  begin
    VList := Polygon^.Vertices;
    wp1 := VList^.Vertex^.WorldPosition;
    VList := VList^.Rest;
    wp2 := VList^.Vertex^.WorldPosition;
    VList := VList^.Rest;
    wp3 := VList^.Vertex^.WorldPosition;
    CalcNorm(wp1, wp2, wp3, Normal, Success);
    while not Success do
    begin
      wp1 := wp2;
      wp2 := wp3;
      VList := VList^.Rest;
      wp3 := VList^.Vertex^.WorldPosition;
      CalcNorm(wp1, wp2, wp3, Normal, Success);
    end;
    Normalise(Normal, Normal);
  end;
end   { CalculateNormal };


begin   { CalculatePolygonNormals }
  Surface := Object^.SurfaceHead;
  while Surface <> nil do
  begin
    Polygon := Surface^.PolygonHead;
    while Polygon <> nil do
    begin
      CalculateNormal(Polygon);
      Polygon := Polygon^.Next;
    end;
    Surface := Surface^.Next;
  end;
end   { CalculatePolygonNormals };


procedure CalculateVertexNormals(Object: ObjectPtr);
var
  Vertex: VertexPtr;


  procedure CalculateNormal(Vertex: VertexPtr);
  var
    PolyL: PolygonList;
    totalvec: Vector;
  begin
    with totalvec do
    begin
      x := 0; y := 0; z := 0;
    end;
    PolyL := Vertex^.Polygons;
    while PolyL <> nil do
```

```
      begin
        with PolyL^.Polygon^ do
        begin
          totalvec.x := totalvec.x + Normal.x;
          totalvec.y := totalvec.y + Normal.y;
          totalvec.z := totalvec.z + Normal.z;
        end;
        PolyL := PolyL^.Rest;
      end;
      Normalise(totalvec, Vertex^.Normal);
    end   { CalculateNormal };

  begin   { CalculateVertexNormals }
    Vertex := Object^.VertexHead;
    while Vertex <> nil do
    begin
      CalculateNormal(Vertex);
      Vertex := Vertex^.Next;
    end;
  end   { CalculateVertexNormals };

begin   { CalculateNormals }
  CalculatePolygonNormals(Object);
  CalculateVertexNormals(Object);
end   { CalculateNormals };

procedure CullObjectPolygons(Object: ObjectPtr);
var
  Surface: SurfacePtr;

  procedure CullSurfacePolygons(Polygon: PolygonPtr);

    procedure CullPolygon(Polygon: PolygonPtr);
    var
      LineOfSight: Vector;
    begin
      with Polygon^.Vertices^.Vertex^.WorldPosition do
      begin
        LineOfSight.x := ProjectionVector.x - x;
        LineOfSight.y := ProjectionVector.y - y;
        LineOfSight.z := ProjectionVector.z - z;
      end;
      with Polygon^ do
        Culled := DotProduct(Normal, LineOfSight) < 0;
    end   { CullPolygon };

  begin   { CullSurfacePolygons }
    while Polygon <> nil do
    begin
      CullPolygon(Polygon);
      Polygon := Polygon^.Next;
    end;
  end   { CullSurfacePolygons };
```

```
begin   { CullObjectPolygons }
  Surface := Object^.SurfaceHead;
  while Surface <> nil do
  begin
    CullSurfacePolygons(Surface^.PolygonHead);
    Surface := Surface^.Next;
  end;
end   { CullObjectPolygons };

procedure CalculateScreenCoords(Object: ObjectPtr);
var
  Vertex: VertexPtr;

  procedure ScreenCoords(w: Vector;
                              var s: Vector);
  var
    f: integer;
  begin
    f := mapworldtondc3(w.x, w.y, w.z, s.x, s.y, s.z);
    with s do
    begin
      x := x*300; y := y*300; z := z*1024;
    end;
  end   { ScreenCoords };

begin { CalculateScreenCoords }
  Vertex := Object^.VertexHead;
  while Vertex <> nil do
    with Vertex^ do
    begin
      ScreenCoords(WorldPosition, ScreenPosition);
      Vertex := Next;
    end;
end   { CalculateScreenCoords };

procedure DrawObject(Object: ObjectPtr);
var
  Surface: SurfacePtr;

  procedure MoveTo3D(p: Vector);
  var
    f: integer;
  begin
    with p do
      f := moveabs3(x, y, z);
  end   { MoveTo3D };

  procedure DrawTo3D(p: Vector);
  var
    f: integer;
  begin
    with p do
      f := lineabs3(x, y, z);
  end   { DrawTo3D };
```

```
procedure DrawSurface(Surface: SurfacePtr);
var
  Polygon: PolygonPtr;


  procedure DrawPolygon(Polygon: PolygonPtr);
  var
    VList: VertexList;
    StartPos: Vector;


    procedure DrawVNormal(Vertex: VertexPtr);
    var
      tvec: Vector;
    begin
      with Vertex^ do
      begin
        tvec.x := WorldPosition.x + 0.1*Normal.x;
        tvec.y := WorldPosition.y + 0.1*Normal.y;
        tvec.z := WorldPosition.z + 0.1*Normal.z;
        MoveTo3D(WorldPosition);
        DrawTo3D(tvec);
      end;
    end   { DrawVNormal };


  begin   { DrawPolygon }
    with Polygon^ do
      if not Culled then
      begin
        VList := Vertices;
        StartPos := VList^.Vertex^.WorldPosition;
        MoveTo3D(StartPos);
        VList := VList^.Rest;
        while VList <> nil do
        begin
          DrawTo3D(VList^.Vertex^.WorldPosition);
          VList := VList^.Rest;
        end;
        DrawTo3D(StartPos);
        if DrawVertexNormals then
        begin
          VList := Vertices;
          while VList <> nil do
          begin
            DrawVNormal(VList^.Vertex);
            VList := VList^.Rest;
          end;
        end;
      end;
  end   { DrawPolygon };
```

385

```
begin   { DrawSurface }
  with Surface^ do
  begin
    Polygon := PolygonHead;
    while Polygon <> nil do
    begin
      DrawPolygon(Polygon);
      Polygon := Polygon^.Next;
    end;
  end;
end   { DrawSurface };

begin   { DrawObject }
  with Object^ do
  begin
    Surface := SurfaceHead;
    while Surface <> nil do
    begin
      DrawSurface(Surface);
      Surface := Surface^.Next;
    end;
  end;
end   { DrawObject };

procedure Termination;
var
  f: integer;
begin
  f := closeretainseg;
  f := deselectvwsurf(DisplayScreen);
  f := terminatecore;
end   { Termination };

begin   { main program }
  Initialisation;
  ReadScene('test.scn');

  Object := ObjectHead;
  while Object <> nil do
  begin
    TransformObject(Object);
    CalculateNormals(Object);
    CullObjectPolygons(Object);
    CalculateScreenCoords(Object);
    Object := Object^.Next;
  end;

  Object := ObjectHead;
  while Object <> nil do
  begin
    DrawObject(Object);
    Object := Object^.Next;
  end;
```

```
    repeat until keypressed;
    Termination;
end.
```

APPENDIX C

An Implementation of a Renderer

The pseudo-code described in Chapter 5 is expanded into a set of Pascal procedures (Program C.1) to be added to the simple wireframe program presented in Appendix B. The complete system Gouraud shades objects using a Z-buffer by-polygon based renderer. (Incidentally, if you are short of array space for the Z-buffer, a possibility is to use half of the screen memory as a Z-buffer.)

The description of the system begins with the extra types and variables specific to the shading process. There is the edge list, which holds for each scan line a list of edge–scanline intersections. Then there is an array to hold the Z-buffer information – one integer per pixel. Note that, for simplicity, the screen resolution is assumed to be 1024×1024, indexed from 0 to 1023. Finally, there is a vector which specifies the direction of the light source.

This listing contains six procedures, and it is best to start with the last one, *RenderObject*, since this is the top level procedure that is called to perform rendering on an entire object. The light vector is initialized to an arbitrary value; in a real system this would be done outside the rendering process, and specified in some interactive way by the user. Then all elements in the Z-buffer are set to the maximum value, signifying that no pixel has yet been set. The procedure then parses through the data structure, and, for each polygon that it finds, it calls *RenderPolygon*.

This procedure renders an entire polygon. It does this in two stages. First, it sets up *EdgeList* for the polygon, by clearing it, then it goes through the polygon's list of vertices, using successive pairs of vertices to define edges which are then passed as parameters to *AddEdgeToList* (more of which in the next paragraph). After the edge list has been created, it is examined in scan line order, and, if the entry for a particular scan line is not empty, the values are read for that line and passed to *RenderSegment*. Note that this assumes the simplified case of convex polygons, where there are exactly two (or zero!) intersections per scan line. For concave polygons, there would be an even number of intersections for each scan line. These would need to be sorted into order of increasing x, and then each pair in turn would be passed to *RenderSegment*.

AddEdgeToList has as its parameters two vertices which jointly define an edge. The first operation to be performed is to swap the the ends, if necessary, and then to make the second point higher than the first. Rounded versions of the two *y* coordinates are evaluated, and are then used to reject horizontal edges. After this, the intensity value for each vertex is calculated (*N·L*), and increments for *x*, *z* and *i* are calculated. Note that this is slightly inefficient, as the intensity for a particular vertex may be calculated several times during subsequent calls to *AddEdgeToList*. This may be avoided by initially processing all vertices and storing the calculated value of *i* with other vertex information. The last operation to be performed is, for each scan line that the edge crosses, to calculate appropriate values of *x*, *z* and *i*, to generate an edge box, and to insert it in the appropriate slot in *EdgeList*. Note that, in accordance with the rasterization rules discussed earlier, the **for** loop proceeds until *Iy2* − 1 rather than *Iy2*.

The last major procedure is *RenderSegment*. This has passed as parameters two edge boxes which together define a horizontal span. Then incremental calculations are performed in much the same manner as for *AddEdgeTolist*, generating *z* and *i* values for each pixel in the span. The *z* value for each pixel is compared with the current *z* value and, if less, the pixel is written to the screen using *CalculatePixel*, and the new *z* value assigned.

CalculatePixel takes the intensity value *i* for a particular pixel and generates red–green–blue RGB values. In this procedure, there are predefined constants specifying the colour of the object (RGB components in the range 0–1) and the ambient lighting level (0–1 also). As in the case of the light vector, these values would in reality be defined elsewhere in the program, and might vary from object to object, or even between polygons. The first task of the procedure is to limit the intensity value to zero if the light is behind the object (that is *N·L* < 0), and then the ambient (all-round) lighting component is added. This modified value of *i* is then used to weight the RGB components of the surface colour. If any of these goes above 1.0, then it is limited to this value, indicating saturation of that colour component. These final values of RGB are passed to a machine-specific procedure *WritePixel* which sends them to the output device.

One last point: the Z-buffer is shown being initialised by a call to *RenderObject*; if there are multiple objects in a scene then this initialization should be performed just once, outside the body of this procedure.

Program C.1   An implementation of a renderer.

```
procedure WritePixel(x, y: integer; r, g, b: real);
begin
   { machine specific }
end;

type EdgeBoxPtr = ^EdgeBox;
     EdgeBox    = record
                     x, z, i: real;
                     next: EdgeBoxPtr;
                  end;
```

```pascal
var EdgeList      : array [0..1023] of EdgeBoxPtr;
    z_buffer      : array [0..1023, 0..1023] of integer;
    LightVector   : vector;

procedure InitialiseZbuffer;

  var
    x, y: integer;

begin
  for x := 0 to 1023 do
    for y := 0 to 1023 do
      z_buffer[x, y] := MaxInt;
end   { InitialiseZbuffer };

procedure AddEdgeToList(vertex1, vertex2: VertexPtr);

var x, dx,
    z, dz,
    i, di,
    y1, y2: real;
y, Iy1, Iy2: integer;
tempvert  : Vertexptr;
box       : EdgeBoxPtr;

begin
  if vertex1^.ScreenPosition.y > vertex2^.ScreenPosition.y
  then   { swap ends }
  begin
    tempvert := vertex1;
    vertex1 := vertex2;
    vertex2 := tempvert;
  end;
  y1 := vertex1^.ScreenPosition.y;
  y2 := vertex2^.ScreenPosition.y;
  Iy1 := round(y1);
  Iy2 := round(y2);
  if Iy1 <> Iy2 then   {not a horizontal line}
  begin
    {set up increments}
    with vertex1^ do
    begin
      x := ScreenPosition.x;
      z := ScreenPosition.z;
      i := DotProduct(normal, LightVector);
    end;
    with vertex2^ do
    begin
      dx := (ScreenPosition.x - x)/(y2 - y1);
      dz := (ScreenPosition.z - z)/(y2 - y1);
      di := (DotProduct(Normal, Lightvector) - i)/(y2 - y1);
    end;
    for y := Iy1 to Iy2 - 1 do
```

```
      begin
        new(box);
        box^.x := x;
        box^.z := z;
        box^.i := i;
        box^.next := EdgeList[y];
        EdgeList[y] := box;
        x := x + dx;
        z := z + dz;
        i := i + di;
      end;
    end   { if };
end   { AddEdgeTolist };


procedure CalculatePixel(x, y: integer; i: real);

const r = 0.8;
      g = 0.4;
      b = 0.6;
      ambient = 0.25;

var rr, gg, bb: real;

begin
  if i < 0.0 then i := 0.0;
  i := i + ambient;
  if i > 1.0 then i := 1.0;
  rr := i*r;
  gg := i*g;
  bb := i*b;
  WritePixel(x, y, rr, gg, bb);
end   { CalculatePixel };


procedure RenderSegment(y: integer;
                        box1, box2: EdgeBoxPtr);

var TempBox: EdgeBoxPtr;
    z, dz,
    i, di,
    dx: real;
    x,
    Iz,
    Ix1, Ix2: integer;

begin
  if box1^.x > box2^.x then
  begin   { swap box1 & box2 }
    TempBox := box1;
    box1 := box2;
    box2 := TempBox;
  end;
  Ix1 := round(box1^.x);
  Ix2 := round(box2^.x);
  if Ix1 <> Ix2 then   {segment not of zero width}
```

```
      begin
         {initialize increments}
         dx := box2^.x − box1^.x;
         z := box1^.z;
         i := box1^.i;
         dz := (box2^.z − z)/dx;
         di := (box2^.i − i)/dx;
         for x := Ix1 to Ix2 − 1 do
         begin
            Iz := round(z);
            if Iz < Z_buffer[x, y] then
            begin
               z_buffer[x, y] := Iz;
               CalculatePixel(x, y, i);
            end   {if};
            z := z + dz;
            i := i + di;
         end   {for};
      end   {if};
   end   { RenderSegment };

procedure RenderPolygon(polygon: PolygonPtr);

var
   y: integer;
   vertex0,
   vertex1,
   vertex2: VertexList;

begin
   {initialize edge list}
   for y := 0 to 1023 do
      EdgeList[y] := nil;
   {create edge list}
   vertex1 := polygon^.vertices;
   vertex0 := vertex1;
   vertex2 := vertex1^.Rest;
   repeat
      AddEdgeToList(vertex1^.vertex, vertex2^.vertex);
      vertex1 := vertex2;
      vertex2 := vertex2^.rest;
   until vertex2 = nil;
   AddEdgeToList(vertex1^.vertex, vertex0^.vertex);
   {render it}
   for y := 0 to 1023 do
      if EdgeList[y] <> nil then
         RenderSegment(y, EdgeList[y], EdgeList[y]^.next);
   end   { RenderPolygon };

procedure RenderObject(object: ObjectPtr);

var surface: Surfaceptr;
    polygon: PolygonPtr;
```

```
begin
  with LightVector do
  begin
    x := 0.53; y := 0.27; z := 0.08
  end;
  surface := object^.Surfacehead;
  while surface <> nil do
  begin
    polygon := surface^.PolygonHead;
    while polygon <> nil do
    begin
      if not polygon^.culled then
        RenderPolygon(polygon);
      polygon := polygon^.next;
    end;
    surface := surface^.next;
  end;
end   { RenderObject };
{ Additions to end of wireframe program main body }

  InitialiseZbuffer;
  Object := ObjectHead;
  while Object <> nil do
  begin
    RenderObject(Object);
    Object := Object^.next;
  end;
```

APPENDIX D

The Utah Teapot

The University of Utah was the centre of research into rendering algorithms in the early 1970s. Various polygon mesh models were set up manually, including a VW Beetle, digitized by Ivan Sutherland's computer graphics class in 1971. This is reproduced in Newman and Sproull (1981) together with another familiar model – the human-like mask.

In 1975 M. Newell developed the Utah teapot, a familiar object that has become a kind of benchmark in computer graphics, and one that has been used frequently in this text. He did this by sketching the profile of the teapot to estimate suitable control points for bicubic Bezier patches. The lid, rim and body of the teapot were then treated as solids of revolution and the spout and handle were modelled as ducted solids. This resulted, eventually, in 32 patches, the data for which is reproduced in Tables D.1 and D.2.

The original teapot is now in the Boston Computer Museum, displayed alongside its computer alter ego. A full description of the model and details on the Computer Museum are given in Crow (1987).

The data consists of 306 world coordinate vertices given in Table D.1. Table D.2 contains 32 patch definitions for bicubic Bezier patches. Each row in the table is a list of 16 vertex numbers that define the control point polyhedron for each patch. The patches are placed into five groups: the body, the handle, the spout, the lid and the bottom.

Table D.1   Vertex table.

Vertex number	x	y	z	Vertex number	x	y	z	Vertex number	x	y	z
1	1.40000	0.00000	2.40000	53	2.00000	0.00000	1.35000	105	−1.50000	0.00000	0.15000
2	1.40000	−0.78400	2.40000	54	2.00000	−1.12000	1.35000	106	−2.00000	1.12000	0.45000
3	0.78400	−1.40000	2.40000	55	1.12000	−2.00000	1.35000	107	−1.12000	2.00000	0.45000
4	0.00000	−1.40000	2.40000	56	0.00000	−2.00000	1.35000	108	0.00000	2.00000	0.45000
5	1.33750	0.00000	2.53125	57	2.00000	0.00000	0.90000	109	−1.50000	0.84000	0.22500
6	1.33750	−0.74900	2.53125	58	2.00000	−1.12000	0.90000	110	−0.84000	1.50000	0.22500
7	0.74900	−1.33750	2.53125	59	1.12000	−2.00000	0.90000	111	0.00000	1.50000	0.22500
8	0.00000	−1.33750	2.53125	60	0.00000	−2.00000	0.90000	112	−1.50000	0.84000	0.15000
9	1.43750	0.00000	2.53125	61	−0.98000	−1.75000	1.87500	113	−0.84000	1.50000	0.15000
10	1.43750	−0.80500	2.53125	62	−1.75000	−0.98000	1.87500	114	0.00000	1.50000	0.15000
11	0.80500	−1.43750	2.53125	63	−1.75000	0.00000	1.87500	115	1.12000	2.00000	0.45000
12	0.00000	−1.43750	2.53125	64	−1.12000	−2.00000	1.35000	116	2.00000	1.12000	0.45000
13	1.50000	0.00000	2.40000	65	−2.00000	−1.12000	1.35000	117	0.84000	1.50000	0.22500
14	1.50000	−0.84000	2.40000	66	−2.00000	0.00000	1.35000	118	1.50000	0.84000	0.22500
15	0.84000	−1.50000	2.40000	67	−1.12000	−2.00000	0.90000	119	0.84000	1.50000	0.15000
16	0.00000	−1.50000	2.40000	68	−2.00000	−1.12000	0.90000	120	1.50000	0.84000	0.15000
17	−0.78400	−1.40000	2.40000	69	−2.00000	0.00000	0.90000	121	−1.60000	0.00000	2.02500
18	−1.40000	−0.78400	2.40000	70	−1.75000	0.98000	1.87500	122	−1.60000	−0.30000	2.02500
19	−1.40000	0.00000	2.40000	71	−0.98000	1.75000	1.87500	123	−1.50000	−0.30000	2.25000
20	−0.74900	−1.33750	2.53125	72	0.00000	1.75000	1.87500	124	−1.50000	0.00000	2.25000
21	−1.33750	−0.74900	2.53125	73	−2.00000	1.12000	1.35000	125	−2.30000	0.00000	2.02500
22	−1.33750	0.00000	2.53125	74	−1.12000	2.00000	1.35000	126	−2.30000	−0.30000	2.02500
23	−0.80500	−1.43750	2.53125	75	0.00000	2.00000	1.35000	127	−2.50000	−0.30000	2.25000
24	−1.43750	−0.80500	2.53125	76	−2.00000	1.12000	0.90000	128	−2.50000	0.00000	2.25000
25	−1.43750	0.00000	2.53125	77	−1.12000	2.00000	0.90000	129	−2.70000	0.00000	2.02500
26	−0.84000	−1.50000	2.40000	78	0.00000	2.00000	0.90000	130	−2.70000	−0.30000	2.02500
27	−1.50000	−0.84000	2.40000	79	0.98000	1.75000	1.87500	131	−3.00000	−0.30000	2.25000
28	−1.50000	0.00000	2.40000	80	1.75000	0.98000	1.87500	132	−3.00000	0.00000	2.25000
29	−1.40000	0.78400	2.40000	81	1.12000	2.00000	1.35000	133	−2.70000	0.00000	1.80000
30	−0.78400	1.40000	2.40000	82	2.00000	1.12000	1.35000	134	−2.70000	−0.30000	1.80000
31	0.00000	1.40000	2.40000	83	1.12000	2.00000	0.90000	135	−3.00000	−0.30000	1.80000
32	−1.33750	0.74900	2.53125	84	2.00000	1.12000	0.90000	136	−3.00000	0.00000	1.80000
33	−0.74900	1.33750	2.53125	85	2.00000	0.00000	0.45000	137	−1.50000	0.30000	2.25000
34	0.00000	1.33750	2.53125	86	2.00000	−1.12000	0.45000	138	−1.60000	0.30000	2.02500
35	−1.43750	0.80500	2.53125	87	1.12000	−2.00000	0.45000	139	−2.50000	0.30000	2.25000
36	−0.80500	1.43750	2.53125	88	0.00000	−2.00000	0.45000	140	−2.30000	0.30000	2.02500
37	0.00000	1.43750	2.53125	89	1.50000	0.00000	0.22500	141	−3.00000	0.30000	2.25000
38	−1.50000	0.84000	2.40000	90	1.50000	−0.84000	0.22500	142	−2.70000	0.30000	2.02500
39	−0.84000	1.50000	2.40000	91	0.84000	−1.50000	0.22500	143	−3.00000	0.30000	1.80000
40	0.00000	1.50000	2.40000	92	0.00000	−1.50000	0.22500	144	−2.70000	0.30000	1.80000
41	0.78400	1.40000	2.40000	93	1.50000	0.00000	0.15000	145	−2.70000	0.00000	1.57500
42	1.40000	0.78400	2.40000	94	1.50000	−0.84000	0.15000	146	−2.70000	−0.30000	1.57500
43	0.74900	1.33750	2.53125	95	0.84000	−1.50000	0.15000	147	−3.00000	−0.30000	1.35000
44	1.33750	0.74900	2.53125	96	0.00000	−1.50000	0.15000	148	−3.00000	0.00000	1.35000
45	0.80500	1.43750	2.53125	97	−1.12000	−2.00000	0.45000	149	−2.50000	0.00000	1.12500
46	1.43750	0.80500	2.53125	98	−2.00000	−1.12000	0.45000	150	−2.50000	−0.30000	1.12500
47	0.84000	1.50000	2.40000	99	−2.00000	0.00000	0.45000	151	−2.65000	−0.30000	0.93750
48	1.50000	0.84000	2.40000	100	−0.84000	−1.50000	0.22500	152	−2.65000	0.00000	0.93750
49	1.75000	0.00000	1.87500	101	−1.50000	−0.84000	0.22500	153	−2.00000	−0.30000	0.90000
50	1.75000	−0.98000	1.87500	102	−1.50000	0.00000	0.22500	154	−1.90000	−0.30000	0.60000
51	0.98000	−1.75000	1.87500	103	−0.84000	−1.50000	0.15000	155	−1.90000	0.00000	0.60000
52	0.00000	−1.75000	1.87500	104	−1.50000	−0.84000	0.15000	156	−3.00000	0.30000	1.35000

Table D.1   *(contd)*

Vertex number	x	y	z	Vertex number	x	y	z	Vertex number	x	y	z
157	−2.70000	0.30000	1.57500	207	0.80000	0.00000	3.15000	257	0.00000	0.40000	2.55000
158	−2.65000	0.30000	0.93750	208	0.80000	−0.45000	3.15000	258	−1.30000	0.72800	2.55000
159	−2.50000	0.30000	1.12500	209	0.45000	−0.80000	3.15000	259	−0.72800	1.30000	2.55000
160	−1.90000	0.30000	0.60000	210	0.00000	−0.80000	3.15000	260	0.00000	1.30000	2.55000
161	−2.00000	0.30000	0.90000	211	0.00000	0.00000	2.85000	261	−1.30000	0.72800	2.40000
162	1.70000	0.00000	1.42500	212	0.20000	0.00000	2.70000	262	−0.72800	1.30000	2.40000
163	1.70000	−0.66000	1.42500	213	0.20000	−0.11200	2.70000	263	0.00000	1.30000	2.40000
164	1.70000	−0.66000	0.60000	214	0.11200	−0.20000	2.70000	264	0.22400	0.40000	2.55000
165	1.70000	0.00000	0.60000	215	0.00000	−0.20000	2.70000	265	0.40000	0.22400	2.55000
166	2.60000	0.00000	1.42500	216	−0.00200	0.00000	3.15000	266	0.72800	1.30000	2.55000
167	2.60000	−0.66000	1.42500	217	−0.45000	−0.80000	3.15000	267	1.30000	0.72800	2.55000
168	3.10000	−0.66000	0.82500	218	−0.80000	−0.45000	3.15000	268	0.72800	1.30000	2.40000
169	3.10000	0.00000	0.82500	219	−0.80000	0.00000	3.15000	269	1.30000	0.72800	2.40000
170	2.30000	0.00000	2.10000	220	−0.11200	−0.20000	2.70000	270	0.00000	0.00000	0.00000
171	2.30000	−0.25000	2.10000	221	−0.20000	−0.11200	2.70000	271	1.50000	0.00000	0.15000
172	2.40000	−0.25000	2.02500	222	−0.20000	0.00000	2.70000	272	1.50000	0.84000	0.15000
173	2.40000	0.00000	2.02500	223	0.00000	0.00200	3.15000	273	0.84000	1.50000	0.15000
174	2.70000	0.00000	2.40000	224	−0.80000	0.45000	3.15000	274	0.00000	1.50000	0.15000
175	2.70000	−0.25000	2.40000	225	−0.45000	0.80000	3.15000	275	1.50000	0.00000	0.07500
176	3.30000	−0.25000	2.40000	226	0.00000	0.80000	3.15000	276	1.50000	0.84000	0.07500
177	3.30000	0.00000	2.40000	227	−0.20000	0.11200	2.70000	277	0.84000	1.50000	0.07500
178	1.70000	0.66000	0.60000	228	−0.11200	0.20000	2.70000	278	0.00000	1.50000	0.07500
179	1.70000	0.66000	1.42500	229	0.00000	0.20000	2.70000	279	1.42500	0.00000	0.00000
180	3.10000	0.66000	0.82500	230	0.45000	0.80000	3.15000	280	1.42500	0.79800	0.00000
181	2.60000	0.66000	1.42500	231	0.80000	0.45000	3.15000	281	0.79800	1.42500	0.00000
182	2.40000	0.25000	2.02500	232	0.11200	0.20000	2.70000	282	0.00000	1.42500	0.00000
183	2.30000	0.25000	2.10000	233	0.20000	0.11200	2.70000	283	−0.84000	1.50000	0.15000
184	3.30000	0.25000	2.40000	234	0.40000	0.00000	2.55000	284	−1.50000	0.84000	0.15000
185	2.70000	0.25000	2.40000	235	0.40000	−0.22400	2.55000	285	−1.50000	0.00000	0.15000
186	2.80000	0.00000	2.47500	236	0.22400	−0.40000	2.55000	286	−0.84000	1.50000	0.07500
187	2.80000	−0.25000	2.47500	237	0.00000	−0.40000	2.55000	287	−1.50000	0.84000	0.07500
188	3.52500	−0.25000	2.49375	238	1.30000	0.00000	2.55000	288	−1.50000	0.00000	0.07500
189	3.52500	0.00000	2.49375	239	1.30000	−0.72800	2.55000	289	−0.79800	1.42500	0.00000
190	2.90000	0.00000	2.47500	240	0.72800	−1.30000	2.55000	290	−1.42500	0.79800	0.00000
191	2.90000	−0.15000	2.47500	241	0.00000	−1.30000	2.55000	291	−1.42500	0.00000	0.00000
192	3.45000	−0.15000	2.51250	242	1.30000	0.00000	2.40000	292	−1.50000	−0.84000	0.15000
193	3.45000	0.00000	2.51250	243	1.30000	−0.72800	2.40000	293	−0.84000	−1.50000	0.15000
194	2.80000	0.00000	2.40000	244	0.72800	−1.30000	2.40000	294	0.00000	−1.50000	0.15000
195	2.80000	−0.15000	2.40000	245	0.00000	−1.30000	2.40000	295	−1.50000	−0.84000	0.07500
196	3.20000	−0.15000	2.40000	246	−0.22400	−0.40000	2.55000	296	−0.84000	−1.50000	0.07500
197	3.20000	0.00000	2.40000	247	−0.40000	−0.22400	2.55000	297	0.00000	−1.50000	0.07500
198	3.52500	0.25000	2.49375	248	−0.40000	0.00000	2.55000	298	−1.42500	−0.79800	0.00000
199	2.80000	0.25000	2.47500	249	−0.72800	−1.30000	2.55000	299	−0.79800	−1.42500	0.00000
200	3.45000	0.15000	2.51250	250	−1.30000	−0.72800	2.55000	300	0.00000	−1.42500	0.00000
201	2.90000	0.15000	2.47500	251	−1.30000	0.00000	2.55000	301	0.84000	−1.50000	0.15000
202	3.20000	0.15000	2.40000	252	−0.72800	−1.30000	2.40000	302	1.50000	−0.84000	0.15000
203	2.80000	0.15000	2.40000	253	−1.30000	−0.72800	2.40000	303	0.84000	−1.50000	0.07500
204	0.00000	0.00000	3.15000	254	−1.30000	0.00000	2.40000	304	1.50000	−0.84000	0.07500
205	0.00000	−0.00200	3.15000	255	−0.40000	0.22400	2.55000	305	0.79800	−1.42500	0.00000
206	0.00200	0.00000	3.15000	256	−0.22400	0.40000	2.55000	306	1.42500	−0.79800	0.00000

Table D.2   Bicubic Bezier patch definitions.

Patch number	Control point polyhedron vertex numbers															
Body																
1	1	2	3	4	5	6	7	8	9	10	11	12	13	14	15	16
2	4	17	18	19	8	20	21	22	12	23	24	25	16	26	27	28
3	19	29	30	31	22	32	33	34	25	35	36	37	28	38	39	40
4	31	41	42	1	34	43	44	5	37	45	46	9	40	47	48	13
5	13	14	15	16	49	50	51	52	53	54	55	56	57	58	59	60
6	16	26	27	28	52	61	62	63	56	64	65	66	60	67	68	69
7	28	38	39	40	63	70	71	72	66	73	74	75	69	76	77	78
8	40	47	48	13	72	79	80	49	75	81	82	53	78	83	84	57
9	57	58	59	60	85	86	87	88	89	90	91	92	93	94	95	96
10	60	67	68	69	88	97	98	99	92	100	101	102	96	103	104	105
11	69	76	77	78	99	106	107	108	102	109	110	111	105	112	113	114
12	78	83	84	57	108	115	116	85	111	117	118	89	114	119	120	93
Handle																
13	121	122	123	124	125	126	127	128	129	130	131	132	133	134	135	136
14	124	137	138	121	128	139	140	125	132	141	142	129	136	143	144	133
15	133	134	135	136	145	146	147	148	149	150	151	152	69	153	154	155
16	136	143	144	133	148	156	157	145	152	158	159	149	155	160	161	69
Spout																
17	162	163	164	165	166	167	168	169	170	171	172	173	174	175	176	177
18	165	178	179	162	169	180	181	166	173	182	183	170	177	184	185	174
19	174	175	176	177	186	187	188	189	190	191	192	193	194	195	196	197
20	177	184	185	174	189	198	199	186	193	200	201	190	197	202	203	194
Lid																
21	204	204	204	204	207	208	209	210	211	211	211	211	212	213	214	215
22	204	204	204	204	210	217	218	219	211	211	211	211	215	220	221	222
23	204	204	204	204	219	224	225	226	211	211	211	211	222	227	228	229
24	204	204	204	204	226	230	231	207	211	211	211	211	229	232	233	212
25	212	213	214	215	234	235	236	237	238	239	240	241	242	243	244	245
26	215	220	221	222	237	246	247	248	241	249	250	251	245	252	253	254
27	222	227	228	229	248	255	256	257	251	258	259	260	254	261	262	263
28	229	232	233	212	257	264	265	234	260	266	267	238	263	268	269	242
Bottom																
29	270	270	270	270	279	280	281	282	275	276	277	278	93	120	119	114
30	270	270	270	270	282	289	290	291	278	286	287	288	114	113	112	105
31	270	270	270	270	291	298	299	300	288	295	296	297	105	104	103	96
32	270	270	270	270	300	305	306	279	297	303	304	275	96	95	94	93

APPENDIX E

Some Theoretical Concepts

E.1 Introduction

Computer graphics is an inexact science; some would say it is more of an art form. Some aspects of three-dimensional graphics – bicubic parametric patches, for example – are mathematically rigorous; certain aspects of shading, as we have seen, are gross simplifications. Many topics have thrived from a sound theoretical base. Anti-aliasing has benefited from a theoretical underpinning with Fourier theory. With some reflection models a formal framework seems an academic nicety because the end result is such an approximation to it.

Algorithms have been developed using those aspects of applied physics and/or geometric optics that produce the desired visual effect on the screen. Sometimes this results in super-reality – ray tracing is a case in point – and this is as valid a goal in computer graphics as the imitation of reality. Such areas as the visualization of scientific phenomena demand super-reality, dealing as they do with images that can represent invisible functions such as medical scans.

The relationship between computer graphics and rigorous physical models is somewhat tenuous. A lot of this is to do with hardware limitations. The drawbacks of the algorithms result in many cases from the lack of processing capability (ray tracing again, for example).

New hardware has spawned the development of certain algorithms. In particular the availability of screen memories motivated the design of shading algorithms and led to the demise of vector and storage tube terminals. Nowadays three-dimensional graphics motivates the hardware design, with the classic rendering algorithms now being made available on silicon. (Note that one of the important theoretical concepts of the first decade of graphics – coherence – is now fading because it militates against parallel realization.)

This appendix presents some theoretical concepts that are pertinent to graphics and looks at models that can be used as a global framework to encompass practical algorithms. The material does not pretend to be a comprehensive overview of the physics of illumination and reflection but is a selection of a few concepts that seem useful.

E.2   Useful definitions

We start by considering that light is a form of energy and introduce a statement of energy equilibrium for light arriving at and leaving a surface. Metrics used in radiative transfer are confusing for non-specialists and such terms as light intensity and energy are used freely and sometimes erroneously in computer graphics.

Luminous flux or simply light is the total **power**, P, radiated by a source over the visible range of the spectrum. Light **energy**, E, is power per unit time. The starting basis in the radiosity method, for example, is in terms of energy, dividing the energy associated with a patch into an emitted and a reflected term. Practical sources emit light over an area, and **radiant emittance**, dP/dS, is the power per unit area or flux density. **Intensity** is defined as power per unit projected area of the source per solid angle:

$$\frac{dP}{dA_p\, d\Omega}$$

In light–surface interaction we are normally concerned with events over the surface of an illuminating hemisphere centred on the point of the surface under consideration. For example, a surface element illuminated by an incident beam will produce reflected beams in every direction and the reflected radiation has to be 'collected' over a hemisphere. A differential solid angle $d\Omega$ is the cone that subtends an area of the hemisphere. A small solid angle is approximated as the projected area divided by the square of the hemisphere radius:

$$d\Omega = dA_p / r^2$$

Finally, **radiance** is power per unit solid angle per unit projected area in the direction of interest. This is related to the power per unit solid angle leaving in the normal direction. If dS is a perfect diffuser then Lambert's law applies – the power in the normal direction and the power in the direction of interest are related by $\cos\theta$. Thus radiance is expressed as:

$$\frac{dP}{d\Omega\, dS \cos\theta}$$

E.3   Hall's model

Hall (1986b) gives an excellent theoretical foundation for reflection models and this treatment is followed here to derive a general equation for the light intensity leaving a surface in a given direction. Hall's treatment is based on considering reflected and transmitted light to consist of a coherent component and an incoherent or scattered component (Beckmann and Spizzichino, 1963).

It is emphasized in Hall (1986b) that a physically accurate model must maintain energy equilibrium, that is the energy arriving at a surface must equal the energy leaving the surface. In general a surface will both reflect and absorb light and the energy leaving a surface splits into two contributions – a reflected and a transmitted component. The transmitted component is that part of the incident energy absorbed by or transmitted into the material. The coherent

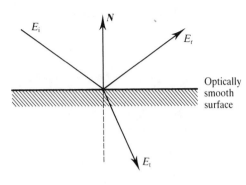

component of the reflected light is that reflected along the mirror direction and
the coherent component of the transmitted light is that transmitted along the
direction given by Snell's law. (A more detailed discussion of coherent reflection
and refraction is to be found in Chapter 7.)

If a surface is optically smooth (Figure E.1) then only coherent behaviour
occurs and we have from energy equilibrium:

$$E_i = E_r + E_t$$
$$= F_r E_i + F_t E_i \qquad F_r + F_t = 1$$

where F_r and F_t are the Fresnel coefficients. Note that although Figure E.1 shows
the usual 'beams' of light, E_i acts through a solid angle.

Incoherent reflection is controlled by a bidirectional reflectivity function
R_{bd} where:

$$R_{bd} = f(N, V, L, \sigma, \lambda)$$

N, V and L determine the geometry of the interaction and have their usual
meanings. N is the surface normal, V the unit view vector and L is the unit light
vector. σ is the surface roughness and λ is the wavelength of the light. As in the
Cook and Torrance model (Chapter 3), the surface roughness function is a
statistical probability function and this causes the incoherent component to
'cluster' about the R vector. Similarly, the transmitted component is controlled by
a function T_{bd} causing a clustering about T, the direction of the coherent refracted
or transmitted component. Figure E.2 shows incoming energy E_i producing
coherent reflected and transmitted components together with incoherent reflected
and transmitted terms. The incoherent terms have components everywhere over
the illuminating hemispheres. To maintain energy equilibrium the reflection and
transmission functions have to be integrated over the entire hemispheres. Note
that in the figure the incoherent transmitted components are shown to have
smaller amplitudes than the reflected components with a discontinuity at the
surface. This is because some of the transmitted light is converted into non-visible
components, a factor taken into account by the dependence of T_{bd} on
wavelength. (This is, of course a wholly classical approach.) Thus we can write:

Figure E.2
Coherent and incoherent
reflection and
transmission. (After Hall
(1986a).)

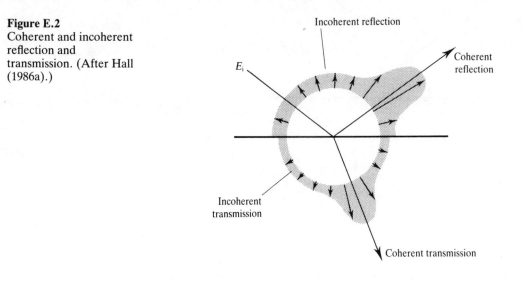

$$E_i = r_\sigma F_r E_i + \frac{E_i}{\mathrm{d}A} \int^{2\pi} R_{bd}\ (\mathbf{N\cdot R})\ \mathrm{d}A\ \mathrm{d}\Omega$$

$$+ t_\sigma F_t E_i + \frac{E_i}{\mathrm{d}A} \int^{2\pi} T_{bd}\ (\mathbf{N\cdot T})\ \mathrm{d}A\ \mathrm{d}\Omega$$

where the two coherent terms are now attenuated by some functions of roughness, r_σ and t_σ. Dividing through by the energy term gives:

$$1 = r_\sigma F_r + t_\sigma F_t + \int^{2\pi} R_{bd}\ (\mathbf{N\cdot R})\ \mathrm{d}\Omega + \int^{2\pi} T_{bd}\ (\mathbf{N\cdot T})\ \mathrm{d}\Omega$$

The reciprocity principle states that the reflective and refractive relationships are independent of the direction of energy into the system. This means that in Figure E.2 the directions can be reversed and the energy leaving the surface in a direction that is the reverse of the incident direction is the sum of the energy incoming in the reverse transmitted direction and the reverse reflected direction. This enables us to write an equation for the intensity of light leaving the surface in a single direction:

$$I = r_\sigma F_r I_r + \int^{2\pi} I_i\ R_{bd}\ (\mathbf{N\cdot R})\ \mathrm{d}\Omega + t_\sigma F_t I_t + \int^{2\pi} I_i\ T_{bd}\ (\mathbf{N\cdot T})\ \mathrm{d}\Omega \qquad \text{(E.1)}$$

This situation is shown in Figure E.4, where we now have I_i, the incoming light, incident and variable over the two hemispheres. The practical reason for the variability in the I_i term is not only the position and geometry of illuminating sources but also the interaction of objects with other objects in the scene. Thus we end up with an equation that is structured into four components, that is two coherent terms and two incoherent terms, and this form is a suitable framework for simple reflection models and ray tracing.

Hall (1986b) points out that the application of this relationship requires a tremendous amount of information and reflection models typically rely on gross

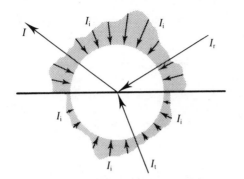

Figure E.3
Intensity in a particular direction due to I_i; (incident from every direction) and I_r and I_t (incident from the reflection and transmission directions). (After Hall (1986a).)

approximations that capture the essence of this relationship to provide visually acceptable results.

Returning to consideration of the Phong reflection model we can now see that this is an approximation to the the incoherent reflection term in Equation E.1. The Cook and Torrance model is again an approximation to this term with a physically based reflectance function and an energy-based formulation.

E.4   The rendering equation

In 1986 Kajiya introduced an equation that he termed the rendering equation. An attempt to unify the various approaches to modelling light in computer graphics theoretically, the equation describes the intensity of light reflected from a surface, in a given direction, in terms of global illumination. The form of the equation is based on studies in radiative heat transfer (Siegel and Howell, 1984) and Kajiya uses the equation as a theoretical base for a new rendering method called 'hierarchical sampling'.

The rendering equation is difficult to understand for non-mathematicians and the form used here is by Wallace *et al.* (1987). The equation is:

$$I_{out}(\phi_{out}) = E(\phi_{out}) + \int^{2\pi} R_{bd}(\phi_{out}, \phi_{in})\, I_{in}(\phi_{in}) \cos\theta \, d\Omega \tag{E.2}$$

where I_{out} is the outgoing intensity for a point on the surface, E is that contribution to the outgoing intensity that is due to emission, R_{bd} is the bidirectional reflectance–transmittance of the surface, I_{in} is the incoming intensity from the rest of the environment, ϕ_{in}, ϕ_{out} are the incoming and outgoing directions and θ is the angle between ϕ_{in} and the surface normal at the point the equation applies. $d\Omega$ is the solid angle of the incoming intensity and the integral is over the sphere of all incoming directions.

The equation states that the outgoing intensity for a differential area leaving the surface in a particular direction is the sum of any light emitted by the surface, in that particular direction, plus any light reflected (or transmitted) in that direction owing to light arriving at that point from all directions above the surface (for reflected light) and from all directions below the surface (for transmitted light).

The local reflection models described in Chapters 2 and 3 assumed that reflected light can be divided into two components – a diffuse component that does not depend on direction and a directional or specular component. So we have:

$$R_{bd}(\phi_{out}, \phi_{in}) = k_s R_s(\phi_{out}, \phi_{in}) + k_d R_d$$

where k_s and k_d are fractions ($k_s + k_d = 1$). In this case equation E.2 reduces to

$$I_{out}(\phi_{out}) = E(\phi_{out}) + I_{d,out} + I_{s,out}(\phi_{out}) \tag{E.3}$$

where:

$$I_{d,out} = k_d R_d \int^{2\pi} I_{in}(\phi_{in}) \cos \theta \, d\Omega \tag{E.4}$$

$$I_{s,out}(\phi_{out}) = k_s \int^{2\pi} R_s(\phi_{out}, \phi_{in}) \, I_{in}(\phi_{in}) \cos \theta \, d\Omega \tag{E.5}$$

In local reflection models we generally consider light only from primary sources and there is no contribution to I_{in} from any other source resulting from interaction between non-emitting surfaces. For simple point light sources $I_{in}(\phi_{in})$ reduces to a constant and Equation E.4 becomes the familiar product term of the diffuse component of the Phong equation depending only on θ. Consider Equation E.5 and the Phong reflection model. R_s depends on ϕ_{out} only and we assume an 'empirical spread' about the mirror direction. In the Cook and Torrance model (Chapter 3), R_s also depends on ϕ_{in}. Generally, then, Equation E.5 reduces to a product term depending on ϕ_{out}, ϕ_{in} and θ.

Equation E.3 also serves as a comparison between direct reflection models and the radiosity method. In the direct reflection models the second and third terms are evaluated but only with respect to direct light sources. In the radiosity method the first two terms are evaluated and in this method $I_{d,out}$ depends on incoming intensities from all other surfaces including light sources that are treated as emitting surfaces.

APPENDIX F

Highlight Detection – the H test

F.1 Introduction

The H test is based on a hierarchy of simple tests that predict the value of the highlight function on the line between two vertices. For there to be a contribution from the specular term $N \cdot H$, we can say: $N \cdot H \geq T$, a threshold term. The value of this term is examined at pairs of vertices to predict the variation in its magnitude along the edge. A hierarchy of five simple tests performs this prediction.

- Test A: to determine whether $N \cdot H$ at any vertex is greater than the threshold value.
- Test B: determines whether $N \cdot H$ reaches a maximum along any polygon edge.
- Test C: determines whether the maximum of test B is greater than zero.
- Test D: determines whether this maximum is greater than the threshold value.
- Test E: is performed once per polygon, and determines whether a polygon has a maximum along each of its edges.

Figure F.1 shows the four distinct highlight possibilities for a polygon:

(1) a highlight can cover one or more vertices, intersecting the lines between this vertex and its two neighbouring vertices,

(2) a highlight can spread over a single line between two vertices, but not over any vertices,

(3) a highlight can be contained within a polygon, or,

(4) there is no highlight associated with the polygon.

It is important to bear in mind that these situations exist because we are

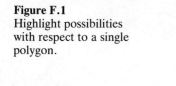

Figure F.1
Highlight possibilities
with respect to a single
polygon.

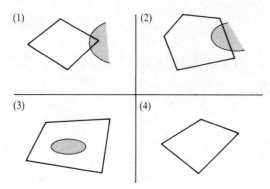

considering averaged vertex normals that are interpolated over the surface of a
polygon, and not the normal vector of a polygon. The Phong interpolation
scheme evaluates the intensity based on the interpolated normal.

The five tests A to E are used to ascertain which of the four highlight cases
has occurred. The way in which the tests are organized to do this is shown in
Figure F.2. The individual tests are now described in more detail.

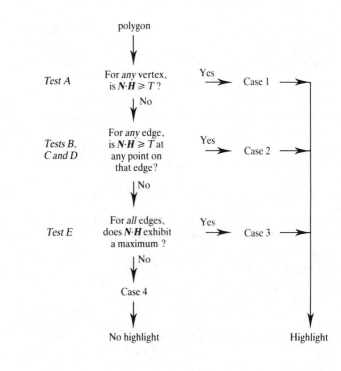

Figure F.2
Relationship between
tests of the highlight
cases for the H
algorithm.

F.2   The tests

F.2.1   Test A

This test simply evaluates $N \cdot H$ at a polygon vertex and compares this with the threshold value. If $N \cdot H$ is greater than the threshold, then the current vertex is within the visible region of a specular highlight. This test is sufficient to determine all polygons matching case (1) of Figure F.1.

F.2.2   Test B

This checks to see whether the intensity of the specular highlight reaches a point of maximum along the current edge. In fact it will find any stationary point, but points of minimum and inflection will be rejected by the subsequent tests. Let the unit normals at the two vertices be A and B. During Phong shading, the normal is linearly interpolated along an edge, that is

$$N(u) = (1 - u)A + uB \qquad \text{for some } u \ (0 \leqslant u \leqslant 1)$$

Let

$$\phi(u) = \frac{N(u) \cdot H}{|N(u)|}$$

A specular contribution should be considered if $\phi(u)$ is greater than the threshold T for some u $(0 < u < 1)$.

Since test A has failed, then $\phi(0) = A \cdot H$ and $\phi(1) = B \cdot H$ are both less than the threshold, and if $\phi(u) > T$ for some u $(0 < u < 1)$ a point of maximum must occur in $\phi(u)$ between the two vertices. Now,

$$\phi(u) = \frac{N(u) \cdot H}{|N(u)|} = \frac{a + u(b - a)}{(pu^2 - pu + 1)^{1/2}}$$

where $a = A \cdot H$, $b = B \cdot H$, $c = A \cdot B$ and $p = 2(1 - c)$. Differentiating, setting $\phi'(u) = 0$ and letting $d = bc - a$ and $e = ac - b$ gives

$$u = \frac{e}{e + d}$$

There are now four possibilities to consider, any of the first three indicating failure and the fourth indicating success.

(1) $d = 0$ and $e = 0$. Then

$$\phi(u) = \text{constant}$$

Thus there is no maximum along that edge.

(2) $de = 0$:

$$\text{if } d = 0 \text{ and } e \neq 0 \text{ then } u = 1$$
$$\text{if } e = 0 \text{ and } d \neq 0 \text{ then } u = 0$$

Thus there is a maximum occurring at a vertex, not between vertices, which is less than T.

(3) $de < 0$ implies that d and e are of opposite signs. So, either $u < 0$ or $u > 1$. Therefore the maximum does not occur between the vertices.

(4) $de > 0$ implies that d and e are of the same sign, and so $0 < u < 1$, and there is a maximum along the edge.

Thus, $de > 0$ is a necessary and sufficient condition for the intensity of the specular highlight to reach a maximum between the two vertices.

F.2.3   Test C

This test determines whether the value of the maximum located by test B is greater than zero. This is a less expensive preliminary to test D, and is also necessary to ensure the validity of subsequent tests.

From test B we have that

$$\phi(u) = \frac{a + u(b - a)}{(pu^2 - pu + 1)^{1/2}}$$

Now, at the point of maximum we require

$$\phi(u) > 0 \qquad \text{that is } a + u(b - a) > 0$$

Rearranging and substituting gives $d(ad + be) > 0$. Setting $g = ad + be$ gives $dg > 0$. Thus, if $dg > 0$, then the value of the maximum from test C is greater than zero.

F.2.4   Test D

All that now remains to be determined is whether the maximum is greater than the threshold. That is

$$\phi(u) \geq T \text{ or } a + u(b - a) \geq T \ (pu^2 - pu + 1)^{1/2}$$

From the previous test, we know that $a + u(b - a) > 0$, and $T > 0$ by definition; thus

$$[a + u(b - a)]^2 \geq T^2(pu^2 - pu + 1)$$

Rearranging and setting $f = de$ gives

$$g^2 \geqslant T^2(d^2 + 2cf + e^2)$$

Thus, if this condition is satisfied, then the value of $N \cdot H$ at the point of maximum is greater than the threshold and there is a visible highlight crossing the edge.

We can now discuss the way in which these tests detect the cases shown in Figure F.1. This discussion is structured in Figure F.2.

- Case 1: one or more of the vertices are within the visible area of the highlight. Test A is applied to each vertex in turn.
- Case 2: one or more of a polygon's edges are within the visible area of a specular highlight. This is found by sequential application of tests B, C and D.
- Case 3: will only occur on large polygons, with very tight specular highlights. This usually means that the object has been defined by insufficient polygons. This will result in very noticeable Mach bands together with piecewise linear silhouette edges. Although this case was not considered to be very important, an extra test (test E) was added. If a maximum occurs on every polygon edge (each such maximum being less than the threshold) then there is a completely enclosed highlight on that polygon. This inexpensive test will trap many such highlights.

F.2.5   Test E

This final test determines whether a polygon completely contains the visible region of a specular highlight.

Consider the polygon of Figure F.3, where the specular highlight is completely contained within the polygon, and centred on C. Along the edge AB the intensity will reach a maximum (with $N \cdot H$ less than the threshold) at M, where M is the point of intersection of the edge AB and the line perpendicular to AB and passing through C. This assumes that the specular highlight is bounded by a convex curve. If there is a maximum on each of the polygon edges then there is a specular highlight present on that polygon.

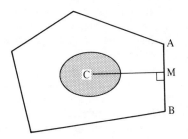

Figure F.3
The position of one of the maxima formed by a completely enclosed specular highlight.

409

Figure F.4
The area of a polygon in which a totally enclosed specular highlight must be centred for test E to succeed.

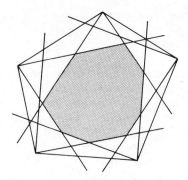

Test E will only detect specular highlights centred within the shaded area of Figure F.4. This area is defined by the perpendiculars to the edges at each of the vertices.

In general, for a reasonably 'regular' polygon (that is, all the sides and angles are of a similar size), this area will lie towards the centre of the polygon. Now, as tests A–D detect all specular highlights crossing a vertex or an edge, test E will trap all the remaining highlights, except for those that are centred on the unshaded portion of Figure F.4 and do not cross the polygon boundary.

Thus the H test will trap the vast majority of highlights, and in general will only fail on large (or irregularly shaped) polygons with small highlights near but not touching the polygon's boundary.

- Case 4: if all the above five tests have failed then the polygon is assumed to have no visible specular highlight, and thus no Phong shading is required.

F.3   Example timings

The times taken to evaluate the H test and to perform the rendering are given in Table F.1 for test torii of increasing 'polygon resolution' of 200, 450 and 800 polygons. Also provided are the timings for the same objects rendered using Phong shading and Gouraud shading using diffuse reflection only. The time labelled 'none' is the base processing time for all operations, database transfer, hidden surface removal etc., apart from shading.

The Phong shading algorithm (used for both the combined shading and the fast Phong shading timings given below) uses efficient incremental calculations which combine the interpolation of the polygon normals with the evaluation of the dot products $L \cdot N$ and $N \cdot H$. The row labelled 'Phong' gives the timings for a standard Phong shading implementation. In this context 'standard' means a direct or 'lazy' implementation of the Phong equation in the form of a direct high level expression of the model.

Table F.1   Example timings.

Object resolution	10×20	15×30	20×40
Number of polygons			
Visible	99	223	393
Highlighted	24	50	74
Shading method			
None	69	87	109
Gouraud	123	146	172
Phong	327	357	389
Fast Phong	278	314	349
H test	187	209	232

These timings are expressed relative to the timings for Gouraud shading in Table F.2 and to Phong shading in Table F.3.

Table F.2   Example timings relative to Gouraud shading.

Object resolution	10×20	15×30	20×40
Gouraud	1.00	1.00	1.00
Phong	4.78	4.58	4.44
Fast Phong	3.87	3.85	3.81
H test	2.19	2.07	1.95

Table F.3   Example timings relative to Phong shading.

Object resolution	10×20	15×30	20×40
Gouraud	0.21	0.22	0.23
Phong	1.00	1.00	1.00
Fast Phong	0.81	0.84	0.86
H test	0.46	0.45	0.44

References

Abram A. G., Westover L. and Whitted T. (1985). Efficient alias-free rendering using bit-masks and lookup tables. *Computer Graphics*, **19** (3), 53–9

Appel A. (1968). Some techniques for machine rendering of solids. *AFIPS Conference Proc.* **32**, 37–45

Atherton P., Weiler K. and Greenberg D. (1978). Polygon shadow generation. *Computer Graphics*, **12** (3), 275–81

Atkin T. (1986). New chip displays its powers. *New Scientist* (March 20, 1986), 43–6

Balakrishnan A. V. (1962). On the problem of time jitter in sampling. *IRE Trans. on Information Theory* (April 1962), pp. 226–36

Barr A. H. (1984). Global and local deformations of solid primitives. *Computer Graphics*, **18** (3), 21–30

Barr A. H. (1986). Ray tracing deformed surfaces. *Computer Graphics*, **20** (4), 287–96

Barksy B. A. and Beatty J. C. (1983). Local control of bias and tension in beta-splines. *ACM Trans. on Graphics*, **2** (2), 109–34

Bartels R. H., Beatty J. C. and Barsky B. A. (1988). *Splines for Use in Computer Graphics and Geometric Modeling*. Los Altos CA: Morgan Kaufmann

Bass D. H. (1981). Using the video lookup table for reflectivity calculations. *Computer Graphics and Image Processing*, **17**, 249–61

Beckmann P. and Spizzichino A. (1963). *Scattering of Electromagnetic Waves from Rough Surfaces*. Basingstoke: Macmillan

Bergeron P. (1986). Une version generale de l'algorithme de ombres projetées de Crow basée sur le concept de volumes d'ombre. *M.Sc. Thesis*. University of Montreal

Bergman L., Fuchs H., Grant E. and Spach S. (1986). Image rendering by adaptive refinement. *Computer Graphics*, **20** (4), 29–38

Bezier P. (1972). *Numerical Control: Mathematics and Applications*. Chichester: Wiley

Bier E. A. and Sloan K. R. (1986). Two-part texture mapping. *IEEE Computer Graphics and Applications*, **6** (9), 40–53

413

Bishop G. and Weimar D. M. (1986). Fast Phong shading. *Computer Graphics*, **20** (4), 103–6

Blinn J. F. (1977). Models of light reflection for computer synthesised pictures. *Computer Graphics*, **11** (2), 192–8

Blinn J. F. (1978a). Computer display of curved surfaces. *Ph.D. Thesis*. University of Utah

Blinn J. F. (1978b). Simulation of wrinkled surfaces. *Computer Graphics*, **12** (3), 286–92

Blinn J. F. (1987). The mechanical universe: an integrated view of a large scale animation project. *SIGGRAPH 87 Course Notes*, **6**

Blinn J. F. (1988). Me and my (fake) shadow. *IEEE Computer Graphics and Applications*, **8** (1), 82–6

Blinn J. F. and Newell M. E. (1976). Texture and reflection in computer generated images. *Comm. ACM*, **19** (10) 362–7

Bloomenthal J. (1985). Modeling the mighty maple. *Computer Graphics*, **19** (3), 305–11

Bouknight W. J. (1970). A procedure for the generation of three-dimensional half-toned computer graphics presentations. *Comm. ACM*, **13** (9), 527–36

Bouknight W. J. and Kelley K. (1970). An algorithm for producing half-tone computer graphics presentations with shadows and moveable light sources. *Proc. AFIPS, Spring Joint Computer Conf.*, **36**, 1–10

Bresenham J. E. (1965). Algorithm for computer control of a digital plotter. *IBM Systems J.* (January 1965), 25–30

Brotman L. S. and Badler N. I. (1984). Generating soft shadows with a depth buffer algorithm. *IEEE Computer Graphics and Applications*, **4** (10), 5–12

Bui-Tuong Phong (1975a). Illumination for computer-generated pictures. *Comm. ACM*, **18** (6), 311–17

Bui-Tuong Phong and Crow F. C. (1975b). Improved rendition of polygonal models of curved surfaces. In *Proc. 2nd USA–Japan Computer Conf.*, pp. 475–80

Carpenter L. C. (1984). The A-buffer, an anti-aliased hidden surface method. *Computer Graphics*, **18** (3), 103–8

Catmull E. (1974). Subdivision algorithm for the display of curved surfaces. *Ph.D. Thesis*. University of Utah

Catmull E. (1975). Computer display of curved surfaces. In *Proc. IEEE Conf. on Computer Graphics, Pattern Recognition and Data Structures*, May 1975 (Reprinted in Freeman H. ed (1980). *Tutorial and Selected Readings in Interactive Computer Graphics*, New York (IEEE) pp. 309–15)

Catmull E. (1978). A hidden surface algorithm with anti-aliasing. *Computer Graphics*, **12** (3), 6–10

Catmull E. (1979). Tutorial on compensation tables. *Computer Graphics*, **13**, 1–7

Chuang R. (1985). Rendering for television. In *SIGGRAPH 85 Course Notes*

Clark J. H. (1976). Hierarchical geometric models for visible surface algorithms. *Comm. ACM*, **19** (10), 547–54

Clark, J. H. (1979). A fast scan line algorithm for rendering parametric surfaces. *Computer Graphics*, **13** (2), 289–99

Cohen M. F. and Greenberg D. P. (1985). A radiosity solution for complex environments. *Computer Graphics*, **19** (3), 31–40

Cohen M. F., Greenberg D. P. and Immel D. S. (1986). An efficient radiosity approach for realistic image synthesis. *IEEE Computer Graphics and Applications*, **6** (2), 26–35

Cohen, M. F., Chen S. E., Wallace J. R. and Greenberg D. P. (1988). A progresive refinement approach to fast radiosity image generation. *Computer Graphics*, **22** (4), 75–84

Cook R. L. (1986). Stochastic sampling in computer graphics. *ACM Trans. on Computer Graphics*, **5** (1), 51–72

Cook R. L. and Torrance K. E. (1982). A reflectance model for computer graphics. *Computer Graphics*, **15** (3), 307–16

Cook R. L., Porter T. and Carpenter L. (1984). Distributed ray tracing. *Computer Graphics*, **18** (3), 137–45

Cook R. L., Carpenter L. and Catmull E. (1987). The REYES image rendering architecture. *Computer Graphics*, **21** (4), 95–102

Cowan W. B. (1983). An inexpensive scheme for the calibration of a colour monitor in terms of CIE standard coordinates. *Computer Graphics*, **17**, 315–21

Crow F. C. (1977). Shadow algorithms for computer graphics. *Computer Graphics*, **13** (2), 242–8

Crow F. C. (1981). A comparison of anti-aliasing techniques. *IEEE Computer Graphics and Applications*, **1** (1), 40–8

Crow F. C. (1984). Summed-area tables for texture mapping. *Computer Graphics*, **18** (3), 207–12

Crow F. C. (1987). The origins of the teapot. *IEEE Computer Graphics and Applications*, **7** (1), 8–19

Dippe M. A. Z. and Wold E. H. (1985). Anti-aliasing through stochastic sampling. *Computer Graphics*, **19** (3), 69–78

Doctor L. J. and Torborg J. G. (1981). Display techniques for octree encoded objects. *IEEE Computer Graphics and Applications*, **1** (3), 29–38

Duff T. (1979). Smoothly shaded renderings of polyhedral objects on raster displays. *Computer Graphics*, **13** (2), 270–5

Duff T. (1985). Compositing 3-D rendered images. *Computer Graphics*, **19** (3), 41–4

Farin G. (1988). Curves and surfaces for CAGD. *SIGGRAPH 88 Course Notes*, **24**

Faux I. D. and Pratt M. J. (1979). *Computational Geometry for Design and Manufacture*. Chichester: Ellis Horwood

Feibush E. A., Levoy M. and Cook R. L. (1980). Synthetic texturing using digital filters. *Computer Graphics*, **14** (3), 294–301

Fiume E., Fournier A. and Rudolph L. (1983). A parallel scan conversion algorithm with anti-aliasing for a general-purpose ultracomputer. *Computer Graphics*, **17** (3), 141–50

Foley J. D. and Van Dam A. (1982). *Fundamentals of Interactive Computer Graphics*. Reading MA: Addison-Wesley

Forsey D. R. and Bartels R. H. (1988). Hierarchical B-spline refinement. *Computer Graphics*, **22** (4), 205–12

Fournier A. and Reeves W. T. (1986). A simple model of ocean waves. *Computer Graphics*, **20** (4), 75–84

Fournier A., Fussell D. and Carpenter L. (1982). Computer rendering of stochastic models. *Comm. ACM*, **25** (6), 371–84

Fuchs H. (1980). On visible surface generation by *a priori* tree structures.

415

Computer Graphics, **14**, 124–33

Fujimoto A., Tanaka T. and Iwata K. (1986). ARTS: Accelerated ray tracing system. *IEEE Computer Graphics and Applications*, **6** (4), 16–26

Gangnet M., Perny D. and Coueignoux P. (1982). Perspective mapping of planar textures. In *Proc. EUROGRAPHICS '82*, pp. 57–71. Amsterdam: North-Holland

Gardener G. Y. (1984). Simulation of natural scenes using textured quadric surfaces. *Computer Graphics*, **18** (3), 11–20

Gardener G. Y. (1985). Visual simulation of clouds. *Computer Graphics*, **19** (3), 297–303

Gardener G. Y. (1988). Functional modeling of natural scenes. *SIGGRAPH 88 Course Notes*, **28**, 44–76

Glassner A. S. (1984). Space subdivision for fast ray tracing. *IEEE Computer Graphics and Applications*, **4** (10), 15–22

Goral C., Torrance K. E., Greenberg D. P. and Battaile B. (1984). Modelling the interaction of light between diffuse surfaces. *Computer Graphics*, **18** (3), 212–22

Gouraud H. (1971). Illumination for computer generated pictures. *Comm. ACM*, **18** (60), 311–17

Greenberg D. P., Cohen M. F. and Torrance K. E. (1986). Radiosity: a method for computing global illumination, *Visual Computer*, **2** (5), 291–7

Greene N. (1984). Environment mapping and other applications of world projections. *IEEE Computer Graphics and Applications*, **6** (11), 21–9

Greene N. and Heckbert P. S. (1986). Creating raster omnimax images using the elliptically weighted average filter. *IEEE Computer Graphics and Applications*, **6** (6), 21–7

Griffiths J. G. (1984). A depth-coherence scan line algorithm for displaying curved surfaces. *Computer Aided Design*, **16** (2), 91–101

Hahn J. K. (1988). Realistic animation of rigid bodies. *Computer Graphics*, **22** (4), 299–308

Haines E. A. and Greenberg D. P. (1986). The light buffer: a shadow-testing accelerator. *IEEE Computer Graphics and Applications*, **6** (9), 6–16

Hall R. (1986a). Colour reproduction and illumination models. *Course Notes*, Computer Graphics Summer Institute, University of Stirling

Hall R. (1986b). A characterization of illumination models and shading techniques. *Visual Computer*, **2** (5), 268–77

Hall R. A. and Greenberg D. P. (1983). A testbed for realistic image synthesis. *IEEE Computer Graphics and Applications*, **3** (8), 10–19

Hanrahan P. (1983). Ray tracing algebraic surfaces. *Computer Graphics*, **17** (3), 83–90

Hanrahan P. and Sturman D. (1985). Interactive animation of parametric models. *Visual Computer*, **1**, 260–6

Harrison K., Mitchell D. and Watt A. (1988). The H-test, a method of high speed interpolative shading. In *New Trends in Computer Graphics, Proc. CG International '88*, pp. 106–16. Berlin: Springer

Heckbert P. S. (1986). Survey of texture mapping. *IEEE Computer Graphics and Applications*, **6** (11), 56–67

Heckbert P. S. and Hanrahan P. (1984). Beam tracing polygonal objects. *Computer Graphics*, **18** (3), 119–27

Hunt R. G. W. (1975). *The Reproduction of Color*. New York: Wiley

Immel D. S., Cohen M. F. and Greenberg D. P. (1986). A radiosity method for non-diffuse environments. *Computer Graphics*, **20** (4), 133–42

Jacklins C. L. and Tanimoto S. L. (1980). Octrees and their use in representing three-dimensional objects. *Computer Graphics and Image Processing*, **14**, 249–70

Joy I. K. and Bhetanabhotla M. N. (1986). Ray tracing parametric surfaces utilizing numeric techniques and ray coherence. *Computer Graphics*, **20** (4), 279–86

Kajiya J. T. (1982). Ray tracing parametric patches. *Computer Graphics*, **16**, 245–54

Kajiya J. T. (1983). New techniques for ray tracing procedurally defined objects. *Computer Graphics*, **17** (3), 91–102

Kajiya J. T. (1985). Anisotropic reflection models. *Computer Graphics*, **19** (3), 15–21

Kajiya J. T. (1986). The rendering equation. *Computer Graphics*, **20** (4), 143–50

Kaplan M. R. (1985). Space Tracing, a constant time ray tracer. *SIGGRAPH 85 Course Notes*, San Fancisco CA, July 1985

Kay D. S. (1979). Transparency, refraction and ray tracing for computer synthesised images. *Masters Thesis*. Cornell University

Kay D. S. and Greenberg D. (1979). Transparency for computer synthesised objects. *Computer Graphics*, **13** (2), 158–64

Kay T. L. and Kajiya J. T. (1986). Ray tracing complex scenes. *Computer Graphics*, **20** (4), 269–78

Korein J. and Badler N. (1983). Temporal anti-aliasing in computer generated animation. *Computer Graphics*, **17** (3), 377–88

Land E. H. (1977). The retinex theory of color vision. *Scientific American* (December 77), 108–28

Lane J. M. and Riesenfeld R. F. (1980). A theoretical development for the computer generation and display of piecewise polynomial surfaces. *IEEE Trans. on Pattern Analysis and Machine Intelligence*, **2** (1), 35–46

Lane J. M., Carpenter L. C., Whitted T. and Blinn J. T. (1980). Scan line methods for displaying parametrically defined surfaces. *Comm. ACM*, **23** (1), 23–34

MacAdam D. L. (1981). *Color Measurement: Theme and Variations*. Berlin: Springer

Magnenat-Thalmann N. and Thalmann D. (1985). *Principles of Computer Animation*. Tokyo: Springer

Mandelbrot B. (1977). *Fractals: Form, Chance and Dimension*. San Francisco CA: Freeman

Mandelbrot B. (1982). *The Fractal Geometry of Nature*. San Francisco CA: Freeman

McCormick B. H. DeFanti T. A. and Brown M. D. (1987). Visualization in scientific computing. *Computer Graphics*, **21** (6)

Meagher D. (1982). Geometric modelling using octree encoding. *Computer Graphics and Image Processing*, **19**, 129–47

Meyer G. W. and Greenberg D. P. (1980). Perceptual color spaces for computer graphics. *Computer Graphics*, **14** 254–61

Miller G. S. and Hoffman C. R. (1984). Illumination and reflection maps:

simulated objects in simulated and real environments. *SIGGRAPH '84 Course Notes*, July 1984

Mitchell D. P. (1987). Generating antialiased images at low sampling densities. *Computer Graphics*, **21** (4), 65–72

Moore M. and Wilhems J. (1988). Collision detection and response for computer animation. *Computer Graphics*, **22** (4), 289–98

Munsell A. H. (1946). *A Color Notation*. Baltimore MD: Munsell Color Co.

Murch G. (1983). The effective use of color. *TEKniques – the IDD Applications Newsletter*, **7** (4) (Winter 1983)

Nakamae E., Harada K., Ishizaki T., and Nishita T. (1986). A montage method: the overlaying of computer generated images onto a background photograph. *Computer Graphics*, **20** (4), 207–14

Nassau K. (1983). *The Physics and Chemistry of Color*. New York: Wiley

Neal C. B. (1973). Television colorimetry for receiver engineers. *IEEE Trans. on Broadcast Television and Receiver* (August 1973)

Newell M. E., Newell R. G. and Sancha T. L. (1972). A new approach to the shaded picture problem. In *Proc. ACM National Conf.*, 443–50

Newman W. M. and Sproull R. F. (1981). *Principles of Interactive Computer Graphics*. New York: McGraw-Hill

Nishita T. and Nakamae E. (1985). Continuous tone representation of three-dimensional objects taking account of shadows and interreflection. *Computer Graphics*, **19** (3), 23–30

Oppenheim A. V. and Shafer R. W. (1975). *Digital Signal Processing*. Englewood Cliffs NJ: Prentice-Hall

Ostwald W. (1931). *Colour Science*. London: Winsor and Winsor

Peachey D. R. (1985). Solid texturing of complex surfaces. *Computer Graphics*, **19** (3), 279–86

Peachey D. R. (1988). Anti-aliasing solid textures. *SIGGRAPH 88 Course Notes*, **28**, 13–35

Perlin K. (1985). An image synthesizer. *Computer Graphics*, **19** (3), 287–96

PHIGS (1988). PHIGS+ functional description. *Computer Graphics*, **22** (3)

Porter T. and Duff T. (1984). Compositing digital images. *Computer Graphics*, **18** (3), 253–9

Potmesil M. and Chakravarty I. (1981). A lens and aperture camera model for synthetic image generation, *Computer Graphics*, **15** (3), 297–306

Potmesil M. and Chakravarty I. (1983). Modelling motion blur in computer generated images. *Computer Graphics*, **17** (3), 389–99

Purdue University (1970). *Thermophysical Properties of Matter* Vols. 7–9

Reeves W. T. (1983). Particle systems – a technique for modelling a class of fuzzy objects. *Computer Graphics*, **17** (3), 359–76

Reynolds C. W. (1982). Computer animation with scripts and actors. *Computer Graphics*, **16** (3), 289–96

Reynolds C. W. (1987). Flocks, herds, and schools: a distributed behavioural model. *Computer Graphics*, **21** (4), 25–34

Rubin S. M. and Whitted T. (1980). A three-dimensional representation for fast rendering of complex schemes. *Computer Graphics*, **14**, 110–16

Samek M., Slean C. and Weghorst H. (1986). Texture mapping and distortion in digital graphics. *Visual Computer*, **2** (5), 313–20

Schachter B. J. (1980). Long crested wave models. *Computer Graphics and Image*

Processing, **12**, 187–201

Schachter B. J. (1983). *Computer Image Generation*. New York: Wiley

Schumacker R. A., Brand B., Guilliland M. and Sharp W. (1969). Study for Applying Computer-generated Images to Visual Simulation. Technical Report AFHRL–TR–69–14, US Air Force Human Resources Lab.

Schweitzer D. and Cobb E. S. (1982). Scan line rendering of parametric surfaces. *Computer Graphics*, **16** (3), 265–71

Shelley K. L. and Greenberg D. (1982). Path specification and path coherence. *Computer Graphics*, **16** (3), 157–66

Shoemake K. (1985). Animating rotation with quaternion curves. *Computer Graphics*, **19** (3), 245–54

Siegel R. and Howell J. R. (1984). *Thermal Radiation Heat Transfer*. Washington DC: Hemisphere Publishing

Smith A. R. (1978). Color gamut transformation pairs. *Computer Graphics*, **12**, 12–19

Sproson W. N. (1983). *Colour Science in Television and Display Systems*. Bristol: Adam Hilger

Steinberg H. A. (1984). A smooth surface based on biquadric patches. *IEEE Computer Graphics and Applications*, **4** (9), 20–3

Steketee S. N. and Badler N. I. (1985). Parametric keyframe interpolation incorporating kinetic adjustment and phrasing control. *Computer Graphics*, **19** (3), 255–62

Sutherland I. E., Sproull R. F. and Schumacker R. (1974). A characterization of ten hidden-surface algorithms. *Computing Surveys*, **6** (1), 1–55

Swanson R. W. and Thayer L. J. (1986). A fast shaded-polygon renderer. *Computer Graphics*, **20** (4), 107–16

Taylor, J. M., Murch G. M. and McManus P. A. (1988). Tektronix HVC: a uniform perceptual colour system for display users. *SIGGRAPH 88 Course Notes*, **17**, 35–8

Terzopoulos D. and Fleischer K. (1988). Modelling inelastic deformation: viscoelasticity, plasticity, fracture. *Computer Graphics*, **22** (4), 269–78

Terzopoulos D. and Witkin A. (1988). Deformable models. *IEEE Computer Graphics and Applications*, **8** (6), 41–51

Terzopoulos D., Platt J., Barr A. and Fleischer K. (1987). Elastically deformable models. *Computer Graphics*, **21** (4), 205–14

Torrance K. E. and Sparrow E. M. (1967). Theory for off-specular reflection from roughened surfaces. *Optical Society of America*, **57** (9), 1105–14

Verbeck C. P. and Greenberg D. P. (1984). A comprehensive light source description for computer graphics. *IEEE Computer Graphics and Applications*, **4** (7), 66–75

Wallace J. R., Cohen M. F. and Greenberg D. P. (1987). A two-pass solution to the rendering equation: a synthesis of ray tracing and radiosity methods. *Computer Graphics*, **21** (4), 311–20

Warn D. R. (1983). Lighting controls for synthetic images. *Computer Graphics*, **17** (3), 13–21

Warnock J. (1969). *A Hidden-Surface Algorithm for Computer Generated Half-Tone Pictures*. Technical Report 4–15, NTIS AD-753 671, University of Utah Computer Science Department

Waters K. (1987). A muscle model for animating three-dimensional facial expression. *Computer Graphics*, **21** (4), 17–24

Weghorst H., Hooper G. and Greenberg D. P. (1984). Improved computational methods for ray tracing. *ACM Trans. on Graphics*, **3** (1), 52–69

Weil J. (1986). The synthesis of cloth objects. *Computer Graphics*, **20** (4), 49–54

Weiler K. and Atherton P. (1977). Hidden surface removal using polygon area sorting. *Computer Graphics*, **11** (2), 214–22

Wentworth J. W. (1955). *Color Television Engineering*. New York: McGraw-Hill

Whitted J. T. (1978). A scan line algorithm for the computer display of curved surfaces. In *Proc. 5th Conf. on Computer Graphics and Interactive Techniques*, Atlanta GA, p. 26

Whitted J. T. (1980). An improved illumination model for shaded display. *Comm. ACM*, **23** (6), 342–9

Wilhems J. (1987). Dynamics for everyone. *SIGGRAPH 87 Course Notes*, **10**, 123–48

Williams D. R. and Collier R. (1983). Consequences of spatial sampling by a human photoreceptor mosaic. *Science*, **221** (July 22, 1983), 385–7

Williams L. (1978). Casting curved shadows on curved surfaces. *Computer Graphics*, **12** (3), 270–4

Williams L. (1983). Pyramidal parametrics. *Computer Graphics*, **17** (3), 1–11

Wintringham W. T. (1951). Colour television for colorimetry. *Proc. IRE* (October 1951)

Wylie C., Romney G. W., Evans D. C. and Erdahl A. (1967). Halftone perspective drawings by computer. *Proc. AFIPS, Fall Joint Computer Conf.*, **31**, 49–58

Wyszecki G. and Stiles W. S. (1967). *Color Science*. New York: Wiley

Yamaguchi K., Kunii T. L., Fujimura K. and Toriya H. (1984). Octree related data structures and algorithms. *IEEE Computer Graphics and Applications*, **4** (1), 53–9

Index

A-buffer 112, 276
active edge list 104, 389
active polygon list 103
adaptive depth control in ray tracing
    181, 198
adaptive refinement in radiosity *see*
    progressive refinement
adaptive subdivision in radiosity 210
ambient light 49
animation
    ANIMEDIT 293
    articulated structure 301
    ASAS 293
    camera choreography 290
    CINEMIRA 293
    collision detection 298
    comparison with traditional 286
    of control points 137, 148
    crawling (aliasing artefact) 269
    double interpolant method 289
    dynamic simulation 295
    Euler angles 291
    facial animation 299
    flocking 287
    key frame approach 288
    key frame interface 290
    kinematics 295
    kinetic control 289
    moments of inertia 297
    parametric approach 291
    particle systems 256, 265, 296
    programming approach 292
    quaternions 291
    rigid bodies 296, 298
    rotation 291
    scintillation (aliasing artefact) 269
    scripting systems 292
    of simple wave models 265
    simulation in 295
    synthetic actors 293
    of terrain 265
    use of splines 288, 289
    ViSC 285
    waves 299
    wireframe 42
ANIMEDIT 293
anti-aliasing
    area sampling 275
    artefacts 268
    Bartlett window 274
    convolution 270, 277
    crawling (in animation) 269
    distributed ray tracing 278
    environment mapping 252
    EWA filters in texture mapping
        243
    and Fourier theory 269, 282, 283
    jittering 279
    manifestations of aliasing 268
    mathematical model 277

Nyquist limit   272
postfiltering   273
prefiltering, general   275
prefiltering in texture mapping   245
mip-mapping   245
in ray tracing   176, 179
REYES renderer   281
sampling theorem   269
scintillation (in animation)   269
silhouette edges   268
space variant filters   243
stochastic sampling   278, 284
supersampling   275, 282
temporal   278, 300
in texture mapping   227, 242, 243,
   245, 247
area sampling   275
area subdivision in hidden surface
   removal   105
artefacts, aliasing   268
articulated structure animation   301
ASAS   293

back clipping plane   24
backface elimination   26
basis functions   120
Bartlett window   274
bending transformation   11
Bezier curves   117
   control points   118
   joining conditions   122
Bezier surfaces   126
   control points   125
   joining conditions   131
bounding volumes in ray tracing
   cost of   185
   efficiency of   184
   hierarchical   185
   void area   184
B-spline curves   123
   non-uniform B-splines   125, 134
B-spline surface patches   133
bicubic representation
   of curves   116
   of surfaces   116, 126
   and texture mapping   236
bidirectional reflectivity function   47,
   401
blending functions

B-spline   124
Bezier   120
knots, knot vector   126
Bresenham's algorithm   98
bump mapping   228, 240

de Casteljau algorithm   143
centre of projection   14
channel, α (in RGBαZ)   111
characteristic polyhedron   127
chromaticity coordinates   338
chromaticity diagram   342, 347
chrominance   316
CIE   332, 339
   chromaticity coordinates   338
   chromaticity diagram   342, 347
   LUV space   351
   1931 standard   340
   primaries   340, 341
   to RGB transformation   348
   standard illuminants   343
   standard observer   340
   XYZ space   340
   xyZ space   347
CINEMIRA   293
clipping plane
   front   24
   back   24
CMY
   colour space   314
   cube   314
   hard copy device   314
   ink jet printer   314
   subtractive primaries   314
coherence   104
   spatial coherence in ray tracing   187
coherent/incoherent reflection   401
collision detection (in animation)   298
convolution   270, 277
colour
   alignment white   350
   applications in computer graphics
      311
   blackbody radiators   343
   bleeding, in diffuse inter-reflection
      202
   chromaticity coordinates   338
   chromaticity diagram   342
   chrominance   316

CIE   332, 339
CIE LUV space   351
CIE primaries   340, 341
CIE XYZ to RGB transformation   348
CIE XYZ space   340
CMY colour space   314
CMY cube   314
CMY model   314
colorimetry   331
use in connectivity   311
dominant wavelength   334, 335
economy in the use of   311
film gamut   344
gamma correction   350, 355
graphics monitor gamut   344
hardcopy devices   314
HLS double hexcone model   322
HLS to RGB transformation   325
HSV single hexcone model   318
HSV to RGB transformation   321
HVC space   352
ink jet printer   314
interface methods   318, 322, 325
interface models   318, 322
interpolation in colour space   326
use in logical relationships   311
luminance   337
luminance (TV)   316
luminous efficiency characteristic   337
matching experiment   333
matching functions   335
in medical images   312
mixing colours   345
monitor calibration   350, 355
monitor colour models   313
Munsell colour solid   318, 331
NTSC   315
Ostwald colour system   322
PAL   317
perceptual non-uniformity   313, 351
photopigments   336
photoreceptors   336
physiological aspects   336
primary colour system   333
printing ink gamut   344
in programmer abstractions   311
pseudo-colour enhancement   327

realistic rendering   348, 353, 355
RGB colour space   313
RGB colour cube   313
RGB monitor model   313
RGB to HLS transformation   324
RGB TO HSV transformation   321
in satellite images   312
spectral distribution   334, 353
standard illuminants   343
standard colour models   330
subtractive primaries   314
and texture   228
in three-dimensional scene synthesis   312
trichromatic generalization   334, 336, 338
tristimulus values   333, 339
TV bandwidth   316
TV transmission spaces   315
undersampling   353, 355
YIQ space   315
YUV space   317
colorimetry   331
compositing (three-dimensional images)   111
continuity
   Bezier curves   122
   Bezier patches   131
   first order   122
   zero order   122
control points
   animation   148
   Bezier curve   118
   Bezier surface   128
   characteristic polyhedron   127
   convex hull   144
convex hull (of control points)   144
Cook and Torrance reflection model   65
coordinate systems
   homogeneous   3
   local   2
   left hand   2
   right hand   2
   viewing   13
   world   2
Cox–deBoor definition   125
crawling, in aliasing   269
culling   36, 104

curves
  Bezier curves   117
  β-spline curves   135
  B-spline curves   123
  NURBS   134
  parametric representation of   116

data structures
  BSP trees   195
  use of pointers in   364
  polygon mesh   31, 364
  octrees   190
  octrees in ray tracing   192
DDA algorithm   98
delta form factor   206
depth control in ray tracing   181
depth list algorithm in hidden surface
      removal   105
diffuse reflection   47, 48, 51
  radiosity method   201
  and texture   228
distance (reflection models)   48
distributed ray tracing   174, 278
dominant wavelength   334, 335
double interpolant method in
      animation   289
ducting   40
dynamic simulation in animation   295

efficiency
  of Phong shading   90
  of ray tracing   181
energy equilibrium (in reflection)   400
environment mapping   247
  anti-aliasing   252
  comparison with ray tracing   250
  cube interior maps   249
  latitude–longitude maps   249
  pixel pre-image   248
  polygon meshes   254, 364
  prefiltered diffuse maps   250, 252
  prefiltered specular maps   250, 252
  reflected view vector   247
  six component maps   249
  sphere interior maps   249
  two-dimensional maps   248

facial animation   299
first hit ray tracing   153, 157

form factors, radiosity   203
  calculation by hemicube method
      204
  calculation by integration   204
  definition of   203
  delta form factors, in hemicube   206
  reciprocity relationship of   203
Fourier synthesis   263
Fourier theory (and anti-aliasing)
      269, 282
fractal systems   257
Fresnel term   72
front clipping plane   24
functional modelling   255
  Fourier synthesis   263
  fractal systems   257
  fuzzy objects   256
  external consistency   260
  internal consistency   260
  particles systems   256, 265, 296
  recursive subdivision   257
  terrain generation   257, 264
  three-dimensional noise function
      234, 261
  trees (natural)   257, 264
fuzzy objects   256

gamma correction   350, 355
gamuts, colour
  film   344
  monitor   344
  printing ink   344
Gauss–Seidel method   216
  relaxation factor   217
general transformation matrix   6
GKS   26, 29, 363
global control (of parametric curves
      and surfaces)   126
global illumination in ray tracing   167
goniometric diagrams   80
Gouraud interpolation   83, 84, 389
  comparison with Phong   89
  errors in   86
  incremental calculations   86
  Mach band visualization   93
  Mach bands   84
  rendering system   369
  vertex intensity   85
  vertex normal   85

graphics languages 29
graphics standards
  GKS 26, 29, 363
  PHIGS 26, 29, 363
  PHIGS+ 84

Hall's integral 400
hard copy devices (and colour) 314
hierarchical bounding volumes, in ray
    tracing 185
hidden surface removal 104
  A-buffer 112, 276
  area subdivision 105
  depth list 105
  hidden surface rays 153, 178
  scan line Z-Buffer 103, 107
  spanning scan line 103, 107
  Z-buffer 103, 107, 389
highlight detection 91, 405
HLS double hexcone model 322
HLS to RGB transformation 325
homogeneous coordinates 3
HSV single hexcone model 318
HSV to RGB transformation 321
H-test 91, 405
HVC space 352
hybrid radiosity 211

illumination models
  goniometric diagrams 80
  multiple point sources 49
  point light sources 48, 53
  Warn's method 79
implicit functions 116
ink jet printer 314
intensity 400
interface, colour 318, 322, 325
intermediate surface texture mapping
    238
interpolation in colour space 326
interpolative shading
  Gouraud 83, 84, 389
  highlight detection 91, 405
  H-test 91, 405
  Phong 83, 87
intersection geometry in ray tracing
  line, sphere 163
  bicubic patches 198
  quadric surfaces 198

inverse mapping (texture) 230

jittering (in sampling) 279

key frame animation 288
key frame animation, interface 290
kinetic control, in animation 289
knot vector (B-splines) 126

Lambert's law 48
left-hand coordinate system 2
light sources see illumination
light source transformation algorithm
    for shadows 226
linear transformations
  rotation 4
  scaling 4
  translation 3
list
  active edge list 104, 389
  active polygon list 103
local coordinate system 2
luminance 337
luminance (TV) 316
luminous flux 400
LUT (in reflection models) 59, 63

Mach bands 84
  visualization of 93
marble texture 233
matching experiment, colour 333
matching functions, colour 335
matrix convention in computer
    graphics 3
masking (in microfacets) 71
metallic surfaces (rendering) 65, 74
microfacet based reflection models
    65, 68
microfacets 68
  masking in 71
  shadowing in 71
mixing colours 345
modelling methods
  CSG 149
  octrees 149
  polygon mesh 31, 149, 364
  quadric surfaces 149
monitor colour models 313
monitor calibration 350, 355

monitor dynamic range 350, 355
monitor gamma correction 350, 355
monitor transformation 348
multiple light sources 48, 53
Munsell colour solid 318, 331

net transformation matrix 6
noise function, three-dimensional 234
NTSC 315
NURBS 134
Nyquist limit 272

octrees 149
Ostwald colour system 322

PAL 317
parallel projection 14
parametric animation 291
parametric curves
  Bezier 117
  B-splines 123
  β-splines 123
  continuity of 122
  control points 118
  NURBS 134
  planarity test 144
parametric patches
  Bezier 126
  B-spline, interactive editor 138
  β-splines 133
  de Casteljau algorithm 143
  continuity of 131
  control points 128
  database considerations 137
  degeneracy of 133
  planarity test 144
  scan conversion 139
  silhouette edges 140
parametric representation
  of curves 116
  of surfaces 127
particle systems 256, 265, 296
perspective projection 14
PHIGS 26, 29, 363
PHIGS+ 84
Phong interpolative shading
  comparison with Gouraud 89
  H test 91, 405
  highlight detection 91, 405

speed ups 90, 405
vertex normal interpolation 85
Phong reflection model 46, 55, 56, 63
physiological aspects of colour 336
pixel 59
  coordinates 98
  geometric extent 101
  pre-image in texture mapping 230
  pre-image in environment mapping 248
polygon mesh 1, 364
  database considerations 31
  environment mapping 254
  Gouraud renderer 389
  highlight detection 91, 405
  shading, Gouraud 83, 84, 389
  shading, Phong 83, 87
  texture mapping 236, 237
  vertex intensities 85
  vertex normals 85
  visibility of, in shading 84
  wireframe renderer 363
polygon normals 36
  surface patches 130
postfiltering 273
postprocessing shaded images 59, 63
power 400
prefiltering 275
primary colours 333, 340, 341
programming approach to animation 292
progressive refinement, in radiosity 213
  ambient contribution 215
  form factor storage requirements 213
  gathering, iterations 214
  Gauss–Seidel method 216
  shooting, iterations 216
projection
  centre of 14, 22
  parallel 14
  perspective 14
pseudo-colour enhancement 327, 359

quadric surfaces 41, 149
quaternions in animation 291

radiant emittance 400

radiance 400
radiosity method 201
   accuracy of solution 209
   adaptive refinement 213
   adaptive subdivision 210
   ambient contribution, progressive
      refinement 215
   calculation time/scene complexity
      208
   colour bleeding 202
   definition of 203
   delta form factors 206
   form factor
      definition of 203
      calculation by integration 204
      storage requirements 213
   gathering, progressive refinement
      iterations 214
   Gauss–Seidel method 216
   hemicube method 205
   hybrid radiosity and ray tracing
      211
   progressive refinement 213
   ray tracing and radiosity 211
   reciprocity relationship, form
      factors 203
   shadows 202
   shooting, progressive refinement
      iterations 214
   specular reflection and radiosity
      211
   storage requirements, form factors
      213
   substructuring method 209
   texture mapping 210
   translucency 211
   two-pass approach 211
   view independence 218
   virtual environment 211
rainbow formation, a ray tracing
      example 154
rasterization
   area filling 98
   of edges 98
   integer arithmetic 99
   linked lists of polygons 101
   pixel coordinates 98
   pixel extent 101
   of polygons 100

ray tracing
   adaptive depth control 181, 198
   anti-aliasing 176, 179
   as a binary tree 158
   bounding volumes 184, 198
   using BSP trees 195
   comparison with environment
      mapping 250
   depth control, adaptive 181, 198
   direct transmitted illumination 169
   direct/global illumination model
      167
   distributed ray tracing 174
   efficiency of process 181
   efficiency of recursion 161
   environment mapping, comparison
      with 250
   first hit rays 153, 178
   first hit speed up 187
   global illumination considerations
      168
   hierarchical bounding volumes 185
   hybrid algorithm 187
   hybrid nature of model 170
   intersection geometry
      bi-cubic patches 198
      line, sphere 163
      quadric surfaces 198
   using octrees 192
   and radiosity 211
   rainbow formation 154
   rational computation time 189
   recursive ray tracing 152, 156
   reflection vector 165
   refraction vector 165
   scattered direct transmitted
      illumination 169
   SEADS 194
   shadow acceleration 174
   shadow computation 173, 178
   space tracking using octrees 193
   spatial coherence 187
   spatial subdivision 188
   3D-DDA 194
   trace depth 156, 157, 172
realistic rendering (colour) 348, 353,
      355
reciprocity relationship, form factors
      203

recursion, efficiency in ray tracing
161
recursive ray tracing   152, 156
recursive subdivision in terrain
generation   257
reflectance distribution   see realistic
rendering
reflection models
colour   55
Cook and Torrance   65
distance   50
energy   67
Fresnel term   72
geometry   53
LUTs   59
masking (in microfacets)   71
metallic surfaces   74
microfacets   68
Phong   46, 55, 56, 63
postprocessing   59, 63
refraction   72
shadowing (in microfacets)   71
solid angles   67
statistical (microfacet distributions)
69
reflection vector   165
refraction   72
refraction vector   165
rendering   83, 97
comparison of methods   110
Gouraud system   389
by polygon   103
order of   102
by scan line   103
scan line Z-Buffer   103, 107
spanning scan line   103, 107
wireframe system   363
Z-Buffer   103, 107, 389
rendering equation   403
REYES renderer   281
RGB
colour space   313
cube   313
disadvantage of   313
to HLS transformation   324
to HSV transformation   321
monitor model   313
RGB to HLS transformation   324
RGB to HSV transformation   321

right-hand coordinate system   2
rigid body animation   296
rotation (in animation)   291
rotation, linear transformation   4

sampling theorem   269
scaling, linear transformation   4
scan conversion
analytical scan conversion (of
patches)   142
of edges   98
integer arithmetic   99
linked lists of polygons   101
parametric surfaces   139, 145
pixel extent   101
of polygons   100
scan line algorithm for shadows   223
scan line Z-Buffer   103, 107
anti-aliasing   275
for patches   145
scene construction   6
scene complexity considerations   110
scintillation, in aliasing   269
screen memory   59
scripting systems (in animation)   293
SEADS   194
shading
interpolative
Gouraud   83, 84, 389
highlight detection   91, 405
H-test   91, 405
Phong   83, 87
speeding up shading   91, 405
patches   130
shadowing (in microfacets)   71
shadows
aspects used in computer graphics
221
effects of diffraction   220
function of   219
isolated objects and planes   221,
251
light source transformation
algorithm   226
penumbra   220
radiosity method   202
in ray tracing   173, 178
scan line algorithm   223
secondary data structure   223

shadow volume algorithm   224
shadow volumes and Z-Buffer   225
shadow Z-Buffer algorithm   227, 251
umbra   220
silhouette edges   140
   anti-aliasing   268
   bump mapping   240
simulation (in animation)   295
Snell's law   166
solid angles   67
solid texture   232
spanning scan line algorithm   103, 107
spectral distribution   334, 353
spectral synthesis   263
specular reflection   47, 50
   radiosity   211
   and texture   228
spherical coordinates (in viewing
      interface)   358
splines, β   135
   bias   135
   tension   136
standard colour models   330, 331
standard illuminants   343
statistical reflection functions   69
stochastic sampling   278, 284
structure deforming transformations
      10
   bending   11
   tapering   11
   twisting   11
subdivision
   area, in hidden surface removal
      105
   in radiosity   210
   recursive, in terrain generation   257
   in scan conversion of patches   143
   tears in patch subdivision   143
substructuring method, radiosity   209
subtractive primaries   314
supersampling   273
surfaces, parametric representation
      126

tangent vectors
   curves   118, 119
   surfaces   128
tapering transformation   11

teapot, the Utah   395
temporal anti-aliasing   278, 300
translation, linear transformation   3
trichromatic generalization   334, 336, 338
tristimulus values   333, 339
TV
   bandwidth   316
   colour spaces   315
   NTSC   315
   PAL   317
   YIQ   315
   YUV   317
terrain generation   257, 264
texture mapping
   anti-aliasing   227, 242, 243, 245, 247, 282
   bicubic parametric patches   236, 251
   bump mapping   228, 240
   and colour   228
   and diffuse reflectivity   228
   texture domain   229
   environment mapping   247
   EWA filters   243
   and Fourier theory   282
   intermediate surface mapping   238
   inverse mapping   230
   polygon meshes   236, 237
   polygon parametrization   236
   pixel pre-image   230
   prefiltering, mip-mapping   245
   marble texture   233
   mip-mapping   245
   normal vector perturbation   228, 240
   radiosity   210
   texture space   229
   thin film interference   231
   three-dimensional procedural
      definitions   232, 252
   three-dimensional texture domain
      technique   232, 252
   using transparency   229
   two-part two-dimensional mapping
      238, 251
   two-dimensional texture domain
      techniques   235
   sculpting metaphor   232
   silhouette edges, bump mapping   240

solid textures   232, 252
space variant filters   243
wood grain   233
thin film interference (texture)   231
3D-DDA   194
three-dimensional texture domain
    technique   232
three-dimensional procedural texture
    232
trace depth in ray tracing   156, 157,
    172
transformations
    bending   11
    of control polyhedra (parametric
        patches)   121
    general transformation matrix   6
    inverse   5
    linear   2
    non-linear   10
    modelling   2
    net transformation matrix   6
    rotation   4
    scaling   4
    scene construction   6
    structure deforming   10
    tapering   11
    translation   3
    twisting   11
translucency, in radiosity   211
transparency   62, 110, 113
    and texture   229
trees (natural)   257, 264
twisting transformation   11
two texture domain mapping   235
two-part texture mapping   238
two-pass radiosity method   211

undersampling
    in colour space   353, 355
    in space   see anti-aliasing
    in time   see temporal anti-aliasing
Utah teapot   395

vertex intensity   85

vertex normal   85
view distance   21
view independence, of radiosity
    solution   208
view plane   22
view plane normal   21
view plane window   24
view point, view reference point   13
viewing coordinate system   13
viewing pipeline   26
viewing systems
    four parameter   17, 357
    general   21
    GKS-3D   26, 363
    interface   39, 357
    PHIGS   26, 363
    practical   19
viewing transformation   357
view up vector   22
view vector (reflected)   247
view volume   23
virtual camera   19
ViSC   286
volume sweeping   39

Warn's method (light sources)   79
wireframe   31
wireframe rendering system   363
wood grain texture   233
world coordinate space   2, 357

XYZ colour space   340
xyZ colour space   347

YIQ space   315, 354
YUV space   317, 354

Z-Buffer   83, 103, 106, 389
    algorithm for shadows   227
    anti-aliasing   273
    efficiency of   106
    hardware implementation   111
    scene complexity   110